The Ultimate Car Book 2001

by Jack Gillis

and Ailis Aaron

Design
by Amy Curran

Foreword by
Clarence Ditlow
Center for Auto Safety

HarperResource
An Imprint of HarperCollinsPublishers

ACKNOWLEDGMENTS

This year *Car Book* assistant Ailis Aaron takes over the compilation of the 21st anniversary edition of what can legitimately be called *The Ultimate Car Book*. Thanks to her hard work, the complex process of compiling the information you need to make a smart, sensible new car choice was expertly accomplished. Longtime *Car Book* graphics maven Amy Curran placed, as she has for ten years, all of this information in an easy-to-use format with her usual calm and grace. These two professionals continue to be the greatest assets this year's car buyers have. Rounding out the team was the hard working and skillful Stephanie Ackerman, who provided invaluable good spirits and sound advice.

Many, many talented professionals enabled Amy and Ailis to successfully accomplish this effort. This year's edition would not have been possible without essential contributions from many talented individuals. Most significant was Clarence Ditlow and the staff of the Center for Auto Safety, including Mike Kido. In addition, valuable insight and information was provided by legal expert Phil Nowicki, president of Nowicki and Associates; Carolyn Gorman of the Insurance Information Institute; Martha Casey, U.S. EPA; Pete Packer, Runzheimer International; Kim Hazelbaker, Highway Loss Data Institute; Debbie Bindeman, Insurance Services Organization; Ashley Cheng, *Car Book* veteran. And finally, the rudder who keeps us on course is my friend and agent, Stuart Krichevsky.

As always, the most important factor in being able to bring this information to the American car buyer for 21 years is the encouragement, support, and love from my brilliant and beautiful wife, Marilyn Mohrman-Gillis.

J.G.

As Always,

for Marilyn &
Katie, John, Brian, and Brennan

THE ULTIMATE CAR BOOK (2001 edition). Copyright © 2000, 1999, 1998, 1997, 1996, 1995, 1994, 1993, 1992, 1991, 1990, 1989, 1988, 1987, 1986, 1985, 1984, 1983, 1982, 1981 by Jack Gillis. All rights reserved. Printed in the United States of America. No part of this book may be used or reproduced in any manner whatsoever without written permission except in the case of brief quotations embodied in critical articles and reviews. For information, address HarperCollins Publishers, Inc., 10 East 53rd Street, New York, NY 10022.

HarperCollins books may be purchased for educational, business, or sales promotional use. For information, please write: Special Markets Department, HarperCollins Publishers, Inc., 10 East 53rd Street, New York, NY 10022.

ISBN: 0-06-27-3705-8
00 01 02   5 4 3 2 1

FOREWORD BY CLARENCE DITLOW

The biggest auto safety scandal since the Corvair jumped on the landscape in 2000 with over 100 deaths due to Ford Explorers rolling over after Firestone tires failed. Yet this pales in comparison to over 1600 deaths in fire crashes of General Motors pickups with side saddle gas that explode on impact. What about the Chrysler minivan with tailgates that popped over and killed over 40 people. And then there's the 20 million Fords with defective ignition module that stall on highways across America. What's going on? Aren't cars suppose to be safer?

They are but as these lethal defects and 42,000 traffic deaths in 2000 show, they aren't safe enough. Auto companies still place sales over safety, particularly when it comes to sport utility vehicles (SUVs) like the Explorer when yield up to $15,000 per SUV in profit. It is no coincidence that most of these defects involve trucks and vans subject to less stringent safety standards than passenger cars. People die when the auto industry lobbies loopholes into our safety laws and cutbacks in the safety budget. With just a penny per vehicle to find safety defects, how can the federal government discover the deadly secrets of companies like Ford and Firestone?

That's were the *Car Book* and the Center for Auto Safety (CAS) come in. The *Car Book* helps you buy the safest vehicles sold. The *Car Book* was the first to publish rollover ratings for every vehicle to help you avoid rollover prone SUVs; the first to publish crashworthiness ratings to help you buy vehicles that sac-

rifice themselves to save you in a crash; and the first to develop consumer complaints into a rating system to help you buy a more reliable vehicle.

The Center for Auto Safety (CAS) is your voice for vehicle safety. CAS was the only consumer group asked to testify before both the House and the Senate on how to overhaul the auto safety program in light of the Ford/Firestone scandal. CAS has gone to the courts on your behalf to take on the auto giants. CAS has sued both Ford and Firestone in Federal District court over the Explorer tire rollovers. CAS was instrumental in getting a California judge to order the recall of millions of stalling Fords. On a shoe string budget, half what an auto company pays for one Super Bowl commercial, CAS has won many victories for consumers, not the least of which was saving the *Car Book* when the auto industry wanted to keep its vital information out of consumers' hands. Other CAS accomplishments for you include:

☑ Lemon laws in every state
☑ Airbags in every vehicle
☑ Citizen right to petition for safety recalls and standards in Motor Vehicle Safety Act
☑ Exposed secret warranties saving consumers billions of dollars and got states to enact secret warranty disclosure laws
☑ Mandatory free repairs in safety recall law
☑ Sued and won landmark case upholding Clean Air Act recalls
☑ Exposed the Ford Pinto, Firestone 500 tire, GM side saddle gas tank, Ford ignition

switch, Evenflo One Step child seat
☑ Passage of Mobile Home Construction and Safety Act
☑ Sued to obtain mandatory bridge inspections
☑ Saved tire treadwear grading standards

And the list goes on. Since our founding in 1970 by Ralph Nader and Consumers Union, CAS has also taken on the oil, insurance and trucking companies and won on leadfree gasoline prices, wrecked vehicle disclosure laws and big trucks safety. If it were not for CAS, auto companies would run roughshod over the consumer. If we hadn't had a CAS these past 30 years, we would have more corporate lawlessness, consumer ripoffs, dirtier air, more lemons, fewer recalls and more deaths and injuries on the highway. No wonder the auto and highway lobbies would be much happier if CAS were not on the job watching our for consumers.

By reading the *Car Book*, you have taken an important first step toward your personal vehicle safety. The next step is to support the Center for Auto Safety which works every day on your behalf to ensure that all Americans ride in safe and reliable vehicles. To find out more about what CAS does for you and how you can support CAS, turn to pages 75-76 or go to our Website, www.autosafety.org.

INTRODUCTION

For 21 years *The Car Book* has been responsible for ensuring that you have all the information you need to purchase a safe, reliable new car. And you've been using this information to send a powerful message to carmakers that you will not tolerate unsafe, poorly made vehicles. And you shouldn't—cars simply cost too much to not insist on getting the best product possible. The good news is that cars today are safer and better performing than ever before. Nevertheless, there are still important differences in how cars protect you in a crash, how much they cost to maintain and how far they'll go on a gallon of very expensive gasoline. Read on to find out how knowing these differences before you buy can save you after.

Last year we added the word *"Ultimate"* to our title because we have greatly expanded the information we are making available to you. In this one volume, you'll find information on the most popular minivans, sport utility vehicles, sedans, station wagons, compacts and sports cars. And because more and more of us are smartly opting for late model used cars, you'll also find out how the 1999 and 2000 models performed.

You'll be able to quickly compare if there have been enough improvements to warrant spending the extra dollars on a brand-new car, versus one that looks almost the same, but is one or two years old.

When it comes to buying a car, the best weapon you have to protect yourself is information. You now have in your hands the best arsenal of facts available to help you wade through the claims and hype from auto companies. If you use the information in *The Ultimate Car Book*, there is no reason why your next car shouldn't last at least 150,000 miles.

In addition to better vehicles, car dealers are beginning to treat us like human beings! Now that customer goodwill has become important, dealerships are competing with each other to see who has the best customer satisfaction ratings. This means that our experience with the buying process can affect their relationship with the carmaker. Suddenly, making us happy has become an important goal of the salesperson. How we rate our buying experience will affect their business, which is really as it should be. In addition, competition from Internet sales outlets is putting pressure on traditional dealers to treat us better if they want our business. But don't be lulled into complacency. Buying a car means you have to stay on your toes, and *The Ultimate Car Book 2001* will help you do just that.

In spite of all the new car technology and the Internet, the fundamentals of buying a good, safe, reliable car remain the same: do your homework; shop around; and remember car companies need you more than you need them!

So how do you buy for safety? Many consumers mistakenly believe that handling and performance are the key elements in the safety of a car. While an extremely unresponsive car could cause an accident, most new cars meet basic handling requirements. In fact, many people actually feel uncomfortable driving high performance cars because the highly responsive steering, acceleration, and suspension systems can be difficult to get used to. But the main reason handling is overrated as a safety measure is that automobile collisions are, by nature, accidents. Once they've begun, they are beyond human capacity to prevent, no matter how well your car handles. So the key to protecting yourself is to purchase a car that offers a high degree of crash protection.

Be careful, too, in buying a new, large sport utility vehicle— they truly do handle differently than a typical passenger car. As our concern for safety has influenced carmakers' attitudes, so have our demands for quality. The result—U.S.-built cars continue to be better built than those of 5–10 years ago. And, because we're demanding that companies stand behind their products, we're seeing better warranties, too. Since *The Car Book* began comparing warranties in 1986, a number of carmakers have told us that they've been forced to improve their warranties now that consumers can tell the difference.

Consumers are learning that they can get better-performing and safer cars by buying the ones with good safety records, low maintenance costs, long warranties, and insurance discounts.

Getting the Most from *The Ultimate Car Book:*

We start off with the "Safety Chapter" which rates crash safety, describes your options for protection, and gives vital information on airbags, the detailed frontal and side crash test results, and tips on protecting your children.

The "Fuel Economy Chapter" uncovers the money-saving gas misers and offers savings advice at the pump as gas prices begin to creep up again.

The "Maintenance Chapter" allows you to compare those inevitable repair costs before you buy. You'll also find advice on dealing with mechanics.

The "Warranties Chapter" offers a critical comparison of the new warranties and lets you know the best and worst before you get into trouble down the road. If you do have trouble, we'll let you know which companies offer roadside assistance and how to find out about secret warranties.

The "Insurance Chapter" will help you save money on an expense that is often forgotten in the showroom.

Because most of us can't tell one tire from another, we've included the "Tires Chapter" to help you select the best.

The "Complaints Chapter" provides a road map to resolving inevitable problems quickly and efficiently. We provide consumers with easy access to the hundreds of thousands of car complaints on file with the U.S. government, thanks to the efforts of the Center for Auto Safety.

Review the "Buying Chapter" for some strategies on getting the best price which for many of us is one of the hardest and most distasteful aspects of car buying.

Use the "Buying Guide" to compare cars, and read the chapters to learn more about each model. The "Buying Guide" is designed to easily compare key information about cars you're considering. It's in color and it's

followed by our "Best Bets" section which lists our top choices for 2001!

Finally, our "Ratings Chapter" provides a detailed review of each of the new cars, minivans, sport utilities, and pickups. These pages provide, at a glance, an overview of all the criteria you need to make a good choice. Here, you'll be able to quickly assess key features and see how the car you're interested in stacks up against its competition so you can make sure your selection is the best car for you. Car prices have more than doubled since 1980, so we've also included the percent

of dealer markup to help you negotiate the very best price. And new for this year is our addition of information on the last two model years, so you can decide if buying new is really best for you.

The information in *The Car Book* is based on data collected and developed by our staff, the United States Department of Transportation, and the Center for Auto Safety. With all of this data in hand, you'll find some great choices for 2001. *The Car Book* will guide you through the trade-offs, promises, facts, and myths to the car that will best meet your needs.

—Jack Gillis

TYPICAL OPERATING COSTS

The table below shows the annual operating costs for fifteen popular cars. Costs include operating expenses (fuel, oil, maintenance, and tires) and ownership expenses (insurance, depreciation, financing, taxes, and licensing) and are based on keeping the car for 3 years, driving 20,000 miles per year. (Costs below are based on 2000 figures. Source: Runzheimer International.)

Vehicle	Operating	Ownership	Total
Mercedes-Benz 500 S	$3,220	$21,983	$25,203
Cadillac DeVille	$3,030	$12,196	$15,226
Lincoln Town Car Exec.	$2,810	$12,273	$15,083
Buick Park Ave. Ultra S.C.	$2,930	$11,172	$14,102
Chrysler LHS	$2,870	$9,300	$12,170
Buick LeSabre Limited	$2,480	$8,440	$10,920
Mercury Grand Marquis GS	$2,790	$7,707	$10,497
Nissan Maxima GXE	$2,430	$7,701	$10,131
Dodge Intrepid	$2,340	$7,137	$9,477
Buick Century Custom	$2,390	$6,926	$9,316
Ford Taurus SE	$2,440	$6,597	$9,037
Toyota Camry CE	$2,130	$6,069	$8,199
Dodge Neon Highline	$2,140	$5,887	$8,027
Honda Accord DX	$2,320	$5,319	$7,639
Chevrolet Metro LSI	$1,760	$5,796	$7,556
Saturn SL2 Sedan	$2,060	$5,176	$7,236

SAFETY

Honda Accord

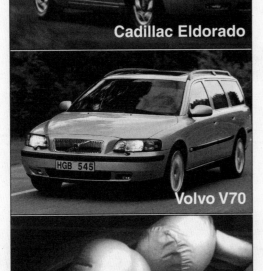
Cadillac Eldorado

Volvo V70

IN THIS CHAPTER

S afety is likely the most important factor that most of us consider when choosing a new car. In the past, evaluating safety was difficult. Now, thanks to the information in *The Ultimate Car Book*, it's much easier to pick a safe car. To provide the greatest possible protection, a car should have a variety of safety features including dual airbags, side airbags, safety belt adjusters and pretensioners, four-wheel anti-lock brakes (ABS), and built-in child safety seats.

Another key factor in occupant protection is how well the car performs in a crash test. In order for you to easily use the government crash tests, we have analyzed the results and presented them in an easy-to-understand format. In the past, crash tests have measured protection in a frontal crash. The government is now testing the performance of cars in side crash tests. Where available, we have also included these results on the following charts.

Also in this chapter, you'll find a review of the current safety features in this year's models including ABS and the latest information about airbags. We also provide a detailed look at an important, and often overlooked, safety feature—the child safety seat. Our section on children and airbags is a must read for any parent.

Crash Test Program: In 1979, the U.S. Department of Transportation began a crash test program to compare the occupant protection of cars called the New Car Assessment Program. These crash tests show significant differences in how well various vehicles protect belted occupants in crashes.

In the frontal crash test, an automobile is sent forward into a concrete barrier at 35 mph, causing an impact similar to two identical cars crashing head-on at 35 mph. The car contains elec-tronically monitored dummies in the driver and passenger seats. This electronic data is analyzed to measure the impact of such a collision on a human being.

For the new side crash tests, a moving barrier is smashed into the vehicle on both sides at 38.5 mph. This test simulates a typical intersection collision between two vehicles. The dummies in the side crash tests are also electronically monitored, and the data collected measures the impact on a human being.

Note that in both crash tests, the dummies are securely belted. Therefore, these test results do not apply to unbelted occupants.

To make it easy for you to compare vehicles, we have presented the results using our *Car Book Crash Test Index*. Using this *Index*, you can easily compare the crash test performance among vehicles.

It is best to compare the results within the same weight class, such as compacts to compacts. Do not compare cars with differing weights. For example, a subcompact that is rated "Good" may not be as safe as a large car with the same rating.

We rate the crash test results of each car relative to all of the cars ever crash tested to give you a better idea of the true top performers among the 2000 models and identify those cars which have room for improvement.

Vehicles missing from this list had not been tested at the time of printing.

NHTSA ON THE WEB

TIP

To get the latest government safety info from the National Highway Traffic Safety Administration go to their website at www.nhtsa.dot.gov. A wealth of information is at your fingertips. Want to know if your car or child is required to have child seat tethers? Having a mechanical problem and want to see if your car has been recalled or has a technical service bulletin? Or perhaps you're looking for some results of crash tests completed after we went to print.

CRASH TESTS: HOW THE CARS ARE RATED

A car's ability to protect you in a crash depends on its ability to absorb the force of impact rather than transfer it to the occupant. Frontal and side crash tests measure the amount of crash forces transferred to the head, chest, and legs of occupants in a 35-mph (frontal) or 38.5-mph (side) crash.

The tables on the following pages indicate how this year's cars can be expected to perform in crash tests. We only included a vehicle if its design has not changed enough to dramatically alter previous results. Twins that are structurally similar can be expected to perform similarly.

The first column provides *The Car Book*'s overall *Crash Test Index* (CTI). This number represents all the forces measured by the test. Lower CTI numbers are better. The CTI is best used to compare cars within the same size and weight class.

The second column provides an overall rating of *Very Good*, *Good*, *Average*, *Poor*, or *Very Poor*. These reflect the car's performance compared to all other models ever tested.

The next two columns indicate the likelihood of each occupant sustaining a life-threatening injury, based on the dummies' head and chest scores. Lower percentages mean a lower likelihood of being seriously injured. This information is taken directly from the government's analysis of the crash test results.

The last two columns indicate how the dummies' legs fared in the crash test. Legs labeled *Poor* did not meet the government's standards. Those that did meet the standards are rated *Moderate*, *Good*, and *Very Good*, reflecting performance relative to all other cars ever tested. The leg injury ratings are not weighted as heavily as the head and chest in determining overall CTI performance.

Crash test results may vary due to differences in the way cars are manufactured, in how models are equipped, and in test conditions. There is no absolute guarantee that a car which passed the test will adequately protect you in an accident. Some two-door models may not perform exactly like their four-door counterparts.

CRASH TESTS

Here are the best crash test performers among the 2001 vehicles. Lower Crash Test Index numbers indicate better performance.

FRONT TESTS

SUBCOMPACT
Ford Focus 2 dr. (1832)
Saturn SL/SW (1927)
VW New Beetle (2348)
Ford Focus 4 dr. (2350)

COMPACT
Honda Civic 2 dr. (1488)
Honda Civic 4 dr. (1463)
Volkswagen Jetta (1865)
Volkswagen Golf (1865)
Mazda 626 (2230)
Oldsmobile Alero (2415)
Pontiac Grand Am (2415)
Subaru Legacy (2525)
Mitsubishi Galant (2547)

INTERMEDIATE
Chevrolet Camaro (1783)
Pontiac Firebird (1783)
Mercury Sable (1793)
Ford Taurus (1793)
Volkswagen Passat (1881)
Nissan Altima (1921)
Toyota Camry (1927)
Chevrolet Impala (1943)
Saturn L/LW (1979)
Volvo S80 (1995)
Lexus ES300 (2521)

LARGE
Audi A8 (1845)
Ford Crown Victoria (1832)
Mercury Grand Marquis (1832)
Buick LeSabre (1948)

MINIVAN
Ford Windstar (1468)
Honda Odyssey (1533)
Mercury Villager (1630)
Nissan Quest (1630)
Toyota Sienna (1863)

COMPACT PICKUP
Ford Ranger (2494)
Mazda B Series Pickup (2494)

MID-SIZE SPORT UTILITY
Nissan Xterra (2336)
Toyota 4Runner (2390)
Infiniti QX4 (2462)
Nissan Pathfinder (2462)
Mercedes-Benz M-Class (2496)

SIDE TESTS

COMPACT
Honda Civic 2 dr. (1042)
Mitsubishi Galant (1157)
Subaru Legacy (1218)
Volkswagen Jetta (1445)

INTERMEDIATE
Honda Accord (950)
Volvo S80 (975)
Chrysler PT Cruiser (1112)
Nissan Maxima (1144)
Toyota Avalon (1216)
Lexus ES300 (1280)
Chevrolet Impala (1398)

LARGE
Infiniti I30 (1144)
Lincoln Town Car (1227)
Mercury Grand Marquis (1481)
Ford Crown Victoria (1481)
Buick LeSabre (1510)

MINIVAN
Mazda MPV (625)
Honda Odyssey (637)
Ford Windstar (884)
Toyota Sienna (1036)
Oldsmobile Silhouette (1068)
Pontiac Montana (1068)
Chevrolet Venture (1068)
Mercury Villager (1160)
Nissan Quest (1160)

SMALL SPORT UTILITY
Honda CR-V (1059)
Chevrolet Tracker (1194)

MID-SIZE SPORT UTILITY
Toyota 4Runner (288)
Nissan Pathfinder (421)
Ford Explorer (552)
Mercury Mountaineer (552)
Isuzu Rodeo (579)
Honda Passport (580)
Infiniti QX4 (765)
Nissan Xterra (715)
Infiniti QX4 (765)
Chevrolet Blazer (829)
GMC Jimmy/Envoy (829)
Pontiac Aztek (1313)
Jeep Grand Cherokee (1067)
Jeep Cherokee (1537)

STANDARD PICKUP
Ford F-Series (714)

Data current as of 10/00.

CRASH TEST RESULTS

Crash Test Performance		Crash Test Index	Car Book Rating	Likelihood of Life Threatening Injury		Leg Injury Rating	
				Driver	Passenger	Driver	Passenger
SUBCOMPACT							
Dodge/Plymouth Neon	FRONT	3753	Average	21%	21%	Good	Good
	SIDE	2587	Average	14%	16%	Good	Moderate
Ford Focus 2 dr.	FRONT	1832	Very Good	8%	9%	Good	Moderate
	SIDE	3826	Poor	9%	36%	Good	Good
Ford Focus 4 dr.	FRONT	2350	Very Good	12%	11%	Good	Good
	SIDE	2022	Good	13%	10%	Good	Very Good
Ford ZX2	FRONT			21%	28%	Good	
2 dr.	SIDE	3191	Poor	27%	10%	Moderate	Moderate
4 dr.	SIDE	2730	Average	18%	14%	Moderate	Good
Honda Insight	FRONT	2960	Good	12%	20%	Good	Good
Mazda Protégé*	FRONT	3119	Good	18%	15%	Good	Good
	SIDE	1705	Good	12%	7%	Very Good	Good
Saturn SL/SW	FRONT	1927	Very Good	10%	10%	Very Good	Good
	SIDE	3154	Average	18%	19%	Moderate	Good
Subaru Impreza*	FRONT	2930	Good	15%	17%	Very Good	Good
Volkswagen Beetle	FRONT	2348	Very Good	11%	12%	Very Good	Good
	SIDE	1750	Good	5%	15%	Good	Very Good
COMPACT							
Chevrolet Cavalier 2 dr.	FRONT	3313	Good	22%	14%	Good	Very Good
	SIDE	5493	Very Poor	49%	22%	Moderate	Good

*Vehicle to be tested in 2001. Results expected to be the same or better.

How to Read the Charts:

1234	**Crash Test Index** is the overall numerical injury rating for front occupants in a frontal and side crash. *Lower numbers mean better performance.*
Very Good	**Car Book Rating** shows how the vehicle compares among all vehicles tested to date. The range is very good, good, moderate, poor, and very poor.
00%	**Likelihood of Life Threatening Injury** is the chance that the occupants would be seriously injured in a frontal and side crash. *Lower percentages mean better performance.*
Good	**Leg Injury Rating** compares occupant leg protection in a frontal and side crash for all cars tested to date.

Note: Front and side crash ratings are included when available.

CRASH TEST RESULTS

Crash Test Performance		Crash Test Index	Car Book Rating	Likelihood of Life Threatening Injury		Leg Injury Rating	
				Driver	Passenger	Driver	Passenger
COMPACT (cont.)							
Chevrolet Cavalier 4 dr.	FRONT	3248	Good	17%	17%	Good	Good
	SIDE	3853	Poor	31%	15%	Poor	Moderate
Chevrolet Prizm	FRONT	2735	Good	15%	13%	Good	Good
	SIDE	2378	Good	14%	14%	Moderate	Good
	SIDE[1]	2066	Good	6%	17%	Moderate	Good
Honda Civic 2 dr.	FRONT	1488	Very Good	8%	7%	Very Good	Very Good
	SIDE	1042	Very Good	6%	6%	Very Good	Very Good
Honda Civic 4 dr.	FRONT	1463	Very Good	8%	6%	Very Good	Good
	SIDE	1536	Very Good	7%	10%	Very Good	Good
Kia Sephia	SIDE	2399	Good	18%	9%	Very Good	Good
Mazda 626	FRONT	2230	Very Good	11%	11%	Good	Good
	SIDE	2554	Average	14%	16%	Poor	Good
Mitsubishi Galant	FRONT	2547	Very Good	14%	13%	Very Good	Good
	SIDE[1]	1157	Very Good	5%	8%	Very Good	Good
Oldsmobile Alero	FRONT	2415	Very Good	13%	11%	Good	Good
	SIDE	2808	Average	15%	18%	Good	Moderate
Pontiac Grand Am	FRONT	2415	Very Good	13%	11%	Good	Good
	SIDE	2808	Average	15%	18%	Good	Moderate
Pontiac Sunfire 2 dr.	FRONT	3313	Good	22%	14%	Good	Very Good
	SIDE	5493	Very Poor	49%	22%	Moderate	Good
Pontiac Sunfire 4 dr.	FRONT	3248	Good	17%	17%	Good	Good
	SIDE	3853	Poor	31%	15%	Poor	Moderate
Subaru Legacy*	FRONT	2525	Very Good	12%	13%	Good	Good
	SIDE	1218	Very Good	8%	6%	Very Good	Very Good
Toyota Corolla	FRONT	2735	Good	15%	13%	Good	Good
	SIDE[1]	2066	Good	6%	17%	Moderate	Good
	SIDE	2378	Good	14%	14%	Moderate	Good
Volkswagen Golf	FRONT	1865	Very Good	9%	8%	Good	Good
Volkswagen Jetta	FRONT	1865	Very Good	9%	8%	Good	Good
	SIDE[1]	1445	Very Good	6%	10%	Very Good	Good

[1]Front Side Airbags; *Vehicle to be tested in 2001. Results expected to be the same or better.

CRASH TEST RESULTS

Crash Test Performance		Crash Test Index	Car Book Rating	Likelihood of Life Threatening Injury		Leg Injury Rating	
				Driver	Passenger	Driver	Passenger
INTERMEDIATE							
Buick Century	FRONT	3829	Average	12%	30%	Good	Good
	SIDE	2763	Average	15%	18%	Moderate	Good
Buick Regal	FRONT	3829	Average	12%	30%	Good	Good
	SIDE	2763	Average	15%	18%	Moderate	Good
Chevrolet Camaro	FRONT	1783	Very Good	11%	7%	Very Good	Very Good
	SIDE	2342	Good	17%	10%	Good	Moderate
Chevrolet Impala*	FRONT	1943	Very Good	7%	10%	Moderate	Good
	SIDE	1398	Very Good	7%	8%	Good	Good
Chevrolet Malibu	FRONT	2633	Good	13%	14%	Good	Good
	SIDE	2657	Average	22%	9%	Good	Good
Chrysler Concorde	FRONT	3418	Good	20%	15%	Moderate	Good
	SIDE	2162	Good	8%	17%	Good	Good
Chrysler PT Cruiser	FRONT	4616	Poor	36%	13%	Moderate	Moderate
	SIDE[2]	1112	Very Good	8%	4%	Very Good	Very Good
Dodge Intrepid	FRONT	3418	Good	20%	15%	Moderate	Good
	SIDE	2232	Good	8%	18%	Very Good	Moderate
Ford Mustang*	FRONT	3063	Good	14%	17%	Good	Good
	SIDE	2558	Average	18%	12%	Good	Very Good
Ford Taurus	FRONT	1793	Very Good	8%	7%	Good	Good
	SIDE	2426	Good	11%	17%	Good	Good
	SIDE[2]	2783	Average	16%	16%	Moderate	Very Good
Honda Accord 2 dr.*	FRONT	2688	Good	15%	15%	Very Good	Good
	SIDE	1895	Good	15%	6%	Very Good	Very Good
	SIDE[1]	1155	Very Good	7%	6%	Good	Very Good
Honda Accord 4 dr.*	FRONT	3083	Good	19%	15%	Very Good	Good
	SIDE[1]	950	Very Good	6%	4%	Very Good	Very Good
	SIDE	1593	Good	9%	8%	Very Good	Very Good
Infiniti I30	FRONT	2577	Good	14%	14%	Very Good	Good
	SIDE	1144	Very Good	6%	6%	Good	Very Good
Lexus ES300*	FRONT	2521	Very Good	14%	13%	Good	Very Good
	SIDE	1280	Very Good	6%	8%	Moderate	Good
Mercury Sable	FRONT	1793	Very Good	8%	7%	Good	Good
	SIDE[2]	2783	Average	16%	16%	Moderate	Very Good
	SIDE	2426	Good	11%	17%	Good	Good

[1]Front Side Airbags; [2]Front Side Airbags and Head Airbags; *Vehicle to be tested in 2001. Results expected to be the same or better.

CRASH TEST RESULTS

Crash Test Performance		Crash Test Index	Car Book Rating	Likelihood of Life Threatening Injury		Leg Injury Rating	
				Driver	Passenger	Driver	Passenger
INTERMEDIATE (cont.)							
Nissan Altima	FRONT	1921	Very Good	11%	9%	Very Good	Good
	SIDE	3009	Average	18%	18%	Good	Good
Nissan Maxima	FRONT	2577	Good	14%	14%	Very Good	Good
	SIDE[2]	1144	Very Good	6%	6%	Good	Very Good
	SIDE	1432	Very Good	10%	6%	Good	Very Good
Oldsmobile Intrigue	FRONT	3829	Very Good	12%	30%	Good	Good
Pontiac Firebird	FRONT	1783	Very Good	11%	7%	Very Good	Very Good
	SIDE	2342	Good	17%	10%	Good	Moderate
Pontiac Grand Prix*	FRONT	3194	Good	20%	14%	Good	Good
Saturn L/LW	FRONT	1979	Very Good	11%	10%	Very Good	Good
	SIDE	2787	Average	25%	6%	Good	Good
Toyota Avalon	SIDE	1216	Very Good	8%	5%	Very Good	Good
Toyota Camry	FRONT	1927	Very Good	12%	8%	Very Good	Very Good
	SIDE[1]			8%		Good	
	SIDE	2341	Good	15%	12%	Good	Good
Toyota Solara	SIDE	1795	Good	16%	3%	Good	Very Good
Volkswagen Passat	FRONT	1881	Very Good	10%	8%	Good	Good
	SIDE	1642	Good	8%	10%	Good	Good
Volvo S80	FRONT	1995	Very Good	10%	10%	Very Good	Good
	SIDE	975	Very Good	5%	5%	Very Good	Very Good
LARGE							
Acura RL	FRONT	3128	Good	20%	17%	Very Good	Very Good
Audi A8	FRONT	1845	Very Good	10%	8%	Good	Good
Buick LeSabre*	FRONT	1948	Very Good	10%	10%	Very Good	Good
	SIDE	1510	Very Good	9%	8%	Very Good	Very Good
Cadillac Deville	FRONT	4543	Average	34%	18%	Moderate	Good
	SIDE	1562	Good	9%	9%	Very Good	Very Good
Cadillac Seville	FRONT	1948	Very Good	10%	10%	Very Good	Good
Chrysler LHS	SIDE	2162	Good	8%	17%	Good	Good
Ford Crown Victoria	FRONT	1832	Very Good	10%	8%	Good	Very Good
	SIDE	1481	Very Good	9%	7%	Good	Good
Lincoln Town Car*	FRONT	2947	Good	20%	11%	Good	Very Good
	SIDE	1227	Very Good	7%	7%	Very Good	Good
Mercury Grand Marquis	FRONT	1832	Very Good	10%	8%	Good	Very Good
	SIDE	1481	Very Good	9%	7%	Good	Good

[1]Front Side Airbags [2]Front Side Airbags and Head Airbags; *Vehicle to be tested in 2001. Results expected to be the same or better.

CRASH TEST RESULTS

Crash Test Performance		Crash Test Index	Car Book Rating	Likelihood of Life Threatening Injury		Leg Injury Rating	
				Driver	Passenger	Driver	Passenger
LARGE (cont.)							
Oldsmobile Aurora	FRONT	1948	Very Good	10%	10%	Very Good	Good
	SIDE	1967	Good	12%	10%	Very Good	Very Good
Pontiac Bonneville	FRONT	1948	Very Good	10%	10%	Very Good	Good
MINIVAN							
Chevrolet Astro	FRONT	4073	Average	29%	13%	Moderate	Moderate
Chevrolet Venture*	FRONT	3416	Good	11	24%	Good	Good
	SIDE	1068	Very Good	6%	6%	Good	Good
Chrysler T & C*	FRONT	3420	Good	18%	18%	Moderate	Good
Dodge Caravan*	FRONT	3370	Good	19%	18%	Good	Good
Ford Windstar*	FRONT	1468	Very Good	5%	9%	Good	Very Good
	SIDE[2]	884	Very Good	5%	4%	Very Good	Very Good
	SIDE	1319	Very Good	6%	8%	Very Good	Moderate
GMC Safari	FRONT	4073	Average	29%	13%	Moderate	Moderate
Honda Odyssey	FRONT	1533	Very Good	8%	7%	Very Good	Very Good
	SIDE	637	Very Good	3%	4%	Very Good	Very Good
Mazda MPV	FRONT	3263	Good	19%	16%	Good	Very Good
	SIDE	625	Very Good	3%	3%	Very Good	Good
Mercury Villager	FRONT	1630	Very Good	8%	8%	Good	Good
	SIDE	1160	Very Good	5%	8%	Very Good	Good
Nissan Quest	FRONT	1630	Very Good	8%	8%	Good	Good
	SIDE	1160	Very Good	5%	8%	Poor	Good

[2]Front Side Airbags and Head Airbags; *Vehicle to be tested in 2001. Results expected to be the same or better.

How to Read the Charts:

1234 **Crash Test Index** is the overall numerical injury rating for front occupants in a frontal and side crash. *Lower numbers mean better performance.*

Very Good **Car Book Rating** shows how the vehicle compares among all vehicles tested to date. The range is very good, good, moderate, poor, and very poor.

00% **Likelihood of Life Threatening Injury** is the chance that the occupants would be seriously injured in a frontal and side crash. *Lower percentages mean better performance.*

Good **Leg Injury Rating** compares occupant leg protection in a frontal and side crash for all cars tested to date.

Note: Front and side crash ratings are included when available.

CRASH TEST RESULTS

Crash Test Performance	Crash Test Index	Car Book Rating	Likelihood of Life Threatening Injury		Leg Injury Rating	
			Driver	Passenger	Driver	Passenger
MINIVAN (cont.)						
Oldsmobile Silhouette* FRONT	3416	Good	11%	24%	Good	Good
SIDE	1068	Very Good	6%	6%	Good	Good
Pontiac Montana FRONT	3416	Good	11%	24%	Good	Good
SIDE	1068	Very Good	6%	6%	Good	Good
Toyota Sienna FRONT	1863	Very Good	10%	9%	Very Good	Good
SIDE	1036	Very Good	6%	5%	Good	Very Good
COMPACT PICKUP						
Chevrolet S-Series FRONT	5132	Poor	30%	30%	Moderate	Good
SIDE			9%		Very Good	
Chev. S-Series Ext. Cab FRONT	5657	Poor	44%	23%	Moderate	Moderate
SIDE			16%		Good	
Dodge Dakota SIDE			5%		Good	
Ford Ranger Stand. Cab* FRONT	2494	Very Good	14%	11%	Good	Very Good
Standard Cab SIDE			4%		Good	
Extended Cab SIDE			9%		Moderate	
GMC Sonoma Stand. Cab FRONT	5424	Poor	33%	32%	Moderate	Good
Standard Cab SIDE			9%		Very Good	
Extended Cab FRONT	5668	Poor	44%	23%	Moderate	Moderate
Extended Cab SIDE			16%		Good	
Mazda B-Series Stand. Cab FRONT	2494	Very Good	14%	11%	Good	Very Good
Standard Cab SIDE			4%		Good	
Extended Cab SIDE			9%		Moderate	
Nissan Frontier SIDE			8%		Moderate	
Toyota Tacoma SIDE			32%		Poor	
STANDARD PICKUP						
Chevrolet Silverado FRONT	3713	Average	22%	18%	Moderate	Good
Dodge Ram FRONT	3226	Good	21%	14%	Good	Good
FRONT	2659	Good	15%	12%	Good	Good
Ford F-Series Stand. Cab* FRONT	2586	Good	12%	13%	Good	Good
Extended Cab SIDE	714	Very Good	3%	4%	Very Good	Very Good
Standard Cab SIDE			2%		Very Good	Very Good
SMALL SPORT UTILITY						
Chevrolet Tracker SIDE	1194	Very Good	9%	4%	Moderate	Very Good
Honda CR-V FRONT	2826	Good	19%	10%	Good	Good
SIDE	1059	Very Good	6%	6%	Good	Very Good

*Vehicle to be tested in 2001. Results expected to be the same or better.

15

Crash Test Performance	Crash Test Index	Car Book Rating	Likelihood of Life Threatening Injury		Leg Injury Rating	
			Driver	Passenger	Driver	Passenger
SM. SP. UTILITY (cont.)						
Jeep Wrangler *FRONT*	3284	Good	19%	16%	Good	Good
MID-SIZE SPORT UTILITY						
Chevrolet Blazer *FRONT*	4612	Poor	33%	19%	Moderate	Good
SIDE	829	Very Good	5%	3%	Very Good	Very Good
Chevrolet Tahoe* *FRONT*	3174	Good	15%	17%	Moderate	Good
Ford Explorer *FRONT*	3520	Average	20%	19%	Good	Good
SIDE[2]	552	Very Good	3%	3%	Very Good	Very Good
GMC Jimmy *FRONT*	4612	Poor	33%	19%	Moderate	Good
SIDE	829	Very Good	5%	3%	Very Good	Very Good
Honda Passport *FRONT*	3491	Average	20%	19%	Good	Good
SIDE	580	Very Good	4%	2%	Good	Very Good
Infiniti QX4 *FRONT*	2462	Very Good	18%	9%	Very Good	Very Good
SIDE	765	Very Good	3%	5%	Very Good	Very Good
Isuzu Rodeo *FRONT*	3491	Average	20%	19%	Good	Good
SIDE	579	Very Good	4%	2%	Good	Very Good
Jeep Cherokee *FRONT*	5138	Poor	29%	29%	Moderate	Moderate
SIDE	1537	Very Good	12%	5%	Moderate	Good
Jeep Grand Cherokee *FRONT*	4748	Poor	30%	22%	Moderate	Moderate
SIDE	1067	Very Good	7%	5%	Good	Good
Mercedes-Benz M-Class *FRONT*	2496	Very Good	14%	10%	Good	Good
Mercury Mountaineer *FRONT*	3520	Average	20%	19%	Good	Good
SIDE[2]	552	Very Good	3%	3%	Very Good	Very Good
Nissan Pathfinder *FRONT*	2462	Very Good	18%	9%	Very Good	Very Good
SIDE[2]	421	Very Good	3%	2%	Very Good	Very Good
Nissan Xterra *FRONT*	2336	Very Good	11%	14%	Very Good	Very Good
SIDE	715	Very Good	6%	1%	Good	Very Good
Oldsmobile Bravada^ *FRONT*	4612	Poor	19%	33%	Moderate	Good
SIDE	829	Very Good	5%	3%	Very Good	Very Good
Pontiac Aztek *SIDE*	1313	Very Good	3%	11%	Very Good	Moderate
Subaru Forester* *FRONT*	2740	Good	15%	12%	Good	Good
Toyota 4Runner* *FRONT*	2390	Very Good	15%	10%	Good	Good
SIDE	288	Very Good	2%	1%	Very Good	Very Good
LARGE SPORT UTILITY						
Cadillac Escalade *FRONT*	3174	Good	15%	17%	Moderate	Good
Ford Expedition* *FRONT*	2600	Good	14%	14%	Good	Very Good
GMC Denali *FRONT*	3174	Good	15%	17%	Moderate	Good
Lincoln Navigator *FRONT*	2600	Good	14%	14%	Good	Very Good

[2]Front Side Airbags and Head Airbags; ^No 2001 model. 2002 model available in early 2001. 2000 model sold until 2002 available. *Vehicle to be tested in 2001. Results expected to be the same or better.

AUTOMATIC CRASH PROTECTION

The concept of automatic safety protection is not new—automatic fire sprinklers in public buildings, release of oxygen masks in airplanes, purification of drinking water, and pasteurization of milk are all commonly accepted forms of automatic safety protection. Ironically, we often incorporate better technology in safely transporting electronic equipment, eggs, and china than we do in packaging humans in automobiles.

Over twenty years ago, in cooperation with the federal government and strong prodding from the insurance companies, the automobile industry developed airbags as a form of automatic safety protection. These devices will not prevent all deaths, but they will cut your chances of being killed or seriously injured in a car accident in half.

The idea behind automatic crash protection is to protect people from what is called the "second collision," when the occupant comes forward and collides with the interior of their own car. Because the "second collision" occurs within milliseconds, and because so many people do not use seat belts, providing automatic rather than manual protection dramatically improves the chances of escaping injury.

Airbags: There are side airbags, rear side airbags, head protection airbags, and advanced airbags on the way. Hidden in the steering wheel, the right side of the dashboard, and other locations, airbags provide unobtrusive and effective protection in frontal crashes. When needed, they inflate instantly to cushion the driver and the front seat passenger. By spreading crash forces over the head and chest, front airbags protect the body from violent contact with the hard surfaces of the car. Cars with airbags also provide manual seat belts to protect occupants in nonfrontal crashes and to keep them in the best position to benefit from an airbag. However, airbags offer protection in frontal crashes even if the safety belt is not fastened. Side airbags work the same way, except they come out of the doors in order to spread crash forces across the driver's or passenger's legs, side, and arms.

Second Generation (De-Powered) Airbags: In an effort to lower the number of improperly buckled children killed by airbag deployment, the government is allowing automakers to de-power their airbags for new models. As a result, automakers began de-powering their airbags on 1999 models, which has safety advocates concerned. Please be warned: de-powered airbags can still be fatal to out-of-position children (children who are not sitting upright and properly buckled in). Additionally, de-powering airbags lowers the amount of protection for adults. De-powering airbags, unfortunately, is a weak solution to a serious problem.

Should I turn my airbag off? The short answer to this question is no. According to government statistics, thousands of people have been saved by airbags. In spite of the tragic stories you have no doubt heard, airbags save lives. If properly belted, an airbag will reduce your risk of a serious head injury by 75 percent!

Because of concern for their children's safety, parents may be considering turning off their airbag—a far better alternative is to keep your children in the back seat and keep the airbag ready to save a larger passenger.

Drivers should note that the ideal position when driving is belted with your chest approximately 10 inches from the center of the steering wheel. If it isn't possible for you to get at least 10 inches away from the wheel, you can try pedal extenders. Call the National Mobility Equipment Dealers Association at 813–932–8566 for more information about pedal extenders.

Airbag Cutoff Switches: Cutoff switches are currently available in pickups. You can also qualify for a waiver that would allow you to install an on-off switch in your vehicle. This waiver is given to the following: 1) individuals with medical conditions where the risk of injury from a deploying airbag is greater than the risk of injury from impacting the steering wheel, 2) individuals who are unable to position themselves at least 10 inches back from the center of the driver airbag cover, 3) individuals who must transport an infant in a rear-facing child seat because the vehicle has no back seat, 4) individuals who routinely transport children younger than 12 in car pools in a vehicle without enough seats in the rear to accommodate all the children.

Consumers can obtain the necessary forms by calling 800-424-9393 or by visiting their website at www.nhtsa.dot.gov. NHTSA has published a list of dealerships and independent shops willing to install on-off switches for those with a valid waiver.

Smart Airbags: The solution to airbag concerns lies with smart airbags. Most automakers are developing smart airbag systems, which will differentiate between an adult, a child, a rear-facing child seat, or an empty seat, using various heat, ultrasonic sound wave, and infrared sensors. Not only will smart airbags save lives, but by preventing the passenger-side airbag from deploying when the seat is empty, they will save thousands in repair costs. We expect these safer airbags to be available in the next few years.

Here are the correct answers to typical airbag questions from the Insurance Institute for Highway Safety:

Is the gas that inflates airbags dangerous? Nitrogen, which makes up 79.8 percent of the air we breathe, is the gas that inflates the bags. A solid chemical, sodium azide, generates this nitrogen gas. Sodium azide does not present a safety hazard in normal driving, in crashes, or in disposal. In fact, occupants of the car will never even come in contact with the sodium azide.

Will airbags inflate by mistake? Airbags will inflate only in frontal impacts equivalent to hitting a solid wall at about 10 mph or higher. They will not inflate when you go over bumps or potholes or when you hit something at low speed. Even slamming on your brakes will not cause the airbags to inflate unless you hit something.

Will airbags protect occupants without seat belts? Airbags are designed to protect unbelted front-seat adults in 30-mph frontal crashes into a wall. However, airbags are not designed to protect unbelted children or the elderly. Equipping cars with airbags reduced the average injury severity for adults in serious frontal crashes by 64 percent, even though over 80 percent of the occupants were unbelted. The best protection, however, is provided by a combination of airbags and lap and shoulder safety belts.

HEAD PROTECTION AIRBAGS

Because head injuries often occur in side impact crashes, automakers have developed new airbags to specifically protect your head in the event of a side crash or rollover. These airbags usually deploy out of the roof or roof pillars. Here are some of the vehicles offering head protection airbags:

2001 DaimlerChrysler PT Cruiser
1999-2001 Ford Windstar
1999-2001 Ford Explorer
1999-2001 Lincoln Continental
1999-2001 Lincoln Town Car
1999-2001 Mercury Cougar
1999-2001 Mercury Mountaineer
2000-2001 Ford Focus
2000-2001 Ford Taurus
2000-2001 Lincoln LS
2000-2001 Mercury Sable
1999–2001 BMW 3-Series
1998–2001 BMW 5-Series
1998–2001 BMW 7-Series
1999-2001 Mercedes E-Class sedan
2000-2001 Mercedes E-Class sedan and wagon
2000-2001 Mercedes S-Class
2000-2001 Mercedes CL coupe
1998–2001 Saab 9-3
1998–2001 Saab 9-5
1999–2001 Volvo S70/V70
1999–2001 Volvo S80
2000-2001 Volvo S40/V40

AIRBAG DEPLOYMENT

In the fall of 1997, the Center for Auto Safety (CAS) revealed major differences in passenger-side airbag design which may affect their safety. The study found auto manufacturers generally chose one of two methods to deploy passenger-side airbags, vertically or horizontally. The horizontally deploying airbags shoot straight out of the dashboard toward the passenger. Vertically deploying airbags mounted in the top of the dash move upward toward the windshield and reflect off the windshield toward the passenger. Vertically deploying airbags can also be mounted from the edge of the dash creating a safety zone between the occupant and the deploying airbag. According to CAS, most passenger-side airbag deaths have been from horizontally deploying airbags. Although vertically deploying airbags will not eliminate the risk of injury, it appears that they may be more effective at reducing the risk of injury during deployment.

Further, some manufacturers have taken the lead in equipping their airbag systems with dual-stage inflators. These systems deploy an airbag with a level of force based on crash severity. In a low-speed collision, the airbag will have a low level of deployment, while in a severe collision, the airbag will deploy more aggressively to protect the occupant. Based on data collected by CAS and responses received from auto companies, we have listed below those manufacturers who have chosen to use vertically deploying airbags and dual-stage inflators. Some additional models may have dual inflators but, unfortunately, auto companies aren't required to disclose this information.

The implementation of smart airbags will dramatically improve airbag performance. At this time, NHTSA is in the process of developing requirements for smart airbag systems.

VERTICALLY DEPLOYING AIRBAGS

1998–2001 Acura CL	2000-2001 Infiniti G20
1998–2001 Acura Integra	1998–2001 Lexus ES300
1998–2001 Acura RL	1998–2001 Lexus GS300/400
1998–2001 Acura TL	1998 Lexus LS400
1998–2001 Acura NSX	1999–2001 Lexus RX300
1998–2001 BMW 318ti	2000-2001 Lincoln LS
1998 Buick Riviera	1998–2001 Mercury Sable
1998–2001 Cadillac Deville	2000-2001 Mazda MPV
1998–2001 Cadillac Seville	1999–2001 Mazda Protégé
1998–2001 Cadillac Eldorado	1999–2001 Mitsubishi Galant
1998–2001 Chev. Cavalier	1998–2001 Nissan Sentra
1998–2001 Chevrolet Malibu	1999–2001 Oldsmobile Alero
1998–2001 Chevrolet Prizm	1999–2001 Pontiac Gr. Am
2000-2001 Ford Focus	1998–2001 Pontiac Sunfire
1998–2001 Ford Taurus	1998–2001 Saturn EV1
1998–2001 Honda Accord	1998–2001 Toyota Camry
1998–2001 Honda Civic	1998–2001 Toyota Corolla
1998–2001 Honda Odyssey	2000-2001 Toyota RAV4
2000-2001 Honda Insight	1998–2001 Toyota Sienna
1998–2001 Infiniti Q45	1999–2001 Toyota Solara

DUAL-STAGE INFLATORS

2000–2001 Acura CL
2000–2001 Acura RL
2000–2001 Acura TL
2000–2001 BMW 3 Series
2000–2001 BMW 5 Series
2000–2001 BMW Z3
2000–2001 BMW X5
2000–2001 Chrys. Voyager/Chrys. T&C/Dodge Caravan
2000–2001 Ford Taurus
2000–2001 Honda Accord (V6 engine models only)
2000–2001 Mercedes-Benz C-Class
2000–2001 Mercedes-Benz E-Class
2000–2001 Mercedes-Benz M-Class
2000–2001 Mercury Sable

SAFETY BELTS

About 60 percent of occupants killed or injured in auto crashes would have been saved from serious harm had they been wearing safety belts. Yet many Americans do not use these life-saving devices.

Safety belts are particularly important in minivans, 4x4s, and pickups because there is a greater chance of being killed or seriously injured in a rollover accident. The simple precaution of wearing your belt greatly improves your odds of survival.

Why don't people wear their belts? They simply don't know the facts. Once you know the facts, you should be willing to buckle up.

While most safety advocates welcome the passage of safety belt usage laws, the ones passed to date are weak and generally unenforced. In addition, most of the laws are based on "secondary" enforcement—meaning that you cannot be stopped for failing to wear your belt. If you are stopped for another reason and the officer notices you don't have your belt on by the time he or she reaches the vehicle, you may be fined. In states with "primary" enforcement, you can be stopped for not wearing a safety belt. Yet, in many cases the fines are less than a parking ticket. In Arkansas, however, you can get a $10 credit toward a primary violation if you are wearing a seat belt and in Wyoming, a $5 credit.

Another unusual feature of these laws is that most of them allow drivers to avoid buckling up if they have a doctor's permission. This loophole was inserted to appease those who were not really in favor of the law. However, many doctors are wondering if they will be held responsible for the injuries of unbuckled patients. In fact, the State of New York Medical Society cautions doctors never to give medical dispensation from the law because "no medical condition has yet been found to warrant a medical exemption for seat belt use."

Even though most state laws are weak, they have heightened awareness and raised the level of usage. Belt use in states that have passed a safety belt law tends to rise sharply after the law is enacted. However, after the law has been on the books a few months, safety belt use drops.

! SAFETY BELT MYTHS !

Myth: "I don't want to be trapped by a seat belt. It's better to be thrown free in an accident."

Fact: The chance of being killed is 25 times greater if you're ejected. A safety belt will keep you from plunging through the windshield, smashing into trees, rocks, or other cars, scraping along the ground, or getting run over by your own or anothers vehicle. If you are wearing your belt, you're far more likely to be conscious after an accident to free yourself and other passengers.

Myth: "Pregnant women should not wear safety belts."

Fact: According to the American Medical Association, "Both the pregnant mother and the fetus are safer, provided the lap belt is worn as low on the pelvis as possible."

Myth: "I don't need it. In case of an accident, I can brace myself with my hands."

Fact: At 35 mph, the impact of a crash on you and your passengers is brutal. There's no way your arms and legs can brace you against that kind of collision—the speed and force are just too great. The force of impact at only 10 mph is roughly equivalent to the force of catching a 200-pound bag of cement dropped from a first-floor window.

Myth: "I just don't believe it will ever happen to me."

Fact: Every one of us can expect to be in a crash once every 10 years. For 1 out of 20 of us, it will be a serious crash. For 1 out of 60 born today, it will be fatal.

CHILD SAFETY SEATS

How many times have you gone out of your way to prevent your children from being injured by keeping household poisons out of reach, watching carefully as they swam, or keeping a good grip on their hand while crossing a street or parking lot? Probably, quite often. Yet, parents ignore the biggest danger of all when they allow their children to lay down in the back of a minivan or roam unrestrained in their car. Ironically, it's your automobile that poses the greatest threat to your child's health.

Child safety seats are the best and only reliable way to protect your child in a vehicle. However, NHTSA estimates that up to 85% of children who ride in a car seat are improperly buckled in. Because of this confusion, NHTSA has phased in regulations for attaching and anchoring child seats into vehicles.

The universal child seat system uses a top tether, an adjustable strap attached to the back of the child seat. The tether system stabilizes the seat and reduces the potential for head injury. The straps are secured via an attachment mounting in the rear shelf area of most passenger cars. Eighty percent of 1999 passenger cars were required to have top tether anchorages for back seats, and all 2000 model passenger cars had the anchor points.

Never place a child in your lap! At 30 mph, a crash or sudden stop will wrench a 10-pound child from your arms with a force of nearly 300 pounds! If you aren't wearing a seat belt, then your own body will be thrown forward with enough force to crush your child against the dashboard or the back of the front seat.

Hand-Me-Down Seats: To ensure that a secondhand child seat will adequately protect your child, see if its identification stickers, belt instructions, and date of manufacture are still visible. Only use seats less than five years old. Make sure no parts or instructions are missing. Most importantly, know the history of the child seat—never use seats that have been in crashes, no matter how perfect they look.

Buying Tips: Purchasing a new child seat for your child is always money well spent. Many vehicles now have built-in child seats which are an excellent option. Child seats with an automatic retracting harness and a shield are typically the easiest to use. Here are more buying tips for a child safety seat:

☑ Try before you buy. Your car's seat belts and the shape of its seats will determine which child seats fit your car so make sure it can be properly installed.

☑ Determine how many straps or buckles must be fastened to use a child seat. The less complicated the seat, the less chance for misuse. The easiest seats require only one strap or buckle after fastening the seat belt around the child seat.

☑ Make sure the seat is wide enough for growth and bulky winter clothes. If possible, let your child sit in the seat to measure for fit.

☑ Is your child comfortable? Can your child move his or her arms freely, sleep in the seat, or see out a window?

☑ Make sure you fill out and mail the owner registration card. This is the best way to find out if your seat is ever recalled.

BUCKLED UP=BETTER BEHAVIOR

Medical researchers have concluded that belted children are better behaved. When not buckled up, children squirm, stand up, complain, fight, and pull at the steering wheel. When buckled into safety seats, however, they displayed 95 percent fewer incidents of bad behavior.

When buckled up, children feel secure. In addition, being in a seat can be more fun because most safety seats are high enough to allow children to see out the window. Also, children are less likely to feel carsick and more likely to fall asleep in a car seat.

Make the car seat your child's own special place, so he or she will enjoy being in it. Pick out some special soft toys or books that can be used only in the car seat to make using the seat a positive experience. Finally, set a good example for your child by using your own safety belt <u>every</u> time you get in the car.

CHILD SAFETY SEAT TYPES

There are six types of child seats: *infant-only, convertible, toddler-only, child/booster, booster, and built-in.*

Infant-Only Seats: Infant-only seats can be used from birth until your baby reaches a weight of 17–20 pounds. This type of seat must be installed facing the rear in a semireclined position. In a collision, the crash forces are spread over the baby's back, the strongest body surface. The seat's harness should come from below the child's shoulders in the rear-facing position.

One benefit of an infant-only seat is that you can easily install and remove the seat with the baby in place. Most infant car seats can also be used as household baby seats. Caution: Some household baby seats look remarkably similar to infant safety seats. These are not crashworthy and should never be used as car safety seats.

Convertible Seats: Buying a convertible seat can save you the expense of buying both an infant seat and a toddler seat. Most convertible seats can be used from birth until the child reaches four years and 40 pounds. When used for an infant, the seat faces rearward in a semireclined position. When the child is at least a year old and 20 pounds or more, the frame can be adjusted upright and the seat turned to face forward.

As with any safety seat, it is extremely important that the straps fit snugly over the child's shoulders. A good way to ensure that the straps are adjusted correctly is to buy a seat with an automatically adjusting harness.

Like a car safety belt, these models automatically adjust to fit snugly on your child. Convertible seats come in three basic types:

The *five-point harness* consists of two shoulder and two lap straps that converge at a buckle connected to a crotch strap. These straps are adjustable, allowing for growth and comfort.

The *T-shield* has a small pad joining the shoulder belts. With only one buckle, many parents find this the simplest and easiest-to-use type of convertible seat, but it will not fit newborns properly.

The *tray shield* is another convenient model, since the safety harness is attached to the shield. As the shield comes down in front of the child, the harness comes over the child's shoulders. The shield is an important part of the restraint system, but, like the T-shield, it will not fit small infants.

Toddler-Only Seats: These are really booster child seats and they may take the place of convertible seats when a child is between 20 and 30 pounds. Weight and size limits vary greatly among seats.

Child/Booster Seats: Some manufacturers are now making a variety of combination child/booster seats. For example, one model can be converted from a 5-point harness to a high-backed, belt-positioning booster seat. They can be used for children ranging from 20 to 40 pounds, making them a very economical choice.

Booster Seats: Booster seats are used when your child is too big for a convertible seat but too small to use safety belts. Most car lap/shoulder belts do not adequately fit children with a seating height less than 28 inches. Booster seats can be used for children over 30 pounds and come in three types:

Belt-positioning booster seats raise the child for a better fit with the car's safety belts. If your child is under three years old, do not use belt-positioning booster seats because your child may be able to unbuckle him or herself.

The *removable-shield booster seat* can be used with a lap/shoulder belt with the shield removed or with a lap belt with the shield on. This seat can be adapted to different cars and seating positions, making it a good choice.

The *shield-type booster seat* has a small plastic shield with no straps and can be used only with lap belts. Typically, the safety belt fastens in front of the shield, anchoring it to the car. Most safety experts recommend using these seats until a child is four years old and 40 pounds.

Built-in Seats: Chrysler, Ford, GM, Volvo, and other auto companies offer the option of a fold-out toddler seat on some of their models. These seats are only for children older than one and come as either a five-point harness or a booster with three-point belt; however, the three-point booster is not recommended for children under three years old. This built-in seat is an excellent feature because it is always in the car and does not pose the problem of compatability that often occurs with separate child seats.

USING YOUR CHILD SAFETY SEAT

The incorrect use of child safety seats has reached epidemic proportions. A stunning 85% of parents misuse their child's safety seat. Problems fall into two categories: incorrect installation of the seat and incorrect use of the seat's straps to secure the child. In most cases, the car's safety belt was improperly routed through the seat.

In addition to following your seat's installation instructions, here are some important usage tips:

☑ The safest place for the seat is the center of the back seat.

☑ Use a locking clip when needed. Check the instructions that come with your seat and those in your car owner's manual.

☑ Keep your child rear-facing for at least a year.

☑ Regularly check the seat's safety harness and the car's seat belt for a tight, secure fit because the straps will stretch on impact.

☑ Don't leave sharp or heavy objects or groceries loose in the car. Anything loose can be deadly in a crash.

☑ In the winter, dress your baby in a legged suit to allow proper attachment of the harness. If necessary, drape an extra blanket over the seat after your baby is buckled.

☑ Be sure all doors are locked.

☑ Do not give your child lollipops or ice cream on a stick while riding. A bump or swerve could jam the stick into his or her throat.

Seat Belts for Kids: How long should children use car seats? For school-age children, a car seat is twice as effective in preventing injury than an adult lap and shoulder harness—use a booster as long as possible. Most children can start using seat belts at 65 pounds and when tall enough for the shoulder belt to cross the chest, not the neck. The lap section of the belt should be snug and as low on the hips as possible. If the shoulder belt does cross the face or neck, use a booster.

Never:

☒ Use the same belt on two children.

☒ Move a shoulder belt behind a child's back or under an arm.

☒ Buckle in a pet or any large toys with the child.

☒ Recline a seat with a belted child.

☒ Use a twisted seat belt. The belt must be straight and flat.

☒ Use pillows or cushions to boost your child.

☒ Place a belt around you with a child in your lap. In an accident or sudden stop, your child would absorb most of the crash force.

LOCKING CLIPS

Locking clips come with most child safety seats and are needed if the latch plate on the car's seat belt slides freely along the belt. If you don't properly install the locking clip, the child seat can move or tip over. Look for heavy-duty locking clips, available at Ford, Toyota, and Nissan dealers. The safest way to use a heavy-duty locking clip is to pull the seat belt entirely out and attach the clip so the child seat is secure with no retracting involved. For more information, contact Safety Belt Safe at 800–745–SAFE.

REAR-FACING CHILD SAFETY SEATS

Never use a rear-facing child safety seat in a seating position that has an airbag. To deploy fast enough to protect adult occupants, an airbag inflates with enough force to potentially cause serious head and chest injuries to a child in a rear-facing safety seat. And remember, airbags do not take the place of child safety seats.

CHILDREN AND AIRBAGS

Will airbags protect children? Studies of actual crashes indicate that children can be protected by airbags—but only if they are properly buckled up! A deploying airbag can be deadly to an unrestrained child. Properly buckling your child has never been more important now that virtually all cars and minivans, and most trucks and sport utilities, offer airbags on the passenger's side where children often sit.

According to the government, airbags have saved thousands of lives. However, to date, 61 children under the age of 12 have been killed by the deployment of an airbag. Last year the National Highway Traffic Safety Administration estimated that about one child per month is killed by airbag deployment, and if certain measures are not implemented, the number could increase to one per week.

Remember—*most children killed by airbags are not properly belted.* The majority of the children killed were either completely unrestrained or improperly restrained. To protect the occupant, an airbag must inflate in a fraction of a second before the occupant hits the dashboard. For a full-size adult, the result is coming forward into a cushion of air. For a child who isn't properly buckled, it can be deadly, especially if the child is standing up or leaning on the dashboard.

! HOW TO BEST PROTECT YOUR CHILD (AND YOURSELF) !

Never place a rear-facing child seat in front of a passenger-side airbag. Even front-facing child seats should be used on a rear seat. The best spot for your children is in the center of the back seat. If you do not have a back seat, here are some tips for keeping your child (and yourself) safe while seated in an airbag seat:

☑ Push the seat as far back as it will go.
☑ Make sure your child is sitting up straight and not leaning forward against the dash.
☑ If you are an adult, sit at least 10–12 inches away from the steering wheel. In the passenger side, slide the seat back as far as it will go.
☑ Use caution if your vehicle has side airbags. Just like frontal airbags, the best way to protect your child is to make sure they are seated and buckled up properly. Again, the safest spot for your child in an accident is the middle of the back seat.

YOUNG DRIVERS

TIP

Each year, teenagers account for about 15 percent of highway deaths. According to the Insurance Institute for Highway Safety (IIHS), the highest driver death rate per 100,000 people is among 18-year-olds. Clearly, parents need to make sure their children are fully prepared to be competent, safe drivers before letting them out on the road. All states issue learner's permits. However, only 35 states and the District of Columbia require permits before getting a driver's license. It isn't difficult for teenagers to get a license and only 14 states prohibit teenagers from driving during night and early morning. Call your MVA for your state's young driver laws.

ANTI-LOCK BRAKES

After airbags, one of the best safety features available is an anti-lock braking system (ABS). ABS shortens stopping distance on dry, wet, and even icy roads by preventing wheel lockup and keeps you from skidding out of control when you "slam" on the brakes.

The ABS works by sensing the speed of each wheel. If one or more of the wheels begins to lock up or skid, it releases that wheel's brakes, allowing the wheel to roll normally again, thus stopping the skid. When the wheel stops skidding, the hydraulic pressure is reapplied instantly. This cycle can be repeated several times per second, keeping each wheel at its optimum braking performance even while your foot keeps pushing on the brake pedal. Although ABS is typically connected to all four wheels, in some light trucks and vans it is connected to only the rear wheels.

The ABS is only active when it senses that the wheels are about to lock up. When an ABS is active, you may notice that the brake pedal pulsates slightly. This pulsation is normal, and it indicates that the brakes are being released and reapplied. *Don't pump your brakes*—the ABS is doing it for you. If there is a failure in the ABS, the vehicle reverts to its conventional braking system and a warning light indicates that the ABS needs repair.

Note: Using tires other than the ones originally on the vehicle may affect the anti-lock braking system. If you are planning to change the size of the tires on your vehicle, first consult your owner's manual.

! WHAT HAPPENS IN A COLLISION? !

A car crash typically involves two collisions. First, the car hits another object and second, the occupant collides with the inside of the car. Injuries result from this second collision. The key to surviving an auto accident is protecting yourself from the second collision. Always wearing your safety belt is the most important defense while having an airbag is a very close second. The whole purpose of the airbag is to protect you in this second collision.

Upon impact, in a typical 35-mph crash, the car begins to crush and slow down. Within 1/10 of a second, the car comes to a stop, but the person keeps moving forward at 35 mph. 1/50 of a second after the car has stopped, the unbelted person slams into the dashboard or windshield.

According to government reports prepared before the widespread use of belts and airbags, these were the major causes of injury in the second collision:

Steering wheel	27%
Instrument panel	11%
Side (doors)	10%
Windshield	5%
Front roof pillar	4%
Glove box area	3%
Roof edges	3%
Roof	2%

FOUR-WHEEL DRIVE

Before you buy four-wheel drive (4WD), you need to ask: do I really need it? 4WD is an expensive option that could require complex repairs should it break down. If you go off-roading on a regular basis, you need 4WD. If road conditions where you regularly drive are consistently slippery, 4WD will help—but so will less expensive options like traction control and anti-lock brakes. For seriously snowy or muddy surfaces, 4WD is best. In addition to adding several thousand dollars to your purchase price, 4WD increases your vehicle's weight, hindering your engine's power and fuel efficiency. If you only plan on using 4WD once or twice a year, it may not be worth the extra cost and headaches. If you need 4WD, here is what you need to know before buying. There are four basic 4WD systems:

Off-Road/Part-Time 4WD: This is the most common and least expensive system. Normally, the vehicle runs in rear two-wheel drive (2WD). The driver must manually switch to 4WD when needed on off-road or slippery road conditions. Remaining in 4WD on dry pavement can cause excessive tire wear, damage to the drive train, and skidding and jerking on turns.

All-Road/Full-Time 4WD: This system also allows the driver to remain in 4WD mode on dry pavement. While in 4WD mode, some of these systems are actually operating in 2WD mode, typically rear wheel drive, until wheel slip is sensed, and then power is transferred to the front wheels. You can manually switch to save fuel when you know 4WD is not needed.

Permanent 4WD: There is no 2WD mode with this system. The vehicle always operates in 4WD mode and runs smoothly on dry pavement. Typically, you have the option to switch to low gear over troublesome terrain or conditions.

All-Wheel Drive (AWD): AWD is similar to Permanent 4WD; however, there is no "High" or "Low" mode for difficult off-road conditions.

4WD: WHAT THE NAME MEANS

TIP

Automakers like to give their 4WD systems special names to make them more marketable. Often, these names do not clearly indicate what kind of system is being offered. The following table deciphers the brand names of popular 4WD systems offered on some of this year's sport utilities and tells you what kind of system they really are. We also list vehicles without brand names to let you compare systems. More than one system may be available for a vehicle.

Vehicle	Brand Name	4WD Systems
Cadillac Escalade	AutoTrac	All-Road
Chevy Blazer/GMC Jimmy	Insta-Trac	Off-Road
Chevy Blazer/GMC Jimmy	None	All-Wheel
Chevy/GMC Suburban	Insta-Trac	Off-Road
Chevy Tahoe/GMC Yukon	Insta-Trac	Off-Road
Ford Explorer (V6)	Control Trac	All-Road
Ford Explorer (V8)	All Wheel Drive	All-Wheel
Ford Expedition	Enhanced Cntrl Trac	All-Road
Honda Passport	None	Off-Road
Isuzu Rodeo/Trooper	None	Off-Road
Jeep Cherokee	Command-Trac	Off-Road
Jeep Cherokee/Gr. Cherokee	Selec-Trac	All-Road
Jeep Grand Cherokee	Quadra-Trac	Permanent
Land Rover (all models)	None	Permanent
Lexus LX470	Full-Time 4WD	Permanent
Mercury Mountaineer	All Wheel Drive	All-Wheel
Mitsubishi Montero	Active Trac	All-Road
Nissan Pathfinder	None	Off-Road
Oldsmobile Bravada	SmartTrack	All-Wheel
Toyota 4Runner	None	Off-Road
Toyota Land Cruiser	Full-Time 4WD	Permanent

OFF-ROAD DRIVING

One reason to buy an off-road vehicle is the ability to take advantage of some of our country's more remote areas. But off-roading also presents some unique hazards. The best way to ensure your safety is to understand the dangers and to be prepared.

Before going out, be sure your vehicle is in top shape. Fill up the tank, and check the spare tire and the fluid levels. Also, find out about the local laws that apply to off-roading through local law enforcement.

Loading up: Be sure to load your vehicle carefully and safely. The heaviest items should be on the floor, as far forward of the rear axle as possible. Secure the load so that loose objects can't hit someone or fall out of the vehicle. And remember, heavy loads on the roof or piled high in the cargo area will raise the vehicle's center of gravity and increase your chances of rolling over.

Controlling your vehicle: On an unpaved surface, the best way to control your vehicle is to control your speed. At a higher speed, you have less time to look for and react to obstacles. Off the road, your vehicle will bounce more and your wheels may leave the ground, so keep a firm grip on the steering wheel. You'll also need more distance for braking.

Off-roading can take you over a wide variety of surfaces, including rocks, grass, sand, mud, snow, and ice. Each of these surfaces affects the control of your vehicle in different ways.

Driving in mud, sand, snow, and ice reduces your traction and increases your braking distance. It is best to use a low gear and keep your vehicle moving so you don't get stuck.

Before driving through water, make sure that it isn't too deep, or your vehicle may be damaged. Drive slowly to prevent water from splashing into your ignition system or tailpipe, causing you to stall. Caution: rushing water is especially dangerous and should be avoided. It can sweep your vehicle away. Even at low speeds, it can wash away the ground from under your tires, causing loss of control.

Driving on hills: Off-road terrain often requires you to drive up, down, or across a hill, each of which presents its own hazards. There are some hills that can't be driven—they are simply too steep for any vehicle. If you have any doubt about the steepness, don't drive the hill. Here are some things to keep in mind as you approach a hill:

Is there a constant incline, or does the hill get sharply steeper in places?

Is there good traction on the hillside, or will the surface cause you to slip?

Is there a straight path up or down the hill?

Are there trees or rocks on the hill that block your path?

What's beyond the hill? Walk it first if you don't know. It's the smart way to see if you'll find a cliff, a fence, or another steep hill.

Is the hill simply too rough? Steep hills often have ruts, gullies, and exposed rocks because they are more susceptible to erosion.

Driving uphill: If you decide you can safely drive up a hill, use a low gear and get a smooth start up the hill. Try to maintain your speed. If you use more power than you need, the wheels may start to spin or slide. Avoid twists and turns and drive as straight a route

as you can. Always slow down as you approach the top of the hill. If your vehicle stalls on the hill, quickly brake to prevent yourself from rolling backwards. Then restart your engine, shift into reverse, and slowly back down the hill. Never shift into neutral to "rev up" the engine and go forward. Your vehicle will roll backwards quickly, and you may lose control. And never attempt to turn around. If the hill is steep enough to stall your vehicle, it is certainly steep enough to make you roll over.

Driving downhill: If you decide you can go down a hill safely, keep your vehicle headed straight down and use a low gear. The engine drag will help your brakes. Never drive downhill with your transmission in neutral, because your brakes will have to do all the work and could overheat and fade. Drive slowly, and avoid turns that take you across the hill. Avoid braking so hard that you lock the wheels or you won't be able to steer your vehicle. If your wheels lock up during downhill braking and the vehicle starts to slide, quickly ease off the brakes and you should straighten out.

Driving across a hill: Even a hill that's not too steep to drive straight up or down can be a problem to drive across. Since your vehicle is not as wide as it is long, driving across a steep hill can cause your vehicle to roll over. Watch out for loose gravel and wet grass which can cause your tires to slip downhill. If the vehicle slips sideways, it could hit something that will trip it and make it roll. If you feel your vehicle starting to slide sideways, turn downhill to help you straighten out and stop slipping.

SAFE TOWING

If you regularly tow a camper, boat, or other trailer, it is important that your vehicle be capable of safely towing the load. Towing a trailer puts considerable strain on a vehicle: the tires, brakes, and engine all experience extra stress.

The most strain is on the automatic transmission. Power from the engine is transmitted to the wheels through a fluid coupling (called a torque converter) that can become extremely hot when towing. If the fluid is burned from overheating, the transmission can be severely damaged. If you do a great deal of towing over long distances, installing an auxiliary transmission cooler will reduce the operating temperature of the fluid and help prevent damage to your transmission.

You can also prolong the life of your vehicle by towing in drive rather than overdrive, except on long stretches of road. Towing in drive provides more power, and it places less stress on the entire vehicle than does overdrive.

1. Never pull more than the maximum allowable trailer weight listed in your owner's manual.

2. Never tow if your engine is not running smoothly.

3. Check tire inflation regularly and keep a spare trailer tire in your vehicle when towing.

4. Service your cooling system regularly.

5. Replace tires, brakes, and shock absorbers well before you normally would. They need to be kept in above-average condition to tow safely.

6. Use overload shocks if the hitch weight requires it.

7. Be especially cautious when towing a boat because tires can be damaged on a ramp.

8. If you tow regularly, change your automatic transmission fluid twice as often as recommended. If your owner's manual suggests 30,000 miles, change it every 15,000 miles or if it is discolored or smells burnt.

9. Install an auxiliary transmission cooler to protect the transmission. Typical costs range from $20 to $100.

BEEP, BEEP

TIP

As car instrument panels become more and more sophisticated, there is growing confusion about the location of horn buttons. No regulations exist requiring a standard location so manufacturers put them in various places around the steering wheel. On your test drive, make sure the horn button is easy to locate and use. Proper use of a car horn can avoid serious accidents. The Center for Auto Safety has been urging the government to standardize horn location since 1980. If you have experienced a problem due to a nonstandard horn location, we urge you to contact the National Highway Traffic Safety Administration, Rulemaking Division, 400 7th St., SW, Washington, DC 20590 and the Center for Auto Safety, 1825 Connecticut Ave., NW, Suite 330, Washington, DC 20009.

ROLLOVER

The risk of rollover is a significant safety issue especially with sport utility vehicles. Because of their relatively high center of gravity, they don't hug the road like smaller, lower automobiles and trucks. As a result, they are more likely to turn over on sharp turns or corners. Not only does a rollover increase the likelihood of injuries, but it also increases the risk of the occupant being thrown from the vehicle. In fact, the danger of rollover with sport utilities is so severe that manufacturers are now required to place a sticker where it can be seen by the driver every time the vehicle is used. Recently, the government decided to update this sticker to make it more noticeable. It will have a new look this year.

To understand the concept behind these vehicles' propensity to roll over, consider this: place a section of 2x4 lumber on its 2-inch side. It is easily tipped over by a force pushing against the side. But if you place it on its 4-inch side, the same force will cause it to slide rather than tip over. Similarly, in a moving vehicle, the forces generated by a turn can cause a narrow, tall vehicle to roll over.

As the trend of buying light trucks, minivans, and sport utility vehicles for private passenger use grows, the Center for Auto Safety (CAS) is fighting to require safety standards for vehicle stability. If you experience a problem with your sport utility vehicle, contact the CAS (page 74) and the Auto Safety Hotline, 800–424–9393 (202–366–0123 in Washington, DC).

SSF ROLLOVER RATING

On the following pages are rollover ratings for the 2001 vehicles. Last year, approximately 10,000 people died in rollover-related accidents. By their nature, certain types of vehicles are more prone to rollover than others. While this is a relatively simple fact of physics, it is not easy for consumers to determine which vehicles are more prone to tip. For many years, members of Congress and consumer advocates have petitioned the government to develop rollover ratings. We first began publishing this information in 1992. This year, the National Highway Traffic Safety Administration (NHTSA) has adopted this rating system. They have also mandated that sport utility vehicles and trucks, because of their higher center of gravity, have the warning label we mention in the box on page 27.

The formula that we used that NHTSA adopted as a rollover rating is called the Static Stability Factor (SSF). This is a formula that uses the track width of the vehicle (tire to tire) and height to determine which vehicles are more or less likely to roll over when compared to each other. You can't use this information to exactly predict rollovers. However, all things being equal, if two vehicles are in the same situation where a rollover could occur, the one with a high SSF is more likely to roll over than a vehicle with a low SSF. Because this formula doesn't consider factors like driver behavior, the weight of the vehicle, and other factors, some experts do not believe it tells the whole story. We agree, and we believe that the government needs to continue its efforts to provide an even better rollover rating system that consumers can use when buying a vehicle.

In the meantime, we have calculated the SSF for this year's models to give you an idea of which vehicles, using this formula, may have a more or less likelihood of rolling over. Keep in mind that driving conditions, the actual weight of the car, and other factors may influence a rollover situation. However, knowing how the vehicles rate using the SSF can be a key consideration in your evaluation of the vehicle.

STATIC STABILITY FACTOR

VEHICLE	SSF	SSF RATING	VEHICLE	SSF	SSF RATING
Acura CL	1.375	Low SSF	Dodge Ram Pickup	1.163	Moderate SSF
Acura Integra	1.377	Low SSF	Dodge Stratus	1.388	Low SSF
Acura MDX	1.208	Moderate SSF	Dodge/Plymouth Neon	1.296	Low SSF
Acura RL	1.346	Low SSF	Ford Excursion	1.064	High SSF
Acura TL	1.355	Low SSF	Ford Expedition	1.068	High SSF
Audi A4	1.315	Low SSF	Ford Explorer	1.080	High SSF
Audi A6	1.337	Low SSF	Ford Focus	1.302	Low SSF
Audi A8	1.378	Low SSF	Ford F-Series Pickup	1.083	High SSF
BMW 3 Series	1.305	Low SSF	Ford Mustang	1.422	Low SSF
BMW 5 Series	1.323	Low SSF	Ford Ranger	1.072	High SSF
BMW X5	1.148	Moderate SSF	Ford Taurus	1.370	Low SSF
BMW Z3	1.379	Low SSF	Ford Windstar	1.213	Moderate SSF
Buick Century	1.359	Low SSF	GMC Jimmy	1.088	High SSF
Buick LeSabre	1.366	Low SSF	GMC Safari	1.088	High SSF
Buick Park Avenue	1.361	Low SSF	GMC Sierra	1.153	Moderate SSF
Buick Regal	1.362	Low SSF	GMC Yukon	1.070	High SSF
Cadillac Catera	1.320	Low SSF	Honda Accord	1.336	Low SSF
Cadillac DeVille	1.377	Low SSF	Honda Civic	1.276	Low SSF
Cadillac Eldorado	1.420	Low SSF	Honda CR-V	1.146	Moderate SSF
Cadillac Escalade	1.062	High SSF	Honda Insight	1.275	Low SSF
Cadillac Seville	1.409	Low SSF	Honda Odyssey	1.250	Low SSF
Chevrolet Astro	1.086	High SSF	Honda Passport	1.088	High SSF
Chevrolet Blazer	1.055	High SSF	Honda Prelude	1.443	Low SSF
Chevrolet Camaro	1.481	Very Low SSF	Honda S2000	1.449	Very Low SSF
Chevrolet Cavalier	1.306	Low SSF	Hyundai Accent	1.282	Low SSF
Chevrolet Impala	1.340	Low SSF	Hyundai Elantra	1.299	Low SSF
Chevrolet Lumina	1.342	Low SSF	Hyundai Santa Fe	1.149	Moderate SSF
Chevrolet Malibu	1.304	Low SSF	Hyundai Sonata	1.337	Low SSF
Chevrolet Metro	1.218	Moderate SSF	Hyundai Tiburon	1.388	Low SSF
Chevrolet Monte Carlo	1.397	Low SSF	Hyundai XG300	1.351	Low SSF
Chevrolet Prizm	1.334	Low SSF	Infiniti G20	1.282	Low SSF
Chevrolet Silverado	1.109	High SSF	Infiniti I30	1.323	Low SSF
Chevrolet S-Series	1.100	High SSF	Infiniti Q45	1.331	Low SSF
Chevrolet Suburban	1.112	High SSF	Infiniti QX4	1.073	High SSF
Chevrolet Tahoe	1.105	High SSF	Isuzu Rodeo	1.124	High SSF
Chevrolet Tracker	1.081	High SSF	Isuzu Trooper	1.034	Very High SSF
Chevrolet Venture	1.157	Moderate SSF	Isuzu VehiCross	1.115	High SSF
Chrysler 300M	1.378	Low SSF	Jeep Cherokee	1.045	High SSF
Chrysler Concorde	1.391	Low SSF	Jeep Grand Cherokee	1.072	High SSF
Chrysler LHS	1.378	Low SSF	Jeep Wrangler	1.042	Very High SSF
Chrysler PT Cruiser	1.156	Moderate SSF	Kia Sephia	1.295	Low SSF
Chrysler Sebring	1.400	Low SSF	Kia Sportage	1.090	High SSF
Chrysler Town and Country	1.152	Moderate SSF	Land Rover Discovery II	0.945	Very High SSF
Chrysler Voyager	1.152	Moderate SSF	Land Rover Range Rover	1.054	High SSF
Daewoo Lanos	1.234	Moderate SSF	Lexus ES300	1.373	Low SSF
Daewoo Leganza	1.313	Low SSF	Lexus GS300	1.321	Low SSF
Daewoo Nubira	1.274	Low SSF	Lexus IS300	1.322	Low SSF
Dodge Caravan	1.152	Moderate SSF	Lexus LS430	1.316	Low SSF
Dodge Dakota	1.131	Moderate SSF	Lexus LX470	1.094	High SSF
Dodge Durango	1.072	High SSF	Lexus RX300	1.166	Moderate SSF
Dodge Intrepid	1.391	Low SSF	Lexus SC300/400	1.407	Low SSF

STATIC STABILITY FACTOR

VEHICLE	SSF	SSF RATING	VEHICLE	SSF	SSF RATING
Lincoln Continental	1.390	Low SSF	Pontiac Aztek	1.185	Moderate SSF
Lincoln LS	1.351	Low SSF	Pontiac Bonneville	1.377	Low SSF
Lincoln Navigator	1.085	High SSF	Pontiac Firebird	1.481	Very Low SSF
Lincoln Town Car	1.387	Low SSF	Pontiac Grand Am	1.340	Low SSF
Mazda 626	1.336	Low SSF	Pontiac Grand Prix	1.403	Low SSF
Mazda B-Series Truck	1.072	High SSF	Pontiac Montana	1.157	Moderate SSF
Mazda Miata	1.453	Very Low SSF	Pontiac Sunfire	1.305	Low SSF
Mazda Millenia	1.362	Low SSF	Saab 9-3	1.268	Low SSF
Mazda MPV	1.106	High SSF	Saab 9-5	1.314	Low SSF
Mazda Protégé	1.295	Low SSF	Saturn L100/L200	1.321	Low SSF
Mazda Tribute	1.086	High SSF	Saturn SC1	1.330	Low SSF
Mercedes-Benz C-Class	1.318	Low SSF	Saturn SL1	1.239	Moderate SSF
Mercedes-Benz E-Class	1.324	Low SSF	Suzuki Esteem	1.313	Low SSF
Mercedes-Benz M-Class	1.080	High SSF	Suzuki Grand Vitara	1.086	High SSF
Mercury Cougar	1.413	Low SSF	Suzuki Swift	1.234	Moderate SSF
Mercury Grand Marquis	1.416	Low SSF	Toyota 4Runner	1.094	High SSF
Mercury Mountaineer	1.037	Very High SSF	Toyota Avalon	1.311	Low SSF
Mercury Sable	1.370	Low SSF	Toyota Camry	1.365	Low SSF
Mercury Villager	1.131	Moderate SSF	Toyota Celica	1.420	Low SSF
Mitsubishi Diamante	1.405	Low SSF	Toyota Echo	1.191	Moderate SSF
Mitsubishi Eclipse	1.439	Low SSF	Toyota Highlander	1.172	Moderate SSF
Mitsubishi Galant	1.332	Low SSF	Toyota Land Cruiser	1.088	High SSF
Mitsubishi Mirage	1.367	Low SSF	Toyota RAV4	1.126	Moderate SSF
Mitsubishi Montero	1.052	High SSF	Toyota Sequoia	1.115	High SSF
Nissan Altima	1.322	Low SSF	Toyota Sienna	1.161	Low SSF
Nissan Frontier	1.091	High SSF	Toyota Solara	1.368	Low SSF
Nissan Maxima	1.323	Low SSF	Toyota Tacoma	1.060	High SSF
Nissan Pathfinder	1.075	High SSF	Toyota Tundra	1.150	Moderate SSF
Nissan Quest	1.234	Moderate SSF	Volkswagen Golf	1.305	Low SSF
Nissan Sentra	1.312	Low SSF	Volkswagen Jetta	1.301	Low SSF
Nissan Xterra	1.074	High SSF	Volkswagen New Beetle	1.243	Moderate SSF
Oldsmobile Alero	1.358	Low SSF	Volkswagen Passat	1.281	Low SSF
Oldsmobile Aurora	1.373	Low SSF	Volvo C70/S70/V70	1.328	Low SSF
Oldsmobile Bravada	1.090	High SSF	Volvo S40/V40	1.295	Low SSF
Oldsmobile Intrigue	1.367	Low SSF	Volvo S60	1.357	Low SSF
Oldsmobile Silhouette	1.157	Moderate SSF	Volvo S80	1.352	Low SSF

! GOVERNMENT WARNING !

To alert consumers to rollover, the following warning is required on certain vehicles:

This is a multipurpose passenger vehicle which will handle and maneuver differently from an ordinary passenger car, in driving conditions which may occur on streets and highways and off road. As with other vehicles of this type, if you make sharp turns or abrupt maneuvers, the vehicle may roll over or may go out of control and crash. You should read driving guidelines and instructions in the Owner's Manual, and wear your seat belt at all times.

THE FUTURE OF SAFETY

Many car manufacturers claim that cars are safe enough today since airbags, anti-lock brakes, and traction control are becoming standard features. The fact is there's lots more that can be done. We continue to pay high prices in personal injury and insurance premiums for accidents that could be less serious if manufacturers would market more advanced safety features.

While these features may increase the car's costs, those increases would be minor in relation to the dramatic reduction in the risk of injuries in crashes. Unfortunately, carmakers are slow to offer us new technology. Following are a few options that will dramatically increase driving safety—if manufacturers choose to offer them.

Tire Pressure Monitors: Maintaining proper tire pressure is one of the most important and overlooked factors in the safety of your vehicle. Because it's not easy to check tire pressure, many of us neglect it. Help is on the way with automatic pressure sensing devices which indicate the pressure of each tire right on the dash.

Radar Brakes: Using radar to detect approaching objects, a warning sounds for the need to brake. It could perhaps be used to automatically apply the brakes when a driver falls asleep, and would be invaluable when parallel parking.

Air Pads: Air pads are double layers of plastic with multiple compartments which look like ordinary trim in the uninflated condition. When the crash sensors for the airbags detect a crash, the air pads inflate out a few inches over all hard surfaces, such as the area over the windshield.

Glass-Plastic Glazing: This adds a layer of thin, strong, transparent plastic on the inside surface of all windows. When the glass breaks, the plastic layer holds the pieces of glass away from the occupants and provides a "safety net" to reduce the chance of ejection.

Pressure-Sensitive Brake Lights: These lights illuminate with varying intensity based on the pressure applied to the brakes and the speed in which it's applied. Slowing for a stop sign triggers a slow progression from dim to bright, full pressure on the brake pedal would issue a bright beacon.

Navigation Computer: Vehicle navigation systems are in widespread use in Japan and becoming available in the U.S. Current systems are expensive options, offering a variety of safety and convenience features. Mercedes (Tele Aid), GM (OnStar), Ford (Rescu), as well as BMW and Nissan currently offer several systems. The automatic crash notification feature is a significant advantage and is expected to be a welcome safety feature. However, current systems only call for assistance if an airbag is deployed and may not work for side impact or rollover crashes. Future systems are expected to alert the Emergency Medical Services with crash occurrence and location information and crash severity so that proper response can be made for serious crashes.

Smart Airbags: Several automakers are devloping smart airbag systems which will differentiate between an adult, a child, a rear-facing child seat, or an empty seat, using various heat, ultrasonic sound wave, and infrared sensors. Not only will they save lives, smart airbags will prevent the passenger-side airbag from deploying when the passenger seat is empty—saving thousands in repair costs.

Black Box Monitor: This device would detect whether the driver is driving drunk or irresponsibly. By monitoring the car's behavior and noting irregular actions, it will shut the car down.

Intelligent Brakes: These brakes sense and compensate for over- or understeering.

Crash Recorder: This would record airbag performance in the event of an accident.

Toyota's Drowsy Driving Warning Sytem: By monitoring the steering and pulse of the driver, this innovation checks the driver to verify alertness. Once it detects drowsiness, the system will warn the driver with lights and sound to wake up, then shake the seat, and finally automatically stop the car.

Self-Dimming Mirrors: A gel-like material placed between two glass sheets darkens and lightens to reduce the headlight glare from mirrors while driving at night.

Honda Civic

Mitsubishi Galant

Toyota Highlander

GASOLINE-ELECTRIC HYBRID

IN THIS CHAPTER

INTRODUCTION

Not only are gas prices reaching new levels, but the trend in overall fuel efficiency doesn't look good. According to the U.S. EPA, the average fuel economy of new vehicles recently dropped to 28.3 miles per gallon. This is the lowest level since 1980. The important fuel economy gains over the past years have been offset by the dramatic increase in heavier, less fuel-efficient vehicles—namely, the popular sport utility vehicles. The increasing market share of these more fuel-inefficient vehicles is bringing the overall averages down.

Using EPA ratings is an excellent way to incorporate fuel efficiency in selecting a new car. By comparing these ratings, even among cars of the same size, you'll find that fuel efficiency varies greatly. One compact car might get 36 miles per gallon (mpg) while another gets only 22 mpg. If you drive 15,000 miles a year and you pay $1.50 per gallon for fuel, the 36 mpg car will save you $319 a year over the "gas guzzler."

Octane Ratings: Once you've purchased your car, you'll be faced with choosing the right gasoline. Oil companies spend millions of dollars trying to get you to buy so-called higher performance or high octane fuels. Because high octane fuel can add considerably to your gas bill, it is important that you know what you're buying.

The octane rating of a gasoline is not a measure of power or quality. It is simply a measure of the gas's resistance to engine knock, which is the pinging sound you hear when the air and fuel mixture in your engine ignites prematurely during acceleration.

The octane rating appears on a yellow label on the fuel pump. Octane ratings vary with different types of gas (premium or regular), in different parts of the country (higher altitudes require lower octane ratings), and even between brands (Texaco's gasolines may have a different rating than Exxon's).

Determining the Right Octane for Your Car: Using a lower-rated gasoline saves money. Most cars are designed to run on a posted octane rating of 87. Check your owner's manual. The following procedure can help you select the lowest octane level for your car.

1 Have your engine tuned to exact factory specifications by a competent mechanic, and make sure it is in good working condition.

2 When the gas in your tank is very low, fill it up with your usual gasoline. After driving 10 to 15 miles, find a safe place to come to a complete stop and then accelerate rapidly. If your engine knocks during acceleration, switch to a higher octane rating. If there is no knocking sound, wait until your tank is very low and fill up with a lower-rated gasoline. Repeat the test. When you determine the level of octane that causes your engine to knock during the test, use gasoline with the next highest rating.

Your engine may knock when accelerating a heavily loaded car uphill or when the humidity is low. This is normal and does not call for a higher-octane gasoline.

FUEL ECONOMY

TIP

Get up-to-date information about fuel economy at www.fueleconomy.gov, a joint website created by the U.S. Department of Energy and the EPA. The EPA's entire Fuel Economy Guide can be found there, allowing you to compare fuel economy among several 2001 model year vehicles. You'll also find out the latest on technological advances pertaining to fuel efficiency. The site's information is extremely useful and easy to navigate. We've added the fuel economy ratings to our car rating pages as well.

FACTORS AFFECTING FUEL ECONOMY

Fuel economy is affected by a number of factors that you can consider before you buy.

Transmission: Manual transmissions are generally more fuel-efficient than automatic transmissions. In fact, a 5-speed manual transmission can add up to 6.5 miles per gallon over a 3-speed automatic. However, the incorrect use of a manual transmission wastes gas, so choose a transmission that matches your preference. Many transmissions now feature an overdrive gear, which can improve a vehicle's fuel economy by as much as 9 percent for an automatic transmission and 3 percent for a manual transmission.

Engine: The size of your car's engine greatly affects your fuel economy. The smaller your engine, the better your fuel efficiency. A 10 percent increase in the size of an engine can increase fuel consumption by 6 percent.

Cruise Control: Cruise control can save fuel because driving at a constant speed uses less fuel than changing speeds frequently.

Air Conditioning: Auto air conditioners add weight and require additional horsepower to operate. They can cost up to 3 miles per gallon in city driving. At highway speeds, however, an air conditioner has about the same effect on fuel economy as the air resistance created by opening the windows.

Trim Package: Upgrading a car's trim, installing sound-proofing, and adding undercoating can increase the weight of a typical car by 150 pounds. For each 10 percent increase in weight, fuel economy drops 4 percent.

Power Options: Power steering, brakes, seats, windows, and roofs reduce your mileage by adding weight. Power steering alone can cause a 1 percent drop in fuel economy.

Here are some tips for after you buy.

Tune-up: If you have a 2 to 3 mpg drop over several fill-ups that is not due to a change of driving pattern or vehicle load, first check tire pressure, then consider a tune-up. A properly tuned engine is a fuel saver.

Tire Inflation: For maximum fuel efficiency, tires should be inflated to the pressure range found on the label in your door well. The tire's maximum pressure may not be suitable for your car. Be sure to check the tire pressure when the tires are cold before you've driven a long distance.

Short Trips: Short trips can be expensive because they usually involve a "cold" vehicle. For the first mile or two before the engine gets warmed up, a cold vehicle only gets 30 to 40 percent of the mileage it gets at full efficiency.

⚠ USING OXYFUELS ⚠

Today's gasoline contains a bewildering array of ingredients touted as octane boosters or pollution fighters. Some urban areas with carbon monoxide pollution problems are requiring the use of oxygen-containing components (called oxyfuels) such as ethanol and MTBE (methyl-tertiary-butylether). The use of these compounds is controversial. Some auto companies recommend their use; others caution against them. Most companies approve the use of gasoline with up to 10% ethanol, and all approve the use of MTBE up to 15%. Many companies recommend against using gasoline with methanol, alleging that it will cause poorer driveability, deterioration of fuel system parts, and reduced fuel economy. These companies may not cover the cost of warranty repairs if these additives are used, so check your owner's manual and warranty to determine what additives are covered. Also check the gas pump, as many states now require the pump to display the percentage of methanol and ethanol in the gasoline.

EMISSIONS OPTIONS

Today's cars are slowly becoming more environmentally friendly. But how do you know which ones? Engine size, fuel type, and emission system all contribute to fuel efficiency and the amount of pollution that your car emits. In addition, cars come with different emission ratings. You do have choices and knowing the different emission options will allow you to better control the impact your car has on our environment. Buying "green" not only lowers air pollution, but sends a strong signal to manufacturers that building "green" cars pays off.

Because it is not easy to evaluate the impact your car has on the environment, experts at the American Council for an Energy-Efficient Economy have developed The Green Car Rating system. This rating system considers a wide variety of items that measure the environmental friendliness of a particular car. Listed in the box are some of the most environmentally friendly cars based on ACEEE's Green Car Rating. We strongly recommend that you get the full story on the green ratings and the details for virtually every new model in ACEEE's *Green Guide to Cars and Trucks*. Copies are available for $8.95 from ACEEE, 1001 Connecticut Ave. NW, Washington, DC 20036 by calling 202–429–0063, or visit www.aceee.org.

Emissions Options: California has traditionally lead the country in requiring environmentally responsible vehicles. These California certified vehicles are available nationwide. By checking

ACEEE's *Green Guide to Cars and Trucks* you can find the emission rating for the cars you are considering. Here is what the ratings mean.

Federal Certification

Tier 1: Current National Standard, the weakest and therefore most polluting of the standards.

California Certification

TLEV: Transitional Low Emission Vehicle, slightly stronger than the Federal Standard.

LEV: Low Emission Vehicle, an intermediate California standard, about twice as strong as Tier 1.

ULEV: Ultra Low Emission Vehicle, emphasizes very low emissions of compounds that cause smog and are toxic and carcinogenic.

ZEV: Zero Emission Vehicle, prohibits any tailpipe emissions.

GREEN MACHINES

The following list is based on ACEEE's 2001 "Green Machine" ratings. We have included the models which didn't change in 2001. This list presents some of the best performing vehicles in various size categories. This list does include hybrid vehicles.

Vehicle	Engine	MPG (city/hwy)	Green Rating
Mazda MX-5 Miata	1.8L, auto	25/29	30
Honda Insight	1.0L, manual	61/70	48
Mitsubishi Mirage	1.5L, auto	38/36	33
Chevrolet Metro	1.3L, manual	36/42	38
Nissan Sentra	1.8L, auto	24/30	36
Toyota Echo	1.5L, manual	34/41	37
Saturn SW wagon	1.9L, auto	37/36	32
Honda Accord	2.3L, auto	23/30	34
Mazda 626	2.0L, manual	26/32	31
Volkswagen Passat Wgn	1.8L, manual	24/31	28
Ford Crown Victoria	4.6L, auto	15/23	32
Chevrolet Venture	3.4L, auto	19/26	21
Isuzu Hombre	2.2L, manual	23/29	25
Ford F150	4.2L, manual	16/21	18
Chevrolet Tracker	1.6L, manual	25/28	29
Jeep Cherokee	2.5L, manual	20/24	23
Toyota 4Runner	2.7L, auto	20/24	21

FUEL ECONOMY MISERS AND GUZZLERS

Every year the Department of Energy publishes the results of the Environmental Protection Agency's (EPA) fuel economy tests in a comparative guide.

Because the success of the EPA program depends on consumers' ability to compare the fuel economy ratings easily, we have included key mileage figures in our ratings page and listed below this year's misers and guzzlers. The complete EPA fuel economy guide is available at www.fueleconomy.gov.

FUEL ECONOMY MISERS AND GUZZLERS

BEST

	MPG (city/hwy)	Annual Fuel Cost
SUBCOMPACT		
Honda Insight man.	61/68	$316
Toyota Prius auto.	52/45	$421
Suzuki Swift man.	36/42	$518
Volkswagen New Beetle auto.	34/44	$513
Toyota Echo man.	34/41	$547
Saturn SC man.	29/33	$614
COMPACT		
Volkswagen Golf/Jetta man.	42/49	$433
Volkswagen Golf/Jetta auto.	34/45	$513
Toyota Corolla man.	32/41	$563
Chevrolet Prizm man.	32/41	$579
Mazda 626 man.	26/32	$699
INTERMEDIATE		
Honda Accord man.	26/32	$723
Saturn L100/L200 man.	25/33	$723
Chevrolet Impala auto.	21/32	$810
Toyota Avalon auto.	21/29	$844
Chrys. Concorde/Ddge Intrepid auto.	20/28	$881
LARGE		
Buick LeSabre/Pont. Bonne. auto.	19/30	$881
Buick Park Avenue auto.	19/30	$881
Chrysler LHS	18/25	$964
Lexus LS430	18/25	$1107
TRUCKS		
Chev. S10/Sonoma/Hombre 2WD man.	22/28	$844
Ford Ranger/Mazda B-Ser. 2WD man.	22/26	$844
Nissan Frontier 2WD man.	22/26	$844
Toyota Tacoma 2WD auto.	21/23	$921
Chev. S10/Sonoma/Hombre auto.	19/25	$964
MINIVANS		
Chev. Venture/Olds Silh. FWD auto.	19/26	$921
Pontiac Montana FWD auto.	19/26	$921
Toyota Sienna auto.	19/24	$964
Chrys. Voyager/T & C auto. 2WD	18/24	$1012
Dodge Caravan 2WD auto.	18/24	$1012
SPORT UTILITY VEHICLES		
Toyota RAV 4 2WD man.	25/31	$749
Suzuki Vitara auto./man.	25/28	$780
Toyota RAV 4 2WD auto.	24/29	$780
Chev. Tracker 2WD hardtop auto.	23/26	$810
Ford Escape 2WD man.	23/28	$810

WORST

	MPG (city/hwy)	Annual Fuel Cost
SUBCOMPACT		
Ferrari 550 Marin./Barchetta man.	8/13	$2325
Lambor. DB132/144 Diablo man.	10/13	$2113
Ferrari 456 MGT/MGTA auto.	10/15	$2113
Ferrari 456 MGT/MGTA man.	10/16	$1937
Ferrari 360 Modena/Spider man.	11/16	$1788
COMPACT		
Volkswagen Jetta	19/26	$964
Bentley Continental R auto.	11/16	$1788
BMW M5 man.	13/21	$1453
Jaguar Vanden Plas S/C auto.	16/22	$1293
INTERMEDIATE		
Rolls Royce Silver Seraph auto.	11/16	$1788
Bentley Arnage auto.	11/16	$1788
Ford Taurus Wagon auto.	14/20	$1500
BMW 740i auto.	15/21	$1367
LARGE		
Rolls Royce Park Ward auto.	12/16	$1660
BMW 750IL auto.	13/20	$1453
Mercedes S600 auto.	15/23	$1293
Ford Crown Victoria auto.	15/23	$709
Mercedes S500 auto.	16/23	$1223
BMW 540i man.	15/23	$1293
TRUCKS		
Ford F 150 Natural Gas auto.	12/16	$910
Dodge Dakota 2WD/4WD auto.	12/17	$1446
Dodge Ram 1500 auto./man.	12/17	$1446
Toyota Tundra 4WD auto.	14/17	$1351
Ford F150 Pick-Up 4WD auto.	14/17	$1351
MINIVANS		
Dodge Ram Wgn 2500 2WD auto.	12/16	$980
Ford E150 Club Wagon auto.	13/17	$1446
GMC G1500/2500 Sav. 2WD auto.	14/17	$1351
Chev. G1500/2500 2WD auto.	14/17	$1351
Chevrolet Astro AWD auto.	15/19	$1266
SPORT UTILITY VEHICLES		
Lincoln Navigator 4WD auto.	12/16	$1788
Land Rover Range Rover auto.	12/15	$1788
GMC K1500 Yukon 4WD auto.	12/16	$1557
Toyota Lnd Cruis. Wgn 4WD auto.	13/16	$1446
Toyota Sequoia 4WD auto.	14/17	$1351

Source: U.S. Environmental Protection Agency

PRODUCTS THAT DON'T WORK

Hundreds of products on the market claim to improve fuel economy. Not only are most of these products ineffective, some may even damage your engine.

Sometimes the name or promotional material associated with these products implies they were endorsed by the federal government. In fact, no government agency endorses any gas saving products. Many products, however, have been tested by the U.S. EPA.

Of the hundreds of so-called gas saving devices on the market, only five tested by the EPA have been shown to slightly improve your fuel economy without increasing harmful emissions. However, these offer limited savings because of their cost. They are the Pass Master Vehicle Air Conditioner P.A.S.S. Kit, Idalert, Morse Constant Speed Accessory Drive, Autotherm, and Kamei Spoilers. We don't recommend these because the increase in fuel economy is not worth the investment in the product.

The following devices were reviewed or tested by the EPA and they did *not* improve fuel economy.

AIR BLEED DEVICES
ADAKS Vacuum Breaker Air Bleed
Air-Jet Air Bleed
Aquablast Wyman Valve Air Bleed
Auto Miser
Ball-Matic Air Bleed
Berg Air Bleed
Brisko PCV
Cyclone-Z
Econo Needle Air Bleed
Econo-Jet Air Bleed Idle Screws
Fuel Max
Gas Saving Device
Grancor Air Computer
Hot Tip
Landrum Mini-Carb
Landrum Retrofit Air Bleed
Mini Turbocharger Air Bleed*
Monocar HC Control Air Bleed
Peterman Air Bleed*
Pollution Master Air Bleed
Ram-Jet
Turbo-Dyne G.R. Valve

DRIVING HABIT MODIFIERS
Fuel Conservation Device
Gastell

FUEL LINE DEVICES
Fuel Xpander
Gas Meiser I
Greer Fuel Preheater
Jacona Fuel System
Malpassi Filter King
Moleculetor
Optimizer
Petro-Mizer
Polarion-X
Russell Fuelmiser
Super-Mag Fuel Extender
Wickliff Polarizer

FUELS AND FUEL ADDITIVES
Bycosin*
EI-5 Fuel Additive*

Fuelon Power Gasoline Fuel Additive
Johnson Fuel Additive*
NRG #1 Fuel Additive
QEI 400 Fuel Additive*
Rolfite Upgrade Fuel Additive
Sta-Power Fuel Additive
Stargas Fuel Additive
SYNeRGy-1
Technol G Fuel Additive
ULX-15/ULX-15D
Vareb 10 Fuel Additive*
XRG #1 Fuel Additive

IGNITION DEVICES
Autosaver
Baur Condenser*
BIAP Electronic Ignition Unit
Fuel Economizer
Magna Flash Ignition Ctrl. Sys.
Paser Magnum/Paser 500/Paser 500 HEI
Special Formula Ignition Advance Springs*

INTERNAL ENGINE MODIFICATIONS
ACDS Auto. Cyl. Deactivation Sys.
Dresser Economizer*
MSU Cylinder Deactivation*

LIQUID INJECTION
Goodman Engine Sys. Model 1800*
Waag-Injection System*

MIXTURE ENHANCERS
Basko Enginecoat
Dresser Economizer
Electro-Dyne Superchoke*
Energy Gas Saver*
Environmental Fuel Saver*
Filtron Urethane Foam Filter*
Gas Saving and Emission Control Improvement Device
Glynn-50*
Hydro-Catalyst Pre-Combustion System

Lamkin Fuel Metering Device
Petromizer System
Sav-A-Mile
Smith Power and Deceleration Governor Spritzer*
Turbo-Carb
Turbocarb

OILS AND OIL ADDITIVES
Analube Synthetic Lubricant
Tephguard*

VAPOR BLEED DEVICES
Atomized Vapor Injector
Econo-Mist Vacuum Vapor Injection System
Frantz Vapor Injection System*
Hydro-Vac
Mark II Vapor Injection System*
Platinum Gasaver
POWER FUeL
Scatpac Vacuum Vapor Induction System
Turbo Vapor Injection System*
V-70 Vapor Injector

MISCELLANEOUS
Brake-Ez*
Dynamix
Fuel Maximiser
Gyroscopic Wheel Cover
Kat's Engine Heater
Lee Exhaust and Fuel Gasification EGR*
Mesco Moisture Extraction Sys.
P.S.C.U. 01 Device
Treis Emulsifier

*For copies of reports on these products, write Test and Evaluation Branch, U.S. EPA, 2565 Plymouth Rd., Ann Arbor, MI 48105. For the other products, contact the National Technical Information Service, Springfield, VA 22161. (703–487–4650)

Lexus LS 430

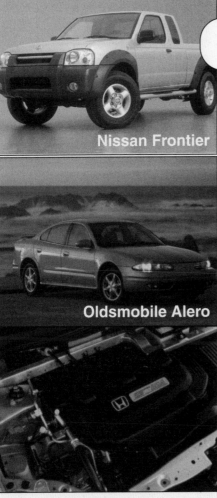

Nissan Frontier

Oldsmobile Alero

IN THIS CHAPTER

INTRODUCTION

After you buy a car, maintenance costs will be a significant portion of your operating expenses. This chapter allows you to consider and compare some of these costs before deciding which car to purchase. These costs include preventive maintenance servicing—such as changing the oil and filters—as well as the cost of repairs after your warranty expires. On the following pages, we compared the costs of preventive maintenance and nine likely repairs for the 2001 models. Since the cost of a repair also depends on the shop and the mechanic, this chapter includes tips for finding a good shop and communicating effectively with a mechanic.

Preventive maintenance is the periodic servicing, specified by the manufacturer, that keeps your car running properly. For example, regularly changing the oil and oil filter. Every owner's manual specifies a schedule of recommended servicing for at least the first 50,000 miles, and the tables on the following pages estimate the cost of following this preventive maintenance schedule.

If for some reason you do not have an owner's manual with the preventive maintenance schedule, contact the manufacturer to obtain one.

The tables also list the costs for nine repairs that typically occur during the first 100,000 miles. There is no precise way to predict exactly when a repair will be needed. But if you keep a car for 75,000 to 100,000 miles, it is likely that you will experience most of these repairs at least once. The last column provides a relative indication of how expensive these nine repairs are for many cars. Repair cost is rated as Very Good if the total for nine repairs is in the bottom fifth of all the cars rated, and Very Poor if the total is in the top fifth.

Most repair shops use "flat-rate manuals" to estimate repair costs. These manuals list the approximate time required for repairing many items. Each automobile manufacturer publishes its own manual and there are several independent manuals as well. For many repairs, the time varies from one manual to another. Some repair shops even use different manuals for different repairs. To determine a repair bill, a shop multiplies the time listed in its manual by its hourly labor rate and then adds the cost of parts.

Our cost estimates are based on flat-rate manual repair times multiplied by a nationwide average labor rate of $50 per hour. All estimates also include the cost of replaced parts and related adjustments, which are based on 1999 figures.

Prices in the following tables may not predict the exact costs of these repairs. For example, the labor rate for your area may be more or less than the national average. However, the prices will provide you with a relative comparison of maintenance costs for various automobiles.

> **! DEALER MAINTENANCE SCHEDULES !**
>
> Some dealers and repair shops create their own maintenance schedules which call for more frequent (and thus more expensive) servicing than the manufacturer's recommendations. If the servicing recommended by your dealer or repair shop doesn't match what the car maker recommends, make sure you understand and agree to the extra items.

MAINTENANCE COSTS

	PM Costs to 50,000 Miles	Water Pump	Alternator	Front Brake Pads	Starter	Fuel Injection	Fuel Pump	Struts/ Shocks	Timing Belt/ Chain	Power Steer. Pump	Relative Maint. Cost
SUBCOMPACT											
Dodge Neon	N/A	247	348	155	265	84	348	166	210	328	Vry. Gd.
Ford Focus	N/A	154		125	202	73	248	255	148		
Ford ZX2	739	154	281	114	346	110	287	250	185	120	Vry. Gd.
Honda Civic	990	205	240	87	302	143	243	322	121	518	Good
Hyundai Accent	398	195	282	80	342	116	180	269	159	557	Good
Kia Rio	N/A	203	354	112	302	204	218	296	158	323	Good
Kia Sephia	787	240	347	87	337	164	314	351	221	400	Good
Mazda Miata	883	252	510	87	238	285	459	320	175	604	Poor
Mitsubishi Mirage	1167	226	265	118	245	108	399	270	117	633	Good
Nissan Sentra	810	185	349	107	357	224	154	252	725	278	Average
Saturn SC	985	144	211	100	181	112	294	172	282	269	Vry. Gd.
Saturn SL/SW	985	144	211	100	181	112	294	172	282	269	Vry. Gd.
Subaru Impreza	658	210	397	114	429	172	317	382	200	462	Average
Suzuki Esteem	880	236	358	111	227	295	535	364	173	644	Poor
Suzuki Swift	880	263	239	135	187	250	771	423	171	667	Vry. Pr.
Toyota Prius	N/A	157	0	145	0	244	0	542	323	0	Vry. Gd.
Volkswagen Beetle	228	310	474	105	429	207	238	397	177	141	Average
COMPACT											
Acura Integra	1224	276	416	87	346	151	401	356	195	510	Poor
BMW 3 Series	98	165	584	136	344	174	166	492	492	484	Poor
BMW Z3	98	136	459	116	130	252	157	469	393	605	Average
Chevrolet Cavalier	785	167	230	114	300	156	543	250	300	374	Good
Chevrolet Prizm	953	179	503	131	423	236	382	430	279	395	Poor
Chrysler Sebring	767	390	358	158	268	247	642	224	234	310	Poor
Honda Prelude	992	299	279	92	350	138	311	332	236	524	Average
AVERAGE	**738**	**237**	**384**	**127**	**324**	**187**	**371**	**298**	**315**	**400**	

MAINTENANCE COSTS

	PM Costs to 50,000 Miles	Water Pump	Alternator	Front Brake Pads	Starter	Fuel Injection	Fuel Pump	Struts/ Shocks	Timing Belt/ Chain	Power Steer. Pump	Relative Maint. Cost
COMPACT (cont.)											
Hyundai Elantra	398	177	298	87	356	114	183	273	181	547	Good
Hyundai Tiburon	398	172	295	72	354	109	178	294	161	544	Good
Infiniti G20	797	184	515	100	263	246	227	251	772	457	Poor
Mazda 626	883	224	257	90	244	247	417	136	164	295	Vry. Gd.
Mitsubishi Eclipse	785	273	375	118	221	195	266	272	177	327	Good
Mitsubishi Galant	1115	320	363	113	339	207	330	239	159	329	Good
Oldsmobile Alero	790	417	302	160	307	170	570	205	269	261	Average
Pontiac Grand Am	790	412	302	160	307	163	570	225	298	281	Average
Pontiac Sunfire	790	167	225	107	300	156	565	250	300	374	Good
Subaru Legacy	637	220	161	114	296	150	315	312	207	230	Vry. Gd.
Toyota Celica	1033	228	361	106	281	231	294	410	145	602	Average
Volkswagen Golf	228	231	710	127	426	184	341	343	141	246	Poor
Volkswagen Jetta	228	231	710	127	426	184	341	333	141	246	Poor
INTERMEDIATE											
Audi A4	0	345	752	159	584	172	271	385	211	465	Vry. Pr.
Audi A6	0	315	599	174	482	129	374	417	171	500	Vry. Pr.
Buick Century	797	131	245	118	297	247	439	218	282	206	Good
Buick Regal	797	155	230	118	328	146	439	218	260	222	Vry. Gd.
Cadillac Catera	611	341	918	180	693	222	420	515	196	630	Vry. Pr.
Chevrolet Camaro	797	276	384	179	308	172	664	313	238	235	Poor
Chevrolet Impala	0	131	252	127	316	256	472	348	332	160	Good
Chevrolet Monte Carlo	804	131	252	127	316	256	472	348	332	160	Good
Chevrolet Malibu	797	141	294	160	282	242	568	353	306	402	Poor
Chrysler Concorde	767	342	218	149	258	126	342	330	300	280	Good
Dodge Intrepid	767	240	218	149	258	126	342	330	289	280	Good
AVERAGE	**738**	**237**	**384**	**127**	**324**	**187**	**371**	**298**	**315**	**400**	

MAINTENANCE COSTS

	PM Costs to 50,000	Water Pump	Alternator	Front Brake Pads	Starter	Fuel Injection	Fuel Pump	Struts/ Shocks	Timing Belt/ Chain	Power Steer. Pump	Relative Maint. Cost
INTERMEDIATE (cont.)											
Dodge Stratus	767	234	325	108	255	89	288	182	209	395	Vry. Gd.
Ford Mustang	811	218	245	130	245	130	311	167	330	283	Vry. Gd.
Ford Taurus	720	206	261	125	262	83	310	212	415	170	Vry. Gd.
Honda Accord	992	211	238	106	378	138	404	246	208	286	Good
Hyundai Sonata	398	200	375	92	272	109	173	239	155	641	Good
Mazda Millenia	881	269	778	121	265	300	458	471	237	915	Vry. Pr.
Mercedes-Benz C-Class	1112	334	816	116	415	170	236	412	257	616	Vry. Pr.
Mercury Sable	720	191	250	118	262	82	328	212	182	170	Vry. Gd.
Nissan Altima	785	167	366	105	294	164	217	252	538	262	Good
Nissan Maxima	818	261	508	110	329	258	291	459	600	537	Vry. Pr.
Oldsmobile Intrigue	797	176	398	116	300	173	436	299	365	370	Average
Pontiac Firebird	797	169	384	159	308	172	664	269	233	399	Poor
Pontiac Grand Prix	797	155	230	116	333	146	413	283	256	222	Vry. Gd.
Saab 9-3	701	175	382	129	222	148	355	198	694	430	Average
Saab 9-5	756	202	500	129	288	112	325	392	410	440	Poor
Saturn L/LW	N/A	215	238	148	237	64	245	262		250	
Toyota Avalon	1033	267	558	91	386	263	279	390	182	534	Poor
Toyota Camry	1033	268	358	99	282	258	279	388	172	535	Average
Toyota Solara	1033	270	407	104	393	252	278	360	98	506	Average
Volkswagen Passat	233	289	698	146	524	177	327	392	211	482	Vry. Pr.
Volvo C70/S70/V70	1229	262	653	116	303	193	354	337	165	539	Poor
Volvo S60	N/A	259	686	94	303	155	284	222	126	500	Average
Volvo S80	1229	247	635	104	438	195	294	371	215	567	Poor
LARGE											
Acura CL	1223	236	380	92	382	133	320	349	175	515	Average
AVERAGE	**738**	**237**	**384**	**127**	**324**	**187**	**371**	**298**	**315**	**400**	

MAINTENANCE COSTS

	PM Costs to 50,000	Water Pump	Alternator	Front Brake Pads	Starter	Fuel Injection	Fuel Pump	Struts/ Shocks	Timing Belt/ Chain	Power Steer. Pump	Relative Maint. Cost
LARGE (cont.)											
Acura RL	1223	508	418	102	572	138	337	518	259	563	Vry. Gd.
Acura TL	1223	317	337	92	392	210	404	284	266	325	Average
Audi A8	0	613	840	198	686	227	436	725	428	510	Vry. Pr.
BMW 5 Series	98	152	586	138	267	148	230	521	546	460	Poor
Buick LeSabre	804	233	538	120	192	141	497	224	268	428	Average
Buick Park Avenue	804	233	170	125	306	144	477	245	268	424	Good
Cadillac DeVille	611	135	375	120	355	136	520	1378	709	352	Vry. Pr.
Cadillac Eldorado	611	138	340	122	377	136	527	1363	709	352	Vry. Pr.
Cadillac Seville	611	138	768	167	387	127	511	890	709	319	Vry. Pr.
Chrysler 300M	N/A	230	232	149	265	154	332	330	228	255	Good
Chrysler LHS	785	230	232	149	265	154	332	330	228	310	Good
Ford Crown Victoria	811	156	257	125	286	122	303	75	324	246	Vry. Gd.
Hyundai XG300	N/A	245	437	78	363	74	163	266	208	288	Vry. Gd.
Infiniti I30	797	277	513	110	329	245	289	493	592	522	Vry. Pr.
Infiniti Q45	797	150	801	120	426	314	333	931	955	417	Vry. Pr.
Lexus ES300	797	269	478	92	400	266	286	408	183	525	Poor
Lexus GS300/400	797	353	923	107	391	316	293	222	188	532	Vry. Pr.
Lexus IS300	797	290	589	85	502	212	266	246	151	456	Poor
Lexus LS430	797	348	642	117	784	328	370	233	259	602	Vry. Pr.
Lexus SC300/400	797	310	621	107	557	353	285	331	234	564	Vry. Pr.
Lincoln Continental	797	183	333	118	205	144	308	866	477	376	Poor
Lincoln LS	797	233	269	118	215	154	298	145	265	266	Vry. Gd.
Lincoln Town Car	797	154	265	118	286	132	340	102	352	241	Vry. Gd.
Mercedes-Benz E-Class	1342	421	978	184	479	148	245	396	305	615	Vry. Pr.
Mercury Cougar	794	121	338	113	316	102	337	240	358	234	Vry. Gd.
AVERAGE	**738**	**237**	**384**	**127**	**324**	**187**	**371**	**298**	**315**	**400**	

MAINTENANCE COSTS

	PM Costs to 50,000	Water Pump	Alternator	Front Brake Pads	Starter	Fuel Injection	Fuel Pump	Struts/ Shocks	Timing Belt/ Chain	Power Steer. Pump	Relative Maint. Cost
LARGE (cont.)											
Mercury Grand Marquis	811	156	257	125	286	117	313	75	324	246	Vry. Gd.
Mitsubishi Diamante	1195	320	312	116	320	209	445	430	247	462	Poor
Oldsmobile Aurora	N/A	130	365	117	360	136	461	188	474	389	Average
Pontiac Bonneville	790	233	538	125	308	141	470	259	264	428	Poor
MINIVAN											
Chevrolet Venture	744	134	449	125	292	235	517	197	359	382	Average
Chrysler Town and Cntry	685	114	362	141	234	134	360	212	241	255	Vry. Gd.
Dodge Caravan	685	354	355	141	272	175	360	212	234	230	Good
Ford Windstar	661	167	249	117	299	161	340	231	242	105	Vry. Gd.
GMC Safari	744	269	292	125	305	210	556	119	293	418	Average
Honda Odyssey	990	324	232	92	405	205	365	398	266	262	Average
Mazda MPV	930	263	263	118	242	366	193	330	234	836	Poor
Mercury Villager	690	243	259	116	176	352	301	265	191	283	Good
Nissan Quest	690	174	438	115	294	409	259	272	158	297	Good
Oldsmobile Silhouette	744	134	449	125	292	235	517	184	359	382	Average
Plymouth Voyager	685	276	300	141	251	147	360	212	214	275	Good
Pontiac Montana	685	134	449	125	292	235	517	184	359	382	Average
Toyota Sienna	1033	305	573	98	322	286	384	408	282	518	Vry. Pr.
COMPACT PICKUP											
Chevrolet S Series	863	171	262	147	256	187	516	189	426	407	Average
Dodge Dakota	811	162	370	100	348	126	388	81	355	345	Good
Ford Ranger	863	249	232	114	200	145	202	80	404	174	Vry. Gd.
GMC Sonoma	863	171	262	147	264	187	516	205	426	407	Average
Mazda B Series Truck	732	267	340	110	264	130	585	121	428	329	Average
Nissan Frontier	904	203	215	100	396	145	283	85	311	235	Vry. Gd.
AVERAGE	**738**	**237**	**384**	**127**	**324**	**187**	**371**	**298**	**315**	**400**	

	PM Costs to 50,000 Miles	Water Pump	Alternator	Front Brake Pads	Starter	Fuel Injection	Fuel Pump	Struts/ Shocks	Timing Belt/ Chain	Power Steer. Pump	Relative Maint. Cost
COMPACT PICKUP (cont.)											
Toyota Tacoma	893	192	335	87	279	216	181	356	493	579	Average
STANDARD PICKUP											
Chevrolet Silverado	853	243	245	202	308	193	505	155	376	418	Average
Ford F Series	732	188	410	91	192	187	392	94	370		
Dodge Ram Pickup	939	164	385	204	325	120	355	104	285		
GMC Sierra	853	255	245	254	313	141	505	116	446	418	Average
MID-SIZE SP. UTILITY											
Oldsmobile Bravada	853	241	257	140	335	188	603	102	523	418	Poor
Subaru Forester	638	220	397	114	429	172	317	382	200	462	Average
Suzuki Grand Vitara	N/A	593	352	120	227	345	555	393	665	599	Vry. Pr.
Toyota 4Runner	904	197	373	87	330	251	234	121	377	559	Average
LARGE SPORT UTILITY											
Cadillac Escalade	N/A	239	240	120	302	218	605	499	344	409	Poor
Chevrolet Suburban	853	245	242	259		182	579		176		
Dodge Durango	939	154	405	104	45	136	348	94	450	335	Vry. Gd.
Ford Excursion	N/A	68		136	195	140	322	84	490	65	Vry. Gd.
Ford Expedition	732	178	294	104	281	206	256	129	484	276	Good
GMC Denali	N/A	244	236	121	295	207	594	151	296	413	Average
GMC Suburban	853	241	247	191	303	170	574	84	232	416	Good
GMC Yukon XL	853	245	242	233	306	182	533	116	341	418	Average
Land Rover Range Rover	1393	269	811	192	560	276	593	267	317	533	Vry. Pr.
Lexus LX470	N/A	274	459	137	556	278	299	286	239	576	Vry. Pr.
Lincoln Navigator	732	164	330	81	355	210	339	94	542		
Toyota Land Cruiser	904	325	456	135	497	276	294	95	238	567	Vry. Gd.
AVERAGE	**738**	**237**	**384**	**127**	**324**	**187**	**371**	**298**	**315**	**400**	

SERVICE CONTRACTS

Service contracts are one of the most expensive options you can buy. In fact, service contracts are a major profit source for many dealers.

A service contact is not a warranty. It is more like an insurance plan that, in theory, covers repairs that are not covered by your warranty or that occur after the warranty runs out. They may also be referred to as an "extended warranty."

Service contracts are generally a poor value. The companies who sell contracts are very sure that, on average, your repairs will cost considerably less that what you pay for the contract—if not, they wouldn't be in business.

Tip: One alternative to buying a service contract is to deposit the cost of the contract into a savings account. If the car needs a major repair not covered by your warranty, the money in your account will cover the cost. Most likely, you'll be building up your down payment for your next car!

Here are some important questions to ask before buying a service contract:

How reputable is the company responsible for the contract? If the company offering the contract goes out of business, you will be out of luck. The company may be required to be insured but they may not. Find out if they are insured and by whom. Check with your Better Business Bureau or office of consumer affairs if you are not sure of a company's reputation. Service contracts from car and insurance companies are more likely to remain in effect than those from independent companies.

Exactly what does the contract cover and for how long? Service contracts vary considerably—different items are covered and different time limits are offered. This is true even among service contracts offered by the same company. For example, one company has plans that range from 4 years/36,000 miles maximum coverage to 6 years/100,000 miles maximum coverage, with other options for only power train coverage. Make sure you know what components are covered because if a breakdown occurs on a part that is not covered, you are responsible for the repairs.

If you plan to resell your car in a few years, you won't want to purchase a long-running service contract. Some service contracts automatically cancel when you resell the car, while others require a hefty transfer fee before extending privileges to the new owner.

Some automakers offer a "menu" format, which lets you pick the items you want covered in your service contract. Find out if the contract pays for preventive maintenance, towing, and rental car expenses. If not written into the contract, assume they are not covered.

Make sure the contract clearly specifies how you can reach the company. Knowing this before you purchase a service contract can save you time and aggravation in the future.

How will the repair bills be paid? It is best to have the service contractor pay bills directly. Some contracts require you to pay the repair bill, and reimburse you later.

Where can the car be serviced? Can you take the car to any mechanic if you have trouble on the road? What if you move?

What other costs can be expected? Most service contracts will have a deductible expense. Compare deductibles on various plans. Also, some companies charge the deductible for each individual repair while other companies pay per visit, regardless of the number of repairs being made.

! TURBOCHARGING !

A turbocharger is an air pump that forces more air into the engine for combustion. Most turbochargers consist of an air compressor driven by a small turbine wheel that is powered by the engine's exhaust. The turbine takes advantage of energy otherwise lost and forces increased efficiency from the engine. Turbochargers are often used to increase the power and sometimes the fuel efficiency of small engines. Engines equipped with turbochargers are more expensive than standard engines. The extra power may not be necessary when you consider the added expense and the fact that turbocharging adds to the complexity of the engine.

TIPS FOR DEALING WITH A MECHANIC

Call around. Don't choose a shop simply because it's nearby. Calling a few shops may turn up estimates cheaper by half.

Don't necessarily go for the lowest price. A good rule is to eliminate the highest and lowest estimates; the mechanic with the highest estimate is probably charging too much, and the lowest may be cutting too many corners.

Check the shop's reputation. Call your local consumer affairs agency and the Better Business Bureau. They don't have records on every shop, but unfavorable reports on a shop disqualify it.

Look for certification. Mechanics can be certified by the National Institute for Automotive Service Excellence, an industry-wide yardstick for competence. Certification is offered in eight areas of repair and shops with certified mechanics are allowed to advertise this fact. However, make sure the mechanic working on your car is certified for the repair.

Take a look around. A well-kept shop reflects pride in workmanship. A skilled and efficient mechanic would probably not work in a messy shop.

Don't sign a blank check. The service order you sign should have specific instructions or describe your vehicle's symptoms. Avoid signing a vague work order. Be sure you are called for final approval before the shop does extra work.

Show interest. Ask about the repair. But don't act like an expert if you don't really understand what's wrong. Express your satisfaction. If you're happy with the work, compliment the mechanic and ask for him or her the next time you come in. You will get to know each other and the mechanic will get to know your vehicle.

Develop a "sider." If you know a mechanic, ask about work on the side—evenings or weekends. The labor will be cheaper.

Take a test-drive. Before you pay for a major repair, you should take the car for a test-drive. The few extra minutes you spend checking out the repair could save you a trip back to the mechanic. If you find that the problem still exists, there will be no question that the repair wasn't properly completed.

REPAIR PROTECTION BY CREDIT CARD

TIP

Paying your auto repair bills by credit card can provide a much needed recourse if you are having problems with an auto mechanic. According to federal law, you have the right to withhold payment for sloppy or incorrect repairs. Of course, you may withhold no more than the amount of the repair in dispute.

In order to use this right, you must first try to work out the problem with the mechanic. Also, unless the credit card company owns the repair shop (this might be the case with gasoline credit cards used at gas stations), two other conditions must be met. First, the repair shop must be in your home state (or within 100 miles of your current address), and second, the cost of repairs must be over $50. Until the problem is settled or resolved in court, the credit card company cannot charge you interest or penalties on the amount in dispute.

If you decide to take action, send a letter to the credit card company and a copy to the repair shop, explaining the details of the problem and what you want as settlement. Send the letter by certified mail with a return receipt requested.

Sometimes the credit card company or repair shop will attempt to put a "bad mark" on your credit record if you use this tactic. Legally, you can't be reported as delinquent if you've given the credit card company notice of your dispute, but a creditor can report that you are disputing your bill, which goes in your record. However, you have the right to challenge any incorrect information and add your side of the story to your file.

For more information, write to the Federal Trade Commission, Credit Practices Division, 601 Pennsylvania Avenue, NW, Washington, DC 20580.

Oldsmobile Bravada

Pontiac Sunfire

Suzuki Grand Vitara

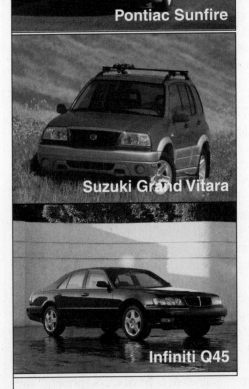

Infiniti Q45

IN THIS CHAPTER

INTRODUCTION

A long with your new car comes a warranty, which is a promise from the manufacturer that the car will perform as it should. Most of us never read the warranty—until it is too late. In fact, because warranties are often difficult to read and understand, most of us don't really know what our warranties offer. This chapter will help you understand what to look for in a new car warranty, tip you off to secret warranties, and provide you with the best and worst among the 2001 warranties.

There are two types of warranties: one provided by the manufacturer and one implied by law.

Manufacturers' warranties are either "full" or "limited." The best warranty you can get is a full warranty because, by law, it must cover all aspects of the product's performance. Any other guarantee is called a limited warranty, which is what most car manufacturers offer. Limited warranties must be clearly marked as such, and you must be told exactly what is covered.

Warranties implied by law are warranties of merchantability and fitness. The "warranty of merchantability" ensures that your new car will be fit for the purpose for which it is used—that means safe, efficient, and trouble-free transportation. The "warranty of fitness" guarantees that if the dealer says a car can be used for a specific purpose, it will perform that purpose.

Many claims made by the salesperson are also considered warranties. They are called expressed warranties and you should have them put in writing if you consider them to be important. If the car does not live up to promises made to you in the showroom, you may have a case against the seller.

The manufacturer can restrict the amount of time the limited warranty is in effect. And in most states, the manufacturer can also limit the time that the warranty implied by law is in effect.

Through the warranty, the manufacturer is promising that the car's parts and design are free from defects, and that for a certain period the car will operate soundly provided it is used in a normal fashion. This period of time is usually measured in both months and miles, whichever comes first is the limit.

While the warranty is in effect, the manufacturer will perform, at no charge, repairs that are necessary because of defects in materials or in the way the car was manufactured.

Any implied warranties, including the warranties of merchantability and fitness, can at most be limited to the duration of the written warranty. Manufacturer warranties try to disclaim responsibility for other problems caused by repairs, such as the loss of time or use of your car, or any expenses they might cause. In at least nine states, such limitations on your warranty rights are invalid.

In addition to the rights granted to you in the warranty, you may have other rights under your state laws.

To keep your warranty in effect, you must operate and maintain your car according to the instructions in your owner's manual. Remember, it is important to keep a record of all maintenance performed on your car.

To have your car repaired under the warranty, take it to an authorized dealer or service center. The work should be done in a reasonable amount of time during normal business hours.

Be careful not to confuse your warranty with a service contract. The service contract must be purchased separately while the warranty is yours at no extra cost when you buy the car.

Corrosion Warranty: All manufacturers warrant against corrosion. The typical corrosion warranty lasts for six years or 100,000 miles, whichever comes first.

Some dealers offer extra rust protection at an additional cost. Before you purchase this option, compare the extra protection offered to the corrosion warranty already included in the price of the car—it probably already provides sufficient protection against rust.

Emission System Warranty: The emission system is warranted by federal law. Any repairs required during the first two years or 24,000 miles will be paid for by the manufacturer if an original engine part fails because of a defect in materials or workmanship, and the failure causes your car to exceed federal emissions standards. Major components are covered for eight years or up to 80,000 miles.

SECRET WARRANTIES

If dealers report a number of complaints about a certain part and the manufacturer determines that the problem is due to faulty design or assembly, the manufacturer may permit dealers to repair the problem at no charge to the customer even though the warranty is expired. In the past, this practice was often reserved for customers who made a big fuss. The availability of the free repair was never publicized, which is why we call these "secret warranties."

Manufacturers deny the existence of secret warranties. They call these free repairs "policy adjustments" or "goodwill service." Whatever they are called, most consumers never hear about them.

Many secret warranties are disclosed in service bulletins that the manufacturers send to dealers. These bulletins outline free repair or reimbursement programs, as well as other problems and their possible causes and solutions.

Service bulletins from many manufacturers may be on file at the National Highway Traffic Safety Administration. Visit their website at www.nhtsa.dot.gov to access NHTSA's Service Bulletin database.

If you find that a secret warranty is in effect and repairs are being made at no charge after the warranty has expired, contact the Center for Auto Safety, 1825 Connecticut Ave., NW, #330, Washington, DC 20009. They will publish the information so others can benefit.

Disclosure Laws: Spurred by the proliferation of secret warranties and the failure of the FTC to take action, California, Connecticut, Virginia, and Wisconsin have passed legislation that requires consumers to be notified of secret warranties on their cars. Several other states have introduced similar warranty bills.

Typically, the laws require the following: direct notice to consumers within a specified time after the adoption of a warranty adjustment policy; notice of the disclosure law to new car buyers; reimbursement, within a number of years after payment, to owners who paid for covered repairs before they learned of the extended warranty service; and dealers must inform consumers who complain about a covered defect that it is eligible for repair under warranty.

New York's bill has another requirement—the establishment of a toll-free number for consumer questions, despite opposition from Ford, GM, Toyota, and other auto manufacturers.

If you live in a state with a secret warranty law already in effect, write your state attorney general's office (in care of your state capital) for information. To encourage passage of such a bill, contact your state representative (in care of your state capital).

Due to past secret warranty problems, three auto companies are required to make their service bulletins public.

Ford: Information on goodwill adjustments is available through Ford's "defect line" at 800–241–3673.

General Motors: Bulletins are available from the past three years for a charge and free indexes to bulletins are available through GM dealers or call 800–551–4123.

Volkswagen: An index of all service bulletins can be ordered by calling 800–544–8021.

LITTLE SECRETS OF THE AUTO INDUSTRY

TIP Every auto company makes mistakes building cars. When they do, they often issue technical service bulletins telling dealers how to fix the problem. Rarely do they publicize these fixes, many of which are offered for free, called secret warranties. The Center for Auto Safety has published a book called *Little Secrets of the Auto Industry*, a consumer guide to secret warranties. This book explains how to find out about secret warranties, offers tips for going to small claims court and getting federal and state assistance, and lists information on state secret warranty laws. To order a copy, send $17.50 to: Center for Auto Safety, Pub. Dept. CB, 1825 Connecticut Ave., NW, Suite 330, Washington, DC 20009.

COMPARING WARRANTIES

Warranties are difficult to compare because they contain lots of fine print and confusing language. The following table will help you understand this year's new car warranties. Because the table does not contain all the details about each warranty, you should review the actual warranty to make sure you understand its fine points. Remember, you have the right to inspect a warranty before you buy—it's the law.

The table provides information on five areas covered by a typical warranty:

The Basic Warranty covers most parts of the car against manufacturer's defects. The tires, batteries, and items you may add to the car are covered under separate warranties. The table describes coverage in terms of months and miles; for example, 36/36,000 means the warranty is good for 36 months or 36,000 miles, whichever comes first. This is the most important part of your warranty.

The Powertrain Warranty usually lasts longer than the basic warranty. Because each manufacturer's definition of the powertrain is different, it is important to find out exactly what your warranty will cover. Powertrain coverage should include parts of the engine, transmission, and drivetrain. The warranty on some luxury cars will often cover some additional systems such as steering, suspension, and electrical systems.

The Corrosion Warranty usually applies only to actual holes due to rust. Read this section carefully, because many corrosion warranties do not apply to what the manufacturer may describe as cosmetic rust or bad paint.

The Roadside Assistance column indicates whether or not the warranty includes a program for helping with problems on the road. Typically, these programs cover such things as lock outs, jump starts, flat tires, running out of gas, and towing. Most of these are offered for the length of the basic warranty. Some have special limitations or added features, which we have pointed out. Because each one is different, check yours out carefully.

The last column contains the **Warranty Rating Index**, which provides an overall assessment of this year's warranties. The higher the Index number, the better the warranty. The Index number incorporates the important features of each warranty. In developing the Index, we gave the most weight to the basic and powertrain components of the warranties. The corrosion warranty was weighted somewhat less, and the roadside assistance features received the least weight. We also considered special features such as whether you had to bring the car in for corrosion inspections, or if rental cars were offered when warranty repairs were being done.

After evaluating all the features of the new warranties, here are this year's best and worst ratings.

2001 WARRANTIES: THE BEST AND THE WORST

THE BEST		THE WORST	
Volkswagen	2154	Honda	954
Audi	1867	Plymouth	932
Kia	1848	Jeep	932
Hyundai	1798	Dodge	932
Infiniti	1718	Chrysler	932

The higher the index number, the better the warranty. See the table on the following pages for complete details.

WARRANTY COMPARISONS

Manufacturer	Basic Warranty	Power Train Warranty	Corrosion Warranty	Roadside Assistance	Index*	Warranty Rating
Acura	48/50,000	48/50,000	60/unlimited	48/50,000	1283	Average
Audi	48/50,000[1]	48/50,000	120/unlimited	48/50,000[2]	1867	Vry. Gd.
BMW	48/50,000[3]	48/50,000	72/unlimited	48/50,000[2]	1429	Good
Buick	36/36,000	36/36,000	72/100,000	36/36,000	956	Very Poor
Cadillac	48/50,000	48/50,000	72/100,000	Lifetime[4,5]	1176	Average
Chevrolet	36/36,000	36/36,000	72/100,000	36/36,000	956	Very Poor
Chrysler	36/36,000	36/36,000	60/100,000	36/36,000	932	Very Poor
Dodge	36/36,000	36/36,000	60/100,000	36/36,000	932	Very Poor
Ford	36/36,000	36/36,000	60/unlimited	36/36,000	1062	Poor
GMC	36/36,000	36/36,000	72/100,000	36/36,000	956	Very Poor
Honda	36/36,000	36/36,000	60/unlimited	None	954	Very Poor
Hyundai	60/60,000	120/100,000	60/100,000	60/unlimited[6]	1798	Vry. Gd.
Infiniti	48/60,000	72/70,000	84/unlimited	48/unlimited	1718	Vry. Gd.
Isuzu	36/50,000	120/120,000	72/100,000	60/60,000	1588	Good
Jeep	36/36,000	36/36,000	60/100,000	36/36,000	932	Very Poor
Kia	60/60,000	120/100,000	60/100,000	60/unlimited[2]	1848	Vry. Gd.
Land Rover	48/50,000	48/50,000	72/unlimited	48/50,000	1373	Average
Lexus	48/50,000	72/72,000	72/unlimited	48/50,000	1511	Good
Lincoln	48/50,000	48/50,000	60/unlimited	48/50,000	1283	Average
Mazda	36/50,000	36/50,000	60/unlimited	36/50,000[7]	1165	Poor
Mercedes-Benz	48/50,000	48/50,000	48/50,000	Lifetime	1032	Poor
Mercury	36/36,000	36/36,000	60/unlimited	36/36,000	1062	Poor

* Higher numbers are better.

[1] Includes all service, repairs, and parts to 36/50,000
[2] Includes all trip interruption expenses
[3] Includes all service, repairs, and parts to 36/36,000
[4] <48/50,000 = free; >48/50,000 = small charge
[5] Covers trip interruption expenses up to 48/50,000 for a warranty failure
[6] Includes towing for accidents
[7] Covers Millenia and MPV only
[8] Limited roadside services
[9] Covers emergency towing, on-site service, and lock out service
[10] Includes all service repairs, and parts to 24/24,000

WARRANTY COMPARISONS

Manufacturer	Basic Warranty	Power Train Warranty	Corrosion Warranty	Roadside Assistance	Index*	Warranty Rating
Mitsubishi	36/36,000	60/60,000	84/unlimited	36/36,000	1124	Poor
Nissan	36/36,000	60/60,000	60/unlimited	36/36,000[8]	1485	Good
Oldsmobile	36/36,000	36/36,000	72/100,000	36/36,000[2]	1006	Poor
Plymouth	36/36,000	36/36,000	60/100,000	36/36,000	932	Very Poor
Pontiac	36/36,000	36/36,000	72/100,000	36/36,000	956	Very Poor
Saab	48/50,000	48/50,000	72/unlimited	48/50,000[2]	1423	Average
Saturn	36/36,000	36/36,000	72/100,000	36/36,000[2]	1006	Poor
Subaru	36/36,000	60/60,000	60/unlimited	36/36,000[9]	1206	Average
Suzuki	36/36,000	36/36,000	36/unlimited	None	954	Very Poor
Toyota	36/36,000	60/60,000	60/unlimited	Optional	978	Very Poor
Volkswagen	24/24,000[10]	120/100,000	144/unlimited	24/24,000[2]	2154	Vry. Gd.
Volvo	48/50,000	48/50,000	96/unlimited	48/50,000[2]	1603	Vry. Gd.

* Higher numbers are better.

[1]Includes all service, repairs, and parts to 36/50,000
[2]Includes all trip interruption expenses
[3]Includes all service, repairs, and parts to 36/36,000
[4]<48/50,000 = free; >48/50,000 = small charge
[5]Covers trip interruption expenses up to 48/50,000 for a warranty failure
[6]Includes towing for accidents
[7]Covers Millenia and MPV only
[8]Limited roadside services
[9]Covers emergency towing, on-site service, and lock out service
[10]Includes all service repairs, and parts to 24/24,000

Honda Prelude

Toyota Sequoia

Mitsubishi Eclipse

Honda Odyssey

IN THIS CHAPTER

INTRODUCTION

Insurance is a big part of ownership expenses, yet it's often forgotten in the show-room. As you shop, remember that the car's design and accident history may affect your insurance rates. Some cars cost less to insure because experience has shown that they are damaged less, less expensive to fix after a collision, or stolen less.

This chapter provides you with the information you need to make a wise insurance purchase. We discuss the different types of insurance, offer special tips on reducing this cost, and include information on occupant injury, theft, and bumper ratings—all factors that can affect your insurance.

More and more consumers are saving hundreds of dollars by shopping around for insurance. In order to be a good comparison shopper, you need to know a few things about automobile insurance.

A number of factors determine what these coverages will cost you. A car's design can affect both the chances and severity of an accident. A car with a well-designed bumper may escape damage altogether in a low-speed crash. Some cars are easier to repair than others or may have less expensive parts. Cars with four doors tend to be damaged less than cars with two doors.

The reason one car may get a discount on insurance while another receives a surcharge also depends upon the way it is traditionally driven. Sports cars, for example, are usually surcharged due, in part, to the typical driving habits of their owners. Four-door sedans and station wagons generally merit discounts.

Insurance companies use this and other information to determine whether to offer a discount on insurance premiums for a particular car or whether to levy a surcharge.

Not all companies offer discounts or surcharges, and many cars receive neither. Some companies offer a discount or impose a surcharge on collision premiums only. Others apply discounts and surcharges on both collision and comprehensive coverage. Discounts and surcharges usually range from 10 to 30 percent. Allstate offers discounts of up to 35 percent on certain cars. Remember that one company may offer a discount on a particular car while another may not.

Check with your insurance agent to find out whether your company has a rating program.

TYPES OF COVERAGE

Collision Insurance: This pays for the damage to your car after an accident.

Comprehensive Physical Damage Insurance: This pays for damages when your car is stolen or damaged by fire, flood, or other perils.

Property Damage Liability: This pays claims and defense costs if your car damages someone else's property.

Medical Payments Insurance: This pays for your car's occupants' medical expenses resulting from an accident.

Bodily Injury Liability: This provides money to pay claims against you and to pay for the cost of your legal defense if your car injures or kills someone.

Uninsured Motorists Protection: This pays for injuries caused by an uninsured or a hit-and-run driver.

NO-FAULT INSURANCE

One of the major expenses of vehicular accidents has been the cost of determining who is "at fault." With the traditional liability system, both parties hire lawyers, wait months or years for court decisions, and incur large legal costs. Aside from economic damages, or out-of-pocket costs, victims can also sue for non-economic, or pain and suffering damages. An award for pain and suffering can account for the gross disparity between awards in similar cases. This was the only method of coverage until consumers, insurers, and state regulators realized that most of the insurance premium dollar was spent on legal fees and non-economic awards.

Attempting to reduce costs, many states have instituted "no-fault" policies. True no-fault applies to state laws that provide for the payment of policyholder benefits and restrict the right to sue.

The concept of no-fault is that each person's losses are covered by their personal insurance protection, regardless of who is at fault. Lawsuits are permitted only under certain conditions, known as a threshold. A verbal threshold allows additional legal action only if certain serious injuries occur. A monetary threshold sets a dollar amount that medical claims must reach before permitting a lawsuit.

No-fault laws vary from state to state. Variations include the conditions of the right to sue, threshold standards, and the inclusion or exclusion of property damage. States with some form of no-fault include: Colorado, Florida, Hawaii, Kansas, Kentucky, Massachusetts, Michigan, Minnesota, New Jersey, New York, North Dakota, Pennsylvania, Utah, and also Puerto Rico. Consult your state Department of Motor Vehicles for details.

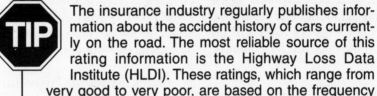

INSURANCE INDUSTRY STATISTICS

TIP

The insurance industry regularly publishes information about the accident history of cars currently on the road. The most reliable source of this rating information is the Highway Loss Data Institute (HLDI). These ratings, which range from very good to very poor, are based on the frequency of medical claims under personal injury protection coverages. A few companies will charge you more to insure a car rated poor than for one rated good.

A car's accident history may not match its crash test performance. Such discrepancies arise because the accident history includes driver performance. A sports car, for example, may have good crash test results but a poor accident history because its owners tend to drive relatively recklessly.

If you want more information about the injury history, bumper performance, and theft rating of today's cars, write to HLDI, 1005 North Glebe Road, Arlington, VA 22201 or visit their website at www.carsafety.org.

GAP INSURANCE

TIP

GAP insurance covers the difference between what you owe on a car and its actual value, should the car be "totaled" or stolen. If you finance or lease through a dealer, he or she will likely suggest you purchase GAP insurance, which can cost up to $500. If you think this situation is likely, then your financing plan is probably too long.

Whether you need GAP or not, be wary of how dealers try to sell GAP. Dealers may insist the only way to give you financing is if you purchase GAP insurance—this is untrue. When negotiating finance terms, be sure to ask if GAP insurance has been added to the cost, as the dealer may not tell you.

REDUCING INSURANCE COSTS

After you have shopped around and found the best deal by comparing the costs of different coverages, consider other factors that will affect your final insurance bill.

Your Annual Mileage: The more you drive, the more your vehicle will be "exposed" to a potential accident. The insurance cost for a car rarely used will be less than the cost for a frequently used car.

Where You Drive: If you regularly drive and park in the city, you will most likely pay more than if you drive in rural areas.

Youthful Drivers: Usually the highest premiums are paid by male drivers under the age of 25. Whether or not the under-25-year-old male is married also affects insurance rates. (Married males pay less.) As the driver gets older, rates are lowered.

In addition to shopping around, take advantage of certain discounts to reduce your insurance costs. Most insurance companies offer discounts of 5 to 30 percent on various parts of your insurance bill. The availability of discounts varies among companies and often depends on where you live. Many consumers do not benefit from these discounts simply because they don't ask about them.

To determine whether you are getting all the discounts that you're entitled to, ask your insurance company for a complete list of the discounts that it offers.

Here are some of the most common insurance discounts:

Driver Education/Defensive Driving Courses: Many insurance companies offer (and in some cases mandate) discounts to young people who have successfully completed a state-approved driver education course. Typically, this can mean a $40 reduction in the cost of coverage. Also, a discount of 5-15 percent is available in some states to those who complete a defensive driving course.

Good Student Discounts: Many insurance companies offer discounts of up to 25 percent on insurance to full-time high school or college students who are in the upper 20 percent of their class, on the dean's list, or have a B or better grade point average.

Good Driver Discounts: Many companies will offer discounts to drivers with an accident and violation-free record.

Mature Driver Credit: Drivers ages 50 and older may qualify for up to a 10 percent discount or a lower price bracket.

Sole Female Driver: Some companies offer discounts of 10 percent for females, ages 30 to 64, who are the only driver in a household, citing favorable claims experience.

Non-Drinkers and Non-Smokers: A limited number of companies offer incentives ranging from 10–25 percent to those who abstain.

Farmer Discounts: Many companies offer farmers either a discount of 10–30 percent or a lower price bracket.

Car Pooling: Commuters sharing driving may qualify for discounts of 5–25 percent or a lower price bracket.

Insuring Driving Children: Children away at school don't drive the family car very often, so it's usually less expensive to insure them on the parents' poli-

---

! DON'T SPEED !

Besides endangering the lives of your passengers and other drivers, speeding tickets will increase your insurance premium. It only takes one speeding ticket to lose your "preferred" or "good driver" discount, which requires a clean driving record. Two or more speeding tickets or accidents can increase your premium by 40% to 200%. Some insurers may simply drop your coverage. According to the Insurance Institute for Highway Safety (IIHS), you are 17% more likely to be in an accident if you have just one speeding ticket. Insurance companies know this and will charge you for it.

cy rather than separately. If you do insure them separately, discounts of 10–40 percent or a lower price bracket are available.

Desirable Cars: Premiums are usually much higher for cars with high collision rates or that are the favorite target of thieves.

Passive Restraints/Anti-Lock Brake Credit: Many companies offer discounts (from 10 to 30 percent) for automatic belts and air bags. Some large companies are now offering a 5 percent discount to owners of vehicles with anti-lock brakes.

Anti-Theft Device Credits: Discounts of 5 to 15 percent are offered in some states for cars equipped with a hood lock and an alarm or a disabling device (active or passive) that prevents the car from being started.

Multipolicy and Multicar Policy Discount: Some companies offer discounts of up to 10–20 percent for insuring your home and auto with the same company, or more than one car.

Long-Term Policy Renewal: Although not available in all states, some companies offer price breaks of 5–20 percent to customers who renew a long-term policy.

First Accident Allowance: Some insurers offer a "first accident allowance," which guarantees that if a customer achieves five accident-free years, his or her rates won't go up after the first at-fault accident.

Deductibles: Opting for the largest reasonable deductible is the obvious first step in reducing premiums. Increasing your deductible to $500 from $200 could cut your collision premium about 20 percent. Raising the deductible to $1,000 from $200 could lower your premium about 45 percent. The discounts may vary by company.

Collision Coverage: The older the car, the less the need for collision insurance. Consider dropping collision insurance entirely on an older car. Regardless of how much coverage you carry, the insurance company will only pay up to the car's "book value." For example, if your car requires $1,000 in repairs, but its "book value" is only $500, the insurance company is required to pay only $500.

Uninsured Motorist Coverage/Optional Coverage:

The necessity of both of these policies depends upon the extent of your health insurance coverage. In states where they are not required, consumers with applicable health insurance may not want uninsured motorist coverage. Also, those with substantial health insurance coverage may not want an optional medical payment policy.

Rental Cars: If you regularly rent cars, special coverage on your personal auto insurance can cover you while renting for far less than rental agencies offer.

Organizations: If you are a member of AARP, AAA, the military, a union, a professional group, an alumni association, or similar organization, you may be able to get a discount. Often insurance companies will enter joint ventures with organizations.

AUTO THEFT

The Highway Loss Data Institute regularly compiles statistics on motor vehicle thefts. Using the frequency of theft and the loss resulting from the theft, HLDI publishes an index based on "relative average loss payments per insured vehicle year." The list below includes the most and least stolen cars among the 2001 models.

Most Stolen		Least Stolen	
1001	Mercedes S Class LWB	4	Honda Odyssey
877	Acura Integra	11	Saturn SW
616	Mitsubishi Montero	13	Buick Century
539	Mercedes SL Class	13	Buick LeSabre
509	Nissan Maxima	13	Oldsmobile Silhouette
421	Lexus GS300/400	22	Saturn SL
409	BMW 3 Series	22	Chevrolet Venture
387	BMW 7 Series	23	Saturn SC
387	Lincoln Navigator	23	Chevrolet Lumina
321	Volkswagen Golf GTI	24	Buick Park Avenue

BUMPERS

The main purpose of the bumper is to protect your car in low-speed collisions. Despite this intention, most of us have been victims of a $200 to $400 repair bill resulting from a seemingly minor impact. Since most bumpers offered little or no damage protection in low-speed crashes, the federal government used to require that automakers equip cars with bumpers capable of withstanding up to 5 mph crashes with no damage. Unfortunately, this is no longer the case.

In the early eighties, while under pressure from car companies, the government rolled back the requirement that bumpers protect cars in collisions up to 5 mph. Now, car companies only build bumpers to protect cars in 2.5 mph collisions—about the speed at which we walk. This

rollback has cost consumers millions of dollars in increased insurance premiums and repair costs. While the rollback satisfied car companies, most car owners were unhappy.

To let consumers know that today's bumpers offer widely varying amounts of protection in 5-mph collisions, each year the Insurance Institute for Highway Safety tests bumpers to see how well they prevent damage. Thankfully, some automobile manufacturers are betting that consumers still want better bumpers on at least some of their models.

These results are rather startling when you consider that the sole purpose of a bumper is to protect a car from damage in low-speed collisions. Only about one-third of the cars tested to date have bumpers which

actually prevented damage in front and rear 5-mph collisions. As the Institute's figures show, there is no correlation between the price of the car and how well the bumper worked.

Unfortunately, we can't simply look at a bumper and determine how good it will be at doing its job—protecting a car from inevitable bumps. The solution to this problem is quite simple—simply require carmakers to tell the consumer the highest speed at which their car could be crashed with no damage.

Following are the results of the IIHS bumper crash tests. We have included the ten best and the ten worst. This should give you a good basis for comparison. For more test results, you can visit the Insurance Institute for Highway Safety on the internet at www.highwaysafety.org.

BUMPER BASHING—DAMAGE REPAIR COSTS IN 5-MPH CRASH TESTS

Source: Insurance Institute for Highway Safety	Front into Flat Barrier	Rear into Flat Barrier	Front into Angle Barrier	Rear into Pole	Total
The Best					
1998 Volkswagen Beetle	$17	$0	$175	$0	$192
1997 Saturn SL	$116	$71	$531	$0	$718
2000 Saturn LS	$0	$138	$390	$295	$823
1998 Toyota Corolla	$0	$351	$281	$262	$894
1998 Volkswagen Passat	$159	$0	$592	$288	$1,039
1999 Honda Odyssey	$462	$258	$175	$168	$1,063
1999 Volkswagen Jetta	$138	$72	$697	$176	$1,083
1999 Nissan Quest	$0	$239	$631	$240	$1,110
1997 Lincoln Continental	$0	$17	$831	$328	$1,176
1997 Toyota Camry	$116	$95	$487	$602	$1,300
The Worst					
2000 Isuzu Trooper	$2,890	$2,618	$2,333	$3,317	$11,158
2001 Mitsubishi Montero	$1,210	$2,495	$2,525	$2,831	$9,061
1997 Nissan Pathfinder/Infiniti QX4	$886	$1,619	$2,685	$3,063	$8,253
2000 Volvo S80	$5,137	$347	$1,028	$1,550	$8,062
1996 Toyota 4Runner	$855	$2,194	$2,076	$2,632	$7,757
1998 Kia Sportage	$691	$2,742	$1,094	$2,971	$7,498
1997 Mercedes E Class	$402	$1,122	$2,233	$2,687	$6,444
1999 Mitsubishi Montero Sport	$1,153	$1,260	$2,159	$1,790	$6,362
1996 Ford Explorer	$999	$1,446	$2,360	$1,130	$5,935
2000 Mazda MPV	$1,710	$1,031	$1,730	$1,198	$5,669

TIRES

Infiniti I30

Toyota Tacoma

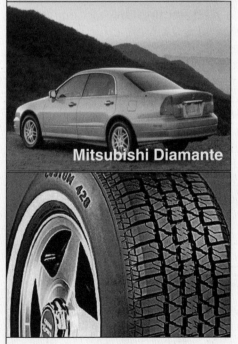

Mitsubishi Diamante

IN THIS CHAPTER

INTRODUCTION

Buying tires has become an infrequent task because today's radial tires last much longer than the tires of the past. Suprisingly, a tire has to perform more functions simultaneously than any other part of the car (steering, bearing the load, cushioning the ride, and stopping). And because there are nearly 1,800 tire lines to choose from, and only a few tire manufacturers, the difference in many tires may only be the brand name.

Because comparing tires is so difficult, many consumers mistakenly use price and brand name to determine quality. But there is help. The U.S. government now requires tires to be rated according to their safety and expected mileage.

Treadwear, traction, and heat resistance grades are printed on the sidewall and are attached to the tire on a paper label. Ask the dealer for the grades of the tires they sell. Using this rating system, we provide a list of the top rated tires on page 65.

Treadwear: The treadwear grade gives you an idea of the mileage you can expect from a tire. It is shown in numbers—300, 310, 320, 330, and so forth. Higher numbers mean longer tire life. Because driving habits vary and tire wear is affected by regional differences in road surfaces, use the treadwear as a relative basis of comparison.

Traction: Traction grades of A, B, and C describe the tire's ability to stop on wet surfaces. Tires graded A will stop on a wet road in a shorter distance than tires graded B or C. Tires rated C have poor traction.

Heat Resistance: Heat resistance is also graded A, B, and C. Hot-running tires can result in blowouts or tread separation. An A rating means the tire will run cooler than one rated B or C, and it is less likely to fail if driven over long distances at highway speeds. In addition, tires that run cooler tend to be more fuel-efficient.

BUYING TIRES

There are two important considerations in selecting the best tire: how long you plan to keep your car and whether the majority of your driving is highway or local. Remember, higher prices do not necessarily mean better tires.

Radial tires are your best buy, which is why they dominate the tire market and are provided on all new vehicles sold in America. In a radial tire, the cords run at right angles to the centerline and may be laid in one to three layers (plies). Over this radial section lies a four-ply belt with cords that run at a slight angle to the center line. The result is a tire with a flexible sidewall (that's why radials often look like they need air), but with stiffness and strength in the tread, giving longer tread life and improved fuel efficiency.

Snow and all-season are two subcategories of tires. Snow tires have an open tread pattern with deep grooves. A snow tire will wear out rapidly on dry roads. Because of this wear and the inconvenience of seasonally changing tires, all-season tires are becoming popular. They are effective in occasional snow, have good traction on wet roads, and outlast snow tires on dry roads.

You can also buy a **retread**. Adding the tread is the last step to building a tire. A retreader takes undamaged used tires, strips off the remaining tread and repeats this last step of the original manufacturing process.

NEW TIRE REGISTRATION

TIP

You may be missing out on free or low-cost replacement tires or driving on potentially hazardous ones if you don't fill out the tire registration form when you buy tires. The law once required all tire sellers to submit buyers' names automatically to the manufacturer, so the company could contact you if the tires were ever recalled. While this is still mandatory for tire dealers and distributors owned by tire manufacturers, it is not required of independent tire dealers. Ask for the tire registration card when you buy tires, and fill it out and send it in. This will allow the company to notify you if the tire is ever recalled.

Pump 'em Up: An estimated 50% of us are driving on under-inflated tires. Because even good tires lose air, it is important to check your tire pressure at least once a month. Under-inflated tires can be dangerous, use more fuel and cause premature tire failure. When checking your tires, be sure to use an accurate guage and inflate to the pressure indicated in your owner's manual, not the maximum pressure printed on your tire.

When to Replace: If any part of Lincoln's head is visible when you insert the top of a penny into a tread groove, it's time to replace the tire. While this old rule of thumb is still valid, today's tires also have a built-in wear indicator. A series of horizontal bars appear across the surface when the tread depth reaches the danger zone.

Tread Design: Look for a tread design that is made up of independent blocks arranged in a staggered fashion. These designs have grooves that run from side to side in order to displace more water for better traction on wet roads. Most all-season tires have this tread pattern.

Load Range: Check the tire's load range to ensure that the tires are adequate for your driving needs. The maximum load is printed on each tire—the higher the load range, the more weight you can carry. To ensure that the tires are adequate, add your vehicle's weight (you'll find it in your owner's manual) and the weight of your average payload (passengers and baggage) and divide by four. This number should never exceed the tire's maximum load range.

Where to Buy: Most tires are sold at one of four outlets: independent dealers (large national chains and small stores which carry a number of brands), department stores (Sears, JC Penney), tire company stores (Goodyear, Uniroyal), and service stations.

The price of the same tire can vary depending on where you shop. It is not uncommon for competing stores on the same street to offer the same tire at different prices. Because of this, shopping around is vital to finding a good buy. Most tire ads are grouped together in the sports section of your Wednesday and Saturday daily newspaper.

The most expensive place to buy tires is at a new car dealership; service stations are a close second. You are most likely to find the best prices at independent tire dealers who carry a variety of tire brands.

GETTING THE BEST PRICE

The price of a tire is based on its size, and tires come in as many as nine sizes. For example, the list price of the same tire can range from $74.20 to $134.35, depending on its size.

The following tips can help you get the best buy.

1. Check to see which manufacturer makes the least expensive "off brand." Only twelve manufacturers produce the over 1,800 types of tires sold in the U.S.
2. Don't forget to inquire about balancing and mounting costs when comparing tire prices. In some stores, the extra charges for balancing, mounting, and valve stems can add up to more than $25. Other stores may offer them as a customer service at little or no cost.
3. Never pay list price for a tire. A good rule of thumb is to pay at least 30 to 40 percent off the suggested list price.
4. Use the treadwear grade the same way you would the "unit price" in a supermarket. The tire with the lowest cost per grade point is the best value. For example, if tire A costs $100 and has a treadwear grade of 300, and tire B costs $80 and has a treadwear grade of 200:

Tire A: $100÷300=$.33 per point
Tire B: $80÷200=$.40 per point

Since 33 cents is less than 40 cents, tire A is the better buy even though its initial cost is more.

SPEED RATINGS

TIP

All passenger car tires meet government standards up to 85 mph. Some tires are tested at higher speeds because certain cars require tires that perform at higher speeds. Consult your owner's manual for the right speed rating for your car. See the tire size: P215/60 SR15. The "S" indicates the tire is tested for speeds up to 112 mph. Other letters include: "T" for up to 118 mph, "H" for up to 130 mph, "V" for up to 149 mph and "Z" for 150 mph or higher.

HOW LONG WILL THEY LAST?

Mileage is an important factor for most of us when we purchase tires. However, few of us realize that where we live is a key factor in how long tires last. In addition to construction and design, tire wear is affected by the level of abrasive material in the road surface. Generally, the road surfaces of the West Coast, Great Lakes region, and northern New England are easiest on tires. The Appalachian and Rocky Mountain areas are usually hardest on tires.

To estimate a tire's treadlife, look at the accompanying map to determine if you live in a high-, medium-, or low-mileage area. Then use the treadwear grade of the tires you are considering to estimate their treadlife for your area. For example, if you are considering tires with a treadwear grade of 300, you can expect those tires to get about 90,000 miles in a high mileage area, 60,000 miles in a medium mileage area, and 45,000 miles in a low mileage area.

Of course, actual mileage depends not only on where you drive but also on how you drive and whether you keep your tires properly inflated and your wheels aligned.

WHAT CAN YOU EXPECT FROM YOUR TIRES?

Treadwear Grade	High Mileage Area	Medium Mileage Area	Low Mileage Area
300	90,000	60,000	45,000
310	93,000	62,000	46,500
320	96,000	64,000	48,000
330	99,000	66,000	49,500
340	102,000	68,000	51,000
350	105,000	70,000	52,500
360	108,000	72,000	54,000
370	111,000	74,000	55,500
380	114,000	76,000	57,000
390	117,000	78,000	58,500
400	120,000	80,000	60,000
410	123,000	82,000	61,500
420	126,000	84,000	63,000
430	129,000	86,000	64,500
440	132,000	88,000	66,000
450	135,000	90,000	67,500
460	138,000	92,000	69,000
470	141,000	94,000	70,500
480	144,000	96,000	72,000
490	147,000	98,000	73,500
500	150,000	100,000	75,000
510	153,000	102,000	76,500
520	156,000	104,000	78,000
530	159,000	106,000	79,500
540	162,000	108,000	81,000
550	165,000	110,000	82,500
560	168,000	112,000	84,000

High Mileage Area

Medium Mileage Area

Low Mileage Area

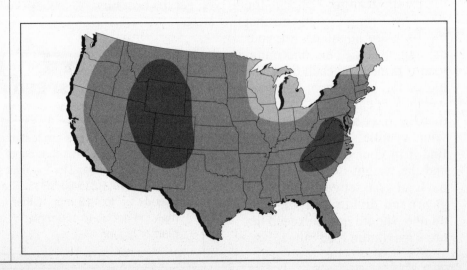

Brand Name	Model	Description	Traction	Grades Heat	Treadwear
TOYO	800 ULTRA	ALL	A	B	700
BIG-O	LEGACY TOUR PLUS 60/65/70 SR	14-16	A	B	660
VOGUE	WIDE TRAC TOURING II	S-RATED	A	B	660
COOPER	LIFELINER STE	ALL	A	B	640
CORDOVAN	GRAND PRIX TOURING LXE	ALL OTHERS	A	B	640
HALLMARK	ULTRA TOURING GT	ALL	A	B	640
KELLY	AQUA TOUR	ALL	A	B	640
LEE	ULTRA TOURING GT	ALL	A	B	640
MASTERCRAFT	TOURING LX	ALL	A	B	640
MULTIMILE	GRAND AM TOURING LSS	ALL OTHERS	A	B	640
SIGMA	SUPREME TOURING SSR	ALL OTHERS	A	B	640
CONTINENTAL	CONTI TOURING CONTACT CT85	ALL	A	B	620
CONTINENTAL	TOURING GT8000	ALL	A	B	620
DAYTON	DAYTONA PREM GT	ALL	A	B	620
DEAN	TOURING EDITION	ALL	A	B	620
GENERAL	AMERI*TOUR	ALL	A	B	620
HERCULES	MEGA TOURING LXT (SR)	ALL	A	B	620
MENTOR	VANTAGE TOURING	ALL	A	B	620
MICHELIN	X ONE	ALL	A	B	620
MICHELIN	X RADIAL PLUS	ALL	A	B	620
MULTIMILE	WILD COUNTRY XRT	ALL	B	C	620
ROAD KING	PREMIUM GT	ALL	A	B	620
ROADMASTER	MENTOR VANTAGE TOURING	ALL	A	B	620
STARFIRE	MENTOR VANTAGE TOURING	ALL	A	B	620
BIG-O	LEGACY TOUR PLUS 75/80 SR	14-16	A	B	600
CORDOVAN	GRAND PRIX TOURING LXE	75 SR	A	B	600
MULTIMILE	GRAND AM TOURING LSS	75 (SR)	A	B	600
SIGMA	SUPREME TOURING SSR	75 SR	A	B	600
MICHELIN	XH4	ALL	A	B	580
TOYO	SPECTRUM	ALL	A	B	580
UNIROYAL	TIGER PAW NAILGARD 70/75 SR	14 & 15	A	B	580
VOGUE	RADIAL VII (S-RATED)	ALL EXCEPT	A	B	580
AMERICAN	GOLD TOUR PLUS 70/75 SR	P205+	A	B	560
CENTENNIAL	INTERCEPTOR TOURING	15 & 16	A	B	560
CONCORDE	TOURING 9000	ALL	A	B	560
CO-OP	GOLDEN MARK 60/65/70	ALL	A	B	560
COOPER	GRAND CLASSIC STE (SR)	ALL	A	B	560
COOPER	LIFELINER CLASSIC II (SR/TR)	ALL	A	B	560
CORDOVAN	GRAND PRIX G/T 70 (RWL)	ALL	A	B	560
CORDOVAN	GRAND PRIX TOURING ST	ALL	A	B	560
CORDOVAN	GRAND PRIX TOURING STX	ALL	A	B	560
DEAN	QUASAR	ALL	A	B	560
DEAN	QUASAR PLUS	ALL OTHERS	A	B	560
DOMINATOR	PT>9	ALL	A	B	560
DOMINATOR	TOURING MR II	ALL	A	B	560
DUNLOP	D65 T	15 & 16	A	B	560
EL DORADO	CRUSADER II (SR)	ALL	A	B	560
EL DORADO	LEGEND	ALL	A	B	560
EMBASSY	DIPLOMAT	ALL	A	B	560
FALKEN	SN812	ALL	A	B	560
GOODRICH	THE ADVANTAGE PLUS 70/75 SR	P205+	A	B	560
GOODYEAR	REGATTA 2	ALL	A	B	560
HERCULES	ULTRA PLUS IV (SR) 55/60/65/70	ALL	A	B	560
KELLY	NAVIGATOR GOLD	ALL EXCEPT	A	B	560
KELLY	NAVIGATOR GOLD	P235/75R15XL	A	C	560
KIRKLAND	SIGNATURE 70/75/80 SR	P205+	A	B	560
MASTERCRAFT	MARK VII (SR)	ALL	A	B	560
MASTERCRAFT	P794 SR/TR	ALL	A	B	560
MEDALIST	PRIMERA 70/75 SR	P205+	A	B	560
MONARCH	ULTRA TRAK A/S	ALL OTHERS	A	B	560
MONARCH	ULTRA TRAK A/S	235/75R15	A	C	560
MULTIMILE	CLASSIC RADIAL SR	ALL	A	B	560
MULTIMILE	GRAND AM SE	ALL	A	B	560
MULTIMILE	GRAND AM TOURING SLE	ALL	A	B	560
MULTIMILE	GRAND AM TOURING ST	ALL	A	B	560
PACEMARK	PREMIUM A/S	ALL EXCEPT	A	B	560

For a complete listing of all the tires on the market, you can call the Auto Safety Hot Line toll free, at 800-424-9393 or 800-424-9153 (TTY). (In Washington, DC, the number is 202-366-7800.)

Brand Name	Model	Description	Traction	Grades Heat	Treadwear
PACEMARK	PREMIUM A/S P235/	75R15 XL	A	C	560
REGUL	SELECT 70/75 SR	P205+	A	B	560
REMINGTON	TOURING XT120	15 & 16	A	B	560
RIKEN	RAPTOR TOURING EDITION 70/75 SR	P205+	A	B	560
ROADMASTER	CONCOURS	ALL	A	B	560
ROADMASTER	MAGIS LXI	ALL	A	B	560
SIGMA	SUPREME TOURING ST	ALL	A	B	560
STARFIRE	CONSTELLATION	ALL	A	B	560
STARFIRE	SPECTRUM LXR	ALL	A	B	560
TBC	CLASSIC RADIAL SE	ALL	A	B	560
TBC	CLASSIC RADIAL SR	ALL	A	B	560
TBC	GRAND SPIRIT RADIAL G/T	ALL	A	B	560
UNIROYAL	TIGER PAW AQUA GRIP 70/75 SR	P205+	A	B	560
VANDERBILT	TURBO TECH TOURING A/S	ALL	A	B	560
WINSTON	SIGNATURE (C)	ALL	A	B	560
AMERICAN	GOLD TOUR PLUS 70/75 SR	THRU P195	A	B	540
CENTENNIAL	INTERCEPTOR TOURING	14	A	B	540
DUNLOP	D65 T	14	A	B	540
DURALON	ULTRA 85	ALL	A	B	540
FALKEN	FK315	ALL	A	B	540
GOODRICH	THE ADVANTAGE PLUS 70/75 SR	THRU P195	A	B	540
GOODYEAR	INFINITRED	ALL OTHERS	A	B	540
HANKOOK	MILEAGE PLUS	ALL	A	B	540
KIRKLAND	SIGNATURE 70/75/80 SR	THRU P195	A	B	540
MEDALIST	PRIMERA 70/75 SR	THRU 195	A	B	540
OHTSU	HS311	ALL	A	B	540
PEERLESS	PREMIUM GT TOURING	ALL	A	B	540
REGUL	SELECT 70/75 SR	THRU P195	A	B	540
REMINGTON	TOURING XT120	14	A	B	540
RIKEN	RAPTOR TOURING EDITION 70/75 SR	THRU P195	A	B	540
TOYO	800 + 75	15 EXCEPT	A	B	540
UNIROYAL	TIGER PAW AQUA GRIP 70/75 SR	THRU P195	A	B	540
UNIROYAL	TIGER PAW NAILGARD 60/65 SR	ALL	A	B	540
UNIROYAL	TIGER PAW TOURING TR	15 &16	A	B	540
UNIROYAL	TIGER PAW TOURING TR 70 SR	14	A	B	540
VOGUE	RADIAL VII (S-RATED)	P215/75R15	A	B	540
AMERICAN	GOLD TOUR PLUS 60/65 SR	ALL	A	B	520
BIG-O	EURO TOUR 65/70 SR	14 &15	A	B	520
CORDOVAN	GRAND SPIRIT AQUA FLOW	ALL	A	B	520
CORDOVAN	ULTREX II	14 & 15	A	B	520
DELTA	SUPREME 70/75	15	A	B	520
GENERAL	AMERI 660AS	ALL	A	B	520
GENERAL	AMERI GS60	ALL	A	B	520
GENERAL	AMERI*G4S	ALL	A	B	520
GOODRICH	EXCENTIA TOURING A/S 65 SR	ALL	A	B	520
GOODRICH	THE ADVANTAGE PLUS 60/65 SR	ALL	A	B	520
GOODYEAR	INFINITRED	13	A	B	520
KIRKLAND	SIGNATURE 60/65 SR	ALL	A	B	520
MEDALIST	PRIMERA 60/65 SR	ALL	A	B	520
NATIONAL	XT5000	15	A	B	520
NATIONAL	XT6000 70/75	15	A	B	520
PIRELLI	P400 AQUAMILE	ALL	A	B	520
REGUL	SELECT 60/65 SR	ALL	A	B	520
RIKEN	RAPTOR TOURING EDITION 60/65 SR	ALL	A	B	520
TOYO	800 + 75	14	A	B	520
TRED TECH	TOURING SUPREME SEII	ALL	A	B	520
UNIROYAL	TIGER PAW AQUA GRIP 60/65 SR	ALL	A	B	520
AMERICAN	PROSPECTOR A/T LT	15	A	B	500
ATLAS	PINNACLE TE 70	13	A	B	500
ATLAS	PINNACLE TE 70/75	14 & 15	A	B	500
BIG-O	EURO TOUR 75 SR	14 & 15	A	B	500
BRIDGESTONE	TURANZA QL20 "T"	ALL	A	B	500
CAVALIER	SPORT LT	15	A	B	500
CORDOVAN	ULTREX II	13	A	B	500
DAYTON	TOURING 70/75S	ALL	A	B	500
DELTA	CHAPARRAL A/T LT	15	A	B	500

For a complete listing of all the tires on the market, you can call the Auto Safety Hot Line toll free, at 800-424-9393 or 800-424-9153 (TTY). (In Washington, DC, the number is 202-366-7800.)

Nissan Altima

Volvo S60

Mitsubishi Mirage

IN THIS CHAPTER

INTRODUCTION

Americans spend billions of dollars on motor vehicle repairs every year. While many of those repairs are satisfactory, there are times when getting your vehicle fixed can be a very difficult process. In fact, vehicle defects and repairs are the number one cause of consumer complaints in the U.S., according to the Federal Trade Commission. This chapter is designed to help you resolve your complaint, whether it's for a new vehicle still under warranty or for one you've had for years. In addition, we offer a guide to arbitration, the names and addresses of consumer groups, federal agencies, and the manufacturers themselves. Finally, we tell you how to take the important step of registering your complaint with the U.S. Department of Transportation.

No matter what your complaint, keep accurate records. Copies of the following items are indispensable in helping to resolve your problems:

☑ your service invoices

☑ bills you have paid

☑ letters you have written to the manufacturer or the repair facility owner

☑ written repair estimates from your independent mechanic.

RESOLVING COMPLAINTS

If you are having trouble, here are some basic steps to help you resolve your problem:

1 First, return your vehicle to the repair facility that did the work. Bring a written list of the problems and make sure that you keep a copy of the list. Give the repair facility a reasonable opportunity to examine your vehicle and attempt to fix it. Speak directly to the service manager (not to the service writer who wrote up your repair order), and ask him or her to test drive the vehicle with you so that you can point out the problem.

2 If that doesn't resolve the problem, take the vehicle to a diagnostic center for an independent examination. This may cost $45 to $60. Get a written statement defining the problem and outlining how it may be fixed. Give your repair shop a copy. If your vehicle is under warranty, do not allow any warranty repair by an independent mechanic; you may not be reimbursed by the manufacturer.

3 If your repair shop does not respond to the independent assessment, present your problem to a mediation panel. These panels hear both sides of the story and try to come to a resolution.

If the problem is with a new vehicle dealer, or if you feel that the manufacturer is responsible, you may be able to use one of the manufacturer's mediation programs discussed on pg. 70.

If the problem is solely with an independent dealer, a local Better Business Bureau (BBB) may be able to mediate your complaint. It may also offer an arbitration hearing. In any case, the BBB should enter your complaint into its files on that establishment.

When contacting any mediation program, determine how long the process takes, who makes the final decision, whether you are bound by that decision, and whether the program handles all problems or only warranty complaints.

4 If there are no mediation programs in your area, contact private consumer groups, local government agencies, or your local "action line" newspaper columnist, newspaper editor, or radio or TV broadcaster. A phone call or letter from them may persuade a repair facility to take action. Send a copy of your letter to the repair shop.

5 One of your last resorts is to bring a lawsuit against the dealer, manufacturer, or repair facility in small claims court. The fee for filing such an action is usually small, and you generally act as your own attorney, saving attorney's fees. There is a monetary limit on the amount you can claim, which varies from state to state. Your local consumer affairs office, state attorney general's office, or the clerk of the court can tell you how to file such a suit.

6 Finally, talk with an attorney. It's best to select an attorney who is familiar with handling automotive problems. Call the lawyer referral service listed in the telephone directory and ask for the names of attorneys who deal with automobile problems. If you can't afford an attorney, contact the Legal Aid Society.

WARRANTY COMPLAINTS

If your vehicle is under warranty or you are having problems with a factory-authorized dealership, here are some special guidelines:

1 Have the warranty available to show the dealer. Make sure you call the problem to the dealer's attention before the end of the warranty period.

2 If you are still unsatisfied after giving the dealer a reasonable opportunity to fix your vehicle, contact the manufacturer's representative (also called the zone representative) in your area. This person can authorize the dealer to make repairs or take other steps to resolve the dispute. Your dealer will have your zone representative's name and telephone number. Explain the problem and ask for a meeting and a personal inspection of your vehicle.

3 If you can't get satisfaction from the zone representative, call or write the manufacturer's owner relations department. Your owner's manual contains this phone number and address. In each case, as you move up the chain, indicate the steps you have already taken.

4 Your next option is to present your problem to a complaint handling panel or to the arbitration program in which the manufacturer of your vehicle participates.

If you complain of a problem during the warranty period, you have a right to have the problem fixed even after the warranty runs out. If your war-ranty has not been honored, you may be able to "revoke acceptance," which means that you return the vehicle to the dealer. If you are successful, you may be entitled to a replacement vehicle or to a full refund of the purchase price and reimburse-ment of legal fees under the Magnuson-Moss Warranty Act. Or, if you are covered by one of the state Lemon Laws, you may be able to return the vehicle and receive a refund or replacement from the manufacturer.

NEED HELP?

TIP

If you need legal assistance with your repair problem, the Center for Auto Safety has a list of lawyers who specialize in helping consumers with auto repair problems. For the names of attorneys in your area, send a stamped, self-addressed envelope to: Center for Auto Safety, 1825 Connecticut Ave., NW, Suite 330, Washington, DC 20009. Check their website at www.autosafety.org for a shorter list of lemon law attorneys.

In addition, the Center has published *The Lemon Book*, a detailed 368-page guide to resolving automobile complaints. The book is available for $17.50 directly from the Center.

Attorneys Take Note: For information on litigation assistance provided by the Center for Auto Safety, including The Lemon Law Litigation Manual, please contact the Center for Auto Safety at the above address.

ARBITRATION

An increasingly popular method of resolving automobile repair problems is through arbitration. This procedure requires that both parties present their cases to an arbitrator or panel that makes a decision based on the merits of the complaint. You can seek repairs, reimbursement of expenses, or a refund or replacement for your car through arbitration.

In theory, arbitration can be an effective means of resolving disputes. It is somewhat informal, relatively speedy, and you do not need a lawyer to present your case. Plus, you avoid the time and expense of going to court.

Almost all manufacturers now offer some form of arbitration, usually for problems that arise during the warranty period. Some companies run their own and others subscribe to programs run by groups like the Better Business Bureau or the National Center for Dispute Settlement. Your owner's manual will identify which programs you can use. Also, contact your state attorney general to find out what programs your state offers.

How It Works: Upon receiving your complaint, the arbitration program will attempt to mediate a resolution between you and the manufacturer or dealer. If you are not satisfied with the proposed solution, you have the right to have your case heard at an arbitration hearing.

These hearings vary among the programs. In the BBB program, each party presents its case in person to a volunteer arbitrator. Other programs decide your case based on written submis-sions from both you and the man-ufacturer.

If an arbitration program is incorporated into your warranty, you may have to use that pro-gram before filing a legal claim. Federal law requires that arbitra-tion programs incorporated into a warranty be nonbinding on the consumer. So, if you do not like the result, you can seek other remedies.

Arbitration programs have different eligibility requirements, so be sure you are eligible for the program you are considering.

Let the Federal Trade Commission, the Center for Auto Safety (their addresses are on pages 71 and 72), and your state attorney general (c/o your state capital) know of your experience with arbitration. It is particularly important to contact these offices if you have a complaint about how your case was handled.

Ford Dispute Settlement Board: Each case is considered by a four-person panel including one dealer, one technician, and two consumer members. Oral presentations are given/available at customer's request. Only cases under warranty are reviewed. Decisions are made within forty days of submission of applica-tion. For information, call 800–392–3673.

Chrysler Customer Arbitration Board: The National Center for Dispute Settlement (NCDS) handles cases in some states. Otherwise, the Customer Arbitration Board will handle the dispute. In both programs, decisions will be based on written submissions by each party. Customers who live in AR, KY, MN, and OH and in states where complaints are handled by NCDS have the right to request oral presentation. The NCDS board consists of a local con-sumer advocate, an independent, A.S.E. certified technical repre-sentative, and a representative from the general public. The Consumer Arbitration Board is a panel whose members have many years of experience in con-sumer affairs and/or automotive service. Both boards will only hear cases under warranty. For information, call 800–992–1997.

Better Business Bureau (BBB) Arbitration Programs (Auto Line): The BBB always tries to mediate a dispute before recommending arbitration. About 12 percent of the disputes it han-dles actually go to arbitration. The arbitrators are selected at random and an impartial techni-cal expert can be present if requested. The consumer can object if conflict exists.

Arbitrators are volunteers from the local community and are not always automobile experts. This can both help and harm your case. As a result, it is important to be well prepared when participating in the BBB program. If you're not, the potential exists for the dealer or manufacturer to appear as the "expert" on automobiles. For more information, contact your local BBB or 800–955–5100.

Automobile Consumer Action Program: AUTOCAP was established by the National Automobile Dealers Association (NADA) to assist consumers in resolving auto sales or service disputes with dealers and manufacturers. The program is sponsored on a voluntary basis by state and local dealer associations. Currently, most AUTOCAPs do not operate under the FTC guidelines required for warranty cases. For more information and for the name of your local panel, contact: AUTOCAP, 8400 Westpark Drive, McLean, Virginia 22102; 703–821–7144.

Arbitration Tips: Arbitration is designed to be easier and less intimidating than going to court. However, the process can still be nerve-racking, especially if you have never been through it before. Here are some tips to help make the process simple and straightforward:

1. Before deciding to go to arbitration, get a written description of how the program works and make sure you understand the details. If you have any questions, contact the local representatives of the program. Remember, the manufacturer or dealer probably has more experience with this process than you do.

2. Make sure the final decision is nonbinding on you. If the decision is binding, you give up your right to appeal.

3. Determine whether the program allows you to appear at the hearing. If not, make sure your written statement is complete and contains all the appropriate receipts and documentation. If you think of something that you want considered after you have sent in your material, send it immediately and specifically request that the additional information be included.

4. Make sure the program follows the required procedures. If the arbitration program is incorporated into the car's warranty, for example, the panel must make a decision on your case within 40 days of receiving your complaint.

5. Contact the manufacturer's zone manager and request copies of any technical service bulletins that apply to your car. Service bulletins may help you prove that your car is defective.

6. Well before the hearing, ask the program representative to send you copies of all material submitted by the other party. You may want to respond to this information.

7. Make sure all your documents are in chronological order, and include a brief outline of the events. Submit copies of all material associated with your problem and a copy of your warranty.

8. Even though you may be very angry about the situation, try to present your case in a calm, logical manner.

9. If you are asking for a refund or a replacement for your car in accordance with your state's Lemon Law, do not assume that the arbitrator is completely familiar with the law. Be prepared to explain how it entitles you to your request.

10. In most programs, you have to reject the decision in order to go to court to pursue other action. If you accept the decision, you may limit your rights to pursue further action. You will, however, have additional claims if the manufacturer or dealer does not properly follow through on the decision or if your car breaks down again.

STATE-RUN ARBITRATION

TIP

State-run arbitration programs are often more fair to consumers than national programs. The following states have set up programs (or guidelines) which are far better than their national counterparts. If you live in one of these areas, contact your attorney general's office (in care of your state capital) for information. If your state is not listed below, you should still contact your state attorney general's office for advice on arbitration.

Arkansas	Massachusetts
Connecticut	Minnesota
Florida	Montana
Georgia	New Hampshire
Hawaii	New Jersey
Idaho	New York
Kentucky	Texas
Maine	Vermont

AUTO SAFETY HOT LINE

One of the most valuable but often unused services of the government is the Auto Safety Hot Line. By calling the hot line to report safety problems, your particular concern or problem will become part of the National Highway Traffic Safety Administration's (NHTSA) complaint database. This complaint program is extraordinarily important to government decision makers who often take action based on this information. In addition, it provides consumer groups, like the Center for Auto Safety, with the evidence they need to force the government to act and get the manufacturers to correct the defect.

Few government services have the potential to do as much for the consumer as this complaint database, so we encourage you to voice your concerns to the government.

Your letter can be used as the basis of safety defect investigations and recall campaigns. When you file a complaint, be sure to indicate that your name and address can be made public. Without names and addresses, it is more difficult for consumer groups to uncover safety defects.

Hot line Complaints: When you call the hot line to report a safety problem, you will be mailed a questionnaire asking for information that the agency's technical staff will need to evaluate the problem. This information also gives the government an indication of which vehicles are causing consumers the most problems. If you have access to the Internet, go to NHTSA's website at www.nhtsa.dot.gov and fill out your complaint online.

You can also use this questionnaire to report defects in tires and child safety seats. In fact, we strongly encourage you to report problems with child safety seats. Now that they are required by law in all fifty states, we have noticed that numerous design and safety problems have surfaced. If the government knows about these problems, they will be more likely to take action so that modifications are made to these life saving devices.

After you complete and return the questionnaire, the following things will happen:
1. A copy will go to NHTSA's safety defect investigators.
2. A copy will be sent to the manufacturer of the vehicle or equipment, with a request for help in resolving the problem.
3. You will be notified that your questionnaire has been received.
4. Your problem will be recorded in the complaint database which we use to provide you with complaint ratings.

Hot Line Services: Hot line operators can also provide information on recalls. If you want recall information on a particular automobile, simply tell the hot line operator the make, model, and year of the vehicle, or the type of equipment involved. You will receive any recall information that NHTSA has about that vehicle or item. This information can be very important if you are not sure whether your vehicle has ever been recalled. If you want a printed copy of the recall information, it will be mailed within 24 hours at no charge.

If you have other vehicle-related problems, the hot line operators can refer you to the appropriate federal, state, and local government agencies. If you need information about federal safety standards and regulations, you'll be referred to the appropriate experts.

AUTO SAFETY HOT LINE
800–424–9393
(IN WASHINGTON, DC: 202–366–0123)
TTY FOR HEARING IMPAIRED:
800–424–9153
(IN WASHINGTON, DC: 202–366–7800)

The toll-free Auto Safety Hot Line can provide information on recalls, record information about safety problems, and refer you to the appropriate government experts on other vehicle related problems. You can even have recall information mailed to you within 24 hours of your call at no charge.

COMPLAINT INDEX

Thanks to the efforts of the Center for Auto Safety, we are able to provide you with the vehicle complaints on file with the National Highway Traffic Safety Administration (NHTSA). Each year, thousands of Americans call the government to register complaints about their vehicles. The federal government collects this information but has never released it to the public.

The complaint index is the result of our analysis of these complaints. It is based on a ratio of the number of complaints for each vehicle to the sales of that vehicle. In order to predict the expected complaint performance of the 2001 models, we have examined the complaint history of that car's series. The term series refers to the fact that when a manufacturer introduces a new model, that vehicle remains essentially unchanged, on average, for four to six years. For example, the Dodge Intrepid was redesigned in 1998 and remains essentially the same car for 2001. As such, we have compiled the complaint experience for that series in order to give you some additional information to use in deciding which car to buy. For those vehicles just introduced, we do not yet have enough data to develop a complaint index.

The following table presents the complaint indexes for the best and worst 2001 models. Higher index numbers mean the vehicle generated a greater number of complaints. Lower numbers indicate fewer complaints.

2001 PROJECTED COMPLAINT RATINGS

THE BEST

Lexus GS300/400	375
Ford F-Series Pickup	827
Lexus LS400	850
Infiniti G20	854
Lexus LX470	881
Acura RL	903
Lexus ES300	1030
Daewoo Leganza	1060
Acura Integra	1095
Honda CR-V	1165
Toyota 4Runner	1211
Subaru Impreza	1397
Infiniti QX4	1439
Daewoo Lanos	1473
Mazda Millenia	1482
Infiniti Q45	1484
Chevrolet Lumina	1634
Saab9-5	1652
Toyota Corolla	1656
Mercedes-Benz E-Class	1727
Nissan Altima	1730
Nissan Pathfinder	1775
Audi A8	1819
Toyota Land Cruiser	1842
Isuzu Trooper	1906

THE WORST

AudiA6	23183
Mercury Cougar	20829
Honda Passport	18049
Lexus SC300/400	16671
Kia Sportage	14100
Mitsubishi Galant	13808
Isuzu Rodeo	13692
Chrysler LHS	12459
Honda Odyssey	12032
Jeep Grand Cherokee	11881
Volkswagen Passat	10458
Mazda Miata	10091
Mercury Villager	9113
Volkswagen Golf	7971
Pontiac Montana	7957
Pontiac Grand Am	7916
Cadillac Catera	7735
Chevrolet Tracker	7572
Ford Windstar	7533
Saab 9-3	7365
Chevrolet Venture	7147
Chrysler 300M	7131
Oldsmobile Intrigue	7060
Lincoln Navigator	6962
Oldsmobile Alero	6952

CENTER FOR AUTO SAFETY

Every year automobile manufacturers spend millions of dollars making their voices heard in government decision making. For example, General Motors and Ford have large staffs in Detroit and Washington that work solely to influence government activity. But who looks out for the consumer?

For over 30 years, the nonprofit Center for Auto Safety (CAS) has told the consumer's story to government agencies, to Congress, and to the courts. Its efforts focus on all consumers rather than only those with individual complaints.

CAS was established in 1970 by Ralph Nader and Consumers Union. As consumer concerns about auto safety issues expanded, so did the work of CAS. It became an independent group in 1972, and the original staff of two has grown to fourteen attorneys and researchers. CAS's activities include:

Initiating Safety Recalls: CAS analyzes over 50,000 consumer complaints each year. By following problems as they develop, CAS requests government investigations and recalls of defective vehicles. CAS was responsible for the Ford Pinto faulty gas tank recall, the Firestone 500 steel-belted radial tire recall, and the record recall of over three million Evenflo One Step child seats.

Representing the Consumer in Washington: CAS follows the activities of federal agencies and Congress to ensure that they carry out their responsibilities to the American taxpayer. CAS brings a consumer's point of view to vehicle safety policies and rule-making. Since 1970, CAS has submitted more than 500 petitions and comments on federal safety standards.

One major effort in this area has been the successful fight for adoption of automatic crash protection in passenger cars. These systems are a more effective and less intrusive alternative to crash protection than mandatory safety belt laws or belts that must be buckled in order to start the car.

In 1992, the Center for Auto Safety uncovered a fire defect that dwarfed the highly publicized flammability of the Ford Pinto. It had to do with the side saddle gas tanks on full size 1973–87 GM pickups and 1988–90 crew cabs that tend to explode on impact. Over 1,600 people have been killed in fire crashes involving these trucks. After mounting a national campaign to warn consumers to steer clear of these GM fire hazards, the U.S. Department of Transportation (DOT) granted CAS' petition and conducted one of its biggest defect investigations in history. The result—GM was asked to recall its pickups. GM, sadly, denied this request.

Exposing Secret Warranties: CAS played a prominent role in the disclosure of secret warranties, "policy adjustments," as they are called by manufacturers. These occur when an automaker agrees to pay for repair of certain defects beyond the warranty period but refuses to notify consumers.

Improving Rust Warranties: Rust and corrosion cost American car owners up to $14 billion annually. CAS has been successful in its efforts to get domestic and foreign auto companies to lengthen their all-important corrosion warranties.

Lemon Laws: CAS's work on Lemon Laws aided in the enactment of state laws which make it easier to return a defective new automobile and get money back.

CENTER FOR AUTO SAFETY ONLINE

TIP The Center for Auto Safety has a website at www.autosafety.org to provide information to consumers and to organize consumer campaigns against auto companies on safety defects. All of the above consumer packages are on CAS's website. Consumers with lemons and safety defects can file electronic complaints with CAS and get referred to lemon lawyers. The best consumer campaigns are on stalling Fords (1983–95 Fords with defective ignition modules that cause stalling on highways) and 1973–87 GM pickups with side saddle gas tanks that can explode on impact.

Tire Ratings: After a suspension between 1982 and 1984, consumers have reliable tread-wear ratings to help them get the most miles for their dollar. CAS's lawsuit overturned DOT's revocation of this valuable tire information program.

Initiating Legal Action: When CAS has exhausted other means of obtaining relief for consumer problems, it will initiate legal action. For example, in 1978 when the Department of Energy attempted to raise the price of gasoline four cents per gallon without notice or comment, CAS succeeded in stopping this illegal move through a lawsuit, thus saving consumers $2 billion for the six-month period that the action was delayed.

A CAS lawsuit against the Environmental Protection Agency (EPA) in 1985 forced the EPA to recall polluting cars, rather than let companies promise to make cleaner cars in the future. As part of the settlement, GM (which was responsible for the polluting cars) funded a $7 million methanol bus demonstration program in New York City.

Help CAS help you: CAS depends on public support. Annual consumer membership is $30 with *The Lemon Book*. All contributions to this non-profit organization are tax-deductible. Annual membership includes a quarterly newsletter called "Lemon Times." To join, send a check to:

Center for Auto Safety
1825 Connecticut Ave., NW
#330
Washington, DC
20009–5708

PUBLICATIONS

CAS has many publications on automobiles, motor homes, recreational vehicles, and fuel economy, and a number of free information packets. For each of the packets listed below, or for a complete description of CAS' publications, send a separate self-addressed, business-sized envelope with 55¢ postage to the address listed. Unless otherwise noted, packets listed below cover all known major problems since 1985 for the models indicated and explain what to do about them. Requests should include make, model, and year of vehicle (with Vehicle Identification Number), as well as the problem you are experiencing. (Allow 2 weeks for delivery.) Publications in bold are available at www.autosafety.org.

Audi
BMW
Cadillac
Chrys. Paint/Water Leaks
Chrys. Ultradrive Trans.
Chrys. Aries Reliant/K-Cars
Chrys. Cirrus/Stratus/Neon/Breeze
Chrys. Dakota/Durango
Chrys. LHS/Intrepid/Concorde/NYe/Vision
Chrys. Minivan
Chrys. Ram Van/Truck
Chrys. Sebring/Avenger
Ford Aerostar/Villager/Windstar
Ford Auto. Trans.: Taurus/Sable/Continental
Ford Bronco II/Explorer/Ranger
Ford Cr. Vic./Gr. Marquis/Thunderbird/Cougar/Lincoln/Town Car/Mark Series
Ford Contour/Mystique
Ford Escort/Lynx/Tracer
Ford E Series (Econoline and Club Wagons)
Ford F-Series Trucks/Broncos
Ford Taurus/Sable
Ford Tempo/Topaz
Ford Mustang/Probe
Ford Paint
GM All Geo's/LeMans/Sprint/Nova
GM Saturn
GM Auto. Trans.: FWD
GM Auto. Trans.: RWD
GM Beretta/Corsica
GM Cut. Supr./Gr. Prix/Lumina/Regal

GM Celebrity/6000/Century/CutCiera & Cruiser
GM Camaro/Firebird
GM Achieva/Calais/Gr. Am/Skylark/Somerset Regal
GM Roadmaster/Caprice/Riviera/Est. Wagon/Custom Cruiser
GM Cavalier/Cimarron/Firenza/Skyhawk/Sunbird/Sunfire/J2000
GM 98/Electra & Park Ave.
GM 88/LeSabre/Bonneville
GM Power Steering Failure
GM C/K PU/Suburban/Tahoe/Yukon/Blazer/Jimmy
GM S-Series/Blazer/Jimmy/Sonoma
GM Big Vans/**GM Astro/Safari/APVs**
GM Pontiac Fiero
GM Paint
Honda/Acura
Hyundai
Jeep–all models
Infinti
Isuzu
Mazda Cars, Mazda Trucks
Mercedes
Mitsubishi
Nissan Cars, Nissan Vans/Trucks/Pathfinder
Renault/Eagle
Saab
Subaru
Toyota
Volkswagen
Volvo

CONSUMER GROUPS AND GOVERNMENT

Here are the names of additional consumer groups which you may find helpful:

Advocates for Highway and Auto Safety
750 First Street, NE, Suite 901
Washington, DC 20002
(202) 408–1711/408–1699 fax
www.saferoads.org
An alliance of consumer, health and safety groups, and insurance companies.

Consumer Action/San Fran.
717 Market St., Suite 310
San Francisco, CA 94103
(415) 777–9635
www.consumer-action.org
General problems of California residents.

Consumers for Auto Reliability and Safety
926 J St., Suite 523
Sacramento, CA 95814
(530) 759–9440
www.carconsumers.com
Auto safety, airbags, and lemon laws.

Highway Loss Data Institute and Insurance Institute for Highway Safety
1005 N. Glebe Rd.
Arlington, VA 22201
(703) 247–1500
www.carsafety.com
Vehicle and highway safety research and advocacy.

SafetyBelt Safe, U.S.A.
P.O. Box 553
Altadena, CA 91003
(800) 745–SAFE or (310) 222–6860
www.carseat.org
Excellent information and training on child safety seats and safety belt usage.

Trunk Releases Urgently Needed Coalition (TRUNC)
537 Jones St., #2514
San Francisco, CA 94102
(415) 789–1000/789–9424 fax
www.netkitchen.com/trunc
Auto safety and consumer advocacy relating to trunk entrapment incidents.

Several federal agencies conduct automobile-related programs. Listed below is each agency with a description of the type of work it performs and how to contact them. Useful web sites are also listed.

National Highway Traffic Safety Administration
400 7th Street, SW, Room 5232
Washington, DC 20590
(202) 366–9550
www.nhtsa.dot.gov
NHTSA issues safety and fuel economy standards for new motor vehicles; investigates safety defects and enforces recall of defective vehicles and equipment; conducts research and demonstration programs on vehicle safety, fuel economy, driver safety, and automobile inspection and repair; provides grants for state highway safety programs in areas such as police traffic services, driver education and licensing, emergency medical services, pedestrian safety, and alcohol abuse.

Environmental Protection Agency
401 M Street, SW
Washington, DC 20460
(202) 260–2090
www.epa.gov
EPA's responsibilities include setting and enforcing air and noise emission standards for motor vehicles and measuring fuel economy in new vehicles (EPA Fuel Economy Guide).

Federal Trade Commission
CRC-240
Washington, DC 20580
(877) FTC–HELP
www.ftc.gov
FTC regulates advertising and credit practices, marketing abuses, and professional services and ensures that products are properly labeled (as in fuel economy ratings). The commission covers unfair or deceptive trade practices in motor vehicle sales and repairs, as well as in non-safety defects.

U.S. Department of Justice
Office of Consumer Litigation
P.O. Box 386
Washington, DC 20044
(202) 307–0092
www.usdoj.gov
The DOJ enforces the federal law that requires manufacturers to label new automobiles and forbids removal or alteration of labels before delivery to consumers. Labels must contain make, model, vehicle identification number, dealer's name, suggested base price, manufacturer option costs, and manufacturer's suggested retail price.

Better Business Bureau
Check your local phone book for the nearest office.
For Auto Line Program, call (800) 955–5100
www.bbb.org
Provides reports on dealers and businesses, operates Auto Line Arbitration Service for defects covered by manufacturer warranty.

AUTOMOBILE MANUFACTURERS

Acura Automobile Division
Mr. Richard Colliver, Exec.V. P.
1919 Torrance Blvd.
Torrance, CA 90501–2746
(310) 783–2000

Audi of America
Mr. Len Hunt, Vice President
3800 Hamlin Road
Auburn Hills, MI 48326
(248) 340-5000

BMW of North America, Inc.
Mr. Tom Purves,
Chairman and CEO
300 Chestnut Ridge Road
Woodcliff Lake, NJ 07675
(201) 307–4000

Chrysler—Jeep Division
Mr. Thomas R. Marinelli,
Vice President
1000 Chrysler Drive
CIMS 485-05-10
Auburn Hills, MI 48326

Daewoo
Mr. Dong Jin Lee,
President and CEO
1055 West Victoria
Compton, CA 90220
(310) 223-5900

DaimlerChrysler Corporation
Mr. James P. Holden, President
Mr. Juergen E. Schrempp, Chairman
1000 Chrysler Drive
Auburn Hills, MI 48326–2766
(248) 576–5741

Ford Motor Company
Mr. William Clay Ford, Jr., Chairman
Mr. Jaques A. Nasser, CEO
The American Road
Dearborn, MI 48126
(313) 322–3000

General Motors Corporation
Mr. John F. Smith, Jr., Chairman
Mr. G. Richard Wagoner, Jr.,
President and CEO
100 Renaissance Center
Detroit, MI 48265
(313) 556–5000

American Honda Motor Co.
Mr. Koichi Amemiya,
President and Chairman
1919 Torrance Blvd.
Torrance, CA 90501–2746
(310) 783–2000

Hyundai Motor America
Mr. Finbarr O'Neill
President and CEO
10550 Talbert Avenue
Fountain Valley, CA 92728
(714) 965–3000

Infiniti
Mr. Thomas Orbe
Vice President and General Mgr.
18501 S. Figueroa St.
Gardena, CA 90248
(310) 771-3111

American Isuzu Motors Inc.
Mr. Yasayuki Sudo, President
13340 183rd St.
Cerritos, CA 90702
(562) 229–5000

Kia Motors America, Inc.
Mr. B.M. Ahn, President and CEO
P.O. Box 52410
Irvine, CA 92619–2410
(949) 470–7000

Land Rover of America
Mr. Howard I. Mosher,
President and CEO
4371 Parliament Place
P.O. Box 1503
Lanham, MD 20706
(301) 731–9040

Lexus Division/Toyota Motor Sales,
U.S.A., Inc.
Mr. Bryan Bergsteinsson,
Group Vice President & GM
19001 S. Western Ave.
Torrance, CA 90509
(310) 328–2075

Mazda Motor of America, Inc.
Mr. Richard Beattie,
President and CEO
7755 Irvine Center Dr.,
PO Box 19734
Irvine, CA 92623–9734
(714) 727–1990

Mercedes-Benz of N.A.
Mr. Michael Jackson,
President and CEO
1 Mercedes Drive
P.O. Box 350
Montvale, NJ 07645
(800) 367–6372

Mitsubishi Motor Sales
Mr. Hiroshi Yajima
Chairman and CEO
6400 Katella Ave.
Cypress, CA 90630–0064
(714) 372–6000

Nissan Motor Corp. U.S.A.
Mr. Norio Mitsumara
President and CEO
18501 S. Figueroa St.
P.O. Box 191
Gardena, CA 90248–0191
(310) 771–3111

Saab Cars USA, Inc.
Mr. Daniel Chasins
President and CEO
4405–A International Drive
Norcross, GA 30093
(770) 279–0100

Subaru of America, Inc.
Mr. Takao Saito
Chairman, CEO and President
Subaru Place
P.O. Box 6000
Cherry Hill, NJ 08034–6000
(856) 488–8500

American Suzuki Motor Corp.
Mr. Rick Suzuki, President
3251 E. Imperial Hwy.
Brea, CA 92621–6722
(714) 996–7040

Toyota Motor Sales, U.S.A., Inc.
Mr. Yoshimi Inaba
President and CEO
19001 S. Western Avenue
Torrance, CA 90509
(310) 618–4000

Volkswagen of America, Inc.
Volkswagen Canada Inc.
Mr. Gerd Klauss
President and CEO
3800 Hamlin Road
Auburn Hills, MI 48326
(810) 340–5000

Volvo Cars of North America
Mr. Mark LaNeve
President and CEO
7 Volvo Drive
Rockleigh, NJ 07647
(201) 768–7300

LEMON LAWS

Sometimes, despite our best efforts, we buy a vehicle that just doesn't work right. There may be little problem after little problem, or perhaps one big problem that never seems to be fixed. Because of the "sour" taste that such vehicles leave in the mouths of consumers who buy them, these vehicles are known as "lemons."

In the past, it's been difficult to obtain a refund or replacement if a vehicle was a lemon. The burden of proof was left to the consumer. Because it is hard to define exactly what constitutes a lemon, many lemon owners were unable to win a case against a manufacturer. However, as of 1993, all states have passed

"Lemon Laws." Although there are some important state-to-state variations, all of the laws have similarities: They establish a period of coverage, usually one year from delivery or the written warranty period, whichever is shorter; they may require some form of non-court arbitration; and most importantly they define a lemon. In most states a lemon is a new car, truck, or van that has been taken back to the shop at least four times for the same repair or is out of service for a total of 30 days during the covered period.

This time does not mean consecutive days. In some states the total time must be for the same repair; in others, it can be based on different repair problems.

Be sure to keep careful records of your repairs since some states now require only one of the three or four repairs to be within the specified time period.

Specific information about laws in your state can be obtained from your state attorney general's office (c/o your state capital) or your local consumer protection office. The following table offers a general description of the Lemon Law in your state and what you need to do to set it in motion (Notification/Trigger). An "L" indicates that the law covers leased vehicles and we indicate where state-run arbitration programs are available. State-run programs are the best type of arbitration.

Alabama	Qualification: 3 unsuccessful repairs or 30 calendar days within shorter of 24 months or 24,000 miles, provided 1 repair attempt or 1 day out of service is within shorter of 1 year or 12,000 miles. Notification/Trigger: Certified mail notice to manufacturer + opportunity for final repair attempt within 14 calendar days.
Alaska	Qualification: 3 unsuccessful repairs or 30 business days out of service within shorter of 1 year or warranty. Notification/Trigger: Written notice by certified mail to manufacturer + dealer (or repair agent) that problem has not been corrected in reasonable number of attempts + refund or replacement demanded within 60 days. Manufacturer has 30 calendar days for final repair attempt. S-C.
Arizona	Qualification: 4 unsuccessful repairs or 30 calendar days out of service within warranty period or shorter of 2 years or 24,000 miles. Notification/Trigger: Written notice + opportunity to repair to manufacturer.
Arkansas	Qualification: 3 unsuccessful repairs, or 1 unsuccessful repair of a problem likely to cause death or serious bodily injury within longer of 24 months or 24,000 miles. Notification/Trigger: Certified or registered mail notice to manufacturer. Manufacturer has 10 days to notify consumer of repair facility. Facility has 10 days to repair.
California	Qualification: 4 times subject to repair or 30 calendar days out of service (can be non-consecutive) within shorter of 18 months or 18,000 miles, or "reasonable" number of attempts during entire express warranty period. Notification/Trigger: Direct written notice to manufacturers at address clearly specified in owner's manual. UPDATE: As of 1/1/01, only 2 times subject to repair allowed for safety defects likely to cause death or serious bodily injury. Coverage also expanded to include small businesses registering up to 5 vehicles, weighing up to 10,000 pounds each.

L   Law specifically applies to leased vehicles
S-C   State has certified guidelines for arbitration
S-R   State-run arbitration mechanism available

LEMON LAWS

Colorado	Qualification: 4 unsuccessful repairs or 30 business days out of service within shorter of 1 year or warranty. Notification/Trigger: Prior certified mail notice for each defect occurrence + opportunity to repair for manufacturer.
Connecticut	Qualification: 4 unsuccessful repairs or 30 calendar days out of service within shorter of 2 years or 24,000 miles, or 2 unsuccessful repairs of a problem likely to cause death or serious bodily injury within warranty period or 1 year. Notification/Trigger: Report to manufacturer, agent, or dealer. Written notice to manufacturer only if required in owner's manual or warranty. S-R, L
Delaware	Qualification: 4 unsuccessful repairs or 30 calendar days out of service within shorter of 1 year or warranty. Notification/Trigger: Written notice + opportunity to repair to manufacturer. L
D.C.	Qualification: 4 unsuccessful repairs or 30 calendar days out of service or 1 unsuccessful repair of safety-related defect, within shorter of 2 years or 18,000 miles. Notification/Trigger: Report of each defect occurrence to manufacturer, agent, or dealer. S-R, Note: Enforcement is suspended until October 1, 2000. L
Florida	Qualification: 3 unsuccessful repairs or 15 calendar days within 24 months from delivery. Notification/Trigger: Written notice by certified or express mail to manufacturer who has 10 calendar days for final repair attempt after delivery to designated dealer. S-C, S-R, L
Georgia	Qualification: 3 unsuccessful repair attempts or 30 calendar days out of service within shorter of 24,000 miles or 24 months, with 1 repair or 15 days out of service within shorter of 1 year or 12,000 miles; or 1 unsuccessful repair of serious safety defect in braking or steering system within shorter of 1 year or 12,000. Notification/Trigger: Certified mail notice return receipt requested. Manufacturer has 7 days to notify consumer of repair facility. Facility has 14 calendar days to repair. S-R, L **Note:** Proceeding under this state's lemon law may cause consumer to lose other important rights regarding the manufacturer and dealer.
Hawaii	Qualification: 3 unsuccessful repair attempts, or 1 unsuccessful repair attempt of defect likely to cause death or serious bodily injury, or out of service for total of 30 days within shorter of 2 years or 24,000 miles. Notification/Trigger: Written notice + opportunity to repair to manufacturer. S-R, L
Idaho	Qualification: 4 repair attempts or 30 business days out of service within shorter of 2 years or 24, 000 miles, or 1 repair of a complete failure of the braking or steering system likely to cause death or serious bodily injury. Notification/Trigger: Written notice to manufacturer or dealer and opportunity to repair. S-R, L.
Illinois	Qualification: 4 unsuccessful repairs or 30 business days out of service within shorter of 1 year or 12,000 miles. Notification/Trigger: Written notice + opportunity to repair to manufacturer. L.
Indiana	Qualification: 4 unsuccessful repairs or 30 business days out of service within the shorter of 18 months or 18,000 miles. Notification/Trigger: Written notice to manufacturer only if required in the warranty. L
Iowa	Qualification: 3 unsuccessful repairs, or 1 unsuccessful repair of a nonconformity likely to cause death or serious bodily injury, or 30 calendar days out of service within shorter of 2 years or 24,000 miles. Notification/Trigger: Written notice by certified registered mail + final opportunity to repair within 10 calendar days of receipt of notice to manufacturer. S-C, L

L   Law specifically applies to leased vehicles
S-C State has certified guidelines for arbitration
S-R State-run arbitration mechanism available

LEMON LAWS

Kansas	Qualification: 4 unsuccessful repairs or 30 calendar days out of service or 10 total repairs within shorter of 1 year or warranty. Notification/Trigger: Actual notice to manufacturer. S-C
Kentucky	Qualification: 4 unsuccessful repairs or 30 calendar days out of service within shorter of 1 year or 12,000 miles. Notification/Trigger: Written notice to manufacturer. S-C
Louisiana	Qualification: 4 unsuccessful repairs or 30 calendar days out of service within shorter of 1 year or warranty. Notification/Trigger: Report to manufacturer or dealer. S-C, L
Maine	Qualification: 3 unsuccessful repairs (when at least 2 times same agent attempted repair) or 15 business days out of service within shorter of warranty or 2 years or 18,000 miles. The Maine statute applies to vehicles within the first 18,000 miles or 2 years regardless of whether the claimant is the original owner. Notification/Trigger: Written notice to manufacturer or dealer. Manufacturer has 7 business days after receipt for final repair attempt. S-R, L
Maryland	Qualification: 4 unsuccessful repairs, 30 calendar days out of service or 1 unsuccessful repair of braking or steering system within shorter of 15 months or 15,000 miles. Notification/Trigger: Certified mail notice, return receipt requested + opportunity to repair within 30 calendar days of receipt of notice to manufacturer or factory branch. L
Mass.	Qualification: 3 unsuccessful repairs or 15 business days out of service within shorter of 1 year or 15,000 miles. Notification/Trigger: Notice to manufacturer or dealer who has 7 business days to attempt final repair. S-R
Michigan	Qualification: Total of 4 unsuccessful repairs within 2 years from the date of the first unsuccessful repair or 30 calendar days within shorter of 1 year or warranty. Notification/Trigger: Certified mail notice, return receipt requested, to manufacturer who has 5 business days to repair after delivery. S-C, L
Minnesota	Qualification: 4 unsuccessful repairs or 30 business days or 1 unsuccessful repair of total braking or steering loss likely to cause death or serious bodily injury within shorter of 2 years or warranty. Notification/Trigger: Written notice + opportunity to repair to manufacturer, agent, or dealer. S-C, L
Mississippi	Qualification: 3 unsuccessful repairs or 15 business days out of service within shorter of 1 year or warranty. Notification/Trigger: Written notice to manufacturer who has 10 business days to repair after delivery to designated dealer.
Missouri	Qualification: 4 unsuccessful repairs or 30 business days out of service within shorter of 1 year or warranty. Notification/Trigger: Written notice to manufacturer who has 10 calendar days to repair after delivery to designated dealer.
Montana	Qualification: 4 unsuccessful repairs or 30 business days out of service after notice within shorter of 2 years or 18,000 miles. Notification/Trigger: Written notice + opportunity to repair to manufacturer. S-R
Nebraska	Qualification: 4 unsuccessful repairs or 40 calendar days out of service within shorter of 1 year or warranty. Notification/Trigger: Certified mail notice + opportunity to repair to manufacturer. S-C
Nevada	Qualification: 4 unsuccessful repairs or 30 calendar days out of service within shorter of 1 year or warranty. Notification/Trigger: Written notice to manufacturer. S-C

L   Law specifically applies to leased vehicles
S-C   State has certified guidelines for arbitration
S-R   State-run arbitration mechanism available

LEMON LAWS

N. H.	Qualification: 3 unsuccessful repairs by same dealer or 30 business days out of service within warranty. Notification/Trigger: Report to manufacturer, distributor, agent, or dealer (on forms provided by manufacturer) + final opportunity to repair before arbitration. S-R, L
New Jersey	Qualification: 3 unsuccessful repairs or 20 calendar days out of service within shorter of 2 years or 18,000 miles. Notification/Trigger: Certified mail notice, return receipt requested to manufacturer who has 10 days to repair. S-C, L
N. Mexico	Qualification: 4 unsuccessful repairs or 30 business days out of service within shorter of 1 year or warranty. Notification/Trigger: Written notice + opportunity to repair to manufacturer, agent, or dealer. S-C
New York	Qualification: 4 unsuccessful repairs or 30 calendar days out of service within shorter of 2 years or 18,000 miles. Notification/Trigger: Notice to manufacturer, agent, or dealer. S-C, L
N. Carolina	Qualification: 4 unsuccessful repairs within shorter of 24 months, 24,000 miles or warranty or 20 business days out of service during any 12 month period of warranty. Notification/Trigger: Written notice to manufacturer + opportunity to repair within 15 calendar days of receipt only if required in warranty or owner's manual. L
N. Dakota	Qualification: 3 unsuccessful repairs or 30 business days out of service within shorter of 1 year or warranty. Notification/Trigger: Direct written notice + opportunity to repair to manufacturer. (Manufacturer's informal arbitration process serves as a prerequisite to consumer refund or replacement.) S-C, L
Ohio	Qualification: 3 unsuccessful repairs of same nonconformity, 30 calendar days out of service, 8 total repairs of any nonconformity, or 1 unsuccessful repair of problem likely to cause death or serious bodily injury within shorter of 1 year or 18,000 miles. Notification/Trigger: Report to manufacturer, its agent, or dealer. L
Oklahoma	Qualification: 4 unsuccessful repairs or 45 calendar days out of service within shorter of 1 year or warranty. Notification/Trigger: Written notice + opportunity to repair to manufacturer. S-C
Oregon	Qualification: 4 unsuccessful repairs or 30 business days within shorter of 1 year or 12,000 miles. Notification/Trigger: Direct written notice + opportunity to repair to manufacturer. S-C, L
Penn.	Qualification: 3 unsuccessful repairs or 30 calendar days within shorter of 1 year, 12,000 miles, or warranty. Notification/Trigger: Delivery to authorized service + repair facility. If delivery impossible, written notice to manufacturer or its repair facility obligates them to pay for delivery. (Manufacturer's informal arbitration process serves as prerequisite to consumer refund or replacement.)
R.I.	Qualification: 4 unsuccessful repairs or 30 calendar days out of service within shorter of 1 year or 15,000 miles. Notification/Trigger: Report to dealer or manufacturer who has 7 days for final repair opportunity. (Manufacturer's informal arbitration process serves as prerequisite to consumer refund or replacement.) L
S. Carolina	Qualification: 3 unsuccessful repairs or 30 calendar days out of service within shorter of 1 year or 12,000 miles. Notification/Trigger: Written notice by certified mail + opportunity to repair (not more than 10 business days) to manufacturer only if manufacturer informed consumer of such at time of sale. S-C, L

L   Law specifically applies to leased vehicles
S-C State has certified guidelines for arbitration
S-R State-run arbitration mechanism available

LEMON LAWS

S. Dakota	Qualification: 4 unsuccessful repairs, 1 of which occurred during the shorter of 1 year or 12,000 miles, or 30 calender days out of service during shorter of 24 months or 24,000 miles. Notification/Trigger: Certified mail notice to manufacturer and final opportunity to repair + 7 calender days to notify consumer of repair facility. (Manufacturer's informal arbitration process serves as a prerequisite to refund or replacement.)
Tennessee	Qualification: 4 unsuccessful repairs or 30 calendar days out of service within shorter of 1 year or warranty. Notification/Trigger: Certified mail notice to manufacturer + final opportunity to repair within 10 calendar days. L
Texas	Qualification: 4 unsuccessful repairs when 2 occurred within shorter of 1 year or 12,000 miles, + other 2 occur within shorter of 1 year or 12,000 miles immediately following second repair attempt; or 2 unsuccessful repairs of a serious safety defect when 1 occurred within shorter of 1 year or 12,000 miles + other occurred within shorter of 1 year or 12,000 miles immediately following first repair; or 30 calendar days out of service within shorter of 2 years or 24,000 miles + at least 2 attempts were made within shorter of 1 year or 12,000 miles. Notification/Trigger: Written notice to manufacturer. S-R, L
Utah	Qualification: 4 unsuccessful repairs or 30 business days out of service within shorter of 1 year or warranty. Notification/Trigger: Report to manufacturer, agent, or dealer. L (Manufacturer's informal arbitration process serves as a prerequisite to consumer refund or replacement.)
Vermont	Qualification: 3 unsuccessful repairs when at least first repair was within warranty, or 30 calendar days out of service within warranty. Notification/Trigger: Written notice to manufacturer (on provided forms) after third repair attempt, or 30 days. Arbitration must be held within 45 days after notice, during which time manufacturer has 1 final repair. S-R, L
Virginia	Qualification: 3 unsuccessful repairs, or 1 repair attempt of serious safety defect, or 30 calendar days out of service within 18 months. Notification/Trigger: Written notice to manufacturer. If 3 unsuccessful repairs or 30 days already exhausted before notice, manufacturer has 1 more repair attempt not to exceed 15 days. S-C, L
Washington	Qualification: 4 unsuccessful repairs, 30 calendar days out of service (15 during warranty period), or 2 repairs of serious safety defects, first reported within shorter of warranty or 24 months or 24,000 miles. One repair attempt + 15 of the 30 days must fall within manufacturer's express warranty of at least 1 year of 12,000 miles. Notification/Trigger: Written notice to manufacturer. S-R, L Note: Consumer should receive replacement or refund within 40 calendar days of request.
W. Virginia	Qualification: 3 unsuccessful repairs or 30 calendar days out of service or 1 unsuccessful repair of problem likely to cause death or serious bodily injury within shorter of 1 year or warranty. Notification/Trigger: Written notice + opportunity to repair to manufacturer.
Wisconsin	Qualification: 4 unsuccessful repairs or 30 calendar days out of service within shorter of 1 year or warranty. Notification/Trigger: Report to manufacturer or dealer. L Note: Consumer should receive replacement or refund within 30 calendar days after offer to return title.
Wyoming	Qualification: 3 unsuccessful repairs or 30 business days out of service within 1 year. Notification/Trigger: Direct written notice + opportunity to repair to manufacturer. (Manufacturer's informal arbitration process serves as a prerequisite to consumer refund or replacement.)

L   Law specifically applies to leased vehicles
S-C   State has certified guidelines for arbitration
S-R   State-run arbitration mechanism available

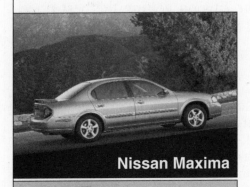

Nissan Maxima

Toyota RAV4

Buick Park Avenue

Honda CR-V

IN THIS CHAPTER

INTRODUCTION

Buying a car means matching wits with a seasoned professional. But if you know what to expect, you'll have a much better chance of getting a really good deal! This chapter offers practical advice on buying a car, tips on getting the best price and financing, information on buying versus leasing, and tips on avoiding lemons.

There's no question that buying a car can be an intimidating experience. But it doesn't have to be. First of all, you have in your hands all of the information you need to make an informed choice. Secondly, if you approach the purchase logically, you'll always maintain control of the decision. Start with the following basic steps:

1 Narrow your choice down to a particular class of car—sports, station wagon, minivan, sedan, large luxury, or economy car. These are general classifications and some cars may fit into more than one category. In most cases, *The Ultimate Car Book* presents the vehicles by size class.

2 Determine what features are really important to you. Most buyers consider safety on the top of their list, which is why the "Safety Chapter" is right up front in *The Ultimate Car Book*. Airbags, power options, ABS, and the number of passengers, as well as "hidden" elements such as maintenance and insurance costs, should be considered at this stage in your selection process.

3 Find three or four cars that meet the needs you outlined above and your pocketbook. It's important not to narrow your choice down to one car because then you lose all your bargaining power in the showroom. (Why? Because you might lose the psychological ability to walk away from a bad deal!) In fact, because cars today are more similar than dissimilar, it's not hard to keep three or four choices in mind. On the car rating pages in the back of the book, we suggest some competitive choices for your consideration. For example, if you are interested in the Honda Accord, you should also consider the Toyota Camry and Ford Taurus.

4 Make sure you take a good, long test drive. The biggest car buying mistake most of us make is to overlook those nagging problems that seem to surface only after we've brought the car home. Spend at least an hour driving the car without a salesperson in the car. If a dealership won't allow you to test-drive a car without a salesperson, go somewhere else. The test-drive should include time on the highway, parking, taking the car in and out of your driveway or garage, sitting in the back seat, and using the trunk or storage area.

TIP: Whatever you do, don't talk price until you're ready to buy!

5 This is the stage most of us dread—negotiating the price. While price negotiation is a car buying tradition, a few carmakers and dealers are trying to break tradition by offering so-called "no-haggle pricing." Since they're still in the minority, and because it's very hard for an individual to establish true competition between dealers, we offer a new means to avoid negotiating altogether by using the non-profit CarBargains pricing service.

Now that you have a quick guide to the steps necessary in making a good choice, use the tables that follow to quickly review the new cars and the pages in the back for a detailed critique of each model. See "Showroom Strategies" on the next page for more details on getting the best price.

For most of us, the auto showroom can be an intimidating environment. We're matching wits with professional negotiators over a very complex product. Being prepared is the best way to turn a potentially intimidating showroom experience into a profitable one. Here's some advice on handling what you'll find in the showroom.

Beware of silence. Silence is often used to intimidate, so be prepared for long periods of time when the salesperson is "talking with the manager." This tactic is designed to make you want to "just get the negotiation over with." Instead of becoming a victim, do something that indicates you are serious about looking elsewhere. Bring the classified section of the newspaper and begin circling other cars or review brochures from other manufacturers. By sending the message that you have other options, you increase your bargaining power and speed up the process.

Don't fall in love with a car. Never look too interested in any particular car. Advise family members who go with you against being too enthusiastic about any one car. Tip: Beat the dealers at their own game— bring along a friend who tells you that the price is "too much compared to the other deal."

Keep your wallet in your pocket. Don't leave a deposit, even if it's refundable. You'll feel pressure to rush your shopping, and you'll have to return and face the salesperson again before you are ready.

Shop at the end of the month. Salespeople anxious to meet sales goals are more willing to negotiate a lower price at this time.

Buy last year's model. The majority of new cars are the same as the previous year, with minor cosmetic changes. You can save considerably by buying in early fall when dealers are clearing space for "new" models. The important trade-off you make using this technique is that the carmaker may have added air bags or anti-lock brakes to an otherwise unchanged vehicle.

Buying from stock. You can often get a better deal on a car that the dealer has on the lot. However, these cars often have expensive options you may not want or need. Do not hesitate to ask the dealer to remove an option (and its accompanying charge) or sell you the car without charging for the option. The longer the car sits there, the more interest the dealer pays on the car, which increases the dealer's incentive to sell.

Ordering a car. Cars can be ordered from the manufacturer with exactly the options you want. Simply offering a fixed amount over invoice may be attractive because it's a sure sale and the dealership has not invested in the car. All the salesperson has to do is take your order.

If you do order a car, make sure when it arrives that it includes only the options you requested. Don't fall for the trick where the dealer offers you unordered options at a "special price," because it was their mistake. If you didn't order an option, don't pay for it.

THE 180-DEGREE TURN

If you try to negotiate a car purchase, remember that you have the most important weapon in the bargaining process: the 180-degree turn. Be prepared to walk away from a deal, even at the risk of losing the "very best deal" your salesperson has ever offered, and you will be in the best position to get a real "best deal." Remember: Dealerships need you, the buyer, to survive.

Don't trade in. Although it is more work, you can usually do better by selling your old car yourself than by trading it in. To determine what you'll gain by selling the car yourself, check the NADA Official Used Car Guide at your credit union or library. On the web, the Kelly Blue Book website at kbb.com is a good source for invoice pricing. The difference between the trade-in price (what the dealer will give you) and the retail price (what you typically can sell it for) is your extra payment for selling the car yourself.

If you do decide to trade your car in at the dealership, keep the buying and selling separate. First, negotiate the best price for your new car, then find out how much the dealer will give you for your old car. Keeping the two deals separate ensures that you know what you're paying for your new car and simplifies the entire transaction.

Question everything the dealer writes down. Nothing is etched in stone. Because things are written down, we tend not to question them. This is wrong—always assume that anything written down is negotiable.

Test-drive without the salesperson. When you test-drive a car, go alone and take a good, long test-drive. If a dealership will not let you take a car without a salesperson, go to another dealership. Test-driving without the distraction of a salesperson is a necessity when trying out a new car.

⚠ AVOIDING LEMONS ⚠

One way to avoid the sour taste of a lemon after you've bought your car is to protect yourself before you sign on the dotted line. These tips will help you avoid problems down the road.

1 Avoid new models. Any new car in its very first year of production often turns out to have a lot of defects. Sometimes the manufacturer isn't able to remedy the defects until the second, third, or even fourth year of production. If the manufacturer has not worked out problems by the third model year, the car will likely be a lemon forever.

2 Avoid the first cars off the line. Most companies close down their assembly lines every year to make annual changes. In addition to adding hundreds of dollars to the price of a new car, these changes can introduce new defects. It can take a few months to iron out these bugs. Ask the dealer when the vehicle you are interested in was manufactured, or look on the metal tag found on the inside of the driver-side door frame to find the date of manufacture.

3 Avoid delicate options. Delicate options have the highest frequency-of-repair records. Power seats, power windows, power antennas, and special roofs are nice conveniences—until they break down. Of all the items on the vehicles, they tend to be the most expensive to repair.

4 Inspect the dealer's checklist. Request a copy of the dealer's pre-delivery service and adjustment checklist (also called a "make-ready list") at the time your new vehicle is delivered. Write the request directly on the new vehicle order. This request informs the dealer that you are aware of the dealer's responsibility to check your new car for defects.

5 Examine the car on delivery. Most of us are very excited when it comes time to take the vehicle home. A few minutes of careful inspection can save hours of misery later. Look over the body for any damage, check for the spare tire and jack equipment, make sure all electrical items work, and all the hubcaps and body molding are on. You may want to take a short test-drive. Finally, make sure you have the owner's manual, warranty forms, and all the legal documents.

DEPRECIATION

Over the past 20 years, new vehicle depreciation costs have steadily increased. A study conducted by Runzheimer International shows that depreciation and interest now account for just over 50% of the costs of owning and operating a vehicle. Recently, however, the increasing cost of depreciation has slowed down. This is due to the relatively stable prices of new vehicles and to the slow increase in finance rates. The higher cost of gasoline consumes a larger percentage of the automotive dollar than ever before. Other costs, including insurance, maintenance, and tires, have remained at relatively steady shares of the automotive dollar.

While there is no foolproof method for predicting retained vehicle value, your best bet is to purchase a popular vehicle model. Chances are it will also be a popular used vehicle model, meaning that the retained value may be higher when you go to sell it.

Most new cars are traded in within four years and are then available on the used car market. The priciest used cars may not be the highest quality. Supply and demand, as well as appearance, are important factors in determining used car prices.

The following table indicates which of the 100 top-selling 1996 cars held their value the best and which did not.

1996 CARS WITH THE BEST AND WORST RESALE VALUE

THE BEST				THE WORST			
Model	1996 Price	2000 Price	Retain. Value	Model	1996 Price	2000 Price	Retain. Value
Chevrolet Suburban	$24,027	$20,000	83%	Chrysler LHS	$30,225	$12,475	41%
Chev. C/K Series PU	$16,883	$13,375	79%	Lincoln Town Car	$41,960	$17,675	42%
Honda Civic	$13,600	$10,200	75%	Geo Tracker	$14,570	$6,250	43%
Chevrolet Camaro	$14,990	$11,200	75%	Ford Taurus	$20,980	$9,050	43%
GMC Sierra (Classic)	$17,991	$13,375	74%	Mercury Sable	$21,295	$9,300	44%
Merc.-Benz E-Class	$43,500	$32,050	74%	Dodge Intrepid	$18,445	$8,225	45%
Dodge Ram Pickup	$14,031	$10,300	73%	Buick Century	$18,383	$8,400	46%
Ford Econo./Club Wgn	$19,695	$14,325	73%	Buick Skylark	$15,890	$7,300	46%
Toyota 4-Runner	$22,448	$15,900	71%	Hyundai Elantra	$12,349	$5,700	46%
Toyota RAV4	$16,698	$11,700	70%	Chevrolet Lumina	$16,355	$7,700	47%

GETTING THE BEST PRICE

One of the most difficult aspects of buying a new car is getting the best price. Most of us are at a disadvantage negotiating because we don't know how much the car actually cost the dealer. The difference between what the dealer paid and the sticker price represents the negotiable amount.

Until recently, the key to getting the best price was finding out the dealer cost. Many shoppers now ask to see the factory invoice, so some dealers promote their cars by offering to sell at only $49 or $99 over invoice. This sounds like a good deal, but these cars often have options you may not want and most invoice prices do not reveal the extra, hidden profit to the dealer.

Now that most savvy consumers know to check the so-called "dealer invoice," the industry has camouflaged this number. Special incentives, rebates, and kickbacks can account for $500 to $2,000 worth of extra profit to a dealer selling a car at "dealer invoice." The non-profit Center for the Study of Services recently discovered that in 37 percent of cases when dealers are forced to bid against each other for the sale, they offered the buyer a price below the "dealer invoice"—an unlikely event if the dealer was actually losing money. The bottom line is that "dealer invoice" doesn't really mean dealer cost.

Because the rules have changed, we believe that most consumers are ill-advised to try and negotiate with a dealer. This is because introducing competition is the best way to get the lowest price on a new car. To do this you have to convince three or four dealers that you are, in fact, prepared to buy a car; that you have decided on the make, model, and features; and that your decision now rests solely on which dealer will give you the best price. You can try to do this by phone, but often dealers will not give you the best price, or will quote you a price over the phone that they will not honor later. Instead, you should try to do this in person. As anyone knows who has ventured into an auto showroom simply to get the best price, the process can be lengthy as well as terribly arduous. Nevertheless, if you can convince the dealer that you are serious and are willing to take the time to go to a number of dealers, it will pay off. Otherwise, we suggest you use the CarBargains service listed on the next page.

Here are some other showroom strategies:

Shop away from home. If you find a big savings at a dealership far from your home or on the Internet, call a local dealer with the price. They may very well match it. If not, pick up the car from the distant dealer, knowing your trip has saved you hundreds of dollars. You can still bring it to your local dealer for warranty work and repairs.

Beware of misleading advertising. New car ads are meant to get you into the showroom. They usually promise low prices, big rebates, high trade-in, and spotless integrity—don't be deceived. Advertised prices are rarely the true selling price. They usually exclude transportation charges, service fees, or document fees. And always look out for the asterisk, both in advertisements and on invoices. It can be a signal that the advertiser has something to hide.

Don't talk price until you're ready to buy. On your first few trips to the showroom, simply look over the cars, decide what options you want, and do your test-driving.

Shop the corporate twins. Page 91 contains a list of corporate twins—nearly identical cars that carry different name plates. Check the price and options of the twins of the car you like. A higher-priced twin may have more options, so it may be a better deal than the lowerpriced car without the options you want.

Watch out for dealer preparation overcharges. Before paying the dealer to clean your car, make sure that preparation is not included in the basic price. The price sticker will state: "Manufacturer's suggested retail price of this model includes dealer preparation."

If you must negotiate . . . negotiate up from the "invoice" price rather than down from the sticker price. Simply make an offer close to or at the "invoice" price. If the salesperson says that your offer is too low to make a profit, ask to see the factory invoice.

CARBARGAINS' BEST PRICE SERVICE

Even with the information that we provide you in this chapter of *The Ultimate Car Book*, many of us still will not be comfortable negotiating for a fair price. In fact, as we indicated on the previous page, we believe it's really very difficult to negotiate the best price with a single dealer. The key to getting the best price is to get dealers to compete with each other.

CarBargains is a service of the non-profit Center for the Study of Services, a Washington, DC, consumer group, set up to provide comparative price information for many products and services.

CarBargains will "shop" the dealerships in your area and obtain at least five price quotes for the make and model of the car that you want to buy. The dealers who submit quotes know that they are competing with other area dealerships and have agreed to honor the prices that they submit. It is important to note that CarBargains is not an auto broker or "car buying" service; they have no affiliation with dealers.

Here's how the service works:

1. You provide CarBargains with the make, model, and style of car you wish to buy (Ford Taurus GL, for example) by phone or mail.

2. Within two weeks, CarBargains will send you dealer quote sheets from at least five local dealers who have bid against one another to sell you that car. The offer is actually a commitment to a dollar amount above (or below) "factory invoice cost" for that model.

You will also receive a printout with the exact dealer cost for the car and each available option including the sales manager honoring the quote.

3. Use the factory invoice cost printout to add up the invoice cost for the base car and the options you want and then determine which dealer offers the best price using the dealer quote sheets. Contact the sales manager of that dealership and arrange to purchase the car.

If a car with the options you want is not available on the dealer's lot, you can have the dealer order the car from the factory or, in some cases, from another dealer at the agreed price.

When you receive your quotes, you will also get some suggestions on low-cost sources of financing and a valuation of your used car (trade-in).

The price for this service may seem expensive, but when you consider the savings that will result by having dealers bid against each other, as well as the time and effort of trying to get these bids yourself, we believe it's a great value. First of all, the dealers know they have a bona fide buyer (you've paid $165 for the service) and they know they are bidding against five to seven of their competitors.

To obtain CarBargains' competitive price quotes, send a check for $165 to CarBargains, 733 15th St., NW, Suite 820CB, Washington, DC 20005. Include your complete mailing address, phone number (in case of questions), and the exact make, model, and year of the car you want to buy. You should receive your bids within two to three weeks. For faster service, call them at 800–475–7283. Or, visit their website at www.checkbook.org.

! AUTO BROKERS !

While CarBargains is a non-profit organization created to help you find the best price for the car you want to purchase, auto brokers are typically in the business to make money. As such, whatever price you end up paying for the car will include additional profit for the broker. While many brokers are legitimately trying to get their customers the best price, others have developed special relationships with certain dealers and may not do much shopping for you. As a consumer, it is difficult to tell which are which. This is why we recommend CarBargains. There have been cases where the auto broker makes certain promises, takes your money, and you never hear from him or her again. If CarBargains is not for you, then we suggest you consider using a buying service associated with your credit union or auto club, which can arrange for the purchase of a car at some fixed price over "dealer invoice."

FINANCING

You've done your test-drive, researched prices, studied crash tests, determined the options you want, and haggled to get the best price. Now you have to decide how to pay for the car.

If you have the cash, pay for the car right away. You avoid finance charges, you won't have a large debt haunting you, and the full value of the car is yours. You can then make the monthly payments to yourself to save up for your next car.

However, most of us cannot afford to pay cash for a car, which leaves two options: financing or leasing. While leasing may seem more affordable, financing will actually cost you less. When you finance a car, you own it after you finish your payments. At the end of a lease, you have nothing. We don't recommend leasing, but if you want more information, see page 88.

Here are some tips when financing your car:

Shop around for interest rates. Most banks and credit unions will knock off at least a quarter of a percent for their customers. Have these quotes handy when you talk financing with the dealer.

The higher your down payment, the less you'll have to finance. This will not only reduce your overall interest charges, but often qualifies you for a lower interest rate. Down payments are typically 10–20% of the final price.

Avoid long car loans. The monthly payments are lower, but you'll pay far more in overall interest charges. For example, a two-year, $15,000 loan at 9% will cost you $1,446.51 in interest; the same amount at five years will cost you $3,682.52 — way over twice as much!

Check out manufacturer promotional rates—the 0.9–2.9% rates you see advertised. These low rates are usually only valid on two- to three-year loans.

Read everything you are asked to sign and ask questions about anything you don't fully understand.

Make sure that an extended warranty has not been added to the purchase price. Dealers will sometimes add this cost without informing the consumer. Extended warranties are generally a bad value. See the "Warranties" chapter for more information.

Credit Unions vs. Banks: Credit unions generally charge fewer and lower fees and offer better rates than banks. In addition, credit unions offer counseling services where consumers can find pricing information on cars or compare monthly payments for financing. You can join a credit union either through

DON'T BE TONGUE-TIED

TIP

Beware of high-pressure phrases like "I've talked to the manager and this is really the best we can do as it is, we're losing money on this deal." Rarely is this true. Dealers are in the business to make money and most do very well. Don't tolerate a take-it-or-leave-it attitude. Simply repeat that you will only buy when you see the deal you want and that you don't appreciate the dealer pressuring you. Threaten to leave if the dealer continues to pressure you to buy today.

Don't let the dealer answer your questions with a question. If you ask, "Can I get air conditioning with this car?" And the salesperson answers, "If I get you air conditioning in this car, will you buy today?" This response tries to force you to decide to buy before you are ready. Ask the dealer to just answer your question and that you'll buy when you're ready. It's the dealer's job to answer questions, not yours.

If you are having a difficult time getting what you want, ask the dealer: "Why won't you let me buy a car today?" Most salespeople will be thrown off by this phrase as they are often too busy trying to use it on you. If they respond in frustration, "OK, what do you want?" then you can say straightforward answers to simple questions.

Get a price; don't settle for: "If you're shopping price, go to the other dealers first and then come back." This technique ensures that they don't have to truly negotiate. Your best response is: "I only plan to come back if your price is the lowest, so that's what I need today, your lowest price."

your employer, an organization or club, or if you have a relative who is part of a credit union.

Low Rate or Cash Back? Sometimes auto manufacturers offer a choice of below market financing or cash back. The following table will tell you if it is better to take the lower rate or the cash back rebate. For example, say you want to finance $18,000. Your credit union or bank offers you 8.5% for an auto loan and the dealer offers either a 6% loan or a $1,500 rebate. Which is better? Find your bank or credit union's rate (8.5%) and the dealer's low rate (6%) on the table. Find where the two intersect on the table and you will find the difference per thousand dollars between the two interest rates (47). When you multiply this number (47) by the number of thousands you're financing (18 for $18,000), you get $846. Since the dealer's $1,500 rebate is more than the breakeven $846, taking your bank's rate (8.5%) and the rebate is a better deal than the dealer's low rate (6%). If the answer had been more than $1,500, then the dealer's rate would have been the better deal. An asterisk (*) means that the bank or credit union's rate is the better deal.

DESTINATION CHARGES

TIP

There once was a time when you could go directly to the factory and buy a car, saving yourself a few hundred dollars in destination and freight charges. Today, destination charges are a non-negotiable part of buying a new car, no matter where you purchase it. They are, however, an important factor when comparing prices. You'll find the destination charges on the price sticker attached to the vehicle. According to automakers, destination charges are the cost of shipping a vehicle from its "final assembly point" to the dealership. The cost of shipping other components for final assembly is sometimes also added.

But, the following table illustrates that there is little correlation between destination charges and where the cars are assembled:

Vehicle	Dest. Charge	Assembly Country
BMW 318i	$570	U.S./Germany
Ford Taurus	$550	U.S.
Hyundai Elantra	$435	Korea
Saturn SC	$440	U.S.

REBATE VS. LOW RATES (FOUR YEAR LOAN)

Multiply the number that intersects your dealer's rate with the rate from your credit union or bank by the number of thousands you are financing. If the result is less than the rebate, take the rebate; if it is above the rebate, go for the dealer financing.

Bank/ C.U. Rate	Dealer Rate						
	2%	3%	4%	5%	6%	7%	8%
7.0	94	76	57	38	19	*	*
7.5	103	85	66	48	29	10	*
8.0	111	93	75	57	38	19	*
8.5	120	102	84	66	47	28	10
9.0	128	111	93	75	56	38	19
9.5	136	119	101	83	65	47	28

Based on data from *Everybody's Money*, a publication of the Credit Union National Association.

LEASING VS. BUYING

As car prices continue to rise, many car buyers are being seduced by the heavily advertised low monthly lease payments. Don't be deceived—in general, leasing costs more than buying outright or financing. When you pay cash or finance a car, you own an asset; leasing leaves you with nothing except all the headaches and responsibilities of ownership with none of the benefits. In addition, leased cars are often not covered by lemon laws. When you lease you pay a monthly fee for a predetermined time in exchange for the use of a car. However, you also pay for maintenance, insurance, and repairs as if you owned the car. Finally, when it comes time to turn in the car, it has to be in top shape—otherwise, you'll have to pay for repairs or body work.

If you are considering a lease, here are some leasing terms you need to know and some tips to get you through the process.

Capitalized Cost is the price of the car on which the lease is based. Negotiate this as if you were buying the cars. Capitalized Cost Reduction is your down payment.

Know the make and model of the vehicle you want. Tell the agent exactly how you want the car equipped. You don't have to pay for options you don't request. Decide in advance how long you will keep the car.

Find out the price of the options on which the lease is based. Typically, they will be full retail price. Their cost can be negotiated (albeit with some difficulty) before you settle on the monthly payment.

Make sure options like a sunroof or stereo are added to the Capitalized Cost. When you purchase dealer-added options, be sure they add the full cost of the option to the Capitalized Cost so that you only pay for the depreciated value of the option, not the full cost.

Find out how much you are required to pay at delivery. Most leases require at least the first month's payment. Others have a security deposit, registration fees, or other "hidden" costs. When shopping around, make sure price quotes include security deposit and taxes—sales tax, monthly use tax, or gross receipt tax. Ask how the length of the lease affects your monthly cost.

Find out how the lease price was determined. Lease prices are generally based on the manufacturer's suggested retail price, less the predetermined residual value. The best values are cars with a high expected residual value. To protect themselves, lessors tend to underestimate residual value, but you can do little about this estimate.

Find out the annual mileage limit. Don't accept a contract with a lower limit than you need. Most standard contracts allow 15,000 to 18,000 miles per year. If you go under the allowance one year, you can go over it the next. Watch out for Excess Mileage fees. If you go over, you'll get charged per mile.

Avoid "capitalized cost reduction" or "equity leases." Here the lessor offers to lower the monthly payment by asking you for more money up front—in other words, a down payment.

Ask about early termination. Between 30 and 40 percent of two-year leases are terminated early, and 40–60 percent of four-year leases are terminated early—this means expensive early termination fees. If you terminate the lease before it is up, what are the financial penalties? Typically, they are very high, so watch out. Ask the dealer exactly what you would owe at the end of each year if you wanted out of the lease. Remember, if your car is stolen, the lease will typically be terminated. While your insurance should cover the value of

LEASEWISE

TIP

If you must lease, why haggle when you can let someone else do it for you? Leasewise, a new service from the Center for the Study of Services, makes dealers bid for your lease. First, they get leasing bids from dealers on the vehicles you're interested in. Next, you'll receive a detailed report with all the bids, the dealer and invoice cost of the vehicle, and a complete explanation of the various bids. Then, you can lease from the lowest bidder or use the report as leverage with another dealer. The service costs $290. For more information, call 800–475–7283, or visit www.check-the car, you still may owe additional amounts per your lease contract.

Avoid maintenance contracts. Getting work done privately is cheaper in the long run—and don't forget, this is a new car with a standard warranty.

Arrange for your own insurance. By shopping around, you can generally find less expensive insurance than what's offered by the lessor.

Ask how quickly you can expect delivery. If your agent can't deliver in a reasonable time, maybe he or she can't meet the price quoted.

Retain your option to buy the car at the end of the lease at a predetermined price. The price should equal the residual value; if it is more, then the lessor is trying to make an additional profit. Regardless of how the end-of-lease value is determined, if you want the car, make an offer based on the current "Blue Book" value of the car at the end of the lease.

Residual Value is the value of your car at the end of the lease.

Here's what First National Lease Systems' Automotive Lease Guide estimates the residual values for a few 2001 cars will be after four years:

Acura TL	51%
Chevy Lumina	32%
Dodge Caravan	39%
Ford F-Series	36%
Honda Accord	48%
Jeep Grand Cherokee	44%
Nissan Altima	38%
Oldsmobile Intrigue	35%
Pontiac Grand Am	36%
Subaru Legacy	44%
Toyota Camry	43%

LEASING VS. BUYING

The following table compares the typical costs of leasing vs. buying the same car over three and six years. Your actual costs may vary, but you can use this format to compare the cars you are considering. Our example assumes the residual value to be about 54% after three years and 36% after six years.

3 Years	Lease	Finance
MSRP	$22,000.00	$22,000.00
Purchase Cost of Car	$20,000.00	$20,000.00
Down Payment		$2,000.00
Monthly Payment	$359.49	$364.98
Total Payments	$12,941.64	$13,139.11[1]
Amount left on loan		$7,758.62
Less value of vehicle		$11,017.90
Overall Cost, first 3 years	$12,941.64	$11,879.83
6 Years		
MSRP	$22,000.00	$22,000.00
Cost of Car	$40,000.00[2]	$20,000.00
Down Payment		$2,000.00
Monthly Payment	$359.49	$364.98
Total Payments	$25,883.28	$21,898.51[3]
Less value of vehicle		$8,000.00
Overall Cost, 6 years	$25,883.28	$15,898.51

[1] First 3 years of 5-year loan with 8% annual percentage rate.
[2] Two 3-year leases.
[3] 5-year loan with 8% annual percentage rate, no monthly payments in 6th year.

USING THE INTERNET

The Internet is changing the way car buyers research and shop for cars. But, the Internet should be used with caution. Remember that anyone—and we mean, *anyone*—can publish a website with no guarantee concerning the accuracy of the information on it. We advise that you only visit websites that have a familiar non-web counterpart. A good example is the Center for Auto Safety's website at www.autosafety.org where you'll find information on auto safety, including publications and newsletters which are typically mailed out to subscribers.

Use the Internet as an information resource. Unfortunately, most automaker websites are nothing more than sophisticated ads with little comparative information.

Good information, like pricing and features, *can* be found online. On this page, we've listed some useful websites.

There are also several online car shopping services that have launched. We view most of them with skepticism. Many online car shopping services are tied to a limited, often non-competitive, group of dealers. They may claim the lowest price, but you'll most likely have a dealer calling you with a price that is not much better than what you'll get if you went into a dealership to haggle.

Auto insurance and financing sites are sometimes no better. Don't rely solely on these online services; getting quotes from other sources is the only way to make sure you truly have the best deal.

Finally, clicking a mouse is no substitute for going out and test-driving a car. If you are shopping for a used car, you must check out the actual car before signing on the dotted line. Do not rely on online photos. In fact, online classifieds for cars are no more reliable than looking in a newspaper.

If you do use a online car shopping service, be sure to shop around on your own. Visit dealerships, get quotes from several car shopping services, and research the value of your used car (see www.kbb.com on this page). Beware that if you give anyone online your phone number, or email address, you are opening yourself up to unwanted email, junk mail, and even sales calls.

ON THE WEB

nhtsa.dot.gov
The National Highway Traffic Safety Administration (NHTSA) website contains useful information on safety standards, crash tests, recalls, technical service bulletins, child seats, and safety advisories.

autosafety.org
The Center for Auto Safety (CAS) provides consumers with a voice for auto safety and quality in Washington and to help lemon owners fight back across the country.

consumer.checkbook.org
The Center for the Study of Services (CSS) is an independent, nonprofit consumer organization and the creator of Consumer Checkbook. One of the few car buying services worth using, CSS's CarBargains pits dealers against each other, keeping you from haggling.

kbb.com
The Kelly Blue Book website is a valuable reference to dealer invoice and retail pricing. Remember that the dealer invoice price is not necessarily how much the dealer has paid for the car; about 2–3% is usually held back. So, even if a dealer sells a car "at cost," they'll still make a few hundred dollars in profit.

edmunds.com/edweb/Incentives.html
Edmund's Car Buying Guide's website offers a page on dealer and consumer rebates. The dealer rebates are especially valuable as dealers will not openly tell you about them.

carfax.com
Used car buyers will want to visit Carfax. Carfax collects information from numerous sources to provide a vehicle history on a specific vehicle, based on the Vehicle Identification Number (VIN). Carfax can help uncover costly and potentially dangerous hidden problems or confirm the clean history of a vehicle.

CORPORATE TWINS AND ASIAN COUSINS

"Corporate twins" refers to vehicles that have different nameplates but share the same mechanics, drivetrain, and chassis. In most cases, the vehicles are identical, like the Dodge and Plymouth Neon. Sometimes the difference is in body style, price, or options as with the Ford Taurus and Mercury Sable. Additionally, there are also "Asian cousins," which are Asian vehicles marketed under a U.S. nameplate. As with corporate twins, Asian cousins are the same vehicle with different nameplates, styles, prices, or options.

CORPORATE TWINS AND ASIAN COUSINS

DiamlerChrysler
Chrysler 300M
Chrysler LHS

Chrysler Concorde
Dodge Intrepid

Chrysler Sebring
Dodge Stratus

Chrysler Town & Country
Dodge Grand Caravan

Chrysler Voyager
Dodge Caravan

General Motors
Cadillac Escalade
Chevrolet Tahoe
GMC Denali
GMC Yukon

Chevrolet Blazer
GMC Jimmy
Oldsmobile Bravada

Chevrolet Camaro
Pontiac Firebird

Chevrolet Impala
Chevrolet Monte Carlo
Pontiac Grand Prix

Chevrolet Prizm
Toyota Corolla*

Chevrolet S-Series Pickup
GMC Sonoma

Chevrolet Silverado
GMC Sierra

Chevrolet Suburban
GMC Yukon XL

Chevrolet Tracker
Suzuki Vitara/Grand Vitara

Chevrolet Venture
Oldsmobile Silhouette
Pontiac Montana

Oldsmobile Alero
Pontiac Grand Am
Chevrolet Malibu

Pontiac Bonneville
Oldsmobile Aurora
Cadillac Seville
Buick LeSabre

Pontiac Sunfire
Chevrolet Cavalier

Ford
Ford Crown Victoria
Lincoln Town Car
Mercury Grand Marquis

Ford Escape
Mazda Tribute*

Ford Expedition
Lincoln Navigator

Ford Explorer
Mercury Mountaineer

Ford Ranger
Mazda B-Series Pickup

Ford Taurus
Mercury Sable

Lincoln LS
Jaguar S

Mercury Villager
Nissan Quest*

Honda
Honda Passport
Isuzu Rodeo

Isuzu
Isuzu Rodeo
Honda Passport

Mazda
Mazda B-Series Pickup
Ford Ranger

Mazda Tribute*
Ford Escape

Nissan
Nissan Maxima
Infiniti I30

Nissan Pathfinder
Infiniti QX4

Nissan Quest*
Mercury Villager

Suzuki
Suzuki Swift*
Chevrolet Metro

Suzuki Vitara/Grand Vitara
Chevrolet Tracker

Toyota
Toyota Camry
Lexus ES300

Toyota Corolla*
Chevrolet Prizm

Toyota Land Cruiser
Lexus LX470

Volkswagen
Volkswagen Golf
Volkswagen Jetta

*Asian cousins

HOW TO BUY A USED CAR

No longer is buying a used car "buying someone else's troubles." In fact, because it is very difficult for most of us to determine even what year a car was made, it is hard to tell a brand new car from a two- to three-year-old model. This is why *The Ultimate Car Book* includes the past two model years for each 2001 model.

Should you consider getting a used car? Absolutely. Thanks to better reliability and the millions of previously leased vehicles hitting the used car market every year, there are more good used cars available than ever before.

Always test drive and carefully inspect a used car. Take it to an independent mechanic and get it checked out. Oftentimes, a trusted friend can be the best source for a used car. You'll always get an honest answer when you ask, "Why are you selling the car?"

Remember these tips when shopping for a used car:

Used cars of the same brand as the new cars that a new car dealer sells are your best bets.

The longer a used car dealer has been in the same location, the better your chances of getting help should a problem arise.

To get a good deal from a rental car company, know the car's fair market value and have it checked by an independent mechanic.

If you know a private owner who trades in a car regularly, contact them and ask if they will sell to you rather than trade in. They will get more selling to you based on wholesale price than they would get from trade-in price. And you'll pay less than retail price.

Visit the used car superstore on a clear, bright day and allow yourself an afternoon's worth of time to peruse. Many superstores will let you sort through their stock via their web page. Take a printout of the models you're interested in with you on your visit.

WHERE TO GET A USED CAR

1 NEW CAR DEALERS Pros: Dealers keep best vehicles to sell; available service facilities **Cons:** Higher price; weaker warranties; be sure to get everything in writing

2 USED CAR DEALERS Pros: Lower price **Cons:** Vehicle is sold "as is"; weak warranties; typically no service facilities; vehicles often from fleets

3 RENTAL CAR COMPANIES Pros: Vehicle history available; good selection; no-haggle pricing **Cons:** Unwanted options; higher mileage; higher price

4 PRIVATE SALES Pros: Lower price **Cons:** Time-consuming; beware of pros masquerading as private sellers

5 USED CAR SUPERSTORES Pros: No-haggle pricing; great selection; good warranty; non-commission salespeople **Cons:** Higher prices

Lexus ES300

Mazda B-Series

Volkswagen Beetle

Pontiac Montana

IN THIS CHAPTER

T he "Buying Guide" provides an overall comparison of the 2001 cars in terms of warranty, safety, fuel economy, complaint ratings, and price range. The cars are arranged by size class based on weight. Based on these comparisons, we have developed *The Ultimate Car Book* Best Bets for 2001—these vehicles rated tops when comparing all the key categories.

USING THE BUYING GUIDE

The "Buying Guide" will allow you to quickly compare the 2001 models.

To fully understand these summary charts, it is important to read the appropriate section of the book. You will note that here and throughout the book, some of the charts contain empty boxes. This indicates that data were unavailable at the time of printing.

Here's how to understand what's included in the "Buying Guide."

Page Reference: The page in the back of the book where you'll find all the details for this car.

Overall Rating: This is the "bottom line." It shows how well this car stacks up on a scale of 1 to 10 when compared to all others on the market. The overall rating considers safety, maintenance, fuel economy, warranty, insurance costs, and complaints. Due to the importance of safety, cars with no crash test results as of our publication date cannot be given an overall rating. More recent results may be available from the Auto Safety Hotline at 1-800-424-9393 (see page 72).

Car Book Crash Test Rating: This indicates how well the car performed in the U.S. government's 35-mph frontal crash test program using a combined rating. We have analyzed and compared all of the crash test results to date and have given them a rating from very good to very poor. These ratings allow you to compare the test results of one car with another. A car with a poor rating may have done well according to government injury ratings but still be among the worst performers of cars being offered in 2001.

Important Note: Recently, the government began a side crash test program. Currently, there are not enough vehicles with side crash test results to enable us to incorporate them into an overall crash test rating combining the front and side crash test results. If, however, a vehicle has been side crash tested and the results are not good, we will not give that vehicle an overall "Best Bet" rating regardless of its other results.

Fuel Economy: This is the EPA-rated fuel economy for city and highway driving measured in miles per gallon. A single model may have a number of fuel economy ratings because of different engine and transmission options. We have included the figure for what is expected to be the most popular model.

Warranty Rating: This is an overall assessment of the car's warranty when compared to all other warranties. The rating considers the important features of each warranty, with emphasis on the length of the basic and power train warranties.

Complaint Rating: This rating is based on the number of complaints about that car on file at the U.S. Department of Transportation. The complaint index will give you a general idea of experiences others have had with models which are essentially unchanged for this model year. All-new vehicles for 2001 are given an average complaint rating, as it is unknown how many complaints they will receive.

Typical Price: This price range will give you a general idea of the "sticker," or asking price of a car. It is based on the lowest to highest retail price of the various models, and it does not include options or the discount that you should be able to negotiate using a service such as CarBargains (see page 89).

Vehicle	Page #	Overall Rating	Overall Crash	Warranty	Fuel Economy	Complaints	Typical Price
SUBCOMPACT							
Dodge/Plymouth Neon	214	5	Average	Very Poor	27/33	Average	$12-13,000
Ford Focus	228	9	Very Good	Poor	25/33	Average	$12-16,000
Ford ZX2	238			Poor	28/37	Average	$12-13,000
Honda Civic	244	7	Very Good	Very Poor	32/39	Average	$10-17,000
Honda Insight	248		Good	Very Poor	61/68	Average	$19-20,000
Honda S2000	256			Very Poor	20/26	Average	$29-32,000
Hyundai Accent	258			Very Good	18/36	Average	$9-11,000
Kia Rio	290			Very Good	22/30	Average	$8-9,000
Kia Sephia	292	8	Good	Very Good	24/29	Average	$10-13,000
Kia Spectrum	294			Very Good	24/29	Average	$10-14,000
Mazda Miata	328			Poor	23/28	Very Poor	$22-24,000
Mazda Protégé	334	4	Good	Poor	29/34	Average	$13-16,000
Mitsubishi Mirage	352			Poor	32/39	Average	$12-15,000
Nissan Sentra	366			Good	27/35	Average	$12-16,000
Saturn SC	398			Poor	28/40	Good	$12-16,000
Saturn SL/SW	400	9	Very Good	Poor	29/40	Good	$10-15,000
Subaru Impreza	404	9	Good	Average	23/29	Very Good	$16-19,000
Suzuki Esteem	410			Very Poor	30/37	Good	$13-17,000
Suzuki Swift	414		Good	Very Poor	36/42	Good	$9-11,000
Toyota Echo	426			Very Poor	34/41	Average	$10-11,000
Toyota Prius	432			Very Poor	52/45	Average	$19-20,000
Volkswagen Beetle	446	9	Very Good	Very Good	24/31	Poor	$16-22,000
COMPACT							
Acura Integra	120			Average	25/31	Very Good	$19-23,000
BMW 3-Series	134			Good	20/29	Average	$27-42,000
BMW Z3	140			Good	21/28	Good	$37-38,000
Chevrolet Cavalier	166	6	Good	Very Poor	23/33	Good	$13-16,000
Chevrolet Prizm	172	4	Good	Very Poor	32/41	Good	$14-16,000
Chrysler Sebring	194			Very Poor	20/27	Average	$18-27,000
Daewoo Lanos	198			Average	26/36	Very Good	$9-13,000
Honda Prelude	254			Very Poor	22/27	Average	$23-26,000
Hyundai Elantra	260			Very Good	25/33	Average	$11-13,000
Hyundai Tiburon	266			Very Good	23/31	Poor	$14-15,000
Infiniti G20	270			Very Good	24/31	Very Good	$22-25,000
Mazda 626	324	5	Very Good	Poor	26/32	Poor	$19-23,000
Mitsubishi Eclipse	348			Poor	22/30	Average	$18-26,000

Vehicle	Page #	Overall Rating	Overall Crash	Warranty	Fuel Economy	Complaints	Typical Price
COMPACT (cont.)							
Mitsubishi Galant	350	3	Very Good	Poor	21/28	Very Poor	$17-24,000
Oldsmobile Alero	370	5	Very Good	Poor	21/29	Very Poor	$17-22,000
Pontiac Grand Am	384	3	Very Good	Very Poor	21/29	Very Poor	$16-22,000
Pontiac Sunfire	390	6	Good	Very Poor	23/32	Good	$14-16,000
Subaru Legacy	406	9	Very Good	Average	21/28	Average	$19-25,000
Toyota Celica	422			Very Poor	28/33	Average	$16-22,000
Toyota Corolla	424	7	Good	Very Poor	32/41	Very Good	$12-14,000
Volkswagen Golf	448	8	Very Good	Very Good	25/31	Very Poor	$15-23,000
Volkswagen Jetta	450	7	Very Good	Very Good	25/31	Poor	$16-25,000
INTERMEDIATE							
Audi A4	128	9	Very Good	Very Good	23/32	Average	$24-32,000
Buick Century	142	7	Average	Very Poor	20/29	Average	$19-23,000
Buick Regal	148	8	Average	Very Poor	19/29	Average	$22-26,000
Cadillac Catera	150			Average	17/24	Very Poor	$31-32,000
Chevrolet Camaro	164	5	Very Good	Very Poor	19/31	Poor	$17-28,000
Chevr. Impala/MonteCarlo	168	7	Very Good	Very Poor	21/32	Average	$19-23,000
Chevrolet Malibu	170	4	Good	Very Poor	20/29	Poor	$17-19,000
Chrysler Concorde	188	6	Good	Very Poor	20/28	Poor	$22-27,000
Chrysler PT Cruiser	192	3	Poor	Very Poor	20/25	Average	$15-16,000
Daewoo Leganza	200			Average	20/28	Very Good	$14-19,000
Dodge Intrepid	208	6	Good	Very Poor	20/28	Good	$21-25,000
Dodge Stratus	212			Very Poor	20/30	Average	$17-21,000
Ford Mustang	230	6	Good	Poor	19/27	Good	$17-27,000
Ford Taurus	234	10	Very Good	Poor	20/27	Good	$18-22,000
Honda Accord	242	5	Good	Very Poor	26/32	Average	$18-24,000
Hyundai Sonata	264			Very Good	22/30	Average	$15-19,000
Lexus ES300	302	10	Very Good	Good	19/26	Very Good	$32-33,000
Mazda Millenia	330	7	Very Good	Poor	20/27	Very Good	$28-31,000
Mercedes-Benz C-Class	336			Poor	20/26	Average	$30-37,000
Nissan Altima	356	9	Very Good	Good	23/31	Very Good	$15-20,000
Nissan Maxima	360	5	Good	Good	22/27	Average	$21-26,000
Oldsmobile Intrigue	376	4	Average	Poor	19/28	Very Poor	$22-26,000
Pontiac Grand Prix	386	7	Good	Very Poor	20/29	Average	$21-25,000
Saab 9-3	392			Average	22/30	Very Poor	$26-45,000
Saab 9-5	394			Average	21/30	Very Good	$34-41,000

Vehicle	Page #	Overall Rating	Overall Crash	Warranty	Fuel Economy	Complaints	Typical Price
INTERMEDIATE (cont.)							
Saturn L/LW	396	7	Very Good	Poor	25/33	Average	$14-21,000
Subaru Outback	408			Average	21/28	Average	$23-31,000
Toyota Avalon	418			Very Poor	21/29	Average	$25-30,000
Toyota Camry	420	7	Very Good	Very Poor	24/33	Average	$17-26,000
Toyota Solara	440			Very Poor	24/33	Average	$18-30,000
Volkswagen Passat	452	8	Very Good	Very Good	22/31	Very Poor	$21-31,000
Volvo C70/V70	454			Very Good	20/27	Average	$29-45,000
Volvo S40/V40	456			Very Good	22/32	Average	$23-25,000
Volvo S60	458			Very Good	20/27	Average	$27-32,000
Volvo S80	460	9	Very Good	Very Good	19/26	Average	$37-41,000
LARGE							
Acura CL	118			Average	19/29	Average	$28-30,000
Acura RL	124	9	Good	Average	18/24	Very Good	$42-44,000
Acura TL	126			Average	19/29	Average	$28-29,000
Audi A6	130			Very Good	17/25	Very Poor	$34-49,000
Audi A8	132	10	Very Good	Very Good	17/25	Very Good	$62-68,000
BMW 5-Series	136			Good	20/29	Good	$35-53,000
Buick LeSabre	144	8	Very Good	Very Poor	19/30	Average	$24-29,000
Buick Park Avenue	146			Very Poor	19/30	Average	$33-37,000
Cadillac DeVille	152	7	Average	Average	17/27	Average	$40-46,000
Cadillac Eldorado	154			Average	17/27	Good	$40-43,000
Cadillac Seville	158	9	Very Good	Average	17/27	Average	$42-48,000
Chrysler 300M	186			Very Poor	18/26	Very Poor	$29-30,000
Chrysler LHS	190			Very Poor	18/26	Very Poor	$28-29,000
Ford Crown Victoria	216	9	Very Good	Poor	17/25	Good	$22-24,000
Hyundai XG300	268			Very Good	19/27	Average	$24-25,000
Infiniti I30	272	7	Good	Very Good	18/26	Average	$30-31,000
Infiniti Q45	274			Very Good	18/23	Very Good	$49-51,000
Lexus GS300/400	304			Good	18/24	Very Good	$38-47,000
Lexus IS300	306			Good	18/23	Average	$30-31,000
Lexus LS430	308			Good	18/25	Very Good	$54-55,000
Lexus SC300/400	314			Good	19/23	Very Poor	$43-56,000
Lincoln Continental	316			Average	17/25	Average	$39-40,000
Lincoln LS	318			Average	18/25	Average	$33-36,000
Lincoln Town Car	322	9	Good	Average	18/25	Average	$39-48,000

Vehicle	Page #	Overall Rating	Overall Crash	Warranty	Fuel Economy	Complaints	Typical Price
LARGE (cont.)							
Mercedes-Benz E-Class	338			Poor	20/28	Very Good	$48-56,000
Mercury Cougar	342			Poor	23/34	Very Poor	$16-22,000
Mitsubishi Diamante	346			Poor	18/25	Good	$25-27,000
Oldsmobile Aurora	372	7	Very Good	Poor	19/28	Average	$30-34,000
Pontiac Bonneville	382	6	Very Good	Very Poor	19/30	Average	$25-32,000
MINIVAN							
Chevrolet Astro	160	5	Average	Very Poor	17/22	Good	$23-25,000
Chevrolet Venture	184	5	Good	Very Poor	19/26	Very Poor	$21-25,000
Chrysler Town & Country	196	6	Good	Very Poor	18/24	Average	$27-37,000
Dodge Caravan	202	6	Good	Very Poor	18/24	Average	$19-23,000
Ford Windstar	236	9	Very Good	Poor	18/23	Very Poor	$20-33,000
Honda Odyssey	250	4	Very Good	Very Poor	18/25	Very Poor	$23-28,000
Mazda MPV	332	3	Good	Poor	18/23	Average	$21-27,000
Mercury Villager	344	5	Very Good	Poor	17/23	Very Poor	$22-27,000
Nissan Quest	364	9	Very Good	Good	17/23	Average	$23-27,000
Oldsmobile Silhouette	378	6	Good	Poor	19/26	Poor	$26-33,000
Pontiac Montana	388	6	Good	Very Poor	19/26	Very Poor	$26-32,000
Toyota Sienna	438	4	Very Good	Very Poor	19/24	Poor	$23-28,000
SMALL SPORT UTILITY							
Chevrolet Tracker	182			Very Poor	23/26	Very Poor	$15-21,000
Ford Escape	218			Poor		Average	$17-21,000
Honda CR-V	246	7	Good	Very Poor	22/25	Very Good	$18-23,000
Hyundai Santa Fe	262			Very Good	21/28	Average	$17-22,000
Jeep Wrangler	288	2	Good	Very Poor	19/20	Poor	$15-23,000
Toyota Highlander	428			Very Poor		Average	
Toyota RAV4	434			Very Poor	25/31	Average	$16-19,000
MID-SIZE SP. UTILITY							
Acura MDX	122			Average	17/23	Average	$35-39,000
BMW X5	138			Good	15/20	Average	$39-49,000
Chevrolet Blazer	162	3	Poor	Very Poor	15/20	Poor	$19-26,000
Chevrolet Tahoe	180	5	Good	Very Poor	14/17	Average	$25-28,000
Ford Explorer	224	5	Average	Poor	15/19	Poor	$21-34,000
GMC Jimmy	240	2	Poor	Very Poor	15/20	Poor	$19-34,000
Honda Passport	252	1	Average	Very Poor	17/20	Very Poor	$23-30,000
Infiniti QX4	276	8	Very Good	Very Good	15/19	Very Good	$34-36,000
Isuzu Rodeo	278	3	Average	Good	17/20	Very Poor	$18-31,000
Isuzu Trooper	280			Good	15/19	Good	$27-35,000
Isuzu VehiCROSS	282			Good	15/19	Average	$30-31,000

Vehicle	Page #	Overall Rating	Overall Crash	Warranty	Fuel Economy	Complaints	Typical Price
MID-SIZE SP. UT. (cont.)							
Jeep Cherokee	284	3	Poor	Very Poor	17/22	Average	$18-24,000
Jeep Grand Cherokee	286	2	Poor	Very Poor	16/20	Very Poor	$28-35,000
Kia Sportage	296			Very Good	20/22	Very Poor	$14-20,000
Land Rov. Disc. Series II	298			Average	13/17	Average	$34-37,000
Lexus RX300	312			Good	18/22	Poor	$33-36,000
Mercedes-Benz M-Class	340	3	Very Good	Poor	17/21	Poor	$36-44,000
Mitsubishi Montero	354			Poor	14/17	Average	$31-35,000
Nissan Pathfinder	362	6	Very Good	Good	15/19	Very Good	$27-31,000
Nissan Xterra	368	5	Very Good	Good	15/19	Average	$18-26,000
Oldsmobile Bravada	374	2	Poor	Poor	15/20	Poor	$31-32,000
Pontiac Aztek	380			Very Poor	19/26	Average	$21-24,000
Subaru Forester	402	5	Good	Average	21/28	Poor	$20-25,000
Suzuki Grand Vitara	412			Very Poor	19/22	Poor	$18-23,000
Toyota 4Runner	416	6	Very Good	Very Poor	16/19	Very Good	$26-37,000
LARGE SPORT UTILITY							
Cadillac Escalade	156	5	Good	Average	13/16	Poor	$46-47,000
Chevrolet Suburban	178			Very Poor	14/16	Average	$26-31,000
Dodge Durango	206			Very Poor	13/18	Poor	$26-29,000
Ford Excursion	220			Poor		Average	$34-41,000
Ford Expedition	222	5	Good	Poor	16/21	Poor	$30-40,000
Land Rover Range Rover	300			Average	13/17	Average	$62-68,000
Lexus LX470	310			Good	13/16	Very Good	$61-62,000
Lincoln Navigator	320	8	Good	Average	23/34	Very Poor	$43-47,000
Toyota Land Cruiser	430			Very Poor	13/16	Good	$52-53,000
Toyota Sequoia	436			Very Poor	14/17	Average	
COMPACT PICKUP							
Chevrolet S-Series	174	3	Poor	Very Poor	22/28	Good	$13-20,000
Dodge Dakota	204			Very Poor	15/20	Poor	$14-22,000
Ford Ranger	232	6	Very Good	Poor	17/20	Good	$11-24,000
Mazda B-Series	326	5	Very Good	Poor	17/20	Good	$13-19,000
Nissan Frontier	358			Good	22/26	Good	$11-25,000
Toyota Tacoma	442			Very Poor	19/21	Average	$11-25,000
STANDARD PICKUP							
Chevrolet Silverado	176	3	Average	Very Poor	15/18	Poor	$16-32,000
Dodge Ram	210	3	Good	Very Poor	15/21	Average	$15-26,000
Ford F-Series	226	8	Good	Poor	15/19	Very Good	$17-24,000
Toyota Tundra	444			Very Poor	16/20	Average	$15-29,000

BEST BETS

Based on information in the "Buying Guide", this list shows the highest-rated cars in each of the size categories. Ratings are based on expected performance in ten important categories (crash tests, safety features, fuel economy, rollover, overall, maintenance and repair costs, warranties, insurance costs, and complaints), with the heaviest emphasis on crash test performance and complaints.

SUBCOMPACTS

SUBCOMPACT: FORD FOCUS   9

Overall	9	Warranty	4
Crash Tests	10	Rollover	8
Safety Features	6	Fuel Econ.	7
Prev. Maint.	8	Complaints	5
Repair Costs	10	Insurance Costs	8

Price Range: $12-16,000

SUBCOMPACT: SATURN SL/SW   9

Overall	9	Warranty	4
Crash Tests	10	Rollover	8
Safety Features	5	Fuel Econ.	7
Prev. Maint.	2	Complaints	5
Repair Costs	10	Insurance Costs	8

Price Range: $10-15,000

SUBCOMPACT: SUBARU IMPREZA   9

Overall	9	Warranty	5
Crash Tests	7	Rollover	7
Safety Features	6	Fuel Econ.	6
Prev. Maint.	9	Complaints	10
Repair Costs	5	Insurance Costs	6

Price Range: $16-19,000

SUBCOMPACTS/COMPACTS

SUBCOMPACT: VW BEETLE   9

Overall	.9	Warranty	.10
Crash Tests	.9	Rollover	.6
Safety Features	.8	Fuel Econ.	.6
Prev. Maint.	.10	Complaints	.3
Repair Costs	.6	Insurance Costs	.8

Price Range: $16-22,000

COMPACT: SUBARU LEGACY   9

Overall	.9	Warranty	.5
Crash Tests	.9	Rollover	.7
Safety Features	.7	Fuel Econ.	.5
Prev. Maint.	.9	Complaints	.5
Repair Costs	.9	Insurance Costs	.8

Price Range: $19-25,000

COMPACT: VW GOLF   8

Overall	.8	Warranty	.10
Crash Tests	.10	Rollover	.7
Safety Features	.8	Fuel Econ.	.7
Prev. Maint.	.10	Complaints	.2
Repair Costs	.4	Insurance Costs	.6

Price Range: $15-23,000

COMPACT: TOYOTA COROLLA   7

Overall	.7	Warranty	.2
Crash Tests	.8	Rollover	.7
Safety Features	.7	Fuel Econ.	.9
Prev. Maint.	.5	Complaints	.9
Repair Costs	.4	Insurance Costs	.6

Price Range: $12-14,000

COMPACTS/INTERMEDIATES

COMPACT: VW JETTA   7

Overall	7	Warranty	10
Crash Tests	10	Rollover	7
Safety Features	3	Fuel Econ.	7
Prev. Maint.	10	Complaints	3
Repair Costs	4	Insurance Costs	6

Price Range: $16-25,000

INTERMEDIATE: FORD TAURUS   10

Overall	10	Warranty	4
Crash Tests	10	Rollover	8
Safety Features	6	Fuel Econ.	5
Prev. Maint.	8	Complaints	7
Repair Costs	9	Insurance Costs	10

Price Range: $18-22,000

INTERMEDIATE: LEXUS ES300   10

Overall	10	Warranty	8
Crash Tests	9	Rollover	8
Safety Features	8	Fuel Econ.	4
Prev. Maint.	6	Complaints	10
Repair Costs	3	Insurance Costs	10

Price Range: $32-33,000

INTERMEDIATE: AUDI A4   9

Overall	9	Warranty	10
Crash Tests	9	Rollover	7
Safety Features	8	Fuel Econ.	6
Prev. Maint.	10	Complaints	5
Repair Costs	2	Insurance Costs	8

Price Range: $24-32,000

INTERMEDIATES

INTERMEDIATE: NISSAN ALTIMA   9

Overall	9	Warranty	7
Crash Tests	10	Rollover	7
Safety Features	6	Fuel Econ.	6
Prev. Maint.	7	Complaints	9
Repair Costs	7	Insurance Costs	6

Price Range: $15-20,000

INTERMEDIATE: VOLVO S80   9

Overall	9	Warranty	7
Crash Tests	10	Rollover	6
Safety Features	7	Fuel Econ.	3
Prev. Maint.	9	Complaints	6
Repair Costs	7	Insurance Costs	5

Price Range: $37-41,000

INTERMEDIATE: CHEV. IMPALA/MC   7

Overall	7	Warranty	2
Crash Tests	10	Rollover	7
Safety Features	6	Fuel Econ.	6
Prev. Maint.	6	Complaints	5
Repair Costs	7	Insurance Costs	8

Price Range: $19-23,000

INTERMEDIATE: SATURN L/LW   7

Overall	7	Warranty	3
Crash Tests	10	Rollover	7
Safety Features	4	Fuel Econ.	7
Prev. Maint.	2	Complaints	5
Repair Costs	10	Insurance Costs	8

Price Range: $14-21,000

INTERMEDIATE: TOYOTA CAMRY   7

Overall	7	Warranty	2
Crash Tests	10	Rollover	8
Safety Features	7	Fuel Econ.	7
Prev. Maint.	2	Complaints	6
Repair Costs	5	Insurance Costs	8

Price Range: $17-26,000

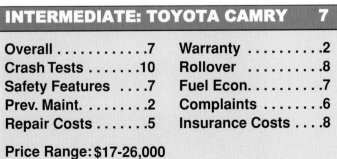

LARGE

LARGE: AUDI A8   10

Overall 10	Warranty 10
Crash Tests 10	Rollover 8
Safety Features 8	Fuel Econ. 4
Prev. Maint. 10	Complaints 9
Repair Costs 1	Insurance Costs 8

Price Range: $62-68,000

LARGE: ACURA RL   9

Overall 9	Warranty 5
Crash Tests 7	Rollover 8
Safety Features 6	Fuel Econ. 4
Prev. Maint. 1	Complaints 10
Repair Costs 10	Insurance Costs . . .10

Price Range: $42-44,000

LARGE: FORD CROWN VICTORIA   9

Overall 9	Warranty 4
Crash Tests 10	Rollover 8
Safety Features 5	Fuel Econ. 4
Prev. Maint. 5	Complaints 7
Repair Costs 10	Insurance Costs . . .10

Price Range: $22-24,000

LARGE: LINCOLN TOWN CAR   9

Overall 9	Warranty 5
Crash Tests 8	Rollover 8
Safety Features 7	Fuel Econ. 4
Prev. Maint. 5	Complaints 6
Repair Costs 10	Insurance Costs . . .10

Price Range: $39-48,000

MINIVANS

MINIVAN: FORD WINDSTAR   9

Overall 9	Warranty 4
Crash Tests 10	Rollover 6
Safety Features 8	Fuel Econ. 3
Prev. Maint. 9	Complaints 2
Repair Costs 10	Insurance Costs . . .10

Price Range: $20-33,000

MINIVAN: NISSAN QUEST   9

Overall 9	Warranty 7
Crash Tests 10	Rollover 6
Safety Features 7	Fuel Econ. 3
Prev. Maint. 9	Complaints 6
Repair Costs 7	Insurance Costs 5

Price Range: $23-27,000

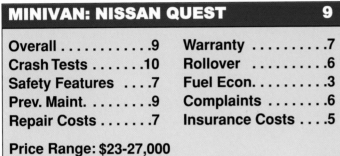

MINIVAN: CHRYSLER TOWN & CTRY 6

Overall 6	Warranty 1
Crash Tests 7	Rollover 5
Safety Features 6	Fuel Econ. 4
Prev. Maint. 9	Complaints 5
Repair Costs 9	Insurance Costs . . .10

Price Range: $27-37,000

MINIVAN: DODGE CARAVAN   6

Overall 6	Warranty 1
Crash Tests 7	Rollover 5
Safety Features 5	Fuel Econ. 2
Prev. Maint. 9	Complaints 5
Repair Costs 7	Insurance Costs . . .10

Price Range: $19-23,000

MINIVAN: OLDS SILHOUETTE   6

Overall 6	Warranty 3
Crash Tests 7	Rollover 5
Safety Features 8	Fuel Econ. 4
Prev. Maint. 8	Complaints 3
Repair Costs 5	Insurance Costs 5

Price Range: $26-33,000

MINIVANS/SPORT UTILITIES

MINIVAN: PONTIAC MONTANA   6

Overall	6	Warranty	2
Crash Tests	7	Rollover	5
Safety Features	8	Fuel Econ.	4
Prev. Maint.	9	Complaints	2
Repair Costs	5	Insurance Costs	5

Price Range: $26-32,000

SM. SPORT UTILITY: HONDA CR-V   7

Overall	7	Warranty	1
Crash Tests	8	Rollover	5
Safety Features	5	Fuel Econ.	5
Prev. Maint.	3	Complaints	10
Repair Costs	6	Insurance Costs	10

Price Range: $18-23,000

MD-SIZE SP. UT.: INFINITI QX4   8

Overall	8	Warranty	9
Crash Tests	9	Rollover	3
Safety Features	8	Fuel Econ.	2
Prev. Maint.	6	Complaints	9
Repair Costs	2	Insurance Costs	10

Price Range: $34-36,000

SPORT UTILITIES

MD-SZ SP. UT.: NISSAN PATHFINDER   6

Overall	6	Warranty	7
Crash Tests	9	Rollover	3
Safety Features	8	Fuel Econ.	2
Prev. Maint.	4	Complaints	9
Repair Costs	3	Insurance Costs	8

Price Range: $27-31,000

MID-SZ SP. UT.: TOYOTA 4RUNNER   6

Overall	6	Warranty	2
Crash Tests	9	Rollover	4
Safety Features	6	Fuel Econ.	2
Prev. Maint.	4	Complaints	10
Repair Costs	6	Insurance Costs	8

Price Range: $26-37,000

LARGE SP. UT.: LINC. NAVIGATOR   8

Overall	8	Warranty	5
Crash Tests	8	Rollover	4
Safety Features	6	Fuel Econ.	7
Prev. Maint.	8	Complaints	2
Repair Costs	10	Insurance Costs	10

Price Range: $43-47,000

PICKUPS

COMPACT PICKUP: FORD RANGER　6

Overall 6	Warranty 4
Crash Tests 9	Rollover 3
Safety Features 5	Fuel Econ. 2
Prev. Maint. 4	Complaints 8
Repair Costs 10	Insurance Costs 8

Price Range: $11-24,000

COMPACT PICKUP: MAZDA B-SER.　5

Overall 5	Warranty 4
Crash Tests 9	Rollover 3
Safety Features 4	Fuel Econ. 2
Prev. Maint. 8	Complaints 8
Repair Costs 6	Insurance Costs 6

Price Range: $13-19,000

STANDARD PICKUP: FORD F-SERIES 8

Overall 8	Warranty 4
Crash Tests 8	Rollover 3
Safety Features 4	Fuel Econ. 2
Prev. Maint. 7	Complaints 10
Repair Costs 10	Insurance Costs . . .10

Price Range: $17-24,000

THE RATINGS

Acura MDX

Daewoo Leganza

Mercedes-Benz C-Class

Saab 9-5

IN THIS CHAPTER

T his chapter provides an overview of the most important features of the new 2001 cars. In this section of *The Ultimate Car Book*, each two-page spread has all the information you'll need to make a smart choice. Here's what you'll find and how to interpret the data we've provided:

THE DESCRIPTION

The vast majority of information in *The Ultimate Car Book* is purely objective—we research and present the facts so that you can make an informed choice among the models that fit your taste and pocketbook. We have, however, included some general information to help you round out the hard facts. Much of the information in our vehicle description is subjective and you may not share our opinion. Nevertheless, like the photo, which gives you a general idea of what the car looks like, the description will give you a snapshot of some of the features we think are worth noting.

GENERAL INFORMATION

New for 2001: While most vehicles are not "all-new" for 2001, here we highlight some new features worth noting.

Corporate Twins: Often a car company will make numerous models on the same platform. This is a list of this car's twins.

Where Made: Here we tell you where the car was assembled and where its parts were manufactured. If more than one country is listed, the first is where the majority of parts originate or where the vehicle was assembled.

Year of Production: We generally recommend against buying a car during its first model year of production. Each year the model is made, the production process is usually improved, and there are fewer defects. Therefore, the longer a car has been made, the less likely you are to be plagued with manufacturing and design defects. On the other hand, the newer a car is, the more likely it is to have the latest in engineering.

Seating: This figure represents the maximum number of seating positions equipped with safety belts. When more than one number is listed (for example, 5/6/7) it means that different models have different seat configurations.

Theft Rating: This rating is given by the Insurance Institute for Highway Safety. It predicts the likelihood of the car being stolen or broken into based on its past history. If no information appears, it means that the car is too new to have a rating.

Prices 2001: This box contains sample price information. When available, we list the base and the most luxurious version of the car. The difference is often substantial. Usually the more expensive versions have fancy trim, larger engines, and lots of automatic equipment. The least expensive versions usually have manual transmissions and few extra features. In addition, some manufacturers try to sell popular options as part of a package.

In addition to the price range, we provide the expected dealer markup. Be prepared for higher retail prices when you get to the showroom. Manufacturers like to load their cars with factory options, and dealers like to add their own items such as fabric protection and paint sealant. Remember, prices and dealer costs can change during the year. Use these figures for general reference and comparisons, not as a precise indication of exactly how much the car you are interested in will cost. See page 92 for a buying service designed to ensure that you get the very best price.

Competition 2001: Here we tell you how the car stacks up with its competition. Use this information to compare the overall rating of similar cars and broaden your choice of new car possibilities. This may help you select a more economical or better performing car than the one you were originally considering. We've added page references so you can easily check out the competition. This list is only a guideline, not an all-inclusive list of every possible alternative.

'00 and '99 Models: One of the new features of *The Ultimate*

HOW TO USE THE RATINGS

Car Book 2001 is that we have included ratings for the '00 and '99 models of the new cars. By buying a used car you will save dramatically on the purchase price and may get protection from the new car warranty left on the car. Because cars today don't change that much from year to year, no one may know that you bought used! In this section we include a brief description of the last two model years, some price ranges, and photos of the vehicles. On the next page we have included the specific ratings for these previous model years.

THE RATINGS

These are ratings in nine important categories, as well as an overall comparative rating. We have adopted the Olympic rating system with "10" being the best.

Comparative Rating: This is the "bottom line." Using a combination of all of the key ratings, this tells how this car stacks up against the others on a scale of 1 to 10. **Due to the importance of crash tests, cars with no crash test results as of our publication date cannot be given an overall rating.** More recent results may be available from the Auto Safety Hotline at 800–424–9393.

Crash Test Performance: This rating compares the 2001 models against all crash test results to date. We give the best performers a 10 and the worst a 1. Remember to compare crash test results relative to other cars

in the same size class. For details, see the "Safety" chapter.

Safety Features: This is an evaluation of how much extra safety is built into the car. We give credit for airbags, ABS, daytime running lights, belt pre-tensioners, and built-in child safety seats. For details, see the "Safety" chapter.

Preventive Maintenance: Each manufacturer suggests a preventive maintenance schedule designed to keep the car in good shape and to protect your rights under the warranty. Those with the lowest PM costs get a 10 and the highest a 1. See the "Maintenance" chapter for the actual costs and more information.

Repair Costs: It is virtually impossible to predict exactly what any new car will cost you in repairs. As such, we take nine typical repairs that you are likely to experience after your warranty expires and compare those costs among this year's models. Those with the lowest cost get a 10 and the highest a 1. For details, see the "Maintenance" chapter.

Warranty: This is an overall assessment of the car's warranty when compared to all warranties. We give the highest-rated warranties a 10 and the lowest a 1. See the "Warranty" chapter for details.

Fuel Economy: Here we compare the EPA mileage ratings of each car. The gas misers get a 10 and the guzzlers get a 1. For more information, see the "Fuel Economy" chapter.

Rollover: Many consumers are aware that vehicles with higher centers of gravity could be more likely to roll over. Comparing the tendency of a vehicle to roll over is very difficult, as there is no agreed upon comparative rating system. Right now the government is in the process of adopting the rating system that we have been using called the static stability formula (SSF). We have compiled the SSF for all of the vehicles. This is by no means a comprehensive means of comparing the vehicles, and it is important to read the details behind the SSF that appear on page 27.

Complaints: This is where you'll find how your car stacks up against hundreds of others on the road, based on the U.S. government complaint data. If the car has not been around long enough to have developed a complaint history, it is given a 5 (average). The least complained about cars get a 10 and the most problematic a 1. See the "Complaints" chapter for details.

Insurance Costs: Insurance companies have rated most of the cars on the road to determine how they plan to charge for insurance. Here, you'll find whether you can expect a discount or a surcharge for what we expect to be the most popular model. If the car is likely to receive neither, we label it regular. Those receiving a discount get a 10; any cars with a surcharge get a 1; any with neither get a 5.

SAFETY

For most of us, safety is a critical consideration in buying a new car. This section will tell you, at a glance, whether or not the car has the safety features you care about.

Frontal Crash Tests: Here's where we tell you if the frontal crash test was either very good, good, average, poor, or very poor. Not all vehicles have been tested.

Side Crash Tests: We've also included the car's performance in side crash tests. Here we indicate whether the side crash test was very good, good, average, poor, or very poor. Not all vehicles have been tested.

Airbags: Here's where you'll find out how the occupants will benefit from this invaluable safety feature. We list the type of airbag system and differentiate de-powered, or next generation, airbags from older airbags which are not de-powered.

Anti-Lock Brakes: Find out if this model has two- or four-wheel anti-lock brakes, and whether you'll have to pay extra for it.

Daytime Running Lamps: Daytime running lights reduce your chances of being in a crash up to 40 percent by increasing the visibility of your vehicle. We indicate whether daytime running lights are standard, optional, or not available (none).

Built-in Child Safety Seats: Some manufacturers are offering "built-in" child safety seats which reduce the chances that your child rides unprotected.

Pretensioners: This valuable safety feature improves the seat belt's effectiveness at protecting occupants in a crash. During the collision, the seat belt not only locks but automatically retracts to keep passengers secure in the seat. Availability is indicated for both front occupants, unless otherwise noted.

SPECIFICATIONS

Here are the "nuts and bolts." In this section we have listed eight key specifications which enable you to evaluate how best that car meets your particular needs. We provide the information for what we expect to be the most popular model.

Fuel Economy: This is the EPA-rated fuel economy for city and highway driving measured in miles per gallon. Most models have a variety of fuel economy ratings because of different engine and transmission options. We've selected the combination expected to be most popular. Electric vehicles are rated in miles per kilowatt hour.

Driving Range: Given the car's expected fuel economy and gas tank size, this gives an idea of how far you can go on a full tank.

Bumpers: Here we indicate the damage-resistance of the car's bumpers. Weak bumpers meet only the basic government requirements at 2.5 mph. Strong bumpers are just as damage-resistant at 5 mph. This information is not available for all vehicles.

Parking Index: Using the car's length, wheelbase, and turning circle, we have calculated how easy it will be to maneuver this car in tight spots. This rating of very easy to very hard is an indicator of how much difficulty you may have parking.

Head/Leg Room: This tells how roomy the front seat is.

Interior Space: This tells how roomy the car is. For minivans and SUV's, see cargo space.

Cargo Space: This gives you the cubic feet available for cargo. For minivans, it's the back of the two front seats to the rear of the vehicle. In cars, it's the trunk space.

Tow Rating: Ratings of very low, low, average, high, and very high indicate the vehicle's relative ability to tow trailers or other loads. The vehicle's tow rating is also given.

YOUR NOTES

MAKE: _____   **MODEL:** _____   **PAGE:** _____

PRICE RANGE: _____

PROS:	CONS:

MAKE: _____   **MODEL:** _____   **PAGE:** _____

PRICE RANGE: _____

PROS:	CONS:

MAKE: _____   **MODEL:** _____   **PAGE:** _____

PRICE RANGE: _____

PROS:	CONS:

The all-new 2001, which was introduced last year, is actually built on the Accord/TL base. This means a larger wheelbase for a smoother, more luxurious ride. A change is the addition of a more powerful 3.2L V-6 as the base engine. If that's not enough, the S version bumps you up to 260 hp. The options include perforated leather seating and an in-dash navigation system. The navigation system comes with a DVD database that covers the entire U.S. On the safety side, dual stage airbags are standard.

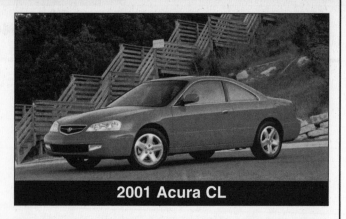

2001 Acura CL

General Information

New for 2001: All-new		**Year of Production:**	1
Twins:		**Seating:**	4
Where Made: U.S.		**Theft Rating:**	High

Prices 2001

Model	Retail	Markup
4-spd. auto.	$27,980	10%
With Navigation System	$29,980	10%
S-Coupe 4-spd. auto.	$30,330	10%
S-Coupe w/Navig. Sys.	$32,330	10%

Competition 2001

Model	POOR				GOOD		pg.
Acura CL							**118**
Infiniti I30					■		272
Lincoln Town Car						■	322
Pontiac Gr. Prix				■			386

'00 and '99 Models

The 1999 CL was sold thru 2000, and there was no actual 2000 model. The CL offers a standard 2.3-liter 4-cylinder engine. You may want to opt for the more powerful 3.0-liter V6, but you will take a slight hit in fuel economy. Standard safety features include dual airbags, 4-wheel ABS, rear headrests, front side window defoggers, keyless entry, and an anti-theft alarm.

Price Ranges 2000–1999

4-speed auto.	$20-$21,000
S-Coupe 4-speed auto.	$22-$23,000

2000 Acura CL

1999 Acura CL

RATINGS

	2001 POOR→GOOD	2000 POOR→GOOD	1999 POOR→GOOD
Comparative Rating			
Frontal Crash Tests			
Safety Features	7	6	6
Preventive Maintenance	1	1	1
Repair Costs	6	5	5
Warranty	5	6	6
Fuel Economy	5	5	5
Rollover (based on SSF; see pg. 30)	8	8	8
Complaints	5	1	10
Insurance Costs	5	10	10

SAFETY

	2001	2000	1999
Frontal Crash Tests	No Govt Results	No Govt Results	No Govt Results
Side Crash Tests	No Govt Results	No Govt Results	No Govt Results
Airbags	Dual/Side	Dual (nextgen)	Dual (nextgen)
Anti-Lock Brakes	4-Wheel	4-Wheel	4-Wheel
Day Running Lamps	None	None	None
Built-In Child Seats	None	None	None
Pretensioners	Standard	Standard	Standard

SPECIFICATIONS

	2001		2000		1999	
Fuel Economy (cty/hwy)	19/29	Average	24/31	Average	24/31	Average
Driving Range (miles)	412.8	Average	473	Vry. Long	473	Very Long
Bumpers	Strong		Strong		Strong	
Parking Index	Hard		Hard		Hard	
Head/Leg Room (in.)	37.5/42.4	Cramped	37.4/42.9	Cramped	37.4/42.9	Cramped
Interior Space (cu. ft.)	90	Cramped	84.7	Vry. Cramp.	84.7	Vry. Cramp.
Cargo Space (cu. ft.)	14	Small	12	Vry. Small	12	Very Small
Tow Rating (lbs.)						

The Integra continues into the 2001 model year unchanged. There are three versions of this Honda Civic-based hatchback: the base RS, mid-level LS, and the top of the line GS-R. The RS and LS trim levels both come with a 1.8-liter 140hp engine, plenty for this fairly light car. The GS-R boasts a beefier 1.8-liter 170hp VTEC which doesn't lose a bit in fuel economy. Handling isn't quite as good as you'd expect from a sports car, but it is better with the VTEC on the GS-R.

2001 Acura Integra

General Information

New for 2001: No major changes		**Year of Production:**	8
Twins:		**Seating:**	4
Where Made: Germany		**Theft Rating:**	Very High

Prices 2001

Model	Retail	Markup
3dr. Coupe LS 5-spd. man.	$19,300	11%
4dr. Sedan GS 5-spd. man.	$21,500	11%
3dr. Coupe GS 4-spd. auto.	$21,750	11%
4dr. Sedan GSR 4-spd. auto.	$22,500	11%

Competition 2001

Model	POOR					GOOD	pg.
Acura Integra							120
Olds Alero				■			370
Pontiac Gr Am		■					384
Pontiac Sunfire				■			390

'00 and '99 Models

An average crash test performer, safety features include dual airbags and 4-wheel ABS. Front seats are comfy and firm, but the back seats are non-existent. The Integra has gone several years without a redesign. Nevertheless, sports car buffs should check out the Integra.

Price Ranges 2000–1999

3dr. Coupe LS 5-sp. man.	$19-20,000
4dr. Sedan GS 5-sp. man.	$21-22,000
3dr. Coupe GS 4-sp. auto.	$20-21,000
4dr. Sedan GSR 4-sp. auto.	$22-23,000

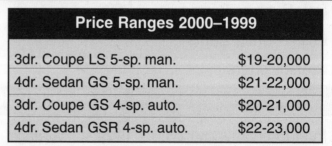

2000 Acura Integra

1999 Acura Integra

Acura Integra — Compact

RATINGS

	2001	2000	1999
	POOR → GOOD	POOR → GOOD	POOR → GOOD
Comparative Rating	—	—	—
Frontal Crash Tests	—	6	6
Safety Features	6	6	6
Preventive Maintenance	1	1	1
Repair Costs	4	4	4
Warranty	5	6	6
Fuel Economy	7	6	6
Rollover (based on SSF; see pg. 30)	8	8	8
Complaints	10	10	9
Insurance Costs	1	1	1

SAFETY

	2001	2000	1999
Frontal Crash Tests	Average	Average	Average
Side Crash Tests	No Govt Results	No Govt Results	No Govt Results
Airbags	Dual (nextgen)	Dual (nextgen)	Dual (nextgen)
Anti-Lock Brakes	4-Wheel	4-Wheel	4-Wheel
Day Running Lamps	None	None	None
Built-In Child Seats	None	None	None
Pretensioners	Standard	None	None

SPECIFICATIONS

	2001		2000		1999	
Fuel Economy (cty/hwy)	25/31	Average	25/32	Average	25/32	Average
Driving Range (miles)	369.6	Short	376.2	Short	376.2	Short
Bumpers	Strong		Strong		Strong	
Parking Index	Vry. Easy		Vry. Easy		Vry. Easy	
Head/Leg Room (in.)	38.6/42.7	Average	38.6/42.7	Average	38.6/42.7	Average
Interior Space (cu. ft.)	83	Vry. Cramp.	77.1	Vry. Cramp.	77.1	Vry. Cramp.
Cargo Space (cu. ft.)	12	Vry. Small	13.3	Small	13.3	Small
Tow Rating (lbs.)						

The all-new MDX blurs the line between sport utility vehicles and sedans. The inside, with standard leather and a dash similar to the Acura 3.2 TL, is like a large European luxury sedan. The suspension system will likely offer a ride more like a sedan than an SUV and the engine is much peppier than your typical off-roader. Acura claims that the all-wheel drive transmission will provide a smoother ride on paved roads. The second and third seats split and fold flat and you can get a 5-speed stick. The MDX is based on the Odyssey.

2001 Acura MDX

General Information

New for 2001: All-new	**Year of Production:** 1
Twins:	**Seating:**
Where Made: Japan	**Theft Rating:**

Prices 2001

Model	Retail	Markup
Base	$34,370	12%
w/Navigation System	$36,370	12%
w/ith Touring Package	$36,970	12%
w/Touring Pack./Navig. Sys.	$38,970	12%

Competition 2001

Model	POOR				GOOD	pg.
Acura MDX						122
Merc-Bz M-Class			■			340
Chev. Blazer						162
Jeep Cherokee			■			284

'00 and '99 Models

Price Ranges 2000–1999

MODEL WAS NOT PRODUCED THIS YEAR

2000 Model

MODEL WAS NOT PRODUCED THIS YEAR

1999 Model

	2001	2000	1999

RATINGS

	POOR — GOOD	POOR — GOOD	POOR — GOOD
Comparative Rating			
Frontal Crash Tests			
Safety Features	7		
Preventive Maintenance			
Repair Costs			
Warranty	5		
Fuel Economy	3		
Rollover (based on SSF; see pg. 30)	6		
Complaints	5		
Insurance Costs	5		

SAFETY

Frontal Crash Tests	No Govt Results		
Side Crash Tests	No Govt Results		
Airbags	Dual/Side		
Anti-Lock Brakes	4-Wheel		
Day Running Lamps	None		
Built-In Child Seats	None		
Pretensioners	Standard		

SPECIFICATIONS

Fuel Economy (cty/hwy)	17/23	Poor	
Driving Range (miles)	384	Short	
Bumpers	Strong		
Parking Index	Vry. Easy		
Head/Leg Room (in.)	38.7/41.5	Cramped	
Interior Space (cu. ft.)	161.5	Vry. Roomy	
Cargo Space (cu. ft.)	49.6	Large	
Tow Rating (lbs.)			

The Acura RL remains one of Acura's most luxurious models. Leather interiors, heated front seats, front and rear headrests, automatic climate control, and heated door mirrors are among the numerous features found on the RL, one of the pricier Acuras. You'll find a 3.5-liter V6 engine with standard ABS brakes. In terms of creature comforts and style, the RL competes with mid-size European luxury sedans.

2001 Acura RL

General Information

New for 2001: No major changes		**Year of Production:**	6
Twins:		**Seating:**	4
Where Made: Japan		**Theft Rating:**	Low

Prices 2001*

Model	Retail	Markup
4-spd. auto.	$42,000	14%
4-spd. auto. w/Navig. Sys.	$44,000	14%

Competition 2001

Model	POOR				GOOD	pg.
Acura RL					■	124
Audi A8				■		132
Ford Cr. Victoria					■	216
Lincoln Town Car					■	322

'00 and '99 Models

In 1999, the RL received side airbags and a sturdier chassis. As Acura's flagship, luxury is a key feature to be found throughout the RL's interior. Along with excellent safety features like side airbags, the RL has good crash tests which carry through to 2001.

Price Ranges 2000–1999

4-speed auto. w/Navigation sys.	$41-42,000
4-speed auto.	$41-42,000

2000 Acura RL

1999 Acura RL

Acura RL   Large

	2001	2000	1999

RATINGS

	POOR ─ GOOD	POOR ─ GOOD	POOR ─ GOOD
Comparative Rating	9	8	8
Frontal Crash Tests	7	7	7
Safety Features	7	7	7
Preventive Maintenance	1	1	1
Repair Costs	10	2	3
Warranty	5	6	6
Fuel Economy	4	3	3
Rollover (based on SSF; see pg. 30)	8	8	8
Complaints	10	10	9
Insurance Costs	10	10	10

SAFETY

	2001	2000	1999
Frontal Crash Tests	Good	Good	Good
Side Crash Tests	No Govt Results	No Govt Results	No Govt Results
Airbags	Dual/Side (nextgen)	Dual/Side (nextgen)	Dual/Side (nextgen)
Anti-Lock Brakes	4-Wheel	4-Wheel	4-Wheel
Day Running Lamps	None	None	None
Built-In Child Seats	None	None	None
Pretensioners	None	None	None

SPECIFICATIONS

	2001		2000		1999	
Fuel Economy (cty/hwy)	18/24	Poor	18/24	Poor	18/24	Poor
Driving Range (miles)	378	Short	378	Short	378	Short
Bumpers	Strong		Strong		Strong	
Parking Index	Average		Average		Average	
Head/Leg Room (in.)	38.8/42.1	Average	38.8/42.1	Average	38.8/42.1	Average
Interior Space (cu. ft.)	96	Average	96.5	Average	96.5	Average
Cargo Space (cu. ft.)	15	Small	14	Small	14	Small
Tow Rating (lbs.)						

The Acura TL, short for "Touring Luxury," is clearly aimed at the luxury entry-level, Lexus ES300 buyer. The TL's only engine choice, a 3.2-liter, gives plenty of power at the expense of fuel economy. Leather interior, automatic climate control, side window defoggers, and other extras contribute to a high base price. The interior is spacious, and the ride is good. Based on the Honda Accord, the TL comes fully loaded with standard features.

2001 Acura TL

General Information

New for 2001: No major changes		**Year of Production:**	3
Twins:		**Seating:**	4
Where Made: U.S.		**Theft Rating:**	Very Low

Prices 2001

Model	Retail	Markup
4-spd. auto.	$28,550	11%
4-spd. auto. w/Navig. Sys.	$30,550	11%

Competition 2001

Model	POOR					GOOD	pg.
Acura TL						■	126
Ford Cr. Victoria					■		216
Audi A8						■	132
Buick Century				■			142

'00 and '99 Models

For 1999, the TL was redesigned completely from bumper to bumper. Standard features include dual airbags and standard ABS, and traction control is also a great option.

Price Ranges 2000–1999

4-speed auto.	$27-29,000

2000 Acura TL

1999 Acura TL

Acura TL   Large

	2001	2000	1999

RATINGS

	POOR → GOOD	POOR → GOOD	POOR → GOOD
Comparative Rating			
Frontal Crash Tests			
Safety Features	7	7	6
Preventive Maintenance	1	1	1
Repair Costs	6	4	3
Warranty	5	6	6
Fuel Economy	5	4	4
Rollover (based on SSF; see pg. 30)	8	8	8
Complaints	5	6	7
Insurance Costs	10	5	5

SAFETY

	2001	2000	1999
Frontal Crash Tests	To Be Tested	No Govt Results	No Govt Results
Side Crash Tests	No Govt Results	No Govt Results	No Govt Results
Airbags	Dual/Side (nextgen)	Dual/Side (nextgen)	Dual (nextgen)
Anti-Lock Brakes	4-Wheel	4-Wheel	4-Wheel
Day Running Lamps	None	None	None
Built-In Child Seats	None	None	None
Pretensioners	None	None	None

SPECIFICATIONS

	2001		2000		1999	
Fuel Economy (cty/hwy)	19/29	Average	19/29	Average	19/27	Poor
Driving Range (miles)	412.8	Average	412.8	Average	395.6	Short
Bumpers	Strong		Strong		Strong	
Parking Index	Average		Average		Average	
Head/Leg Room (in.)	39.9/42.4	Roomy	39.9/42.4	Roomy	39.9/42.4	Roomy
Interior Space (cu. ft.)	96	Average	96.5	Average	96.5	Average
Cargo Space (cu. ft.)	14	Small	14.3	Small	14.3	Small
Tow Rating (lbs.)						

There are no appearance changes for the A4 for 2001. The power on the base 1.8T engine was increased to 170 hp and the engine is classified as an UltraLow Emission Vehicle. A head airbag system and better warranty are also available. There is a sport package which lowers the car, tightens the suspension, and adds some sporty wheels. Another option is to have the shift controls added to the steering wheel. The interior comes in three styles, and a "cold weather" package is available that includes a heated door lock.

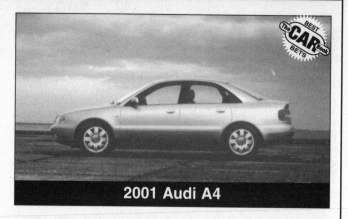

2001 Audi A4

General Information

New for 2001: All-new		**Year of Production:**	1
Twins:		**Seating:**	5
Where Made: Germany		**Theft Rating:**	

Prices 2001

Model*	Retail	Markup
1.8T Sdn man./FrontTrak	$24,540	12%
1.8T Avant man./Quattro	$27,300	12%
2.8 Sdn auto. tip/FrontTrak	$30,300	12%
2.8 Avant man./Quattro	$31,900	12%

*All 5 spd.

Competition 2001

Model	POOR				GOOD	pg.
Audi A4					■	128
Buick Century			■			142
Lexus ES300					■	302
Ford Taurus					■	234

'00 and '99 Models

The S4 comes with a powerful 2.8-liter V6 engine. For the A4, the engine choices are a 1.8-liter 4-cylinder or a 2.8-liter V6. Audi's all wheel drive system, called Quattro, offers fine handling and traction on slick roads and is available on both models. The A4/S4's top-notch design and excellent safety features make it an excellent, albeit pricey, choice.

Price Ranges 2000–1999

1.8T Sedan 5-speed man.	$23-24,000
1.8T Avant 5-speed man./Quattro	$25-26,000
2.8 Sedan 5-speed auto. tip	$28-29,000
2.8 Avant 5-speed man./Quattro	$31-32,000

2000 Audi A4

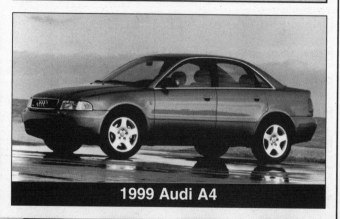

1999 Audi A4

Audi A4   Intermediate

	2001	2000	1999

RATINGS

	POOR → GOOD	POOR → GOOD	POOR → GOOD
Comparative Rating	9	7	5
Frontal Crash Tests	9	9	9
Safety Features	8	8	8
Preventive Maintenance	10	10	5
Repair Costs	2	2	2
Warranty	10	9	10
Fuel Economy	6	5	5
Rollover (based on SSF; see pg. 30)	7	7	7
Complaints	5	2	1
Insurance Costs	5	5	5

SAFETY

	2001	2000	1999
Frontal Crash Tests	No Govt Results	Very Good	Very Good
Side Crash Tests	No Govt Results	No Govt Results	No Govt Results
Airbags	Dual/Head	Dual/Side (nextgen)	Dual/Side (nextgen)
Anti-Lock Brakes	Standard	4-Wheel	4-Wheel
Day Running Lamps		None	None
Built-In Child Seats	None	None	None
Pretensioners	Standard	Standard	Standard

SPECIFICATIONS

	2001		2000		1999	
Fuel Economy (cty/hwy)	23/32	Average	23/32	Average	23/32	Average
Driving Range (miles)	456.5	Vry. Long	437.25	Long	451	Long
Bumpers	Strong		Strong		Strong	
Parking Index	Easy		Easy		Easy	
Head/Leg Room (in.)	38.2/41.3	Vry. Cramp.	38.2/41.3	Vry. Cramp.	38.1/41.3	Vry. Cramp.
Interior Space (cu. ft.)	88	Cramped	120.2	Vry. Roomy	87.7	Cramped
Cargo Space (cu. ft.)	14	Small	31.3	Average	14	Small
Tow Rating (lbs.)						

Like the A4, the Audi A6 is available in a sedan and Avant wagon version. In addition to the standard 2.8-liter V6, you can now choose from a 2.7-liter V6 or a 4.2-liter V8 engine. You'll find several safety features including next generation front airbags, frontal side airbags, lockable head rests for front passengers, rear side airbags, and optional all-wheel drive. It's too bad the government has not crash tested the A6.

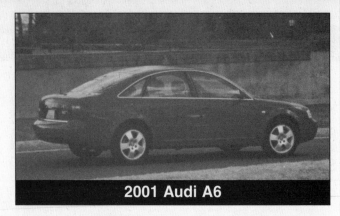
2001 Audi A6

General Information

New for 2001: No major changes		**Year of Production:**	4
Twins:		**Seating:**	5
Where Made: Germany		**Theft Rating:**	

Prices 2001

Model	Retail	Markup
2.8L FrontTrak Sedan 4-dr.	$34,400	12%
2.8L Quattro Avant wgn. 4-dr.	$37,350	12%
2.7T Quattro Sedan 4-dr.	$39,500	12%
4.2 Quattro Sedan 4-dr.	$49,400	12%

Competition 2001

Model	POOR				GOOD	pg.
Audi A6						130
Lexus ES300					■	302
Lincoln Town Car					■	322
Buick Regal			■			148

'00 and '99 Models

First introduced in 1995, the A6 is essentially a stretched-out A4. The roofline was lowered to give the A6 a sportier coupe look. This is essentially a performance car disguised as a luxury sedan. A wagon version, the Avant, joined the sedan in 1999.

Price Ranges 2000–1999

Sedan 5-speed auto. tip	$33-34,000
Avant 5-speed auto. tip	$36-37,000
2.7T Sedan 5-speed auto. tip	$38-39,000
4.2 Sedan 5-speed auto. tip	$48-49,000

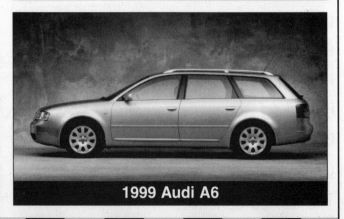
2000 Audi A6   **1999 Audi A6**

Audi A6 — Intermediate

	2001	2000	1999

RATINGS

	POOR → GOOD	POOR → GOOD	POOR → GOOD
Comparative Rating			
Frontal Crash Tests			
Safety Features	8	8	8
Preventive Maintenance	10	10	5
Repair Costs	2	2	2
Warranty	10	9	10
Fuel Economy	4	3	3
Rollover (based on SSF; see pg. 30)	7	7	7
Complaints	1	1	1
Insurance Costs	10	10	10

SAFETY

	2001	2000	1999
Frontal Crash Tests	No Govt Results	No Govt Results	No Govt Results
Side Crash Tests	No Govt Results	No Govt Results	No Govt Results
Airbags	Dual/Side (nextgen)	Dual/Side (nextgen)	Dual/Side (nextgen)
Anti-Lock Brakes	4-Wheel	4-Wheel	4-Wheel
Day Running Lamps	None	None	None
Built-In Child Seats	None	None	None
Pretensioners	Standard	Standard	Standard

SPECIFICATIONS

	2001		2000		1999	
Fuel Economy (cty/hwy)	17/25	Poor	17/27	Poor	17/27	Poor
Driving Range (miles)	388.5	Short	407	Average	407	Average
Bumpers	Strong		Strong		Strong	
Parking Index	Hard		Hard		Hard	
Head/Leg Room (in.)	39.3/41.3	Cramped	39.3/41.3	Cramped	39.3/41.3	Cramped
Interior Space (cu. ft.)	98	Average	98.3	Average	108.3	Roomy
Cargo Space (cu. ft.)	15	Small	17.2	Average	17.2	Average
Tow Rating (lbs.)						

Audi A8 Large

Audi's luxury flagship comes with lots of extras. Its unique aluminum frame is 40% lighter than steel frames. Nevertheless, the A8 performed excellently in government crash tests, proving that lighter weight does not have to compromise safety. Passengers are protected by front and side airbags for front and rear occupants. The A8 comes with a 3.7-liter V8 engine or an all-wheel drive 4.2-liter V8 Quattro version.

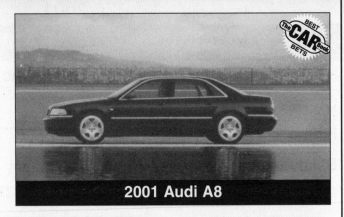

2001 Audi A8

General Information

New for 2001: No major changes	Year of Production:	5
Twins:	Seating:	5
Where Made: Germany	Theft Rating:	

Prices 2001

Model	Retail	Markup
4.2 Base Quattro Sedan 4-dr.	$62,200	13%
L 4.2 Quattro Sedan 4-dr.	$67,900	13%

Competition 2001

Model	POOR					GOOD		pg.
Audi A8							■	**132**
Cadillac Deville					■			152
Infiniti I30					■			272
Buick LeSabre						■		144

'00 and '99 Models

With an all-aluminum body and the choice of two V8 engines, the A8 is Audi's best hope for taking on the big, luxury sedans of Mercedes, BMW, and Lexus. While expensive, the A8 illustrates the best of what luxury automaker Audi has to offer.

Price Ranges 2000–1999

4.2 Sedan 5-speed auto. tip	$62-65,000
L 4.2 Sdn 5-speed auto. tip	none

2000 Audi A8

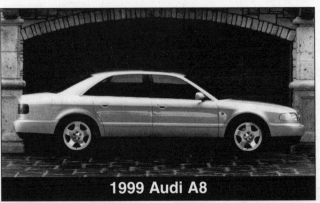

1999 Audi A8

Audi A8 — Large

	2001	2000	1999

RATINGS

	POOR — GOOD	POOR — GOOD	POOR — GOOD
Comparative Rating	10	10	10
Frontal Crash Tests	10	10	10
Safety Features	8	8	8
Preventive Maintenance	10	10	10
Repair Costs	1	1	1
Warranty	10	9	10
Fuel Economy	4	3	3
Rollover (based on SSF; see pg. 30)	8	8	8
Complaints	9	9	
Insurance Costs	5	5	5

SAFETY

	2001	2000	1999
Frontal Crash Tests	Very Good	Very Good	Very Good
Side Crash Tests	No Govt Results	No Govt Results	No Govt Results
Airbags	Dual/Side (nextgen)	Dual/Side (nextgen)	Dual/Side (nextgen)
Anti-Lock Brakes	4-Wheel	4-Wheel	4-Wheel
Day Running Lamps	None	None	None
Built-In Child Seats	None	None	None
Pretensioners	Standard	Standard	Standard

SPECIFICATIONS

	2001		2000		1999	
Fuel Economy (cty/hwy)	17/25	Poor	17/25	Poor	17/25	Poor
Driving Range (miles)	483	Vry. Long	483	Vry. Long	483	Vry. Long
Bumpers	Strong		Strong		Strong	
Parking Index	Vry. Hard		Vry. Hard		Vry. Hard	
Head/Leg Room (in.)	38.9/41.3	Cramped	38.9/41.3	Cramped	38.9/41.3	Cramped
Interior Space (cu. ft.)	104	Roomy	99.8	Average	99.8	Average
Cargo Space (cu. ft.)	18	Average	17.6	Average	17.6	Average
Tow Rating (lbs.)						

For 2001, BMW's entry level 3-Series gains a new range of engine choices for 6-cylinder engines. The sport wagon and coupe were redesigned in 2000 and the sedans in 1999. Engine choices range from the base 2.5-liter inline 6 to the optional 2.8-liter inline 6. The 1.8-liter 4-cylinder was dropped. Safety features include front and side airbags, adjustable rear headrests, and traction control along with 4-wheel ABS and dual airbags.

2001 BMW 3-Series

General Information

New for 2001: No major changes	**Year of Production:** 3
Twins:	**Seating:** 5
Where Made: Germany	**Theft Rating:** Very High

Prices 2001

Model	Retail	Markup
325i Sedan 5-spd. man.	$26,990	10%
325i Sport wgn. 5-spd. auto.	$30,700	12%
330i Sedan 5-spd. man.	$33,990	11%
330Ci Conv. 5-spd. auto.	$43,700	11%

Competition 2001

Model	POOR				GOOD		pg.
BMW 3-Series							**134**
Mitsu. Galant		■					350
Olds Alero			■				370
Pontiac Gr. Am		■					384

'00 and '99 Models

The coupe and sport wagon received their redesign in 2000. The engine selection is extensive, ranging from a 1.8-liter base to a 2.5-liter engine. No crash tests have been performed on the redesigned models.

Price Ranges 2000–1999

325i Sedan 5-speed auto.	$26-27,000
325Ci Coupe 5-speed auto.	$28-29,000
325i Sport Wagon 5-speed auto.	$29-30,000
325Ci Convertible 5-speed auto.	$34-35,000

2000 BMW 3-Series

1999 BMW 3-Series

BMW 3-Series — Compact

	2001	2000	1999

RATINGS

	POOR — GOOD	POOR — GOOD	POOR — GOOD
Comparative Rating			
Frontal Crash Tests			
Safety Features	8	9	8
Preventive Maintenance	10	10	10
Repair Costs	3	4	4
Warranty	7	9	8
Fuel Economy	5	4	5
Rollover (based on SSF; see pg. 30)	7	7	7
Complaints	5	5	7
Insurance Costs	5	1	1

SAFETY

	2001	2000	1999
Frontal Crash Tests	No Govt Results	No Govt Results	No Govt Results
Side Crash Tests	No Govt Results	No Govt Results	No Govt Results
Airbags	Dual/Side (nextgen)	Dual/Side (nextgen)	Dual/Side
Anti-Lock Brakes	4-Wheel	4-Wheel	4-Wheel
Day Running Lamps	Optional	Standard	None
Built-In Child Seats	None	None	None
Pretensioners	Standard	Standard	Standard

SPECIFICATIONS

	2001		2000		1999	
Fuel Economy (cty/hwy)	20/29	Average	21/29	Average	23/32	Average
Driving Range (miles)	406.7	Average	415	Average	456.5	Vry. Long
Bumpers	Weak		Weak		Strong	
Parking Index	Easy		Easy		Easy	
Head/Leg Room (in.)	38.4/37.5	Vry. Cramp.	38.4/37.5	Vry. Cramp.	38.4/37.5	Vry. Cramp.
Interior Space (cu. ft.)	91	Cramped	90.8	Cramped	90.8	Cramped
Cargo Space (cu. ft.)	11	Vry. Small	10.7	Vry. Small	10.7	Vry. Small
Tow Rating (lbs.)						

BMW 5-Series Large

Since its redesign, the 5-Series is roomier, more luxurious, and loaded with safety features. Like the 3-Series, the 5-Series has a range of 6-cylinder engines. Choose from a 2.8-liter inline 6 or the more powerful 4.4-liter V8 engine. Standard safety features include dual and side airbags and a head airbag for protection in a rollover. Also standard is dynamic stability control, which helps on slippery roads. Two more side airbags are optional for rear seats.

2001 BMW 5-Series

General Information

New for 2001: No major changes	**Year of Production:** 5
Twins:	**Seating:** 5
Where Made: Germany	**Theft Rating:** Very High

Prices 2001

Model	Retail	Markup
525i Sedan man	$35,400	11%
525i Wagon auto	$38,500	11%
540iT Wagon auto	$54,700	11%
540i Sedan man	$53,900	11%

Competition 2001

Model	POOR					GOOD	pg.
BMW 5-Series							**136**
Chrys. Concorde				■			188
Audi A8						■	132
Buick Regal					■		148

'00 and '99 Models

In 1997, BMW gave the 5-Series a much-needed redesign. 2000 saw BMW introduce the highly anticipated M5, featuring a muscular 5.0-liter 400 hp V8 engine. Unfortunately, no crash test results are available.

Price Ranges 2000–1999

525i Sedan	$38-39,000
525i Wagon	$40-41,000
540iT Wagon	$53-54,000
540i Sedan	$51-53,000

2000 BMW 5-Series

1999 BMW 5-Series

	2001	2000	1999

RATINGS

	POOR → GOOD	POOR → GOOD	POOR → GOOD
Comparative Rating			
Frontal Crash Tests			
Safety Features	8	9	8
Preventive Maintenance	10	10	10
Repair Costs	3	2	3
Warranty	7	9	8
Fuel Economy	5	4	4
Rollover (based on SSF; see pg. 30)	7	7	7
Complaints	7	8	10
Insurance Costs	5	5	5

SAFETY

	2001	2000	1999
Frontal Crash Tests	No Govt Results	No Govt Results	No Govt Results
Side Crash Tests	No Govt Results	No Govt Results	No Govt Results
Airbags	Dual/Side (nextgen)	Dual/Side (nextgen)	Dual/Side (nextgen)
Anti-Lock Brakes	4-Wheel	4-Wheel	4-Wheel
Day Running Lamps	Optional	Standard	None
Built-In Child Seats	None	None	None
Pretensioners	Standard	Standard	Standard

SPECIFICATIONS

	2001		2000		1999	
Fuel Economy (cty/hwy)	20/29	Average	21/29	Average	20/29	Average
Driving Range (miles)	453.25	Long	462.5	Vry. Long	453.25	Long
Bumpers	Weak		Weak		Weak	
Parking Index	Average		Average		Average	
Head/Leg Room (in.)	38.7/41.7	Cramped	38.7/41.7	Cramped	38.7/41.7	Cramped
Interior Space (cu. ft.)	93	Cramped	94.9	Average	92.5	Cramped
Cargo Space (cu. ft.)	11	Vry. Small	11.1	Vry. Small	11.1	Vry. Small
Tow Rating (lbs.)						

Introduced in May 2000, the X5 zips into 2001 unchanged. With a fairly unique inline 6-cylinder engine, which BMW claims is smoother and quieter, this is the sports car of the sport ute crowd. In addition to the solid BMW feel and their brand of no-nonsense luxury, the X5 comes with options such as a high-pressure liquid headlight cleaning system and rain-sensing wipers. Rear side airbags are an option and other safety features include dual deployment airbags and standard front side airbags.

2001 BMW X5

General Information

New for 2001: All-new	**Year of Production:** 1
Twins:	**Seating:** 5
Where Made: Germany	**Theft Rating:**

Prices 2001

Model	Retail	Markup
3.0i 5-spd. auto.	$38,900	11%
4.4i 5-spd. auto.	$49,400	11%

Competition 2001

Model	POOR				GOOD	pg.
BMW X5						**138**
Honda Passport	■					252
Merc-Bz M-Class		■				340
Ford Explorer			■			224

'00 and '99 Models

This five-passenger off-roader comes with a choice of engines, although the standard 3.0 should be fine and more fuel-efficient. A spot for a built-in phone, programmable key locks, and a variety of trailering and roof rack assemblies mean lots of choices will be on the used car lots.

Price Ranges 2000–1999

PHOTO NOT AVAILABLE

2000 Model

MODEL WAS NOT PRODUCED THIS YEAR

1999 Model

BMW X5 — Mid-Size Sport Utility

	2001	2000	1999

RATINGS

	POOR — GOOD	POOR — GOOD	POOR — GOOD
Comparative Rating			
Frontal Crash Tests			
Safety Features	6	6	
Preventive Maintenance			
Repair Costs			
Warranty	7	9	
Fuel Economy	2	2	
Rollover (based on SSF; see pg. 30)	5	5	
Complaints	5	5	
Insurance Costs	5	5	

SAFETY

	2001	2000	1999
Frontal Crash Tests	No Govt Results	No Govt Results	
Side Crash Tests	No Govt Results	No Govt Results	
Airbags	Dual	Dual	
Anti-Lock Brakes	4-Wheel	4-Wheel	
Day Running Lamps	Optional	Optional	
Built-In Child Seats	None	None	
Pretensioners	Standard	Standard	

SPECIFICATIONS

	2001		2000		1999
Fuel Economy (cty/hwy)	15/20	Vry. Poor	15/20	Vry. Poor	
Driving Range (miles)	425.25	Long	425.25	Long	
Bumpers	Weak				
Parking Index	Hard		Hard		
Head/Leg Room (in.)	38.9/		38.9/		
Interior Space (cu. ft.)					
Cargo Space (cu. ft.)					
Tow Rating (lbs.)					

For 2001, there are no major changes for this popular roadster. The Z3 is a convertible based on the 3-Series platform. The engine choices include the base 2.5-liter inline 6 engine, an optional 2.8-liter inline 6, and a beefier 3.2-liter inline 6. Dual and side airbags are standard as well as 4-wheel ABS. The Z3 is an attractive and popular sports car. This vehicle is extremely (many say too) fast, so be careful!

2001 BMW Z3

General Information

New for 2001: No major changes	**Year of Production:**	6
Twins:	**Seating:**	2
Where Made: Germany	**Theft Rating:**	

Prices 2001

Model	Retail	Markup
Coupe 5-spd. man.	$37,700	11%
Coupe 5-spd. auto.	$39,000	11%
Roadster 3.0i 5-spd. man.	$37,900	11%
Roadster 3.0i 5-spd. auto.	$39,200	11%

Competition 2001

Model	POOR				GOOD		pg.
BMW Z3							**140**
Pontiac Gr. Prix					■		386
Ford Mustang				■			230
Pontiac Sunfire				■			390

'00 and '99 Models

Ever since its splashy debut in a James Bond film, the Z3 has become a surefire way to turn heads on the road. The original 1.9-liter 4-cylinder engine was upgraded to the 2.8-liter inline 6 or the powerful 3.2-liter engine.

Price Ranges 2000–1999

Coupe 5-speed auto.	$36-37,000
Roadster 3.0i 5-speed auto.	$36-37,000

2000 BMW Z3

1999 BMW Z3

BMW Z3 — Compact

	2001	2000	1999

RATINGS

	2001 (POOR–GOOD)	2000 (POOR–GOOD)	1999 (POOR–GOOD)
Comparative Rating		10	
Frontal Crash Tests*		10	
Safety Features	8	9	8
Preventive Maintenance	10	10	10
Repair Costs	5	2	3
Warranty	7	9	8
Fuel Economy	5	4	4
Rollover (based on SSF, see pg. 25)	8	8	8
Complaints	8	8	9
Insurance Costs	10	10	10

SAFETY

	2001	2000	1999
Frontal Crash Tests	No Govt Results	Very Good	No Govt Results
Side Crash Tests	No Govt Results	No Govt Results	No Govt Results
Airbags	Dual/Side (nextgen)	Dual (nextgen)	Dual/Side
Anti-Lock Brakes	4-Wheel	4-Wheel	4-Wheel
Day Running Lamps	Optional	Standard	None
Built-In Child Seats	None	None	None
Pretensioners	Standard	Standard	Standard

SPECIFICATIONS

	2001		2000		1999	
Fuel Economy (cty/hwy)	21/28	Average	19/26	Poor	19/26	Poor
Driving Range (miles)	330.75	Vry. Short	303.75	Vry. Short	303.75	Vry. Short
Bumpers	Weak		Weak		Weak	
Parking Index	Vry. Easy		Vry. Easy		Vry. Easy	
Head/Leg Room (in.)	37.6/41.8	Vry. Cramp.	37.6/41.8	Vry. Cramp.	37.6/41.8	Vry. Cramp.
Interior Space (cu. ft.)	47	Vry. Cramp.	47	Vry. Cramp.	47	Vry. Cramp.
Cargo Space (cu. ft.)	5	Vry. Small	5	Vry. Small	5	Vry. Small
Tow Rating (lbs.)						

*To be tested in 2001.

Buick Century Intermediate

The 2001 Century continues unchanged this year. Last year the base 3.1-liter V6 received more horsepower and dual airbags; traction control, 4-wheel ABS and daytime running lamps are standard. The optional child safety seat is a must-have for parents. The interior is fairly spacious. The optional OnStar communications system lets you get directions or get help in an emergency. Although an average performer in government crash tests, the Century competes well.

2001 Buick Century

General Information

New for 2001: No major changes		**Year of Production:**	5
Twins: Regal, Intrigue, Grand Prix		**Seating:**	6
Where Made: U.S.		**Theft Rating:**	Very Low

Prices 2001

Model	Retail	Markup
Custom 4-spd. Auto	$19,840	9%
Limited 4-spd. Auto	$22,871	9%

Competition 2001

Model	POOR				GOOD	pg.
Buick Century				■		**142**
Chev. Malibu			■			170
Ford Taurus					■	234
Lexus ES300					■	302

'00 and '99 Models

Buick brought the Century into the next century with a drastic and much-needed redesign in 1997. 2000 saw an increase in horsepower and a change in exterior. The redesign offered sleeker styling and more safety features. Great attention was paid to interior comfort.

Price Ranges 2000–1999

4-sp. auto.	$18-20,000
Limited 4-sp. auto.	$20-22,000

2000 Buick Century

1999 Buick Century

	2001	2000	1999

RATINGS

	POOR — GOOD	POOR — GOOD	POOR — GOOD
Comparative Rating	7	6	8
Frontal Crash Tests	6	6	6
Safety Features	7	7	7
Preventive Maintenance	6	5	6
Repair Costs	8	3	8
Warranty	2	2	2
Fuel Economy	5	4	4
Rollover (based on SSF; see pg. 30)	8	8	8
Complaints	5	6	6
Insurance Costs	10	10	10

SAFETY

	2001	2000	1999
Frontal Crash Tests	Average	Average	Average
Side Crash Tests	Average	Average	Average
Airbags	Dual (nextgen)	Dual (nextgen)	Dual
Anti-Lock Brakes	4-Wheel	4-Wheel	4-Wheel
Day Running Lamps	Standard	Standard	Standard
Built-In Child Seats	Optional	Optional	Optional
Pretensioners	None	None	None

SPECIFICATIONS

	2001		2000		1999	
Fuel Economy (cty/hwy)	20/29	Average	20/30	Average	20/29	Average
Driving Range (miles)	428.75	Long	437.5	Long	428.75	Long
Bumpers	Strong		Strong		Strong	
Parking Index	Hard		Hard		Hard	
Head/Leg Room (in.)	39.4/42.4	Average	39.4/42.4	Average	39.4/42.4	Average
Interior Space (cu. ft.)	102	Roomy	118.5	Vry. Roomy	118.5	Vry. Roomy
Cargo Space (cu. ft.)	17	Average	16.7	Average	16.7	Average
Tow Rating (lbs.)	1000	Vry. Low	1000	Vry. Low	1000	Vry. Low

Buick LeSabre Large

The LeSabre was all-new for last year, getting a stiffer body and new safety innovations. It continues into 2001 with no changes. Most notably, side airbags were added to the list of standard safety features. Seats were engineered to protect from whiplash, and ABS and dual airbags are still standard. StabiliTrak, an added option, helps the driver maintain control in all conditions.

2001 Buick LeSabre

General Information

New for 2001: No major changes	**Year of Production:** 2
Twins: Pontiac Bonneville	**Seating:** 6
Where Made: U.S.	**Theft Rating:** Very Low

Prices 2001

Model	Retail	Markup
4-spd. auto.	$24,107	9%
Limited 4-spd. auto.	$28,796	9%

Competition 2001

Model	POOR				GOOD	pg.
Buick LeSabre					▉	144
Ford Cr. Victoria				▉		216
VW Passat				▉		452
Infiniti I30			▉			272

'00 and '99 Models

In 2000, Buick introduced the all-new LeSabre. Equipped with the powerful 3.8-liter V6 engine, the LeSabre offers improved handling, passenger comfort, and solid performance. The '99 model is definitely dated.

Price Ranges 2000–1999

4-sp. auto.	$22-24,000
Limited 4-sp. auto.	$25-28,000

2000 Buick LeSabre

1999 Buick LeSabre

Buick LeSabre — Large

	2001	2000	1999

RATINGS

	POOR → GOOD	POOR → GOOD	POOR → GOOD
Comparative Rating	8	9	9
Frontal Crash Tests*	10	10	8
Safety Features	8	8	6
Preventive Maintenance	6	5	5
Repair Costs	5	8	10
Warranty	2	2	2
Fuel Economy	5	4	4
Rollover (based on SSF, see pg. 25)	8	8	8
Complaints	5		6
Insurance Costs	10	10	10

SAFETY

	2001	2000	1999
Frontal Crash Tests	No Govt Results	No Govt Results	Good
Side Crash Tests	Very Good	Very Good	Good
Airbags	Dual/Side (nextgen)	Dual/Side (nextgen)	Dual (nextgen)
Anti-Lock Brakes	4-Wheel	4-Wheel	4-Wheel
Day Running Lamps	Standard	Standard	Standard
Built-In Child Seats	None	None	None
Pretensioners	None	None	None

SPECIFICATIONS

	2001		2000		1999	
Fuel Economy (cty/hwy)	19/30	Average	19/30	Average	19/30	Average
Driving Range (miles)	441	Long	441	Long	441	Long
Bumpers	Strong		Strong		Strong	
Parking Index	Vry. Hard		Vry. Hard		Vry. Hard	
Head/Leg Room (in.)	38.8/42.4	Average	38.8/42.4	Average	38.8/42.6	Average
Interior Space (cu. ft.)	108	Roomy	125.6	Vry. Roomy	125.5	Vry. Roomy
Cargo Space (cu. ft.)	18	Average	17	Average	17	Average
Tow Rating (lbs.)	1000	Vry. Low	1000	Vry. Low	1000	Vry. Low

*To be tested in 2001.

Buick's "executive sedan" enters 2001 unchanged, save a new Ultra Special Edition. A high-end audio system and an optional StabiliTrak (all-weather control) system are available. The Park Avenue strives to provide a smooth ride and lounge-chair comfort without sacrificing handling. Dual airbags and 4-wheel ABS come standard. You'll find two versions of the 3.8-liter V6, a standard and a turbocharged version. Despite its great size, the Park Avenue is only an average crash test performer.

2001 Buick Park Avenue

General Information

New for 2001: No major changes	**Year of Production:** 5
Twins: Cadillac Seville	**Seating:** 6
Where Made: Canada	**Theft Rating:** Very Low

Prices 2001

Model	Retail	Markup
4-spd. auto.	$32,980	10%
Ultra 4-spd. auto.	$37,490	10%

Competition 2001

Model	POOR					GOOD	pg.
Buick Park Ave.							**146**
Chrys. Concorde				■			188
Lincoln Town Car						■	322
Ford Cr. Victoria						■	216

'00 and '99 Models

The Park Avenue was redesigned in 1997 to share a platform with the Riviera and the Oldsmobile Aurora. Aimed at the car buyers looking for an affordable luxury car, the ride is quiet and the interior spacious. Traction control is optional and highly recommended.

Price Ranges 2000–1999

4-sp. auto.	$31-32,000
Ultra 4-sp. auto.	$35-37,000

2000 Buick Park Avenue

1999 Buick Park Avenue

Buick Park Avenue — Large

RATINGS

	2001 POOR–GOOD	2000 POOR–GOOD	1999 POOR–GOOD
Comparative Rating			
Frontal Crash Tests			
Safety Features	8	8	6
Preventive Maintenance	6	5	5
Repair Costs	7	7	9
Warranty	2	2	2
Fuel Economy	5	4	4
Rollover (based on SSF; see pg. 30)	8	8	8
Complaints	5	5	7
Insurance Costs	10	10	10

SAFETY

	2001	2000	1999
Frontal Crash Tests	To Be Tested	No Govt Results	No Govt Results
Side Crash Tests	No Govt Results	No Govt Results	No Govt Results
Airbags	Dual/Side (nextgen)	Dual/Side (nextgen)	Dual (nextgen)
Anti-Lock Brakes	4-Wheel	4-Wheel	4-Wheel
Day Running Lamps	Standard	Standard	Standard
Built-In Child Seats	None	None	None
Pretensioners	None	None	None

SPECIFICATIONS

	2001		2000		1999	
Fuel Economy (cty/hwy)	19/30	Average	19/30	Average	19/28	Poor
Driving Range (miles)	453.25	Long	453.25	Long	434.75	Long
Bumpers	Strong		Strong		Strong	
Parking Index	Vry. Hard		Vry. Hard		Vry. Hard	
Head/Leg Room (in.)	39.8/41.4	Average	39.8/41.4	Average	39.8/42.4	Roomy
Interior Space (cu. ft.)	111	Roomy	131.2	Vry. Roomy	131.2	Vry. Roomy
Cargo Space (cu. ft.)	19	Average	19.1	Average	19.1	Average
Tow Rating (lbs.)	1000	Vry. Low	1000	Vry. Low	1000	Vry. Low

The Regal gets a spiffy 2001 Olympic version this year, and look for another special edition from the same designer, Joseph Abboud, later this year. A 3.8-liter V6 comes standard or get the super-charged version of the 3.8-liter V6 with more horsepower. Dual airbags and 4-wheel ABS are standard; rear side airbags are optional. Steering and trunk space are ample since its redesign in 1997 which gave the Regal an expanded wheel-base while steering and suspension were also improved.

2001 Buick Regal

General Information

New for 2001: No major changes		**Year of Production:**	5
Twins: Century, Intrigue, Grand Prix		**Seating:**	5
Where Made: Canada		**Theft Rating:**	Very Low

Prices 2001

Model	Retail	Markup
LS 4-spd. auto.	$22,845	9%
GS 4-spd. auto.	$26,095	9%

Competition 2001

Model	POOR					GOOD		pg.
Buick Regal						■		**148**
Chrys. Concorde					■			188
Ford Taurus							■	234
Dodge Intrepid					■			208

'00 and '99 Models

Introduced in 1997 as a 1997 1/2 model, the redesigned Regal joined the same platform as the Century, Oldsmobile Intrigue, and Pontiac Grand Prix. In 2000, the Regal got adjustments for a quieter ride and met California LEV standards.

Price Ranges 2000–1999

LS 4-sp. auto.	$21-22,000
GS 4-sp. auto.	$24-25,000

2000 Buick Regal

1999 Buick Regal

	2001	2000	1999

RATINGS

	POOR — GOOD	POOR — GOOD	POOR — GOOD
Comparative Rating	8	7	8
Frontal Crash Tests	6	6	6
Safety Features	6	6	6
Preventive Maintenance	6	5	6
Repair Costs	9	5	7
Warranty	2	2	2
Fuel Economy	5	4	4
Rollover (based on SSF; see pg. 30)	8	8	8
Complaints	6	6	7
Insurance Costs	10	10	10

SAFETY

	2001	2000	1999
Frontal Crash Tests	Average	Average	Average
Side Crash Tests	Average	Average	Average
Airbags	Dual (nextgen)	Dual	Dual (nextgen)
Anti-Lock Brakes	4-Wheel	4-Wheel	4-Wheel
Day Running Lamps	Standard	Standard	Standard
Built-In Child Seats	None	None	None
Pretensioners	None	None	None

SPECIFICATIONS

	2001		2000		1999	
Fuel Economy (cty/hwy)	19/29	Average	20/29	Average	19/30	Average
Driving Range (miles)	420	Average	428.75	Long	428.75	Long
Bumpers	Strong		Strong		Strong	
Parking Index	Hard		Hard		Hard	
Head/Leg Room (in.)	39.4/42.4	Average	39.4/42.4	Average	39.4/42.4	Average
Interior Space (cu. ft.)	102	Roomy	118.5	Vry. Roomy	118.5	Vry. Roomy
Cargo Space (cu. ft.)	17	Average	16.7	Average	16.7	Average
Tow Rating (lbs.)	1000	Vry. Low	1000	Vry. Low	1000	Vry. Low

The Catera continues into 2001 unchanged. Last year the Catera received a new front and rear fascias, a new hood, and new front and rear lights. The 3.0-liter V6 carries over from 1999. The traction control feature prevents slipping by providing more power to the wheels with the best traction. Dual airbags and 4-wheel ABS are standard. Despite the un-Cadillac modern styling, the Catera continues Cadillac's tradition of excellent interior comfort and ride.

2001 Cadillac Catera

General Information

New for 2001: No major changes		**Year of Production:**	5
Twins:		**Seating:**	5
Where Made: Germany		**Theft Rating:**	Low

Prices 2001

Model	Retail	Markup
4-spd. auto.	$31,305	8%

Competition 2001

Model	POOR					GOOD	pg.
Cadillac Catera							**150**
Dodge Intrepid					■		208
Chev.Malibu			■				170
Saturn L/LW					■		396

'00 and '99 Models

The Catera is based on the German-designed Opel Omega. Cadillac hoped to attract a younger car buyer with the Catera. The Catera sports a nimble 3.0-liter V6 engine and dual airbags were standard for 2000. No crash tests results are available for the Catera.

Price Ranges 2000–1999

4-speed auto.	$30-34,000

2000 Cadillac Catera

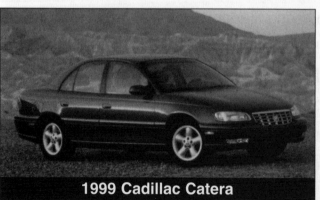
1999 Cadillac Catera

Cadillac Catera — Intermediate

	2001	2000	1999

RATINGS

(Scale: POOR → GOOD, 1–10)

	2001	2000	1999
Comparative Rating	—	—	—
Frontal Crash Tests	—	—	—
Safety Features	8	9	7
Preventive Maintenance	10	1	9
Repair Costs	1	1	2
Warranty	5	4	7
Fuel Economy	3	3	3
Rollover (based on SSF; see pg. 30)	7	7	7
Complaints	2	2	2
Insurance Costs	10	10	10

SAFETY

	2001	2000	1999
Frontal Crash Tests	No Govt Results	No Govt Results	No Govt Results
Side Crash Tests	No Govt Results	No Govt Results	No Govt Results
Airbags	Dual/Side	Dual/Side	Dual
Anti-Lock Brakes	4-Wheel	4-Wheel	4-Wheel
Day Running Lamps	Standard	Standard	Standard
Built-In Child Seats	None	None	None
Pretensioners	Standard	None	Standard

SPECIFICATIONS

	2001		2000		1999	
Fuel Economy (cty/hwy)	17/24	Poor	18/24	Poor	18/24	Poor
Driving Range (miles)	328	Vry. Short	336	Vry. Short	336	Vry. Short
Bumpers	Weak		Weak		Weak	
Parking Index	Easy		Easy		Easy	
Head/Leg Room (in.)	38.7/42.2	Average	38.7/42.2	Average	38.7/42.2	Average
Interior Space (cu. ft.)	99	Average	98.2	Average	98.2	Average
Cargo Space (cu. ft.)	14	Small	14.5	Small	14.5	Small
Tow Rating (lbs.)	1000	Vry. Low	1000	Vry. Low	1000	Vry. Low

Cadillac DeVille   Large

The 2001 DeVille doesn't change from last year's all-new model. The DeVille offers one of the most comprehensive safety packages you can find with standard ABS, front and side airbags, optional rear side airbags, night vision, and traction control. Still standard is Cadillac's Northstar 4.6-liter V8 engine, which provides plenty of power. Three models are available—DeVille, DeVille High Luxury Sedan and, DeVille Touring Sedan.

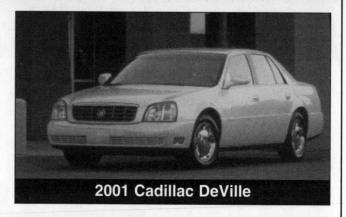

2001 Cadillac DeVille

General Information

New for 2001: No major changes	**Year of Production:**	2
Twins:	**Seating:**	6
Where Made: U.S.	**Theft Rating:**	Very Low

Prices 2001

Model	Retail	Markup
Base 4-spd. auto.	$40,495	9%
DHS/DTS 4-spd. auto.	$46,267	9%

Competition 2001

Model	POOR				GOOD	pg.
Cadillac DeVille				■		**152**
Buick LeSabre					■	144
Ford Cr. Victoria					■	216
Acura RL					■	124

'00 and '99 Models

The 1999 DeVille came in three versions: DeVille Concours, DeVille, and DeVille d'Elegance. Cadillac's Northstar V8 engine (4.6 liter, 300 hp) provides plenty of power. Extras include new exterior and interior colors and massaging lumbar seats for the Concours and d'Elegance. 2000 brought the all-new DeVille with its many standard safety features.

Price Ranges 2000–1999

Base 4-speed auto.	$38-40,000
DHS/DTS 4-speed auto.	$42-45,000

2000 Cadillac DeVille

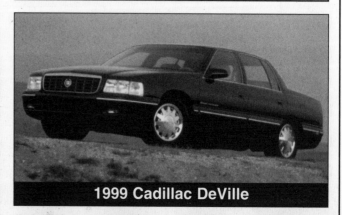

1999 Cadillac DeVille

Cadillac DeVille — Large

	2001	2000	1999

RATINGS

	POOR → GOOD (2001)	POOR → GOOD (2000)	POOR → GOOD (1999)
Comparative Rating	7	7	9
Frontal Crash Tests	5	5	9
Safety Features	7	8	8
Preventive Maintenance	10	1	9
Repair Costs	1	1	2
Warranty	5	4	7
Fuel Economy	4	3	3
Rollover (based on SSF; see pg. 30)	8	8	8
Complaints	5		6
Insurance Costs	10	10	10

SAFETY

	2001	2000	1999
Frontal Crash Tests	Average	Average	Very Good
Side Crash Tests	Good	Good	Very Good
Airbags	Dual/Side	Dual/Side	Dual/Side
Anti-Lock Brakes	4-Wheel	4-Wheel	4-Wheel
Day Running Lamps	Standard	Standard	Standard
Built-In Child Seats	None	None	None
Pretensioners	None	None	Optional

SPECIFICATIONS

	2001		2000		1999	
Fuel Economy (cty/hwy)	17/27	Poor	17/26	Poor	17/26	Poor
Driving Range (miles)	440	Long	430	Long	430	Long
Bumpers	Weak		Weak		Weak	
Parking Index	Vry. Hard		Vry. Hard		Vry. Hard	
Head/Leg Room (in.)	39.1/42.4	Average	39.1/42.4	Average	38.5/42.6	Average
Interior Space (cu. ft.)	115	Vry. Roomy	114.3	Roomy	116.8	Vry. Roomy
Cargo Space (cu. ft.)	19	Average	19.1	Average	20	Average
Tow Rating (lbs.)	2000	Vry. Low	2000	Vry. Low	3000	Low

Another year with no changes, this coupe remains a favorite of the over-50 crowd. The reason: a comfortable interior that features leather and wood trim, a true "by-car" ride, and the hint of sportiness with only two doors. Two trim levels are available: base and up-level Touring Coupe. The standard engine is a 4.6-liter V8 which is adequate; the optional engine is also a 4.6-liter V8 but only offers 25 more hp.

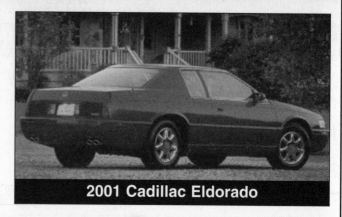

2001 Cadillac Eldorado

General Information

New for 2001: No major changes	**Year of Production:**	10
Twins:	**Seating:**	5
Where Made: U.S.	**Theft Rating:**	Very High

Prices 2001

Model	Retail	Markup
ESC 4-spd. auto.	$40,036	9%
ETC 4-spd. auto.	$43,611	9%

Competition 2001

Model	POOR				GOOD	pg.
Cad. Eldorado						**154**
Lincoln Town Car					■	322
Audi A8						132
Ford Cr. Victoria					■	216

'00 and '99 Models

The last of the luxury coupes, the Eldorado seems dated in styling, but its niche market loves it just the way it is. The front seats are comfy, but it's tough to get in and out of the cramped rear seats. For years, the engine choices have been a 4.6-liter V8 or more powerful 4.6-liter V8.

Price Ranges 2000–1999

ESC 4-speed auto.	$39-40,000
ETC 4-speed auto.	$42-43,000

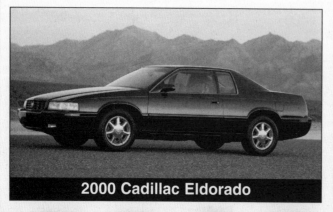

2000 Cadillac Eldorado

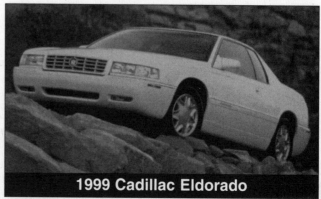

1999 Cadillac Eldorado

Cadillac Eldorado — Large

	2001	2000	1999

RATINGS

	POOR → GOOD (2001)	POOR → GOOD (2000)	POOR → GOOD (1999)
Comparative Rating			
Frontal Crash Tests			
Safety Features	6	6	6
Preventive Maintenance	10	1	9
Repair Costs	1	1	1
Warranty	5	4	7
Fuel Economy	4	3	3
Rollover (based on SSF; see pg. 30)	8	8	8
Complaints	7	7	7
Insurance Costs	10	10	10

SAFETY

	2001	2000	1999
Frontal Crash Tests	No Govt Results	No Govt Results	No Govt Results
Side Crash Tests	No Govt Results	No Govt Results	No Govt Results
Airbags	Dual	Dual	Dual
Anti-Lock Brakes	4-Wheel	4-Wheel	4-Wheel
Day Running Lamps	Standard	Standard	Standard
Built-In Child Seats	None	None	None
Pretensioners	None	None	None

SPECIFICATIONS

	2001		2000		1999	
Fuel Economy (cty/hwy)	17/27	Poor	17/26	Poor	17/26	Poor
Driving Range (miles)	440	Long	430	Long	430	Long
Bumpers	Weak		Weak		Weak	
Parking Index	Vry. Hard		Vry. Hard		Vry. Hard	
Head/Leg Room (in.)	37.8/42.6	Cramped	37.8/42.6	Cramped	37.8/42.6	Cramped
Interior Space (cu. ft.)	100	Average	99.56	Average	99.56	Average
Cargo Space (cu. ft.)	15	Small	15.3	Small	15.3	Small
Tow Rating (lbs.)	1000	Vry. Low	1000	Vry. Low	1000	Vry. Low

Introduced in 1999, Cadillac's entry into the popular sport utility market is actually an upscale Chevy Tahoe/GMC Yukon and continues into 2001 with few changes. Keeping in the Cadillac tradition, the Escalade offers plenty of leather, CD player, alarm system, and the OnStar navigation system. Unlike other Caddys you get cargo space. The Denali gives GMC's buyers an upscale Yukon. The 5.7-liter V8 engine is powerful but a gas guzzler. While you won't get the Cadillac name, a Yukon with leather interior and upgraded sound may be just as good.

2001 Cadillac Escalade

General Information

New for 2001: No major changes		**Year of Production:**	3
Twins: Chev. Tahoe, GMC Yukon		**Seating:**	5
Where Made: U.S.		**Theft Rating:**	

Prices 2001

Model	Retail	Markup
Escalade 4-spd. auto.	$46,225	9%
Denali 4dr. AWD	$45,950	14%

Competition 2001

Model	POOR				GOOD		pg.
Cad. Escalade				■			**156**
Infiniti QX4						■	276
Merc-Bz M-Class		■					340
Olds Bravada	■						374

'00 and '99 Models

In 1999, Cadillac took the popular Tahoe/Yukon line of SUVs, jazzed it up and called it the Cadillac Escalade. GMC called their twin version the Denali. Compared to other large sport utilities, the Escalade/Denali fares well and has decent crash test scores.

Price Ranges 2000–1999

Escalade	$45-47,000

2000 Cadillac Escalade

1999 Cadillac Escalade

	2001	2000	1999

RATINGS

	POOR → GOOD	POOR → GOOD	POOR → GOOD
Comparative Rating	5	2	3
Frontal Crash Tests	7	7	7
Safety Features	6	7	7
Preventive Maintenance	5		
Repair Costs	3		
Warranty	5	4	7
Fuel Economy	1	1	1
Rollover (based on SSF; see pg. 30)	3	3	3
Complaints	4	4	5
Insurance Costs	10	5	5

SAFETY

	2001	2000	1999
Frontal Crash Tests	Good	Good	Good
Side Crash Tests	No Govt Results	No Govt Results	No Govt Results
Airbags	Dual (nextgen)	Dual (nextgen)	Dual (nextgen)
Anti-Lock Brakes	4-Wheel	4-Wheel	4-Wheel
Day Running Lamps	Standard	Standard	Standard
Built-In Child Seats	None	None	None
Pretensioners	None	None	None

SPECIFICATIONS

	2001		2000		1999	
Fuel Economy (cty/hwy)	13/16	Vry. Poor	13/16	Vry. Poor	13/16	Vry. Poor
Driving Range (miles)	435	Long	435	Long	435	Long
Bumpers						
Parking Index	Vry. Hard		Vry. Hard		Vry. Hard	
Head/Leg Room (in.)	39.9/41.7	Average	39.9/41.7	Average	39.9/41.7	Average
Interior Space (cu. ft.)						
Cargo Space (cu. ft.)						
Tow Rating (lbs.)	6600	Vry. High	6600	Vry. High	6600	Vry. High

The Cadillac Seville lumbers into 2001 with only minor changes. These include an optional enhanced sport package and the new Cadillac infotainment system. Only available in a sedan, the Seville comes with a 4.6-liter V8 engine. Ride and handling are good, and the interior room is comfortable. The OnStar communication system helps with directions and emergencies. Dual airbags, traction control, and 4-wheel ABS are standard. Luxuries include heated and massaging seats, which can adjust to the body and position of the occupant.

2001 Cadillac Seville

General Information

New for 2001: No major changes	**Year of Production:** 4
Twins: Aurora, Bonneville, LeSabre	**Seating:** 5
Where Made: U.S.	**Theft Rating:** Average

Prices 2001

Model	Retail	Markup
SLS 4-spd. auto.	$41,935	9%
STS 4-spd. auto.	$48,045	9%

Competition 2001

Model	POOR						GOOD	pg.
Cadillac Seville							■	**158**
Ford Cr. Victoria							■	216
Infiniti I30					■			272
Audi A8							■	132

'00 and '99 Models

The Seville underwent a redesign in 1998. Side airbags were added as a standard safety feature along with dual airbags, traction control, and 4-wheel ABS. The SLS gets 4.6-liter V8; the STS comes with a 300 hp version of the same engine.

Price Ranges 2000–1999

SLS 4-speed auto.	$43-44,000
STS 4-speed auto.	$47-49,000

2000 Cadillac Seville

1999 Cadillac Seville

Cadillac Seville — Large

RATINGS	2001	2000	1999
	POOR → GOOD	POOR → GOOD	POOR → GOOD
Comparative Rating	9	9	
Frontal Crash Tests	10	10	
Safety Features	8	9	9
Preventive Maintenance	10	1	9
Repair Costs	1	1	2
Warranty	5	4	7
Fuel Economy	4	3	3
Rollover (based on SSF; see pg. 30)	8	8	8
Complaints	5	6	6
Insurance Costs	10	10	10

SAFETY

	2001	2000	1999
Frontal Crash Tests	Very Good	No Govt Results	No Govt Results
Side Crash Tests	No Govt Results	No Govt Results	No Govt Results
Airbags	Dual/Side	Dual/Side	Dual/Side
Anti-Lock Brakes	4-Wheel	4-Wheel	4-Wheel
Day Running Lamps	Standard	Standard	Standard
Built-In Child Seats	None	None	None
Pretensioners	Standard	None	Standard

SPECIFICATIONS

	2001		2000		1999	
Fuel Economy (cty/hwy)	17/27	Poor	17/26	Poor	17/26	Poor
Driving Range (miles)	407	Average	397.75	Average	397.75	Average
Bumpers	Weak		Weak		Weak	
Parking Index	Vry. Hard		Vry. Hard		Vry. Hard	
Head/Leg Room (in.)	38.2/42.5	Cramped	38.2/42.5	Cramped	38.2/42.5	Cramped
Interior Space (cu. ft.)	104	Roomy	104.18	Roomy	104.18	Roomy
Cargo Space (cu. ft.)	15	Small	15.7	Small	15.7	Small
Tow Rating (lbs.)	3000	Low	3000	Low	3000	Low

The Chevrolet Astro/GMC Safari really don't compare with other minivans in handling and performance. They are more like the cargo vans they were designed to be. No changes for 2001. The 4.3-liter V6 engine remains the same and it has all-wheel drive which automatically kicks in when the rear wheels begin to slip. You can seat up to seven with multiple storage bins and cup holders. If you're looking for a cargo carrier, the Astro/Safari is a great choice. However, for the most part, the Astro/Safari is outclassed by other minivan competitors.

2001 Chevrolet Astro

General Information

New for 2001: No major changes	Year of Production:	17
Twins:	Seating:	5-8
Where Made: U.S.	Theft Rating:	Very Low

Prices 2001

Model	Retail	Markup
2WD 4-spd. auto.	$23,241	10%
AWD 4-spd. auto.	$25,056	10%

Competition 2001

Model	POOR				GOOD	pg.
Chev. Astro				■		**160**
Chev. Venture				■		184
Ford Windstar					■	236
Toyota Sienna		■				438

'00 and '99 Models

For over fifteen years, Chevrolet has produced this basic van. Offering one of the largest cargo and towing capacities in the van market, the Astro and Safari finally come with all the typical safety features: dual airbags, 4-wheel ABS, and daytime running lamps.

Price Ranges 2000–1999

2WD 4-sp. auto.	$21-22,000
AWD 4-sp. auto.	$23-24,000

2000 Chevrolet Astro

1999 Chevrolet Astro

Chevrolet Astro/GMC Safari · Minivan

	2001	2000	1999

RATINGS

	POOR — GOOD	POOR — GOOD	POOR — GOOD
Comparative Rating	5	5	4
Frontal Crash Tests	5	5	5
Safety Features	6	6	7
Preventive Maintenance	5	8	7
Repair Costs		5	7
Warranty	2	2	2
Fuel Economy	3	2	2
Rollover (based on SSF; see pg. 30)	4	4	4
Complaints	7	8	6
Insurance Costs	10	10	10

SAFETY

	2001	2000	1999
Frontal Crash Tests	Average	Average	Average
Side Crash Tests	No Govt Results	No Govt Results	No Govt Results
Airbags	Dual (nextgen)	Dual (nextgen)	Dual (nextgen)
Anti-Lock Brakes	4-Wheel	4-Wheel	4-Wheel
Day Running Lamps	Standard	Standard	Standard
Built-In Child Seats	None	None	Optional
Pretensioners	None	None	None

SPECIFICATIONS

	2001		2000		1999	
Fuel Economy (cty/hwy)	17/22	Poor	16/21	Vry. Poor	16/21	Vry. Poor
Driving Range (miles)	487.5	Vry. Long	462.5	Vry. Long	462.5	Vry. Long
Bumpers	Strong		Strong		Strong	
Parking Index	Hard		Hard		Hard	
Head/Leg Room (in.)	39.2/41.6	Average	39.2/41.6	Average	39.2/41.6	Average
Interior Space (cu. ft.)						
Cargo Space (cu. ft.)	170.4	Vry. Large	170.4	Vry. Large	170.4	Vry. Large
Tow Rating (lbs.)	5500	High	5500	High	5500	High

Chevrolet Blazer   Mid-Size Sport Utility

The Blazer lineup has three trim levels, the LS, LT, and the Trailblazer, all of which move into 2001 unchanged. The Trailblazer, only available with 4 doors, has a leather interior, better suspension, and upgraded creature comforts. The standard 4.3-liter V6 provides plenty of power. The packages come in many flavors so shop carefully and beware of mediocre crash test results.

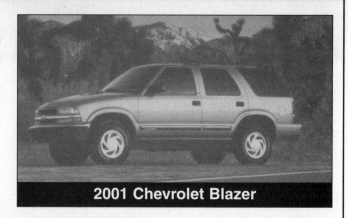

2001 Chevrolet Blazer

General Information

New for 2001: No major changes		**Year of Production:**	7
Twins: GMC Jimmy, Olds Bravada		**Seating:**	4
Where Made: Canada		**Theft Rating:**	Average

Prices 2001

Model	Retail	Markup
2WD 2dr. 5-spd. man.	$19,170	10%
4WD 2dr. 5-spd. man.	$22,170	10%
2WD 4dr. 4-spd. auto.	$24,770	10%
4WD 4dr. 4-spd. auto.	$26,770	10%

Competition 2001

Model	POOR				GOOD		pg.
Chev. Blazer			■				**162**
Ford Explorer				■			224
Jeep Cherokee			■				284
Honda Passport	■						252

'00 and '99 Models

The '99 and '00 models benefit from a minor facelift including a new grill, headlights, and optional fog lamps. You'll find a variety of models and packages to choose from. A special ZR2 package is tailored toward off-roaders, giving the Blazer more ground clearance and an upgraded suspension.

Price Ranges 2000–1999

2WD 2dr. 5-sp. man.	$18-19,000
4WD 2dr. 5-sp. man.	$21-22,000
2WD 4dr. 4-sp. auto.	$23-24,000
4WD 4dr. 4-speed auto.	$25-26,000

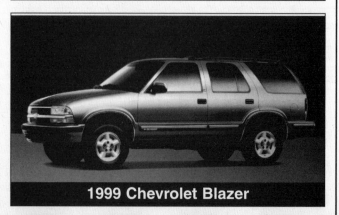

2000 Chevrolet Blazer   **1999 Chevrolet Blazer**

Chevrolet Blazer — Mid-Size Sport Utility

	2001	2000	1999

RATINGS

	POOR → GOOD	POOR → GOOD	POOR → GOOD
Comparative Rating	3	2	3
Frontal Crash Tests	4	4	4
Safety Features	6	6	6
Preventive Maintenance	5	4	5
Repair Costs	6	6	6
Warranty	2	2	2
Fuel Economy	2	2	2
Rollover (based on SSF; see pg. 30)	3	3	3
Complaints	4	5	6
Insurance Costs	10	10	10

SAFETY

	2001	2000	1999
Frontal Crash Tests	Poor	Poor	Poor
Side Crash Tests	Very Good	Very Good	Very Good
Airbags	Dual (nextgen)	Dual (nextgen)	Dual (nextgen)
Anti-Lock Brakes	4-Wheel	4-Wheel	4-Wheel
Day Running Lamps	Standard	Standard	Standard
Built-In Child Seats	None	None	None
Pretensioners	None	None	None

SPECIFICATIONS

	2001		2000		1999	
Fuel Economy (cty/hwy)	15/20	Vry. Poor	16/21	Vry. Poor	16/20	Vry. Poor
Driving Range (miles)	332.5	Vry. Short	351.5	Vry. Short	342	Vry. Short
Bumpers						
Parking Index	Vry. Easy		Easy		Easy	
Head/Leg Room (in.)	39.6/42.4	Roomy	39.6/42.4	Roomy	39.6/42.4	Roomy
Interior Space (cu. ft.)						
Cargo Space (cu. ft.)	66.9	Large	66.9	Large	66.9	Large
Tow Rating (lbs.)	5500	High	5500	High	5500	High

Camaro blasts into 2001 with no major changes. If you're looking for a sports car with lots of power, the Camaro is a great choice. The 3.8-liter V6 engine sports 200 hp, but speed demons will opt for the more powerful Z28 model's 5.7-liter V8 engine. The sports appearance package gets you bigger wheels and extensions for the front fascia and rear spoiler. Warning: while the Camaro does very well in frontal crash tests, because of the way it tends to be driven, its accident rate is high.

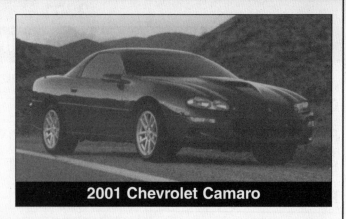

2001 Chevrolet Camaro

General Information

New for 2001: No major changes	**Year of Production:** 9
Twins: Pontiac Firebird	**Seating:** 4
Where Made: U.S.	**Theft Rating:** Very High

Prices 2001

Model	Retail	Markup
Coupe 5-spd. man.	$17,075	9%
Z28 Coupe 4-spd. auto.	$21,645	9%
Convertible 5-spd. man.	$24,370	9%
Z28 Conv. 4-spd. auto.	$28,750	9%

Competition 2001

Model	POOR					GOOD	pg.
Chev. Camaro				■			**164**
Dodge Intrepid					■		208
Ford Mustang				■			230
Lexus ES300						■	302

'00 and '99 Models

For over 30 years, the Camaro has been one of America's favorite muscle cars. For the 1999 and 2000 model years, the Camaro received only minor exterior restyling with no major changes. Dual airbags and 4-wheel ABS are standard features. While roomy up front, the rear seat is almost too small even for young children.

Price Ranges 2000–1999

Coupe 5-sp. man.	$16-17,000
Z28 Coupe 4-sp. auto.	$20-21,000
Convertible 5-sp. man.	$22-24,000
Z28 Convertible 4-sp. auto.	$27-28,000

2000 Chevrolet Camaro   **1999 Chevrolet Camaro**

Chevrolet Camaro/Pontiac Firebird — Intermediate

	2001	2000	1999

RATINGS

	POOR — GOOD	POOR — GOOD	POOR — GOOD
Comparative Rating	5	4	4
Frontal Crash Tests	10	10	10
Safety Features	6	6	6
Preventive Maintenance	6	5	6
Repair Costs	4	4	4
Warranty	2	2	2
Fuel Economy	5	4	4
Rollover (based on SSF; see pg. 30)	10	10	10
Complaints	4	4	3
Insurance Costs	1	1	1

SAFETY

	2001	2000	1999
Frontal Crash Tests	Very Good	Very Good	Very Good
Side Crash Tests	Good	Good	Good
Airbags	Dual (nextgen)	Dual	Dual (nextgen)
Anti-Lock Brakes	4-Wheel	4-Wheel	4-Wheel
Day Running Lamps	Standard	Standard	Standard
Built-In Child Seats	None	None	None
Pretensioners	None	None	None

SPECIFICATIONS

	2001		2000		1999	
Fuel Economy (cty/hwy)	19/31	Average	19/30	Average	19/30	Average
Driving Range (miles)	420	Average	411.6	Average	411.6	Average
Bumpers	Strong		Strong		Strong	
Parking Index	Vry. Hard		Vry. Hard		Vry. Hard	
Head/Leg Room (in.)	37.2/43	Cramped	37.2/43	Cramped	37.2/43	Cramped
Interior Space (cu. ft.)	84	Vry. Cramp.	94.8	Average	94.8	Average
Cargo Space (cu. ft.)	12	Vry. Small	12.9	Vry. Small	12.9	Vry. Small
Tow Rating (lbs.)						

For 2001 the Cavalier continues forward unchanged but in a variety of configurations including a base sedan and coupe, LS sedan, Z24 coupe, and a Z24 convertible. Traction control is optional and highly recommended. A 2.2-liter engine comes standard on the base models; on the LS and Z24 trim levels, a more powerful 2.4-liter engine is available. Fully loaded with safety features including dual airbags, ABS, and daytime running lamps, the Cavalier holds its own against its compact competitors.

2001 Chevrolet Cavalier

General Information

New for 2001: No major changes		**Year of Production:**	7
Twins: Pontiac Sunfire		**Seating:**	5
Where Made: U.S.		**Theft Rating:**	Very Low

Prices 2001

Model	Retail	Markup
2dr. Coupe 4-spd. auto.	$13,860	7%
4dr. Sedan 5-spd. man.	$13,260	7%
4dr. Sedan LS 4-spd. auto.	$14,855	7%
2dr.Coupe Z24 5-spd. man.	$16,365	7%

Competition 2001

Model	POOR					GOOD	pg.
Chev. Cavalier				■			166
VW Jetta					■		450
Mitsu. Galant		■					350
Saturn SL						■	400

'00 and '99 Models

In 2000, the Cavalier got minor revisions throughout—a redesigned instrument panel, an improved security system, and a smoother 4-wheel ABS system. The Cavalier is aimed squarely at budget-conscious car buyers and did fairly well in the crash tests.

Price Ranges 2000–1999

2dr. Coupe 5-sp. man.	$11-13,000
4dr. Sedan 4-sp. auto.	$11-13,000
4dr. Sedan LS 4-sp. auto.	$14-15,000
2dr. Coupe Z24 5-sp. man.	$15-16,000

2000 Chevrolet Cavalier   **1999 Chevrolet Cavalier**

	2001	2000	1999

RATINGS

	POOR — GOOD	POOR — GOOD	POOR — GOOD
Comparative Rating	6	5	5
Frontal Crash Tests	7	7	7
Safety Features	6	6	6
Preventive Maintenance	7	6	6
Repair Costs	7	7	7
Warranty	2	2	2
Fuel Economy	7	6	6
Rollover (based on SSF; see pg. 30)	7	7	7
Complaints	8	8	8
Insurance Costs	1	1	1

SAFETY

	2001	2000	1999
Frontal Crash Tests	Good (2dr./4dr.)	Good (2dr./4dr.)	Good (2dr./4dr.)
Side Crash Tests	Poor (4dr.), Vry. Pr. (2dr.)	Poor (4dr.), Vry. Pr. (2dr.)	Poor (4dr.), Vry. Pr. (2dr.)
Airbags	Dual	Dual	Dual
Anti-Lock Brakes	4-Wheel	4-Wheel	4-Wheel
Day Running Lamps	Standard	Standard	Standard
Built-In Child Seats	None	None	None
Pretensioners	None	None	None

SPECIFICATIONS

	2001		2000		1999	
Fuel Economy (cty/hwy)	23/33	Average	24/34	Good	24/34	Good
Driving Range (miles)	420	Average	435	Long	435	Long
Bumpers	Strong		Strong		Strong	
Parking Index	Easy		Easy		Easy	
Head/Leg Room (in.)	38.9/41.9	Average	38.9/41.9	Average	38.9/41.9	Average
Interior Space (cu. ft.)	92	Cramped	105.1	Roomy	105.1	Roomy
Cargo Space (cu. ft.)	13	Vry. Small	13.6	Small	13.6	Small
Tow Rating (lbs.)						

Standard on the base model is a 3.4-liter V6; the LS model comes with a 3.8-liter V6, and both continue into 2001 unchanged. They have dual airbags and 4-wheel ABS, but the SS gets standard traction control, giving it more powerful handling and control. Comfortable seating and beefier engines bring the Impala into the next century even though fuel prices continue to rise.

2001 Chevrolet Impala

General Information

New for 2001: No major changes	**Year of Production:** 2
Twins: Pontiac Grand Prix	**Seating:** 6
Where Made: Canada	**Theft Rating:** Very Low

Prices 2001

Model	Retail	Markup
Impala 4-spd. auto.	$19,149	9%
Impala LS 4-spd. auto.	$23,225	9%
Monte Carlo LS 4-spd. auto.	$19,570	9%
Monte Carlo SS 4-spd. auto.	$22,400	9%

Competition 2001

Model	POOR				GOOD	pg.
Chev. Impala				■		**168**
Ford Cr. Victoria					■	216
Audi A8						132
Buick Century			■			142

'00 and '99 Models

The Monte Carlo carried over through 2000 with few changes beyond new paint choices and de-powered airbags. The Impala came back in 2000 as the all-new sedan counterpart to the Monte Carlo coupe. The standard engine is a 3.1-liter V6; the Z34 has a 3.8-liter V6. The '99-'00 Monte Carlo is essentially a two-door version of the Lumina.

Price Ranges 2000–1999

4-speed auto.	$17-18,000
LS 4-sp. auto.	$22-23,000

2000 Chevrolet Impala

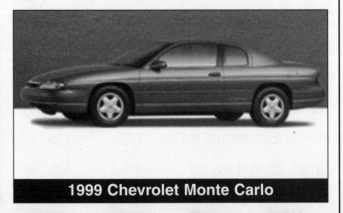

1999 Chevrolet Monte Carlo

Chevrolet Impala/Monte Carlo

Intermediate

	2001	2000	1999

RATINGS

	POOR — GOOD	POOR — GOOD	POOR — GOOD
Comparative Rating	7	6	9
Frontal Crash Tests*	10	10	9
Safety Features	6	6	6
Preventive Maintenance	6	5	5
Repair Costs	7	4	8
Warranty	2	2	2
Fuel Economy	6	5	4
Rollover (based on SSF, see pg. 25)	7	8	8
Complaints	5		10
Insurance Costs	5	5	5

SAFETY

	2001	2000	1999
Frontal Crash Tests	Very Good	Very Good	Very Good
Side Crash Tests	Very Good	Very Good	No Govt Results
Airbags		Dual	Dual
Anti-Lock Brakes		4-Wheel	4-Wheel
Day Running Lamps	Standard	Standard	Standard
Built-In Child Seats	None	None	None
Pretensioners	None	None	None

SPECIFICATIONS

	2001		2000		1999	
Fuel Economy (cty/hwy)	21/32	Average	20/32	Average	20/29	Average
Driving Range (miles)	450.5	Long	442	Long	406.7	Average
Bumpers					Strong	
Parking Index	Hard		Hard		Hard	
Head/Leg Room (in.)	39.2/42.2	Average	38.1/42.4	Cramped	37.9/42.4	Cramped
Interior Space (cu. ft.)	105	Roomy	114	Roomy	111.6	Roomy
Cargo Space (cu. ft.)	18	Average	15.8	Small	15.5	Small
Tow Rating (lbs.)	1000	Vry. Low	1000	Vry. Low	1000	Vry. Low

*To be tested in 2001.

Chevrolet Malibu   Intermediate

The 2001 Chevrolet Malibu comes with a standard 3.1-liter V6 engine but few other changes. You'll find good interior room and fine handling. The Malibu is Chevy's challenge to the best-selling Taurus, Camry, and Accord trio. You can choose between base and LS trim levels. The LS comes with cruise control and a rear defogger.

2001 Chevrolet Malibu

General Information

New for 2001: No major changes	**Year of Production:** 5
Twins: Pontiac Grand Am, Oldsmobile Alero	**Seating:** 5
Where Made: U.S.	**Theft Rating:** Very Low

Prices 2001

Model	Retail	Markup
4-spd. auto.	$17,020	9%
LS 4-spd. auto.	$19,300	9%

Competition 2001

Model	POOR				GOOD	pg.
Chev. Malibu			■			**170**
Buick Regal					■	148
Ford Taurus						234
Honda Accord			■			242

'00 and '99 Models

Introduced in 1997, the Malibu is available in a base and LS. The base has a 2.4-liter engine, which delivers 150 hp. Optional on the base and standard on the LS is a 3.1-liter V6 engine. For 1999, leather seats and a power seat for the driver were added to the LS model. A revised grille, which it borrowed from the Impala, was new for 2000.

Price Ranges 2000–1999

4-speed auto.	$15-16,000
LS 4-speed auto.	$18-19,000

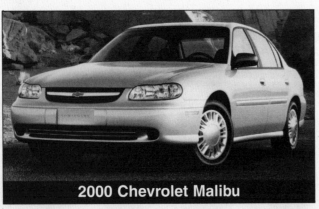

2000 Chevrolet Malibu

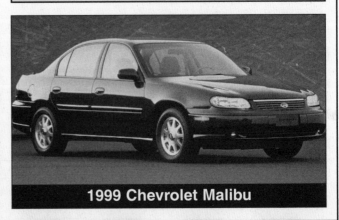

1999 Chevrolet Malibu

Chevrolet Malibu — Intermediate

	2001	2000	1999

RATINGS

	POOR → GOOD (2001)	POOR → GOOD (2000)	POOR → GOOD (1999)
Comparative Rating	4	3	3
Frontal Crash Tests*	8	8	8
Safety Features	6	6	6
Preventive Maintenance	6	5	6
Repair Costs	4	4	1
Warranty	2	2	2
Fuel Economy	5	4	5
Rollover (based on SSF, see pg. 25)	7	7	7
Complaints	3	4	4
Insurance Costs	5	5	5

SAFETY

	2001	2000	1999
Frontal Crash Tests	Good	Good	Good
Side Crash Tests	Average	Average	Poor
Airbags	Dual (nextgen)	Dual (nextgen)	Dual (nextgen)
Anti-Lock Brakes	4-Wheel	4-Wheel	4-Wheel
Day Running Lamps	Standard	Standard	Standard
Built-In Child Seats	None	None	None
Pretensioners	None	None	None

SPECIFICATIONS

	2001		2000		1999	
Fuel Economy (cty/hwy)	20/29	Average	20/30	Average	22/30	Average
Driving Range (miles)	367.5	Vry. Short	375	Short	390	Short
Bumpers	Strong		Strong		Strong	
Parking Index	Average		Average		Average	
Head/Leg Room (in.)	39.4/41.9	Average	39.4/41.9	Average	39.4/42.2	Average
Interior Space (cu. ft.)	99	Average	115	Vry. Roomy	116	Vry. Roomy
Cargo Space (cu. ft.)	16	Small	17.1	Average	16.4	Small
Tow Rating (lbs.)						

*To be tested in 2001.

Chevrolet Prizm Compact

Available in a base or LSi model, the Prizm remains unchanged for 2001. Air conditioning and an upgraded stereo are standard on the base model. The 1.8-liter dual overhead cam engine provides adequate power. Built on the same assembly line as the Toyota Corolla, the Prizm costs much less than its more popular cousin. The Prizm offers top-quality craftsmanship with great safety features like side airbags for a low price. The Prism is likely to be discontinued after 2002.

2001 Chevrolet Prizm

General Information

New for 2001: No major changes	**Year of Production:**	4
Twins: Toyota Corolla	**Seating:**	5
Where Made: Mexico	**Theft Rating:**	Very Low

Prices 2001

Model	Retail	Markup
5-spd. man.	$13,995	5%
LSi 5-spd. man.	$16,060	8%

Competition 2001

Model	POOR					GOOD	pg.
Chev. Prizm			■				**172**
Pontiac Gr. Am		■					384
Mazda 626				■			324
Toyota Corolla					■		424

'00 and '99 Models

The Prizm went through a major makeover in 1998, receiving new engines, a new interior and exterior, additional safety features, and a new nameplate. With the demise of Geo, the Prizm joined the Chevrolet lineup. The Prizm is one of the few cars under $15,000 offering side airbags.

Price Ranges 2000–1999

5-sp. man.	$12-13,000
LSi 5-sp. man.	$14-15,000

2000 Chevrolet Prizm

1999 Chevrolet Prizm

Chevrolet Prizm   Compact

	2001	2000	1999

RATINGS

	POOR — GOOD	POOR — GOOD	POOR — GOOD
Comparative Rating	4	4	4
Frontal Crash Tests	8	8	8
Safety Features	8	8	8
Preventive Maintenance	3	3	4
Repair Costs	3	4	3
Warranty	2	2	2
Fuel Economy	10	7	7
Rollover (based on SSF; see pg. 30)	7	7	7
Complaints	4	4	4
Insurance Costs	1	1	1

SAFETY

Frontal Crash Tests	Good	Good	Good
Side Crash Tests	Good	Good	Good
Airbags	Dual and Opt. Side	Dual and Opt. Side	Dual
Anti-Lock Brakes	4-Wheel (optional)	4-Wheel (optional)	4-Wheel (Optional)
Day Running Lamps	Standard	Standard	Standard
Built-In Child Seats	Optional	Optional	Optional
Pretensioners	Standard	Standard	Standard

SPECIFICATIONS

Fuel Economy (cty/hwy)	32/41 Vry. Good	31/37 Good	31/37 Good
Driving Range (miles)	481.8 Vry. Long	448.8 Long	448.8 Long
Bumpers	Strong	Strong	Strong
Parking Index	Vry. Easy	Vry. Easy	Vry. Easy
Head/Leg Room (in.)	39.3/42.5 Average	39.3/42.5 Average	39.3/42.5 Average
Interior Space (cu. ft.)	88 Cramped	100.1 Average	100.1 Average
Cargo Space (cu. ft.)	12 Vry. Small	12.1 Vry. Small	12.1 Vry. Small
Tow Rating (lbs.)	1500 Vry. Low	1500 Vry. Low	1500 Vry. Low

For 2001, the basic S-10 receives no major changes but a "crew cab" version with four full-size doors joins the line up. The other versions include a base and LS, 2- and 4-wheel drive, regular and extended cab, and several suspension choices. The Xtreme appearance package gives the S-10 a "street rod" look. The 2.2-liter 4-cylinder engine takes care of most needs, but the optional 4.3-liter V6 offers more tow power. Look at the numerous packages carefully because they vary greatly in price.

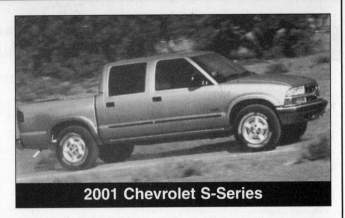

2001 Chevrolet S-Series

General Information

New for 2001: No major changes	**Year of Production:** 8
Twins:	**Seating:** 2-3
Where Made: U.S.	**Theft Rating:** Very Low

Prices 2001

Model	Retail	Markup
2WD 5-spd. man.	$12,749	6%
4WD Ext. Cab 5-spd. man.	$18,906	6%
LS Crew Cab 4WD 4-spd. auto.	$24,809	10%

Competition 2001

Model	POOR				GOOD	pg.
Chev. S-Series		■				**174**
Mazda B-Series				■		326
Ford Ranger					■	232

'00 and '99 Models

In 1998, the S-Series received a new front end, redesigned seats with integrated head rests, and an improved engine. The S-Series finally got a passenger-side airbag, too. With the extended cabs, there is an optional third door, but the back seat is too cramped for adults.

Price Ranges 2000–1999

2WD 5-sp. man.	$12-13,000
4WD 5-sp. man.	$16-19,000
Crew Cab 4WD 4-sp. auto.	$23-25,000

2000 Chevrolet S-Series

1999 Chevrolet S-Series

Chevrolet S-Series/GMC Sonoma — Compact Pickup

	2001	2000	1999

RATINGS

	2001 (POOR→GOOD)	2000 (POOR→GOOD)	1999 (POOR→GOOD)
Comparative Rating	3	2	2
Frontal Crash Tests	4	3	3
Safety Features	6	6	6
Preventive Maintenance	5	4	5
Repair Costs	6	7	7
Warranty	2	2	2
Fuel Economy	5	4	4
Rollover (based on SSF; see pg. 30)	4	4	4
Complaints	9	8	8
Insurance Costs	1	1	1

SAFETY

	2001	2000	1999
Frontal Crash Tests	Poor	Poor	Poor
Side Crash Tests	No Govt Results	No Govt Results	No Govt Results
Airbags	Dual	Dual	Dual
Anti-Lock Brakes	4-Wheel	4-Wheel	4-Wheel
Day Running Lamps	Standard	Standard	Standard
Built-In Child Seats	None	None	None
Pretensioners	None	None	None

SPECIFICATIONS

	2001		2000		1999	
Fuel Economy (cty/hwy)	22/28	Average	19/26	Poor	22/28	Average
Driving Range (miles)	475	Vry. Long	427.5	Long	475	Vry. Long
Bumpers						
Parking Index	Average		Average		Average	
Head/Leg Room (in.)	39.5/42.4	Average	39.5/42.4	Average	39.5/42.4	Average
Interior Space (cu. ft.)						
Cargo Space (cu. ft.)						
Tow Rating (lbs.)	2000	Vry. Low	2000	Vry. Low	2000	Vry. Low

This year, while basically unchanged, the Silverado and the Sierra get 3/4 ton and 1-ton versions. These replace their counterparts in the dropped C/K series. There are also two new engines this year, a 6.6-liter diesel and an 8.1-liter V-8, in addition to the 4.3-liter V6, 4.8-liter V8, 5.3-liter V8, 6.0-liter V8, and a 6.5-liter turbo-diesel V8. With so many engine choices, the Silverado is great for towing. Be careful when using or turning off the passenger-side airbag switch.

2001 Chevrolet Silverado

General Information

New for 2001: No major changes	**Year of Production:** 3
Twins:	**Seating:** 2
Where Made: Canada	**Theft Rating:** Average

Prices 2001

Model	Retail	Markup
1500 2WD 5-spd. man.	$15,880	10%
1500 4WD 4-spd. auto.	$20,040	10%
2500 2WD 5-spd. man.	$21,079	14%
2500 4WD 4-spd. auto.	$27,540	14%

Competition 2001

Model	POOR				GOOD	pg.
Chev. Silverado		■				**176**
Dodge Ram		■				210
Ford F-Series					■	226

'00 and '99 Models

In 1998, the Sierra was based on the C/K Series and rated highly among standard pickups, thanks to excellent frontal crash test scores. In 1999, the Sierra was redesigned, moving to the newly introduced Silverado's platform. The 2000 Sierra and Silverado did not change from 1999.

Price Ranges 2000–1999

1500 2WD 5-sp. man.	$15-16,000
1500 4WD 5-sp. man.	$17-18,000
2500 4WD 5-sp. man.	$23-24,000

2000 Chevrolet Silverado

1999 Chevrolet Silverado

Chevrolet Silverado/GMC Sierra — Full-Size Pickup

	2001	2000	1999

RATINGS

	POOR → GOOD	POOR → GOOD	POOR → GOOD
Comparative Rating	3	2	3
Frontal Crash Tests	6	6	6
Safety Features	6	6	6
Preventive Maintenance	5	4	5
Repair Costs	5	7	9
Warranty	2	2	2
Fuel Economy	1	2	2
Rollover (based on SSF; see pg. 30)	4	4	4
Complaints	3	4	5
Insurance Costs	10	5	5

SAFETY

	2001	2000	1999
Frontal Crash Tests	Average	Average	Average
Side Crash Tests	No Govt Results	No Govt Results	No Govt Results
Airbags	Dual	Dual	Dual
Anti-Lock Brakes	4-Wheel	4-Wheel	4-Wheel
Day Running Lamps	Standard	Standard	Standard
Built-In Child Seats	None	None	None
Pretensioners	None	None	None

SPECIFICATIONS

	2001		2000		1999	
Fuel Economy (cty/hwy)	15/18	Vry. Poor	15/18	Vry. Poor	15/18	Vry. Poor
Driving Range (miles)	429	Long	429	Long	429	Long
Bumpers						
Parking Index	Vry. Hard		Vry. Hard		Vry. Hard	
Head/Leg Room (in.)	41/41.3	Roomy	41/41.3	Roomy	41/41.3	Roomy
Interior Space (cu. ft.)						
Cargo Space (cu. ft.)						
Tow Rating (lbs.)	3946	Low	3946	Low	3946	Low

The Suburban and the Yukon XL enter 2001 essentially unchanged. To provide a more comfortable and safer ride, body stiffness and interior passenger space were increased, and ease of entry was improved last year. 2000 also introduced a 5.3-liter V8 as standard, and a 6-liter V8 provided 15 more horses. ABS, daytime running lamps, and dual airbags are still standard, but front seat side airbags are also standard, which few sport utility vehicles have. Fuel prices could dampen the popularity of these gas eaters, which may make the high price a bit more negotiable.

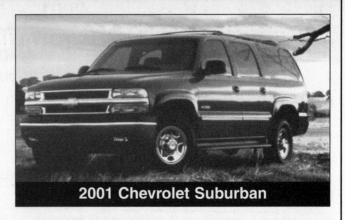
2001 Chevrolet Suburban

General Information

New for 2001: No major changes		**Year of Production:**	2
Twins:		**Seating:**	9
Where Made: Canada		**Theft Rating:**	High

Prices 2001

Model	Retail	Markup
1500 2WD 4-spd. auto.	$25,921	14%
2500 2WD 4-spd. auto.	$27,780	14%
1500 4WD 4-spd. auto.	$28,831	14%
2500 4WD 4-spd. auto.	$30,780	14%

Competition 2001

Model	POOR				GOOD	pg.
Chev. Suburban					■	**178**
Linc. Navigator					■	320
Ford Expedition			■			222
Toyota 4Runner				■		416

'00 and '99 Models

The Suburban and Yukon XL were redesigned for 2000. An unloaded Suburban weighs close to 5,000 pounds, so the standard 5.7-liter V8 has a lot of work to do. Optional engines include a 7.4-liter V8 and a 6.5-liter turbo-diesel V8; all engines come with 4-speed automatic overdrive. The '99 version of the GMC Yukon was called the GMC Suburban.

Price Ranges 2000–1999

1500 2WD 4-sp. auto.	$25-26,000
2500 2WD 4-sp. auto.	$27-28,000
1500 4WD 4-sp. auto.	$28-29,000
2500 4WD 4-sp. auto.	$29-31,000

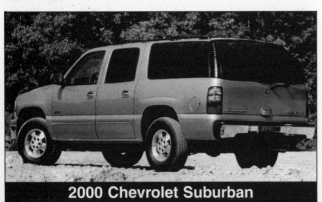
2000 Chevrolet Suburban

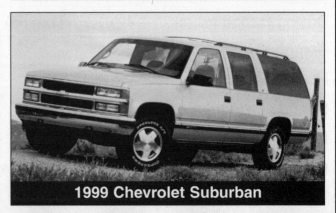
1999 Chevrolet Suburban

Chevrolet Suburban/GMC Yukon XL — Large Sport Utility

	2001	2000	1999

RATINGS

	POOR → GOOD (2001)	POOR → GOOD (2000)	POOR → GOOD (1999)
Comparative Rating			
Frontal Crash Tests			
Safety Features	8	8	6
Preventive Maintenance	5	4	5
Repair Costs	10	7	7
Warranty	2	2	2
Fuel Economy	1	1	1
Rollover (based on SSF; see pg. 30)	4	4	4
Complaints	5		2
Insurance Costs	10	10	10

SAFETY

	2001	2000	1999
Frontal Crash Tests	To Be Tested	No Govt Results	No Govt Results
Side Crash Tests	No Govt Results	No Govt Results	No Govt Results
Airbags	Dual/Side (nextgen)	Dual/Side (nextgen)	Dual (nextgen)
Anti-Lock Brakes	4-Wheel	4-Wheel	4-Wheel
Day Running Lamps	Standard	Standard	Standard
Built-In Child Seats	None	None	None
Pretensioners	None	None	None

SPECIFICATIONS

	2001		2000		1999	
Fuel Economy (cty/hwy)	14/16	Vry. Poor	14/18	Vry. Poor	14/18	Vry. Poor
Driving Range (miles)	495	Vry. Long	528	Vry. Long	672	Vry. Long
Bumpers						
Parking Index	Vry. Hard		Vry. Hard		Vry. Hard	
Head/Leg Room (in.)	40.7/41.3	Roomy	40.7/41.3	Roomy	39.9/41.3	Average
Interior Space (cu. ft.)						
Cargo Space (cu. ft.)	138.4	Vry. Large	138.4	Vry. Large	149.5	Vry. Large
Tow Rating (lbs.)	8800	Vry. High	8800	Vry. High	6500	Vry. High

Chevrolet Tahoe/GMC Yukon — Mid-Size Sport Utility

For 2000, the Tahoe and Yukon got a full makeover so you won't see much difference in the 2001. The stiffer body on the Suburban is also a feature of the Tahoe/Yukon. The base model comes with a 4.8-liter V8, but for more power you can go for the 5.3-liter version. And although the exterior size has not increased, the already comfortable interior has even more space now. Dual airbags, ABS, and front passenger side airbags are all standard.

2001 Chevrolet Tahoe

General Information

New for 2001: No major changes	**Year of Production:** 2
Twins: Cad. Escalade, GMC Denali	**Seating:** 5-6
Where Made: U.S.	**Theft Rating:** Very High

Prices 2001

Model	Retail	Markup
2WD 4-spd. auto.	$24,941	14%
4WD 4-spd. auto.	$27,857	10%
LS 2WD 4-spd. auto.	$31,305	15%
LS 4WD 4-spd. auto.	$34,021	15%

Competition 2001

Model	POOR				GOOD	pg.
Chev. Tahoe			■			180
Ford Explorer			■			224
Jeep Gr. Cher.	■					286
Toyota 4Runner			■			416

'00 and '99 Models

Though the Tahoe/Yukon shares its chassis with the C/K pickups, the engine choices and options list are limited to a 5.7-liter V8 or a weaker 6.5-liter turbo-diesel. The Tahoe/Yukon has one of the largest cargo spaces in the market and the benefit of de-powered airbags.

Price Ranges 2000–1999

2WD 4-sp. auto.	$23-25,000
4WD 4-sp. auto.	$26-28,000

2000 Chevrolet Tahoe

1999 Chevrolet Tahoe

Chevrolet Tahoe/GMC Yukon — Mid-Size Sport Utility

RATINGS

(POOR → GOOD)	2001	2000	1999
Comparative Rating	5	4	4
Frontal Crash Tests*	7	7	
Safety Features	8	8	6
Preventive Maintenance	5	4	5
Repair Costs	6	7	7
Warranty	2	2	2
Fuel Economy	1	1	1
Rollover (based on SSF, see pg. 25)	4	4	4
Complaints	5		2
Insurance Costs	10	10	10

SAFETY

	2001	2000	1999
Frontal Crash Tests	Good	Good	Good
Side Crash Tests	No Govt Results	No Govt Results	No Govt Results
Airbags	Dual/Side (nextgen)	Dual/Side (nextgen)	Dual (nextgen)
Anti-Lock Brakes	4-Wheel	4-Wheel	4-Wheel
Day Running Lamps	Standard	Standard	Standard
Built-In Child Seats	None	None	None
Pretensioners	None	None	None

SPECIFICATIONS

	2001		2000		1999	
Fuel Economy (cty/hwy)	14/17	Vry. Poor	15/19	Vry. Poor	14/18	Vry. Poor
Driving Range (miles)	403	Average	442	Long	480	Vry. Long
Bumpers						
Parking Index	Hard		Hard		Hard	
Head/Leg Room (in.)	40.7/41.3	Roomy	40.7/41.3	Roomy	39.9/41.9	Average
Interior Space (cu. ft.)						
Cargo Space (cu. ft.)	108.2	Vry. Large	108.2	Vry. Large	99.4	Vry. Large
Tow Rating (lbs.)	7100	Vry. High	7100	Vry. High	6000	High

*To be tested in 2001.

Chevrolet Tracker

Small Sport Utility

The Tracker continues into 2001 unchanged, except for minor engine changes, since its makeover in 1999. Chevrolet dropped the 1.6-liter 4-cylinder engine that was standard for the convertible. The 2.0L 4-cylinder engine is now standard on both the 2-door convertible and the 4-door hardtop version. There is also an optional 2.5-liter V6 for the 2001 Tracker. 4-wheel ABS is optional, but dual de-powered airbags are standard in the front seats.

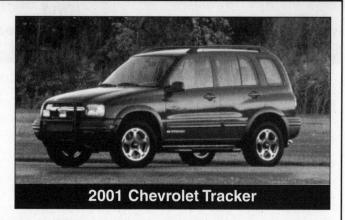

2001 Chevrolet Tracker

General Information

New for 2001: No major changes	**Year of Production:**	2
Twins: Suzuki Grand Vitara	**Seating:**	4
Where Made: U.S.	**Theft Rating:**	

Prices 2001

Model	Retail	Markup
2WD 2dr. Conv. 5-spd. man.	$15,235	6%
4WD 2dr. Conv. 5-spd. man.	$16,335	6%
2WD 5-spd. auto.	$16,885	6%
4WD 5-spd. auto.	$17,955	6%

Competition 2001

Model	POOR				GOOD	pg.
Chev. Tracker						**182**
Honda CR-V				■		246
Jeep Wrangler	■					288

'00 and '99 Models

The Tracker got new rack and pinion steering in 1999, as well as a four-wheel drive system that can be engaged while driving. Interior room is adequate up front, tight in back. The exterior design gives the 2-door convertible and 4-door hardtop versions of this sport utility very different looks.

Price Ranges 2000–1999

2WD 5-sp. man.	$13-14,000
2WD 2dr. Convertible 5-sp. man.	$13-15,000
4WD 2dr. Convertible 5-sp. man.	$14-15,000
4WD 5-sp. man.	$15-16,000

2000 Chevrolet Tracker

1999 Chevrolet Tracker

Chevrolet Tracker — Small Sport Utility

	2001	2000	1999

RATINGS

(Scale: POOR to GOOD)

Rating	2001	2000	1999
Comparative Rating			
Frontal Crash Tests			
Safety Features	5	6	6
Preventive Maintenance		8	8
Repair Costs	10		1
Warranty	2	2	2
Fuel Economy	5	5	5
Rollover (based on SSF; see pg. 30)	3	3	3
Complaints	2		3
Insurance Costs	1	1	1

SAFETY

	2001	2000	1999
Frontal Crash Tests	No Govt Results	No Govt Results	No Govt Results
Side Crash Tests	No Govt Results	No Govt Results	No Govt Results
Airbags	Dual	Dual	Dual
Anti-Lock Brakes	4-Wheel (optional)	4-Wheel (optional)	4-Wheel (optional)
Day Running Lamps	Standard	Standard	Standard
Built-In Child Seats	None	None	None
Pretensioners	None	None	None

SPECIFICATIONS

	2001		2000		1999	
Fuel Economy (cty/hwy)	23/26	Average	25/28	Average	25/28	Average
Driving Range (miles)	362.6	Vry. Short	392.2	Short	392.2	Short
Bumpers						
Parking Index	Vry. Easy		Vry. Easy		Vry. Easy	
Head/Leg Room (in.)	40.9/41.4	Roomy	40.9/41.4	Roomy	40.9/41.4	Roomy
Interior Space (cu. ft.)	96.8	Average	96.8	Average	96.8	Average
Cargo Space (cu. ft.)	10.2	Vry. Small	10.2	Vry. Small	10.2	Vry. Small
Tow Rating (lbs.)	1000	Vry. Low	1000	Vry. Low	1000	Vry. Low

With few changes for 2001, the Venture continues to give car buyers an alternative to the popular Chrysler minivans. Like the Chrysler, the Venture offers sliding doors on both sides. You'll also find standard dual airbags, 4-wheel ABS, and daytime running lamps. Side airbags are optional and recommended. The only engine is a 3.4-liter V6. Seating for seven is comfortable, and removing seats is relatively easy. With good crash tests, family car buyers should check out the Venture.

2001 Chevrolet Venture

General Information

New for 2001: No major changes	**Year of Production:**	5
Twins: Olds Silhouette, Pontiac Montana	**Seating:**	7-8
Where Made: U.S.	**Theft Rating:**	Very Low

Prices 2001

Model	Retail	Markup
Value 4-spd. auto.	$20,975	8%
LS 4-spd. auto.	$22,510	9%
Plus 4-spd. auto.	$24,455	10%

Competition 2001

Model	POOR				GOOD	pg.
Chev. Venture				■		**184**
Honda Odyssey			■			250
Ford Windstar					■	236
Toyota Sienna		■				438

'00 and '99 Models

In 1997, GM took steps to catch up in the highly competitive minivan market by offering the Venture, along with its twins, the Olds Silhouette and Pontiac Montana (formerly called the Transport). The cargo space is one of the largest in the industry, and the 3.4-liter V6 is plenty powerful.

Price Ranges 2000–1999

Value 4-sp. auto.	$21-22,000
LS 4-sp. auto.	$23-24,000

2000 Chevrolet Venture   **1999 Chevrolet Venture**

	2001	2000	1999

RATINGS

	POOR — GOOD	POOR — GOOD	POOR — GOOD
Comparative Rating	5	5	5
Frontal Crash Tests*	7	7	7
Safety Features	9	10	10
Preventive Maintenance	8	8	7
Repair Costs	5	5	5
Warranty	2	2	2
Fuel Economy	4	3	3
Rollover (based on SSF, see pg. 25)	5	5	5
Complaints	2	2	2
Insurance Costs	10	10	10

SAFETY

	2001	2000	1999
Frontal Crash Tests	Good	Good	Good
Side Crash Tests	Very Good	Very Good	Very Good
Airbags	Dual (nextgen)	Dual (nextgen)	Dual (nextgen)
Anti-Lock Brakes	4-Wheel	4-Wheel	4-Wheel
Day Running Lamps	Standard	Standard	Standard
Built-In Child Seats	Optional	Optional	Optional
Pretensioners	Standard	Standard	Standard

SPECIFICATIONS

	2001		2000		1999	
Fuel Economy (cty/hwy)	19/26	Poor	18/25	Poor	18/25	Poor
Driving Range (miles)	450	Long	430	Long	430	Long
Bumpers	Strong		Strong		Strong	
Parking Index	Hard		Hard		Hard	
Head/Leg Room (in.)	39.9/39.9	Cramped	39.9/39.9	Cramped	39.9/39.9	Cramped
Interior Space (cu. ft.)						
Cargo Space (cu. ft.)	133	Vry. Large	133	Vry. Large	126.6	Vry. Large
Tow Rating (lbs.)	3500	Low	3500	Low	3500	Low

*To be tested in 2001.

The Chrysler 300M continues to be Chrysler's flagship vehicle, unchanged since its introduction in 1999. The 300M is powered by an aluminum 3.5-liter V6 engine with 253 hp. Dual airbags, 4-wheel ABS, and traction control are all standard. The sole engine choice, a 3.5-liter V6, is quick. Luxurious standard features include heated leather seats, a four-disc stereo system, and the Autostick manual/automatic transmission. No crash test scores are available, but optional side air bags are available for 2001.

2001 Chrysler 300M

General Information

New for 2001: No major changes		**Year of Production:**	3
Twins: Chrysler LHS		**Seating:**	5
Where Made: U.S., Canada		**Theft Rating:**	Very High

Prices 2001

Model	Retail	Markup
Base	$29,640	10%

Competition 2001

Model	POOR					GOOD		pg.
Chrysler 300M							■	**186**
Buick Century					■			142
Lexus ES300							■	302
Saturn L/LW					■			396

'00 and '99 Models

Introduced in 1999, the 300M is available with leather interior, an anti-theft system, fog lamps, heated rearview mirrors, dual airbags, 4-wheel ABS, and a CD player all are standard. Surprisingly, side airbags weren't available until 2001.

Price Ranges 2000–1999

Base	$28-29,000

2000 Chrysler 300M

1999 Chrysler 300M

Chrysler 300M — Large

	2001	2000	1999

RATINGS

	POOR → GOOD (2001)	POOR → GOOD (2000)	POOR → GOOD (1999)
Comparative Rating	—	5	5
Frontal Crash Tests	—	5	5
Safety Features	5	5	6
Preventive Maintenance	7	7	7
Repair Costs	8	—	—
Warranty	1	1	2
Fuel Economy	4	4	4
Rollover (based on SSF; see pg. 30)	8	8	8
Complaints	2	2	4
Insurance Costs	5	5	5

SAFETY

	2001	2000	1999
Frontal Crash Tests	To Be Tested	Average	Average
Side Crash Tests	No Govt Results	No Govt Results	No Govt Results
Airbags	Dual & Opt. Side (nextgen)	Dual (nextgen)	Dual
Anti-Lock Brakes	4-Wheel	4-Wheel	4-Wheel
Day Running Lamps	None	None	None
Built-In Child Seats	None	None	None
Pretensioners	None	None	None

SPECIFICATIONS

	2001		2000		1999	
Fuel Economy (cty/hwy)	18/26	Poor	18/27	Poor	18/27	Poor
Driving Range (miles)	374	Short	382.5	Short	387	Short
Bumpers						
Parking Index	Hard		Hard		Hard	
Head/Leg Room (in.)	38.3/42.2	Cramped	38.3/42.2	Cramped	38/43.5	Average
Interior Space (cu. ft.)	105	Roomy	121.9	Vry. Roomy	121.9	Vry. Roomy
Cargo Space (cu. ft.)	17	Average	16.8	Average	31	Average
Tow Rating (lbs.)						

Chrysler Concorde

Intermediate

With no major changes for 2001, the Concorde is carrying forward Chrysler's innovative styling and design. The base LX engine is a 2.7-liter V6; a 3.2-liter V6 comes with the up-level LXi. Both engines are all-aluminum and offer great performance without sacrificing fuel economy. Dual airbags are standard but 4-wheel ABS is optional. Interior room is ample.

2001 Chrysler Concorde

General Information

New for 2001: No major changes	**Year of Production:** 4
Twins: Dodge Intrepid	**Seating:** 5
Where Made: Canada	**Theft Rating:** Very Low

Prices 2001

Model	Retail	Markup
LX	$22,500	9%
LXI	$26,500	10%

Competition 2001

Model	POOR					GOOD		pg.
Chrys. Concorde				■				**188**
Buick Century					■			142
Lexus ES300							■	302
VW Passat						■		452

'00 and '99 Models

The Concorde, along with its twin, the Dodge Intrepid, were redesigned in 1998 with an aggressive round shape and a stylish new front and rear end, while maintaining the cab-forward design inside. The '99-'00 version contained few changes.

Price Ranges 2000–1999

LX	$21-22,000
LXi	$24-26,000

2000 Chrysler Concorde

1999 Chrysler Concorde

	2001	2000	1999

RATINGS

	2001 (POOR–GOOD)	2000 (POOR–GOOD)	1999 (POOR–GOOD)
Comparative Rating	6	7	8
Frontal Crash Tests	7	7	7
Safety Features	5	5	4
Preventive Maintenance	7	7	7
Repair Costs	7	8	9
Warranty	1	1	2
Fuel Economy	5	5	5
Rollover (based on SSF; see pg. 30)	8	8	8
Complaints	4	5	5
Insurance Costs	10	10	10

SAFETY

	2001	2000	1999
Frontal Crash Tests	Good	Good	No Govt Results
Side Crash Tests	Good	Good	Good
Airbags	Dual (nextgen)	Dual (nextgen)	Dual
Anti-Lock Brakes	4-Wheel (optional)	4-Wheel (optional)	4-Wheel (optional)
Day Running Lamps	None	None	None
Built-In Child Seats	None	None	None
Pretensioners	None	None	None

SPECIFICATIONS

	2001		2000		1999	
Fuel Economy (cty/hwy)	20/28	Average	21/30	Average	21/30	Average
Driving Range (miles)	408	Average	433.5	Long	433.5	Long
Bumpers	Strong		Strong		Strong	
Parking Index	Hard		Hard		Hard	
Head/Leg Room (in.)	38.3/42.2	Cramped	38.3/42.2	Cramped	38.3/42.1	Cramped
Interior Space (cu. ft.)	107	Roomy	126.3	Vry. Roomy	126.3	Vry. Roomy
Cargo Space (cu. ft.)	19	Average	18.7	Average	18.7	Average
Tow Rating (lbs.)	1500	Vry. Low	1500	Vry. Low	1500	Vry. Low

Completely redesigned in 1999, the LHS continues into 2001 with no major changes. As Chrysler's flagship sedan, the LHS features numerous luxury and safety features like dual airbags, an anti-theft system, traction control, and 4-wheel ABS. Inside, you'll find heated leather seats which are power operated. Its 3.5-liter V6 engine offers 253 hp. An optional touring suspension provides a better ride.

2001 Chrysler LHS

General Information

New for 2001: No major changes	**Year of Production:** 2
Twins: Chrysler 300M	**Seating:** 5
Where Made: Canada	**Theft Rating:**

Prices 2001

Model	Retail	Markup
Base	$28,680.	9%

Competition 2001

Model	POOR				GOOD	pg.
Chrysler LHS						**190**
Buick LeSabre				■		144
Lincoln Town Car					■	322
Audi A8					■	132

'00 and '99 Models

The upscale version of the Concorde and Intrepid, the LHS was redesigned in mid-1998 as a 1999 model. For the redesigned 1999 model, Chrysler drew on the stylish designs of the new Concorde/Intrepid. The cab-forward design allows for excellent interior space, and luxury options abound.

Price Ranges 2000–1999

Base	$22,300-28,000

2000 Chrysler LHS

1999 Chrysler LHS

Chrysler LHS — Large

	2001	2000	1999

RATINGS

(POOR → GOOD)	2001	2000	1999
Comparative Rating	—	5	5
Frontal Crash Tests	—	5	5
Safety Features	5	6	5
Preventive Maintenance	7	6	6
Repair Costs	8	9	9
Warranty	1	1	2
Fuel Economy	4	4	4
Rollover (based on SSF; see pg. 30)	8	8	8
Complaints	1	1	2
Insurance Costs	10	10	10

SAFETY

	2001	2000	1999
Frontal Crash Tests	To Be Tested	Average	Average
Side Crash Tests	Good	Good	Good
Airbags	Dual (nextgen)	Dual (nextgen)	Dual
Anti-Lock Brakes	4-Wheel	4-Wheel	4-Wheel
Day Running Lamps	None	Standard	None
Built-In Child Seats	None	None	None
Pretensioners	None	None	None

SPECIFICATIONS

	2001		2000		1999	
Fuel Economy (cty/hwy)	18/26	Poor	18/27	Poor	18/27	Poor
Driving Range (miles)	374	Short	382.5	Short	382.5	Short
Bumpers						
Parking Index	Hard		Hard		Hard	
Head/Leg Room (in.)	38.3/42.2	Cramped	38.3/42.2	Cramped	38.3/42.2	Cramped
Interior Space (cu. ft.)	107	Roomy	108	Roomy	108	Roomy
Cargo Space (cu. ft.)	19	Average	18.7	Average	18.7	Average
Tow Rating (lbs.)	2000	Vry. Low	2000	Vry. Low	2000	Vry. Low

Chrysler PT Cruiser

Intermediate

Chrysler took a risk with its retro design, but loaded it with lots of very practical features and made it fun to drive. In addition to its remarkable looks, the PT features great interior space, a Rubik's Cube of possibilities with its folding seats, and no bargains due to its popularity. Officially, Chrysler and the government call it a light truck; we think it's much more like a wagon or small minivan. We put it in the intermediate size class because of its weight. A peppy engine, ease of handling, and quiet ride contribute to its popularity.

2001 Chrysler PT Cruiser

General Information

New for 2001: All-new		**Year of Production:**	1
Twins:		**Seating:**	5
Where Made: Canada		**Theft Rating:**	

Prices 2001

Model	Retail	Markup
Base	$15,935	9%

Competition 2001

Model	POOR					GOOD		pg.
Chrys. PT Cruis.			■					**192**
Buick Regal						■		148
Chev. Malibu			■					170
VW Passat						■		452

'00 and '99 Models

Price Ranges 2000–1999

MODEL WAS NOT PRODUCED THIS YEAR

2000 Model

MODEL WAS NOT PRODUCED THIS YEAR

1999 Model

Chrysler PT Cruiser — Intermediate

	2001	2000	1999

RATINGS

	POOR — GOOD	POOR — GOOD	POOR — GOOD
Comparative Rating	3		
Frontal Crash Tests	4		
Safety Features	5		
Preventive Maintenance	7		
Repair Costs			
Warranty	1		
Fuel Economy	4		
Rollover (based on SSF; see pg. 30)	5		
Complaints	5		
Insurance Costs	5		

SAFETY

Frontal Crash Tests	Poor		
Side Crash Tests	No Govt Results		
Airbags	Dual & Opt. Side (nextgen)		
Anti-Lock Brakes	4-Wheel (optional)		
Day Running Lamps	None		
Built-In Child Seats	None		
Pretensioners	None		

SPECIFICATIONS

Fuel Economy (cty/hwy)	20/25	Poor	
Driving Range (miles)	337.5	Vry. Short	
Bumpers			
Parking Index	Easy		
Head/Leg Room (in.)	40.4/40.6	Average	
Interior Space (cu. ft.)	120.2	Vry. Roomy	
Cargo Space (cu. ft.)	19	Average	
Tow Rating (lbs.)	1000	Vry. Low	

All-new for 2001, the Sebring aims to compete with the Grand Am and Camry. The sedan and convertible share the same platform and engine configurations. The Coupe is actually a different car, made at the Mitsubishi plant in Illinois, and comes with a different engine. The safety belts are integrated into the front seats for greater comfort, and the vehicle has been designed to reduce road noise. The sedan has split, folding rear seats and side airbags available.

2001 Chrysler Sebring

General Information

New for 2001: All-new; Sedan model replaces Cirrus	**Year of Production:**	1
Twins: Dodge Stratus	**Seating:**	5
Where Made: U.S.	**Theft Rating:**	Very High

Prices 2001

Model	Retail	Markup
Sedan LX	$17,945	9%
Sedan LXI	$20,830	9%
Coupe LXI	$21,475	10%
LXi Convertible	$26,830	10%

Competition 2001

Model	POOR				GOOD	pg.
Chrys. Sebring						**194**
Ford Mustang				■		230
Pontiac Gr. Am		■				384
Chev. Impala					■	168

'00 and '99 Models

Available in a coupe and convertible; the coupe comes in two trim levels: LX and LXi and the convertible features three: JX, JXi, and Limited. Despite their similar names, the coupe shares a platform with the Avenger, while the Sebring convertible shares the Cirrus platform. The front seat is roomy; the rear is a squeeze for adults.

Price Ranges 2000–1999

Coupe LX	$19-20,000
JXi Convertible	$26-27,000

2000 Chrysler Sebring

1999 Chrysler Sebring

Chrysler Sebring — Compact

	2001	2000	1999
RATINGS (POOR → GOOD)			
Comparative Rating		5	6
Frontal Crash Tests		10	10
Safety Features	4	5	4
Preventive Maintenance	7	7	7
Repair Costs	4	6	8
Warranty	1	1	2
Fuel Economy	5	4	5
Rollover (based on SSF; see pg. 30)	8	8	8
Complaints	5	3	5
Insurance Costs	1	1	1

SAFETY

	2001	2000	1999
Frontal Crash Tests	No Govt Results	Very Good	Very Good
Side Crash Tests	No Govt Results	No Govt Results	No Govt Results
Airbags	Dual (nextgen)	Dual (nextgen)	Dual
Anti-Lock Brakes	4-Wheel (optional)	4-Wheel (optional)	4-Wheel (optional)
Day Running Lamps	None	None	None
Built-In Child Seats	None	None	None
Pretensioners	None	None	None

SPECIFICATIONS

	2001		2000		1999	
Fuel Economy (cty/hwy)	20/27	Poor	19/27	Poor	22/31	Average
Driving Range (miles)	383.05	Short	365.7	Vry. Short	421.35	Average
Bumpers	Strong		Strong		Strong	
Parking Index	Average		Hard		Hard	
Head/Leg Room (in.)	38.5/42.3	Average	39.1/43.3	Roomy	39.1/43.3	Roomy
Interior Space (cu. ft.)	94	Cramped	91	Cramped	91	Cramped
Cargo Space (cu. ft.)	16	Small	13.1	Vry. Small	13.1	Vry. Small
Tow Rating (lbs.)						

Chrysler Town and Country — Minivan

The Town and Country, redesigned for 2001, is the upscale version of the Chrysler minivans, featuring luxury features such as leather and suede interior, heated power seats and lots of power equipment. The T&C comes with an array of new features including power liftgate, removable center console, 3-zone temperature controls, and a rear seat video system with wireless earphones. With the demise of the Plymouth nameplate, Chrysler takes over the Voyager model as the downscale (and shorter) version of the T&C.

2001 Chrysler Town and Country

General Information

New for 2001: All-new		Year of Production:	1
Twins: Grand Caravan		Seating:	7
Where Made: Mexico		Theft Rating:	Average

Prices 2001

Model	Retail	Markup
LX	$24,400	10%
LXi	$29,180	11%
LX AWD	$30,850	11%
Limited(AWD)	$37,180	11%

Competition 2001

Model	POOR				GOOD		pg.
Chrys. T&C				■			**196**
Olds Silhouette				■			378
Honda Odyssey			■				250
Toyota Sienna			■				438

'00 and '99 Models

The 1999-2000 Town and Country is more aerodynamic than the previous version of the Chrysler minivan. There were two engine choices, the 3.3 and 3.8—most drivers preferred the latter, especially if they wanted to tow. Some models come with a suede interior. For the Voyager, the 1999 and 2000 versions were named Plymouth.

Price Ranges 2000–1999

LX	$26-27,000
LX AWD	$28-29,000
Limited	$33-34,000
Limited AWD	$35-36,000

2000 Chrysler Town and Country

1999 Chrysler Town and Country

Chrysler Town and Country

Minivan

	2001	2000	1999
RATINGS			
	POOR — GOOD	POOR — GOOD	POOR — GOOD
Comparative Rating	6	6	7
Frontal Crash Tests*	7	7	5
Safety Features	6	6	6
Preventive Maintenance	9	9	8
Repair Costs	9	9	10
Warranty	1	1	2
Fuel Economy	4	3	3
Rollover (based on SSF, see pg. 25)	5	5	5
Complaints	5	4	6
Insurance Costs	10	10	10

SAFETY

	2001	2000	1999
Frontal Crash Tests	Good	Good	Average
Side Crash Tests	No Govt Results	Good	Good
Airbags		Dual (nextgen)	Dual (nextgen)
Anti-Lock Brakes		4-Wheel	4-Wheel
Day Running Lamps	None	None	None
Built-In Child Seats	Optional	Optional	Optional
Pretensioners	None	None	None

SPECIFICATIONS

	2001		2000		1999	
Fuel Economy (cty/hwy)	18/24	Poor	18/24	Poor	18/24	Poor
Driving Range (miles)	420	Average	420	Average	420	Average
Bumpers			Strong		Strong	
Parking Index	Hard		Hard		Hard	
Head/Leg Room (in.)	39.7/40.6	Cramped	39.8/40.6	Cramped	39.8/40.6	Cramped
Interior Space (cu. ft.)			113.6	Roomy	113.6	Roomy
Cargo Space (cu. ft.)	146.7	Vry. Large	162.9	Vry. Large	162.9	Vry. Large
Tow Rating (lbs.)	3500	Low	2000	Vry. Low	2000	Vry. Low

*To be tested in 2001.

CAR BOOK 2001   197

Daewoo Lanos   Compact

This entry-level vehicle remains unchanged for 2001 but expands its models to include a 3-door coupe, 4-door sedan and 3-door sport model. Using what Daewoo calls "guest engineering" the chassis was developed by Porsche, the power train by GM and the engine controls by Delphi. The engine is adequate and the color choices are distinctive. Power door locks, windows, and mirrors are options. A very basic vehicle.

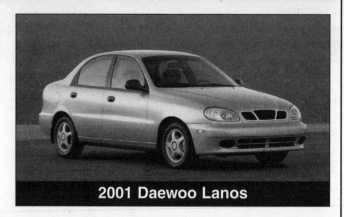

2001 Daewoo Lanos

General Information

New for 2001: No major changes	Year of Production:	3
Twins:	Seating:	4
Where Made: Korea	Theft Rating:	

Prices 2001

Model	Retail	Markup
S-Hatchback	$9,199	18%
S-Sedan	$10,099	15%
Sport-Hatchback	$12,999	18%

Competition 2001

Model	POOR					GOOD	pg.
Daewoo Lanos						■	198
Subaru Legacy					■		406
Chev. Cavalier			■				166
Pontiac Sunfire			■				390

'00 and '99 Models

The Korean-built Lanos is a simple vehicle designed to appeal to first-time buyers. While basic, the car comes with a McPherson suspension system, and Daewoo has added lots of sound-dampening material to reduce road noise.

Price Ranges 2000–1999

S-Hatchback	$8-9,000
S-Sedan	$9-10,000
Sport-Hatchback	$11-12,000

PHOTO NOT AVAILABLE

2000 Model

PHOTO NOT AVAILABLE

1999 Model

Daewoo Lanos — Compact

	2001	2000	1999

RATINGS

	POOR — GOOD	POOR — GOOD	POOR — GOOD
Comparative Rating			
Frontal Crash Tests			
Safety Features	5	5	5
Preventive Maintenance			
Repair Costs			
Warranty			
Fuel Economy	8	8	8
Rollover (based on SSF; see pg. 30)	6	6	6
Complaints	9	9	10
Insurance Costs	5	5	5

SAFETY

	2001	2000	1999
Frontal Crash Tests	No Govt Results	No Govt Results	No Govt Results
Side Crash Tests	No Govt Results	No Govt Results	No Govt Results
Airbags	Dual	Dual	Dual
Anti-Lock Brakes	4-Wheel (optional)	4-Wheel (optional)	4-Wheel (optional)
Day Running Lamps	None	None	None
Built-In Child Seats	Standard	Standard	Standard
Pretensioners	None	None	None

SPECIFICATIONS

	2001		2000		1999	
Fuel Economy (cty/hwy)	26/36	Good	26/36	Good	26/36	Good
Driving Range (miles)	393.7	Short	393.7	Short	393.7	Short
Bumpers						
Parking Index						
Head/Leg Room (in.)	38.9/42.8	Average	38.9/42.8	Average	38.9/42.8	Average
Interior Space (cu. ft.)	91	Cramped				
Cargo Space (cu. ft.)	11	Vry. Small				
Tow Rating (lbs.)						

Unchanged for 2001, the Leganza comes with two additional color choices. It has an automatic interior temperature control system, optional moon roof, and a fuel gauge, which stays active even when the car is turned off. In the event of an accident or sudden stop, doors automatically unlock. An alarm system is standard on the pricier models, and the engine is adequate for the size of the vehicle.

2001 Daewoo Leganza

General Information

New for 2001: No major changes	Year of Production:	3
Twins:	Seating:	4
Where Made: Korea	Theft Rating:	

Prices 2001

Model	Retail	Markup
SE	$13,999	18%
SX	$17,499	8%
CDX	$18,999	11%

Competition 2001

Model	POOR					GOOD	pg.
Daewoo Leganza							200
Chev. Malibu			■				170
Nissan Altima						■	356
Chrys. Concorde					■		188

'00 and '99 Models

These are Daewoo's luxury vehicles, designed to compete with fancy Accords and Camrys. While sales are limited, there is a network of 450 dealers. The ride, handling, and feel are surprisingly good, but the car's general availability is limited.

Price Ranges 2000–1999

SE	$13-14,000
SX	$16-17,000
CDX	$18-19,000

PHOTO NOT AVAILABLE

2000 Model

PHOTO NOT AVAILABLE

1999 Model

	2001	2000	1999

RATINGS

	POOR — GOOD	POOR — GOOD	POOR — GOOD
Comparative Rating			
Frontal Crash Tests			
Safety Features	5	5	5
Preventive Maintenance			
Repair Costs			
Warranty			
Fuel Economy	5	5	5
Rollover (based on SSF; see pg. 30)	7	7	7
Complaints	10	10	10
Insurance Costs	5	5	5

SAFETY

	2001	2000	1999
Frontal Crash Tests	No Govt Results	No Govt Results	No Govt Results
Side Crash Tests	No Govt Results	No Govt Results	No Govt Results
Airbags	Dual	Dual	Dual
Anti-Lock Brakes	4-Wheel (optional)	4-Wheel (optional)	4-Wheel (optional)
Day Running Lamps	None	None	None
Built-In Child Seats	Standard	Standard	Standard
Pretensioners	None	None	None

SPECIFICATIONS

	2001		2000		1999	
Fuel Economy (cty/hwy)	20/28	Average	20/28	Average	20/28	Average
Driving Range (miles)	379.2	Short	379.2	Short	379.2	Short
Bumpers						
Parking Index	Easy					
Head/Leg Room (in.)	39.3/42.3	Average	39.3/42.3	Average	39.3/42.3	Average
Interior Space (cu. ft.)	100	Average				
Cargo Space (cu. ft.)	14	Small				
Tow Rating (lbs.)						

Dodge Caravan/Chrysler Voyager   Minivan

All new for 2001, the Caravan continues to be offered in the regular and longer Grand Caravan lengths. Most minivan buyers will opt for the longer wheelbase to get the additional storage. Dodge and Chrysler have tried to address the problem of easily removable seats by putting them on rollers. This is the nearly identical twin of the Chrysler Voyager (Caravan) and Town and Country (Grand Caravan) and comes with the same new options including power doors, removable center console, 3-zone temperature control, and a sleek (for minivans) new design.

2001 Dodge Caravan

General Information

New for 2001: All-new	**Year of Production:** 1
Twins: Town and Country	**Seating:** 7
Where Made: US	**Theft Rating:** Very Low

Prices 2001

Model	Retail	Markup
SE-SWB	$19,160	10%
Sport	$23,525	10%
Grand Caravan Sport	$29,695	10%
Grand Caravan ES	30,2235	10%

Competition 2001

Model	POOR				GOOD	pg.
Dodge Caravan				■		**202**
Chev. Venture			■			184
Ford Windstar					■	236
Toyota Sienna		■				438

'00 and '99 Models

With over 11 trim levels to choose from, the 1999-2000 Caravans come in plenty of varieties. The standard 2.4-liter, 4-cylinder engine is OK, but the optional 3.3-liter V6 engine is better. Comfort is good for seven and the optional child seats are a must. After a major redesign in 1996, the Caravan remains relatively unchanged through the 2000 model year.

Price Ranges 2000–1999

SE-SWB	$17-19,000
Sport	$21-23,000

2000 Plymouth Voyager

1999 Dodge Caravan

Dodge Caravan/Chrysler Voyager — Minivan

RATINGS

	2001 (POOR–GOOD)	2000 (POOR–GOOD)	1999 (POOR–GOOD)
Comparative Rating	6	7	8
Frontal Crash Tests*	7	7	7
Safety Features	5	6	6
Preventive Maintenance	9	9	8
Repair Costs	7	9	9
Warranty	1	1	2
Fuel Economy	4	4	4
Rollover (based on SSF, see pg. 25)	5	5	5
Complaints	5	4	7
Insurance Costs	5	10	10

SAFETY

	2001	2000	1999
Frontal Crash Tests	Good	Good	Good
Side Crash Tests	No Govt Results	Good	Good
Airbags	Dual/Opt. Side (nextgen)	Dual (nextgen)	Dual (nextgen)
Anti-Lock Brakes	4-Wheel (optional)#	4-Wheel (optional)	4-Wheel (optional)
Day Running Lamps	None	None	None
Built-In Child Seats	Optional	Optional	Optional
Pretensioners	None	None	None

SPECIFICATIONS

	2001		2000		1999	
Fuel Economy (cty/hwy)	18/24	Poor	19/26	Poor	20/26	Poor
Driving Range (miles)	420	Average	450	Long	460	Vry. Long
Bumpers			Strong		Strong	
Parking Index	Hard		Hard		Hard	
Head/Leg Room (in.)	39.7/40.6	Cramped	39.8/40.6	Cramped	39.8/40.6	Cramped
Interior Space (cu. ft.)			158.7	Vry. Roomy	158.7	Vry. Roomy
Cargo Space (cu. ft.)	142.3	Vry. Large	142.9	Vry. Large	142.9	Vry. Large
Tow Rating (lbs.)	1800#	Vry. Low	1000	Vry. Low	1000	Vry. Low

*To be tested in 2001, #Standard on SE.

Nothing has changed for 2001 with the Dakota. The 2.5-liter 4-cylinder engine is standard, and it produces only 120 hp. For heavier work, you'll be happier with the optional 3.9-liter V6, a 5.2-liter V8, or the 5.9-liter V8. You'll have to choose between two- or four-wheel drive, short or long bed, manual or automatic transmission, regular or club cab, and several optional packages. Ride is smoother than typical for compact trucks, and handling is more responsive than larger pickups.

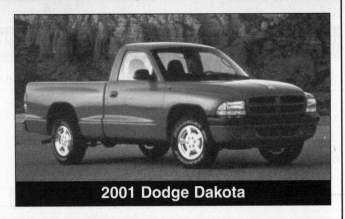

2001 Dodge Dakota

General Information

New for 2001: No major changes		**Year of Production:**	5
Twins:		**Seating:**	2
Where Made: U.S.		**Theft Rating:**	Low

Prices 2001

Model	Retail	Markup
4X2 Regular Cab	$13,910	10%
4X2 Club Cab	$17,235	11%
4X4 Regular Cab	$17,505	11%
4X4 Quad Cab	$22,370	11%

Competition 2001

Model	POOR					GOOD	pg.
Dodge Dakota							204
Chev. S-Series		■					174
Ford Ranger				■			232
Mazda B-Series			■				326

'00 and '99 Models

For 1999 the Dakota received dual de-powered airbags and a passenger airbag cutoff switch. Use caution when using the cutoff switch; remember to turn it back on when an adult gets in. 4-wheel ABS is optional on all models.

Price Ranges 2000–1999

4X2 Regular Cab	$13-14,000
4X2 Club Cab	$16-17,000
4X4 Club Cab	$20-21,000
4X4 Quad Cab	$21-22,000

2000 Dodge Dakota

1999 Dodge Dakota

Dodge Dakota — Compact Pickup

	2001	2000	1999

RATINGS

	2001 (POOR–GOOD)	2000 (POOR–GOOD)	1999 (POOR–GOOD)
Comparative Rating		2	3
Frontal Crash Tests		8	8
Safety Features	5	5	5
Preventive Maintenance	5	5	6
Repair Costs	7	9	8
Warranty	1	1	2
Fuel Economy	2	2	2
Rollover (based on SSF; see pg. 30)	5	5	4
Complaints	3	3	3
Insurance Costs	1	1	1

SAFETY

	2001	2000	1999
Frontal Crash Tests	To Be Tested	Good	Good
Side Crash Tests	No Govt Results	No Govt Results	No Govt Results
Airbags	Dual (nextgen)	Dual (nextgen)	Dual (nextgen)
Anti-Lock Brakes	4-Wheel (optional)	4-Wheel (optional)	4-Wheel (optional)
Day Running Lamps	None	None	None
Built-In Child Seats	None	None	None
Pretensioners	None	None	None

SPECIFICATIONS

	2001		2000		1999	
Fuel Economy (cty/hwy)	15/20	Vry. Poor	15/19	Vry. Poor	15/19	Vry. Poor
Driving Range (miles)	385	Short	374	Short	374	Short
Bumpers					Average	
Parking Index	Average		Average			
Head/Leg Room (in.)	40/41.9	Average	40/41.9	Average	40/41.9	Average
Interior Space (cu. ft.)						
Cargo Space (cu. ft.)	56.3	Large	56.3	Large	56.3	Large
Tow Rating (lbs.)	4000	Average	4000	Average	4000	Average

The Durango moves into 2001 unchanged, save some small appearance items. Dodge joined the parade of sport utilities by introducing the Durango in 1999 as a 4-door challenger to the best-selling Explorer. Based on the Dakota pick-up, the Durango boasts an extra, raised third row to accommodate up to eight passengers. Dual de-powered airbags and 2-wheel ABS are standard; 4-wheel ABS is optional.

2001 Dodge Durango

General Information

New for 2001: No major changes	**Year of Production:** 4
Twins:	**Seating:** 7-8
Where Made: U.S.	**Theft Rating:** Very High

Prices 2001

Model	Retail	Markup
4X2	$26,650	10%
4X4	$28,770	11%

Competition 2001

Model	POOR					GOOD	pg.
Dodge Durango							206
Ford Explorer				■			224
GMC Jimmy		■					240
Jeep Cherokee			■				284

'00 and '99 Models

Assembled in Newark, Delaware, the Durango comes with three engine choices: a base 3.9-liter V6, a 5.2-liter V8, and a 5.9-liter V8. New this year is a rear wheel drive version. The roof in the rear is higher than in the front to increase head-room for the passengers in the third row.

Price Ranges 2000–1999

4X2	$25-27,000
4X4	$27-29,000

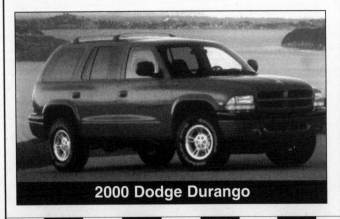

2000 Dodge Durango

1999 Dodge Durango

	2001	2000	1999

RATINGS

	POOR — GOOD	POOR — GOOD	POOR — GOOD
Comparative Rating		1	1
Frontal Crash Tests		4	4
Safety Features	5	5	5
Preventive Maintenance	3	3	3
Repair Costs	9	8	9
Warranty	1	1	2
Fuel Economy	1	1	2
Rollover (based on SSF; see pg. 30)	3	3	3
Complaints	3	3	3
Insurance Costs	5	5	5

SAFETY

	2001	2000	1999
Frontal Crash Tests	To Be Tested	Poor	Average
Side Crash Tests	No Govt Results	No Govt Results	No Govt Results
Airbags	Dual (nextgen)	Dual (nextgen)	Dual (nextgen)
Anti-Lock Brakes	4-Wheel (optional)	4-Wheel (optional)	4-Wheel (optional)
Day Running Lamps	None	None	None
Built-In Child Seats	None	None	None
Pretensioners	None	None	None

SPECIFICATIONS

	2001		2000		1999	
Fuel Economy (cty/hwy)	13/18	Vry. Poor	14/17	Vry. Poor	15/18	Vry. Poor
Driving Range (miles)	387.5	Short	387.5	Short	412.5	Average
Bumpers						
Parking Index	Vry. Hard		Vry. Hard		Vry. Hard	
Head/Leg Room (in.)	39.8/41.9	Average	39.8/41.9	Average	39.8/41.9	Average
Interior Space (cu. ft.)						
Cargo Space (cu. ft.)	88	Vry. Large	88	Vry. Large	88	Vry. Large
Tow Rating (lbs.)	4450	Average	4450	Average	4400	Average

Dodge Intrepid

The Intrepid continues into 2001 with no changes since its minor updates last year. As twin of the Concorde, it mimics Chrysler's innovative styling and design. The base engine is a 2.7-liter V6; a 3.2-liter V6 or 3.5-liter V6 come optional. The engines are all-aluminum and offer great performance without sacrificing fuel economy. Dual airbags are standard, but 4-wheel ABS is optional. Interior room is ample and the dual mode Autostick is an option.

2001 Dodge Intrepid

General Information

New for 2001: No major changes	**Year of Production:** 4
Twins: Chrysler Concorde	**Seating:** 5
Where Made: U.S.	**Theft Rating:** High

Prices 2001

Model	Retail	Markup
SE	$20,910	10%
ES	$22,605	8%
R/T	$24,975	10%

Competition 2001

Model	POOR							GOOD	pg.
Dodge Intrepid						■			208
Buick Century							■		142
Lexus ES300								■	302
Toyota Camry						■			420

'00 and '99 Models

For the 1998 model year, the Intrepid, along with its twin, the Chrysler Concorde, were redesigned into an aggressive round shape with a stylish new front and rear end, while maintaining the cab-forward design inside. Dual airbags are standard, but 4-wheel ABS is optional. The airbags were de-powered in 1999.

Price Ranges 2000–1999

SE	$19-20,000
ES	$22-23,000
R/T	none

2000 Dodge Intrepid

1999 Dodge Intrepid

Dodge Intrepid — Intermediate

	2001	2000	1999

RATINGS

	2001 (POOR–GOOD)	2000 (POOR–GOOD)	1999 (POOR–GOOD)
Comparative Rating	6	7	8
Frontal Crash Tests	7	7	7
Safety Features	5	5	5
Preventive Maintenance	7	7	7
Repair Costs	8	8	10
Warranty	1	1	2
Fuel Economy	5	5	5
Rollover (based on SSF; see pg. 30)	8	8	8
Complaints	7	7	7
Insurance Costs	5	5	5

SAFETY

	2001	2000	1999
Frontal Crash Tests	Good	Good	Good
Side Crash Tests	Good	Good	Good
Airbags	Dual (nextgen)	Dual (nextgen)	Dual (nextgen)
Anti-Lock Brakes	4-Wheel (optional)	4-Wheel (optional)	4-Wheel (optional)
Day Running Lamps	None	None	None
Built-In Child Seats	None	None	None
Pretensioners	None	None	None

SPECIFICATIONS

	2001		2000		1999	
Fuel Economy (cty/hwy)	20/28	Average	21/30	Average	21/30	Average
Driving Range (miles)	408	Average	433.5	Long	433.5	Long
Bumpers	Strong		Strong		Strong	
Parking Index	Hard		Hard		Hard	
Head/Leg Room (in.)	38.3/42.2	Cramped	38.3/42.2	Cramped	38.3/42.2	Cramped
Interior Space (cu. ft.)	104	Roomy	122.9	Vry. Roomy	104.5	Roomy
Cargo Space (cu. ft.)	18	Average	18.4	Average	18.4	Average
Tow Rating (lbs.)	1500	Vry. Low	1500	Vry. Low	1500	Vry. Low

This still distinctive pickup has not changed. The Ram has a massive front end that sets it apart from the competition. This look, combined with old-fashioned power and "big truck" performance, makes it a popular choice in the full-size pickup market. A quad cab configuration comes with extra doors on both sides of the truck. The rear doors open opposite the front allowing for easier access to the rear seat.

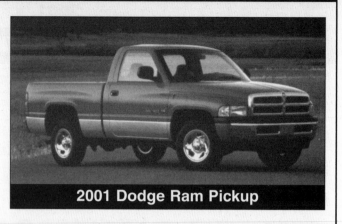

2001 Dodge Ram Pickup

General Information

New for 2001: No major changes		**Year of Production:**	8
Twins:		**Seating:**	3
Where Made: U.S.		**Theft Rating:**	Very High

Prices 2001

Model	Retail	Markup
1500 2WD Regular Cab	$15,285	14%
2500 2WD Regular Cab	$21,000	10%
1500 4WD Club Cab	$23,100	15%
3500 4WD Quad Cab	$28,800	9%

Competition 2001

Model	POOR			GOOD	pg.
Dodge Ram	■				210
Chev. Silverado	■				176
Ford F-Series				■	226

'00 and '99 Models

Engines range from a 3.9-liter V6, two V8s, a turbo-diesel V6, and a thirsty 8.0-liter V10 which is a heavier version of the Dodge Viper's engine. They all get dismal gas mileage. The extended cab version increases seating to six.

Price Ranges 2000–1999

1500 2WD	$14-15,000
2500 2WD	$19-21,000
1500 4WD	$20-21,000
3500 4WD	$24-25,000

2000 Dodge Ram Pickup

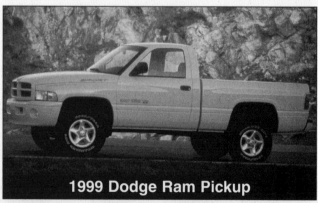

1999 Dodge Ram Pickup

Dodge Ram Pickup

Standard Pickup

	2001	2000	1999

RATINGS

	POOR → GOOD	POOR → GOOD	POOR → GOOD
Comparative Rating	3	4	3
Frontal Crash Tests*	7	8	8
Safety Features	6	6	6
Preventive Maintenance	3	3	3
Repair Costs	10	8	6
Warranty	1	1	2
Fuel Economy	2	2	2
Rollover (based on SSF, see pg. 25)	5	5	5
Complaints	5	6	4
Insurance Costs	1	5	5

SAFETY

	2001	2000	1999
Frontal Crash Tests	Good	Good	Good
Side Crash Tests	No Govt Results	No Govt Results	No Govt Results
Airbags	Dual/Side (nextgen)	Dual/Side (nextgen)	Dual/Side (nextgen)
Anti-Lock Brakes	4-Wheel (optional)	4-Wheel (optional)	4-Wheel (optional)
Day Running Lamps	None	None	None
Built-In Child Seats	None	None	None
Pretensioners	None	None	None

SPECIFICATIONS

	2001		2000		1999	
Fuel Economy (cty/hwy)	15/21	Vry. Poor	15/21	Vry. Poor	15/21	Vry. Poor
Driving Range (miles)	468	Vry. Long	468	Vry. Long	468	Vry. Long
Bumpers						
Parking Index	Vry. Hard		Vry. Hard		Vry. Hard	
Head/Leg Room (in.)	40.2/41	Average	40.2/41	Average	40.2/41	Average
Interior Space (cu. ft.)	62.8	Vry. Cramp.	62.8	Vry. Cramp.	63	Vry. Cramp.
Cargo Space (cu. ft.)						
Tow Rating (lbs.)	3500	Low	3500	Low	3300	Low

*To be tested in 2001.

Dodge Stratus   Intermediate

The Stratus is all-new for 2001. The Stratus coupe and sedan are really different cars, built on different platforms at different factories with different engines. The key difference between the Stratus and its Chrysler Sebring twins is in the front grille and taillights. Otherwise, shop them both. Nice features include such things as a battery saver to save the battery if you leave your lights on, inside lights that turn on when your remove the key, and access to the trunk with split, folding rear seats. The standard engine is larger than last year's standard, and you can upgrade to a powerful 3.0L V6.

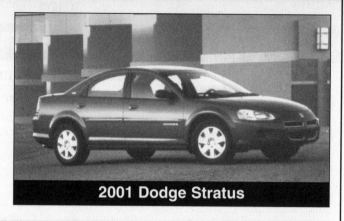
2001 Dodge Stratus

General Information

New for 2001: All-new Coupe model replaces Avenger		**Year of Production:**	1
Twins: Chrysler Sebring		**Seating:**	5
Where Made: Canada		**Theft Rating:**	Average

Prices 2001

Model	Retail	Markup
SE	$17,800	10%
Coupe	$17,810	10%
ES	$20,435	6%
R/T	$20,705	6%

Competition 2001

Model	POOR			GOOD	pg.
Dodge Stratus					212
Buick Regal			■		148
Ford Taurus				■	234
Nissan Altima			■		356

'00 and '99 Models

The base Stratus and ES come with a 2.0-liter with manual transmission, which may not be enough; look for the larger V6. A/C, dual airbags, tilt steering, and power everything are standard, but 4-wheel ABS is optional. The Stratus is the sportier version of its 1999 and 2000 model twins, the Cirrus and Breeze. In 1999, the Stratus received a better suspension and an anti-theft system.

Price Ranges 2000–1999

SE	$15-16,000
Coupe	none
ES	$18-20,000
R/T	none

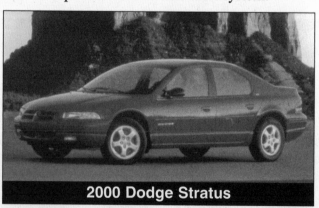
2000 Dodge Stratus

1999 Dodge Stratus

Dodge Stratus — Intermediate

	2001	2000	1999

RATINGS

	POOR → GOOD (2001)	POOR → GOOD (2000)	POOR → GOOD (1999)
Comparative Rating		6	8
Frontal Crash Tests		6	6
Safety Features	5	5	4
Preventive Maintenance	7	7	7
Repair Costs	9	9	10
Warranty	1	1	2
Fuel Economy	5	4	7
Rollover (based on SSF; see pg. 30)	8	8	8
Complaints	5	5	8
Insurance Costs	1	5	5

SAFETY

	2001	2000	1999
Frontal Crash Tests	No Govt Results	Average	Average
Side Crash Tests	No Govt Results	Average	Average
Airbags	Dual (nextgen)	Dual (nextgen)	Dual
Anti-Lock Brakes	4-Wheel (optional)	4-Wheel (optional)	4-Wheel (optional)
Day Running Lamps	None	None	None
Built-In Child Seats	None	None	None
Pretensioners	None	None	None

SPECIFICATIONS

	2001		2000		1999	
Fuel Economy (cty/hwy)	20/30	Average	20/29	Average	26/37	Good
Driving Range (miles)	400	Average	392	Short	504	Vry. Long
Bumpers	Weak		Weak		Weak	
Parking Index	Average		Average		Average	
Head/Leg Room (in.)	37.6/42.3	Cramped	38.1/42.3	Cramped	38.1/42.3	Cramped
Interior Space (cu. ft.)	94	Cramped	111.6	Roomy	51.5	Vry. Cramp.
Cargo Space (cu. ft.)	16	Small	15.7	Small	15.7	Small
Tow Rating (lbs.)			1000	Vry. Low	1000	Vry. Low

After a redesign in 2000, the Neon continues into 2001 with no changes. The 2000 change updated the exterior and provided an all-new interior. The result was reduced noise and more interior space. A 2-liter 4-cylinder engine and manual transmission are standard with an optional automatic. Dual airbags are standard, ABS is optional, and this Neon also has child seat tether anchors—important new safety features which parents will want to have.

2001 Dodge Neon

General Information

New for 2001: No major changes		**Year of Production:**	2
Twins:		**Seating:**	5
Where Made: U.S.		**Theft Rating:**	Average

Prices 2001

Model	Retail	Markup
Base	$12,715	8%

Competition 2001

Model	POOR					GOOD	pg.
Dodge Neon			■				214
Ford Focus						■	228
VW Beetle						■	446
Saturn SL						■	400

'00 and '99 Models

The 1999 Neon benefits from its cab-forward design, which provides excellent interior space for a small car. In 1999, dual de-powered airbags became standard. The single-cam version of the 2-liter engine provides adequate power, but the dual-cam version has even more zing.

Price Ranges 2000–1999

Base	$11-13,000

2000 Dodge Neon

1999 Plymouth Neon

Dodge/Plymouth Neon — Subcompact

	2001	2000	1999

RATINGS

Scale: POOR ... GOOD (1 = Poor, 10 = Good)

	2001	2000	1999
Comparative Rating	5	4	6
Frontal Crash Tests	6		7
Safety Features	4	4	4
Preventive Maintenance	6	6	6
Repair Costs	9		9
Warranty	1	1	2
Fuel Economy	7	7	7
Rollover (based on SSF; see pg. 30)	7	7	7
Complaints	5		9
Insurance Costs	1	1	1

SAFETY

	2001	2000	1999
Frontal Crash Tests	Average	Good	No Govt Results
Side Crash Tests	Average	No Govt Results	No Govt Results
Airbags	Dual	Dual	Dual
Anti-Lock Brakes	4-Wheel (optional)	4-Wheel (optional)	4-Wheel (optional)
Day Running Lamps	None	None	None
Built-In Child Seats	None	None	None
Pretensioners	None	None	None

SPECIFICATIONS

	2001		2000		1999	
Fuel Economy (cty/hwy)	27/33	Good	27/36	Good	28/39	Good
Driving Range (miles)	375	Short	393.75	Short	418.75	Average
Bumpers	Strong		Strong		Strong	
Parking Index	Easy		Easy		Easy	
Head/Leg Room (in.)	39.1/42.4	Average	39.1/42.4	Average	39.6/42.5	Roomy
Interior Space (cu. ft.)	90	Cramped	103.4	Roomy	89.9	Cramped
Cargo Space (cu. ft.)	13	Vry. Small	13.1	Vry. Small	11.8	Vry. Small
Tow Rating (lbs.)	2000	Vry. Low	2000	Vry. Low	1000	Vry. Low

While the exterior remains the same, the safety features of the Crown Vic have changed dramatically. Although ABS is no longer standard, dual stage airbags, crash-severity sensors, seat-postion sensors, and safety belt pretensioners are all standard. The 4.6-liter V8 engine is more powerful with an increase in horsepower. A handling and performance package increases engine hp by 20. In spite of its size, it is one of the most environmentally friendly vehicles on the road. Traction control is an option.

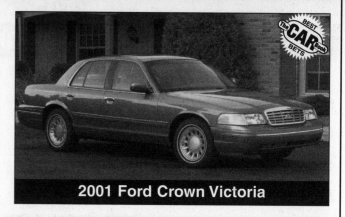

2001 Ford Crown Victoria

General Information

New for 2001: No major changes	Year of Production:	10
Twins: Lincoln Town Car	Seating:	6
Where Made: U.S.	Theft Rating:	Very Low

Prices 2001

Model	Retail	Markup
Base	$22,970	7%
LX	$24,100	7%

Competition 2001

Model	POOR				GOOD	pg.
Ford Cr. Victoria					■	216
Buick Century			■			142
Lincoln Town Car					■	322
Cadillac Deville			■			152

'00 and '99 Models

In 1999, the Crown Victoria got ABS as a standard feature. After 1998's improvements, the exterior of the Crown Victoria was more contemporary and the suspension, tires, and brakes were improved. The base-level model comes with plenty of equipment, but to get more options, you have to move up to the LX.

Price Ranges 2000–1999

Base	$21-22,000
LX	$23-24,000

2000 Mercury Grand Marquis

1999 Ford Crown Victoria

Ford Crown Victoria/Mercury Grand Marquis — Large

	2001	2000	1999

RATINGS

	POOR → GOOD	POOR → GOOD	POOR → GOOD
Comparative Rating	9	9	8
Frontal Crash Tests	10	10	10
Safety Features	5	5	5
Preventive Maintenance	5	5	5
Repair Costs	10	9	6
Warranty	4	2	2
Fuel Economy	4	3	3
Rollover (based on SSF; see pg. 30)	8	8	8
Complaints	7	7	6
Insurance Costs	10	10	10

SAFETY

	2001	2000	1999
Frontal Crash Tests	Very Good	Very Good	Very Good
Side Crash Tests	Very Good	Very Good	Very Good
Airbags	Dual	Dual	Dual
Anti-Lock Brakes	4-Wheel	4-Wheel	4-Wheel
Day Running Lamps	None	None	None
Built-In Child Seats	None	None	None
Pretensioners	None	None	None

SPECIFICATIONS

	2001		2000		1999	
Fuel Economy (cty/hwy)	17/25	Poor	17/25	Poor	17/24	Poor
Driving Range (miles)	399	Average	399	Average	389.5	Short
Bumpers	Strong		Strong		Strong	
Parking Index	Vry. Hard		Vry. Hard		Vry. Hard	
Head/Leg Room (in.)	39.4/42.5	Average	39.4/42.5	Average	39.4/42.5	Average
Interior Space (cu. ft.)	111	Roomy	112	Roomy	111.4	Roomy
Cargo Space (cu. ft.)	21	Average	20.6	Average	20.6	Average
Tow Rating (lbs.)			1000	Vry. Low	1000	Vry. Low

Capitalizing on the longtime demand for the Explorer, Ford has introduced the all-new Escape for 2001, which is a mini version of the Explorer. Built like a car, with unibody construction, the Escape has a variety of engines and automatic 4-wheel drive. The rear seats fold down for a flat storage area, and the back has access via a flip-up glass rear window. There is a cover for the storage area and hooks to tie things down. Aimed at the Toyota RAV4 and the Honda CR-V, this is based on the Mazda Tribute. The two engines are markedly different in power and output.

2001 Ford Escape

General Information

New for 2001: All-new		Year of Production:	1
Twins:		Seating:	5
Where Made:		Theft Rating:	

Prices 2001

Model	Retail	Markup
XLS FWD	$17,645	7%
XLT FWD	$19,195	7%
XLS 4WD	$19,270	5%
XLT 4WD	$20,820	6%

Competition 2001

Model	POOR				GOOD	pg.
Ford Escape				■		**218**
Honda CR-V			■			246
Jeep Wrangler	■					288

'00 and '99 Models

Price Ranges 2000–1999

MODEL WAS NOT PRODUCED THIS YEAR

2000 Model

MODEL WAS NOT PRODUCED THIS YEAR

1999 Model

Ford Escape/Mazda Tribute — Small Sport Utility

	2001	2000	1999

RATINGS

	POOR — GOOD	POOR — GOOD	POOR — GOOD
Comparative Rating			
Frontal Crash Tests			
Safety Features			
Preventive Maintenance			
Repair Costs			
Warranty	4		
Fuel Economy	5		
Rollover (based on SSF; see pg. 30)	4		
Complaints	5		
Insurance Costs			

SAFETY

	2001	2000	1999
Frontal Crash Tests	To Be Tested		
Side Crash Tests	No Govt Results		
Airbags			
Anti-Lock Brakes			
Day Running Lamps			
Built-In Child Seats			
Pretensioners			

SPECIFICATIONS

	2001		2000	1999
Fuel Economy (cty/hwy)	22/26	Average		
Driving Range (miles)	360	Vry. Short		
Bumpers				
Parking Index	Easy			
Head/Leg Room (in.)	40.4/41.6	Roomy		
Interior Space (cu. ft.)	100.1	Average		
Cargo Space (cu. ft.)	33	Average		
Tow Rating (lbs.)	1000	Vry. Low		

This, the largest of all sport utility vehicles at over 19 feet long, continues into 2001 unchanged, save two new color choices. Capable of seating up to nine adults and accommodating their luggage, the two-wheel drive version of this huge vehicle comes standard with a 5.4-liter Triton V8, and the four-wheel drive version has a 6.8-liter Triton V10. Even so, the Excursion's still a Low Emission Vehicle. With the cargo space opened up you can lay out a 4x8 foot sheet of plywood. Towing capacity is great and the hatchback glass rear window opens separately.

2001 Ford Excursion

General Information

New for 2001: No major changes	**Year of Production:**	2
Twins:	**Seating:**	6-9
Where Made: Canada	**Theft Rating:**	

Prices 2001

Model	Retail	Markup
2WD XLT	$34,245	13%
4WD XLT	$37,560	13%
2WD Limited	$37,885	13%
4WD Limited	$40,985	13%

Competition 2001

Model	POOR					GOOD	pg.
Ford Excursion							220
Cad. Escalade				■			156
Linc. Navigator						■	320

'00 and '99 Models

Introduced in 2000, this vehicle is so large that you need to ensure that it can fit in your garage. For more towing capacity, a 7.4-liter V8 diesel is available. The Excursion is equipped with dual airbags and child seat tether anchors. For the beverage-minded it has 10 cup holders and 5 power points for the game players.

Price Ranges 2000–1999

2WD XLT	$33-34,000
4WD XLT	$36-37,000
2WD Limited	$37-38,000
4WD Limited	$40-41,000

2000 Ford Excursion

MODEL WAS NOT PRODUCED THIS YEAR

1999 Model

Ford Excursion — Large Sport Utility

	2001	2000	1999

RATINGS

POOR ◻ GOOD (scale 1–10)

	2001	2000	1999
Comparative Rating			
Frontal Crash Tests			
Safety Features	5	5	
Preventive Maintenance	6	5	
Repair Costs	10		
Warranty	4	2	
Fuel Economy			
Rollover (based on SSF; see pg. 30)	3	3	
Complaints	5		
Insurance Costs	5	5	

SAFETY

	2001	2000	1999
Frontal Crash Tests	No Govt Results	No Govt Results	
Side Crash Tests	No Govt Results	No Govt Results	
Airbags	Dual	Dual	
Anti-Lock Brakes	4-Wheel	4-Wheel	
Day Running Lamps	None	None	
Built-In Child Seats	None	None	
Pretensioners	None	None	

SPECIFICATIONS

	2001	2000	1999
Fuel Economy (cty/hwy)			
Driving Range (miles)			
Bumpers			
Parking Index	Vry. Hard	Vry. Hard	
Head/Leg Room (in.)	41/42.3 Vry. Roomy	41/42.3 Vry. Roomy	
Interior Space (cu. ft.)			
Cargo Space (cu. ft.)	146.4 Vry. Large	100.7 Vry. Large	
Tow Rating (lbs.)	7200 Vry. High	7200 Vry. High	

Ford's smaller capacity/smaller answer to the Chevrolet Suburban is based on the F-Series pick-up and provides seating for up to nine people. There are many options available on four different trim levels. A 240-horsepower 4.6-liter V8 engine now powers this large sport utility. There is an optional 5.4-liter V8, which may be a good choice if you are planning to do heavy towing. The storage area behind the third seat is much smaller than in the Suburban.

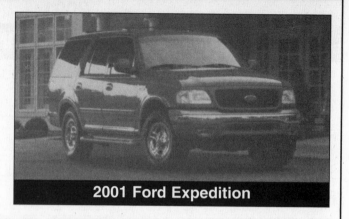

2001 Ford Expedition

General Information

New for 2001: No major changes	**Year of Production:** 5
Twins: Lincoln Navigator	**Seating:** 6-9
Where Made: U.S.	**Theft Rating:** Very High

Prices 2001

Model	Retail	Markup
2WD XLT	$29,845	13%
4WD XLT	$32,715	14%
2WD Eddie Bauer	$36,255	9%
2WD XLT	$40,400	9%

Competition 2001

Model	POOR						GOOD	pg.
Ford Expedition				■				**222**
Infiniti QX4						■		276
Cad. Escalade			■					156
Linc. Navigator						■		320

'00 and '99 Models

Based on the best-selling F-Series pickup, the Ford Expedition was first introduced in 1997. Offering excellent towing and ride, the Expedition was designed to be a more refined competition to the Suburban. The Expedition performed well on frontal crash tests, but no side tests are available.

Price Ranges 2000–1999

2WD XLT	$28-30,000
4WD XLT	$31-32,000
2WD Eddie Bauer	$35-36,000
4WD Eddie Bauer	$38-40,000

2000 Ford Expedition

1999 Ford Expedition

	2001	2000	1999

RATINGS

	POOR ... GOOD	POOR ... GOOD	POOR ... GOOD
Comparative Rating	5	4	4
Frontal Crash Tests*	8	8	9
Safety Features	5	5	5
Preventive Maintenance	8	8	7
Repair Costs	8	7	4
Warranty	4	2	2
Fuel Economy	2	2	2
Rollover (based on SSF, see pg. 25)	3	4	4
Complaints	3	3	4
Insurance Costs	10	10	10

SAFETY

	2001	2000	1999
Frontal Crash Tests	Good	Good	Very Good
Side Crash Tests	No Govt Results	No Govt Results	No Govt Results
Airbags	Dual	Dual	Dual
Anti-Lock Brakes	4-Wheel	4-Wheel	4-Wheel
Day Running Lamps	None	None	None
Built-In Child Seats	None	None	None
Pretensioners	None	None	None

SPECIFICATIONS

	2001		2000		1999
Fuel Economy (cty/hwy)	16/21	Vry. Poor	15/20	Vry. Poor	
Driving Range (miles)	481	Vry. Long	455	Long	
Bumpers					
Parking Index	Vry. Hard		Vry. Hard		
Head/Leg Room (in.)	39.8/40.9	Cramped	39.8/40.9	Cramped	
Interior Space (cu. ft.)					
Cargo Space (cu. ft.)	82.2	Large	118.3	Vry. Large	
Tow Rating (lbs.)	5800	High	5900	High	

*To be tested in 2001.

Ford Explorer/Mercury Mountaineer   Mid-Size Sport Utility

There aren't any changes for America's most popular sport utility for the 2001 model year. Next year Ford is planning a new version. This is the standard by which all other sport utilities are judged; the Explorer is one of the best sport utilities on the road. Dual airbags and 4-wheel ABS are standard. You can opt for side airbags for front occupants. The Explorer's standard engine is a 4-liter V6; an optional 5.0-liter V8 is available. It came with a restyled front end in 1999. Gas mileage on the standard engine is better than larger utility vehicles.

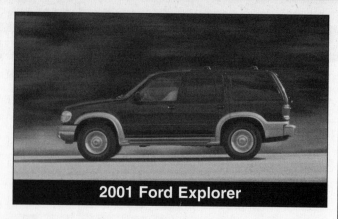
2001 Ford Explorer

General Information

New for 2001: No major changes		**Year of Production:**	7
Twins:		**Seating:**	5
Where Made: U.S.		**Theft Rating:**	Average

Prices 2001

Model	Retail	Markup
2WD XLS	$25,115	9%
4WD XLS	$26,995	10%
AWD XLT	$30,090	5%
4WD Limited	$34,150	5%

Competition 2001

Model	POOR						GOOD	pg.
Ford Explorer				■				**224**
Honda Passport	■							252
Toyota 4Runner						■		416
Jeep Gr. Cher.		■						286

'00 and '99 Models

There are two body styles, 2- and 4-door; the 4-door has more room for adults in back. While it doesn't have the luxury touches of some of the European or Japanese SUVs, with leather seating, an upgraded sound system, and power seats you'll come close. The Firestone fiasco damped sales a bit, but it's still the most popular SUV in its class.

Price Ranges 2000–1999

2WD Sport	$20-21,000
4WD XLS	$23-26,000
AWD XLT	$25-29,000
4WD Limited	$31-34,000

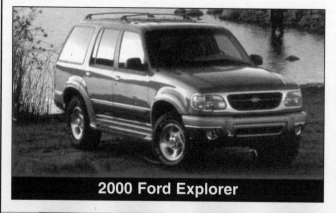
2000 Ford Explorer

1999 Mercury Mountaineer

Ford Explorer/Mercury Mountaineer Mid-Size Sport Utility

	2001	2000	1999

RATINGS

Rating scale: POOR → GOOD

	2001	2000	1999
Comparative Rating	5	3	2
Frontal Crash Tests	6	6	6
Safety Features	7	6	5
Preventive Maintenance	8	8	7
Repair Costs	7	7	7
Warranty	4	2	2
Fuel Economy	2	2	2
Rollover (based on SSF; see pg. 30)	3	3	3
Complaints	4	4	2
Insurance Costs	10	5	5

SAFETY

	2001	2000	1999
Frontal Crash Tests	Average	Average	Average
Side Crash Tests	Very Good	Very Good	Very Good
Airbags	Dual and Side	Dual	Dual
Anti-Lock Brakes	4-Wheel	4-Wheel	4-Wheel
Day Running Lamps	None	None	None
Built-In Child Seats	None	None	None
Pretensioners	None	None	None

SPECIFICATIONS

	2001		2000		1999	
Fuel Economy (cty/hwy)	15/19	Vry. Poor	16/20	Vry. Poor	15/20	Vry. Poor
Driving Range (miles)	357	Vry. Short	378	Short	455	Long
Bumpers						
Parking Index	Hard		Hard		Vry. Hard	
Head/Leg Room (in.)	39.9/42.4	Roomy	39.9/42.4	Roomy	39.8/40.9	Cramped
Interior Space (cu. ft.)						
Cargo Space (cu. ft.)	71.4	Large	79.8	Large	118.3	Vry. Large
Tow Rating (lbs.)					5900	High

Again, no changes this year for Ford's best-selling truck, except the addition of a new Super Duty F-650 Super Cruiser and a new F-150 Supercrew to the series. Important standard features on the F-Series include dual airbags with a deactivation system for turning off the passenger side airbag when there is a rear-facing child seat present. Be sure to turn the switch back on when an adult takes the seat. ABS is optional. Powering the F-Series is a 4.2-liter V6 which should deliver good horse-power.

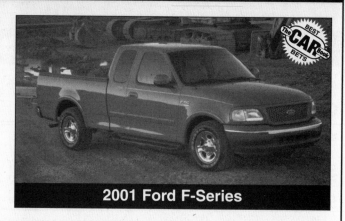

2001 Ford F-Series

General Information

New for 2001: No major changes	**Year of Production:**	5
Twins:	**Seating:**	3
Where Made: U.S.	**Theft Rating:**	Average

Prices 2001

Model	Retail	Markup
F-150 XL 2WD	$16,870	11%
F-150 XL 4WD	$20,170	12%
F-250 XL 2WD	$20,535	12%
F-350 XL 4WD	$24,065	8%

Competition 2001

Model	POOR				GOOD	pg.
Ford F-Series					▮	**226**
Chev. Silverado		▮				176
Dodge Ram		▮				210

'00 and '99 Models

The F-Series pickups have more powerful engine choices which include the new 5.4-liter V8 engine, the 7.5-liter gas or 7.3-liter diesel engines, and the 265hp 6.8-liter V10 that powers the Econoline. The interior is very comfortable, and the ride is what you'd expect from a pickup. There is an optional third door which makes getting into the back of a club cab much easier.

Price Ranges 2000–1999

F-150 XL 2WD	$16-17,000
F-150 XL 4WD	$19-20,000
F-250 XL 4WD	$22-23,000
F-350 XL 4WD	$22-24,000

2000 Ford F-Series

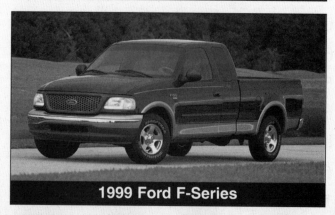

1999 Ford F-Series

Ford F-Series — Standard Pickup

	2001	2000	1999

RATINGS

	2001 (POOR–GOOD)	2000 (POOR–GOOD)	1999 (POOR–GOOD)
Comparative Rating	8	4	2
Frontal Crash Tests*	8	8	8
Safety Features	4	4	4
Preventive Maintenance	8	7	7
Repair Costs	10	10	5
Warranty	4	2	2
Fuel Economy	2	2	2
Rollover (based on SSF, see pg. 25)	3	3	3
Complaints	10	10	3
Insurance Costs	10	5	5

SAFETY

	2001	2000	1999
Frontal Crash Tests	Good	Good	Good
Side Crash Tests	No Govt Results	No Govt Results	No Govt Results
Airbags	Dual	Dual	Dual
Anti-Lock Brakes	2-Wheel (4-whl opt.)	2-wheel (4-whl opt.)	2-wheel (4-whl opt.)
Day Running Lamps	None	None	None
Built-In Child Seats	None	None	None
Pretensioners	None	None	None

SPECIFICATIONS

	2001		2000		1999	
Fuel Economy (cty/hwy)	15/19	Vry. Poor	16/21	Vry. Poor	16/20	Vry. Poor
Driving Range (miles)	425	Long	462.5	Vry. Long	378	Short
Bumpers						
Parking Index	Vry. Hard		Vry. Hard		Hard	
Head/Leg Room (in.)	40.8/40.9	Average	40.8/40.9	Average	39.9/42.4	Roomy
Interior Space (cu. ft.)						
Cargo Space (cu. ft.)					81	Large
Tow Rating (lbs.)	1900	Vry. Low	1900	Vry. Low		

The 2001 Focus is unchanged from the initial 2000 model. However, the ZTS and ZX3 editions now operate with an Advance Trac transmission, and a manual transmission option is now available in the wagon. In addition, a fancier "limited" edition version of the Focus will be offered this year. With the most space in its class, the Focus is available in a three-door, four-door sedan, and wagon, as well as four series - the ZX3, LX, SE, and ZTS.

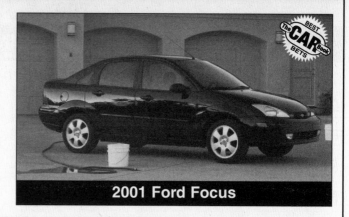

2001 Ford Focus

General Information

New for 2001: No major changes	**Year of Production:** 2
Twins:	**Seating:** 5
Where Made: U.S.	**Theft Rating:**

Prices 2001

Model	Retail	Markup
ZX3 3-door hatchback	$12,125	6%
LX Sedan	$12,385	6%
ZTS Sedan	$15,260	12%
Wagon SE	$16,235	12%

Competition 2001

Model	POOR				GOOD	pg.
Ford Focus					■	**228**
Mazda Protégé		■				334
Subaru Impreza					■	404
Saturn SL					■	400

'00 and '99 Models

Introduced with great fanfare in 2000, the Focus comes with two engines: a 2.0-liter 4-cylinder SOHC and a DOHC version. The main difference is the DOHC provides 20 more horses. Dual airbags and available head-and-chest side airbags provide occupant protection.

Price Ranges 2000–1999

Hatchback	$11-13,000
LX Sedan	$12-13,000
SE Sedan	$13-14,000
ZTS Sedan	$15-16,000

2000 Ford Focus

MODEL WAS NOT PRODUCED THIS YEAR

1999 Model

Ford Focus — Subcompact

	2001	2000	1999

RATINGS

	POOR — GOOD	POOR — GOOD	POOR — GOOD
Comparative Rating	9	8	
Frontal Crash Tests	9	9	
Safety Features	6	6	
Preventive Maintenance	8	8	
Repair Costs	10	10	
Warranty	4	2	
Fuel Economy	7	6	
Rollover (based on SSF; see pg. 30)	7	7	
Complaints	5		
Insurance Costs	5	5	

SAFETY

	2001	2000	1999
Frontal Crash Tests	Very Good	Very Good	
Side Crash Tests	Good	Good	
Airbags	Dual (nextgen)	Dual (nextgen)	
Anti-Lock Brakes	Optional	4-Wheel (optional)	
Day Running Lamps	None	None	
Built-In Child Seats	None	None	
Pretensioners	Standard	Standard	

SPECIFICATIONS

	2001		2000		1999
Fuel Economy (cty/hwy)	25/33	Good	26/33	Good	
Driving Range (miles)	382.8	Short	389.4	Short	
Bumpers					
Parking Index	Vry. Easy		Easy		
Head/Leg Room (in.)	39.3/43.1	Roomy	39.3/43.1	Roomy	
Interior Space (cu. ft.)	95	Average	107	Roomy	
Cargo Space (cu. ft.)	17	Average	12.9	Vry. Small	
Tow Rating (lbs.)	1000	Vry. Low			

The 2001 Mustang is very similar to the 2000 model. A new interior console comes with all Mustangs, and a new hood and side scoops have been added to the GT. A new SVT Cobra model has also been added. The engines are powerful: the 3.8-liter V6 engine now has 190 hp, the 4.6-liter V8 has 260 hp. The 3.8-liter engine actually meets Low Emission Vehicle requirements. A traction control system helps to prevent wheel spin, and chassis improvements reduce noise and vibration. Coupes and convertibles are available in 3 trim levels.

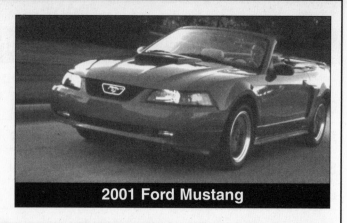
2001 Ford Mustang

General Information

New for 2001: No major changes	**Year of Production:**	8
Twins:	**Seating:**	5
Where Made: U.S.	**Theft Rating:**	High

Prices 2001

Model	Retail	Markup
Coupe Standard	$16,805	8%
Convertible Deluxe	$22,220	9%
GT Coupe Deluxe	$22,440	3%
GT Convertible Premium	$27,850	9%

Competition 2001

Model	POOR				GOOD	pg.
Ford Mustang				■		230
Chev. Camaro			■			164
Dodge Intrepid				■		208
Pontiac Gr. Prix				■		386

'00 and '99 Models

The 1999 Mustang was given a slightly new design and a new power train. In 2000 better traction control and a quieter, smoother ride were added. All models have dual airbags, but ABS, standard on the other models, costs extra on base Mustangs. The Mustang has a high theft rate, which is no surprise.

Price Ranges 2000–1999

Coupe	$16-17,000
Convertible	$21-22,000
GT Coupe	$20-22,000
GT Convertible	$24-26,000

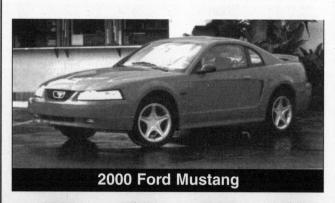
2000 Ford Mustang

1999 Ford Mustang

	2001	2000	1999

RATINGS

	2001 (POOR–GOOD)	2000 (POOR–GOOD)	1999 (POOR–GOOD)
Comparative Rating	6	5	4
Frontal Crash Tests*	7	7	7
Safety Features	5	5	4
Preventive Maintenance	5	5	5
Repair Costs	9	8	7
Warranty	4	2	2
Fuel Economy	5	4	4
Rollover (based on SSF, see pg. 25)	8	8	8
Complaints	7	7	5
Insurance Costs	1	1	1

SAFETY

	2001	2000	1999
Frontal Crash Tests	Good	Good	Good
Side Crash Tests	Average	Average	Average
Airbags	Dual	Dual (nextgen)	Dual
Anti-Lock Brakes	Standard	4-Wheel (optional)	4-Wheel (optional)
Day Running Lamps	None	None	None
Built-In Child Seats	None	None	None
Pretensioners	None	None	None

SPECIFICATIONS

	2001		2000		1999	
Fuel Economy (cty/hwy)	19/27	Poor	20/29	Average	20/29	Average
Driving Range (miles)	361.1	Vry. Short	384.65	Short	384.65	Short
Bumpers	Strong		Strong		Strong	
Parking Index	Average		Average		Average	
Head/Leg Room (in.)	38.1/42.6	Cramped	38.1/42.6	Cramped	38.1/42.6	Cramped
Interior Space (cu. ft.)	79	Vry. Cramp.	83	Vry. Cramp.	83	Vry. Cramp.
Cargo Space (cu. ft.)	9	Vry. Small	10.9	Vry. Small	10.9	Vry. Small
Tow Rating (lbs.)	1000	Vry. Low	1000	Vry. Low	1000	Vry. Low

*To be tested in 2001.

Ford Ranger
Compact Pickup

The Ranger has no major changes for 2001. The 2.5-liter engine on the 2WD is strong, but you'll want to opt for the 4WD's 3.0-liter. Better yet, the V6 upgrades are best for serious load carrying. The Supercab is a longer version of the Ranger, but room in back is tiny. To save money, get the options you want in a complete package. The Ranger performed well on frontal crash tests and is worth checking out.

2001 Ford Ranger

General Information

New for 2001: No major changes		**Year of Production:**	9
Twins: B-Series		**Seating:**	3
Where Made: U.S.		**Theft Rating:**	Very Low

Prices 2001

Model	Retail	Markup
XL 2WD 2.5L Styleside man.	$11,840	10%
XLT 2WD 2.5L Styleside man.	$13,950	10%
XL 4WD Supercab 3.0L V6 auto.	$20,090	7%
XLT 4WD Supercab man.	$20,595	8%

Competition 2001

Model	POOR					GOOD	pg.
Ford Ranger					■		232
Chev. S-Series		■					174
Mazda B-Series				■			326

'00 and '99 Models

In 1998, numerous improvements were implemented to the suspension, engine, and ride that carried over into 1999 and 2000. The 2.5-liter on the 2WD and the 3.0-liter on the 4WD remain standard engines.

Price Ranges 2000–1999

XL 2WD	$11-12,000
XLT 2WD	$11-13,000
XL 4WD Supercab	$18-20,000
XLT 4WD	$18-21,000

2000 Ford Ranger

1999 Ford Ranger

	2001	2000	1999

RATINGS

	POOR ▸ GOOD	POOR ▸ GOOD	POOR ▸ GOOD
Comparative Rating	6	5	5
Frontal Crash Tests*	9	9	9
Safety Features	5	4	4
Preventive Maintenance	4	4	7
Repair Costs	10	5	8
Warranty	4	2	2
Fuel Economy	2	3	3
Rollover (based on SSF, see pg. 25)	3	4	4
Complaints	8	8	4
Insurance Costs	5	5	5

SAFETY

	2001	2000	1999
Frontal Crash Tests	Very Good	Very Good	Very Good
Side Crash Tests	No Govt Results	No Govt Results	No Govt Results
Airbags	Dual	Dual	Dual
Anti-Lock Brakes	4-Wheel	2-wheel (4-whl opt.)	2-wheel (4-whl opt.)
Day Running Lamps	None	None	None
Built-In Child Seats	None	None	None
Pretensioners	Optional	None	None

SPECIFICATIONS

	2001		2000		1999	
Fuel Economy (cty/hwy)	17/20	Vry. Poor	17/22	Poor	17/22	Poor
Driving Range (miles)	305.25	Vry. Short	321.75	Vry. Short	331.5	Vry. Short
Bumpers						
Parking Index	Hard		Hard		Vry. Hard	
Head/Leg Room (in.)	39.2/42.4	Average	39.2/42.2	Average	39.2/42.2	Average
Interior Space (cu. ft.)						
Cargo Space (cu. ft.)						
Tow Rating (lbs.)	4760	Average				

Ford's best-selling Taurus moves into 2001 unchanged. Last year's dual threshold airbags continue on the 2001 model. There are minor changes to the exterior and interior, but the 3.0-liter V6 remains standard and offers more power than the prior version. Child seat tether anchors are an excellent addition and a must-have for parents. Other safety features include traction control and an emergency trunk release. The Taurus does well against competitors like the Accord and Camry in features; however the handling and feel are different.

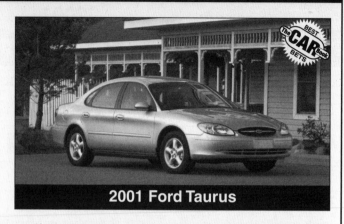

2001 Ford Taurus

General Information

New for 2001: No major changes	Year of Production:	6
Twins:	Seating:	5
Where Made: U.S.	Theft Rating:	Very Low

Prices 2001

Model	Retail	Markup
LX	$18,260	8%
SES	$20,050	8%
SE Wagon	$20,190	8%
SEL	$21,535	6%

Competition 2001

Model	POOR					GOOD	pg.
Ford Taurus						■	**234**
Chev. Malibu			■				170
Honda Accord					■		242
Toyota Camry					■		420

'00 and '99 Models

In both 1999 and 2000, the Taurus received a few cosmetic changes such as new wheels, new consoles, and some comfort items. The Taurus is very spacious inside, and the once-unique oval-shaped headlights are its most remarkable design feature. All come standard with dual airbags, but ABS is optional.

Price Ranges 2000–1999

LX	$17-18,000
SE	$18-19,000
SES	$19-20,000
SE Wagon	$19-20,000

2000 Mercury Sable

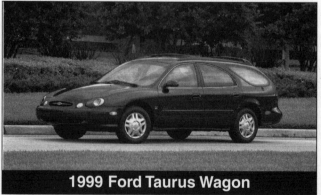

1999 Ford Taurus Wagon

Ford Taurus/Mercury Sable — Intermediate

	2001	2000	1999

RATINGS

	POOR – GOOD	POOR – GOOD	POOR – GOOD
Comparative Rating	10	9	8
Frontal Crash Tests	10	10	10
Safety Features	6	6	6
Preventive Maintenance	8	8	8
Repair Costs	9	10	8
Warranty	4	2	2
Fuel Economy	5	4	4
Rollover (based on SSF; see pg. 30)	8	8	8
Complaints	7	7	6
Insurance Costs	10	5	5

SAFETY

	2001	2000	1999
Frontal Crash Tests	Very Good	Very Good	Very Good
Side Crash Tests	Good	Good	Good
Airbags	Dual (nextgen)	Dual (nextgen)	Dual (nextgen)
Anti-Lock Brakes	4-Wheel (optional)	4-Wheel (optional)	4-Wheel (optional)
Day Running Lamps	None	None	None
Built-In Child Seats	None	None	Optional
Pretensioners	Standard	Standard	None

SPECIFICATIONS

	2001		2000		1999	
Fuel Economy (cty/hwy)	20/27	Poor	20/28	Average	20/28	Average
Driving Range (miles)	376	Short	384	Short	384	Short
Bumpers	Strong		Strong		Strong	
Parking Index	Vry. Hard		Vry. Hard		Hard	
Head/Leg Room (in.)	40/42.2	Roomy	40/42.2	Roomy	39.2/42.2	Average
Interior Space (cu. ft.)	105	Roomy	104.7	Roomy	101.5	Average
Cargo Space (cu. ft.)	17	Average	17	Average	15.8	Small
Tow Rating (lbs.)	1250	Vry. Low	1250	Vry. Low	1250	Vry. Low

2001 brings a variety of new safety features to the Windstar. Occupant weight and height are now taken into account before airbags are deployed; side mirror turn signals and sliding door warning lights have also been added. Optional safety features include the Advance Trac system and adjustable pedals. The Windstar runs on either a 3.0-liter or a 3.8-liter V6. The 3.0 meets Low Emission Vehicle standards; the 3.8 meets Ultra Low Emission Vehicle standards for a clean running engine.

2001 Ford Windstar

General Information

New for 2001: No major changes		**Year of Production:**	7
Twins:		**Seating:**	7
Where Made: U.S.		**Theft Rating:**	Very Low

Prices 2001

Model	Retail	Markup
Van 3-door	$19,910	9%
LX Wagon 3-door	$21,875	10%
SEL Wagon 4-door	$30,805	10%
Limited Wagon 4-Door	$33,455	10%

Competition 2001

Model	POOR → GOOD	pg.
Ford Windstar	GOOD	236
Chev. Venture	middle	184
Honda Odyssey	middle	250
Toyota Sienna	POOR	438

'00 and '99 Models

For 1999, the Windstar got a fourth, sliding, door, bringing it up to speed with other minivans in its class. For safety, Ford offers head-and-chest side impact airbags and great optional built-in child restraints; dual airbags and 4-wheel ABS are both standard. The interior is very roomy.

Price Ranges 2000–1999

Model	Price
Van 3-door	$18-20,000
LX Wagon 3-door	$23-24,000
LX Wagon 4-door	$24-25,000
Limited Wagon 4-door	$33-34,000

2000 Ford Windstar   **1999 Ford Windstar**

Ford Windstar — Minivan

RATINGS

	2001	2000	1999
	POOR — GOOD	POOR — GOOD	POOR — GOOD
Comparative Rating	9	7	6
Frontal Crash Tests*	10	10	10
Safety Features	8	7	6
Preventive Maintenance	9	9	9
Repair Costs	10	9	5
Warranty	4	2	2
Fuel Economy	3	3	3
Rollover (based on SSF, see pg. 25)	6	6	6
Complaints	2	2	2
Insurance Costs	10	10	10

SAFETY

	2001	2000	1999
Frontal Crash Tests	Very Good	Very Good	Very Good
Side Crash Tests	Very Good	Very Good	Very Good
Airbags	Dual (nextgen)	Dual (nextgen)	Dual
Anti-Lock Brakes	4-Wheel	4-Wheel	4-Wheel
Day Running Lamps	None	None	None
Built-In Child Seats	Standard	Standard	Optional
Pretensioners	None	None	None

SPECIFICATIONS

	2001		2000		1999	
Fuel Economy (cty/hwy)	18/23	Poor	17/23	Poor	17/23	Poor
Driving Range (miles)	533	Vry. Long	520	Vry. Long	520	Vry. Long
Bumpers	Strong		Strong		Strong	
Parking Index	Vry. Hard		Vry. Hard		Vry. Hard	
Head/Leg Room (in.)	39.3/40.7	Cramped	39.3/40.7	Cramped	39.3/40.7	Cramped
Interior Space (cu. ft.)						
Cargo Space (cu. ft.)	145.7	Vry. Large	145.7	Vry. Large	145.7	Vry. Large
Tow Rating (lbs.)	3500	Low	3500	Low	3500	Low

*To be tested in 2001.

The ZX2 carries on to 2001 unchanged. It is based on the Escort, which will only be sold as a fleet vehicle, unavailable in the showroom. The Ford Focus will become the new entry-level offering from Ford. ABS is optional, and the rear seat folds down for trunk access. The ZX2 has a glow-in-the-dark inside trunk handle to prevent entrapment and optional tilt steering wheel and cruise control. Manual transmission is standard on this front wheel drive car, and the 2001 model gets some new color choices.

2001 Ford ZX2

General Information

New for 2001: No major changes	**Year of Production:** 5
Twins:	**Seating:** 5
Where Made: Mexico	**Theft Rating:** Very Low

Prices 2001

Model	Retail	Markup
ZX2 Coupe	$12,050	13%

Competition 2001

Model	POOR					GOOD	pg.
Ford ZX2			■				**238**
Mazda Protégé			■				334
Subaru Impreza					■		404
Saturn SL					■		400

'00 and '99 Models

For 1999, the Escort lost its child safety seat. The Escort comes in three flavors: a ZX2 coupe, introduced in 1999, sedan, and wagon, as well as a base 'Cool' version and a well-equipped 'Hot' version. The sedan and wagon are available in a base LX or up-level SE and come standard with a 2-liter 110 hp engine; the ZX2 gets a peppier Zetec 2-liter 130 hp engine.

Price Ranges 2000–1999

ZX2 Coupe	$12-13,000
Sedan	$11-12,000

2000 Ford Escort

1999 Ford Escort

Ford ZX2 — Subcompact

	2001	2000	1999
RATINGS			
	POOR — GOOD	POOR — GOOD	POOR — GOOD
Comparative Rating			
Frontal Crash Tests			
Safety Features	5	4	4
Preventive Maintenance	8	8	7
Repair Costs	10	10	10
Warranty	4	2	2
Fuel Economy	8	7	7
Rollover (based on SSF; see pg. 30)	7	7	7
Complaints	6	6	5
Insurance Costs	1	1	1
SAFETY			
Frontal Crash Tests	No Govt Results	No Govt Results	Poor
Side Crash Tests	Poor (2dr.), Ave. (4dr.)	Ave. (2dr), Poor (4dr)	Ave. (2dr), Poor (4dr)
Airbags	Dual	Dual	Dual
Anti-Lock Brakes	4-Wheel (optional)	4-Wheel (optional)	4-Wheel (optional)
Day Running Lamps	None	None	None
Built-In Child Seats	None	None	None
Pretensioners	None	None	None
SPECIFICATIONS			
Fuel Economy (cty/hwy)	28/37 Good	28/37 Good	28/37 Good
Driving Range (miles)	412.75 Average	412.75 Average	416 Average
Bumpers	Strong	Strong	Strong
Parking Index	Vry. Easy	Vry. Easy	Vry. Easy
Head/Leg Room (in.)	39/42.5 Average	39/42.5 Average	39/42.5 Average
Interior Space (cu. ft.)	87 Cramped	87.2 Cramped	87.2 Cramped
Cargo Space (cu. ft.)	13 Vry. Small	12.8 Vry. Small	12.8 Vry. Small
Tow Rating (lbs.)		1000 Vry. Low	1000 Vry. Low

Now in its 7th year of production, the Jimmy remains unchanged for 2001. Its former twin, the GMC Envoy, is taking a rest and will not be sold as a 2001. The 4.3-liter V6 engine is fine, and you'll have to choose between 2- and 4-door models, four different suspensions, and 2- or 4-wheel drive. Choosing among the various suspension packages will help you tailor the ride and handling to your preference. It seats four comfortably, and you can squeeze in up to six with the optional bench seat in front.

2001 GMC Jimmy

General Information

New for 2001: No major changes		**Year of Production:**	7
Twins: Blazer, Bravada		**Seating:**	
Where Made: Canada		**Theft Rating:**	

Prices 2001

Model	Retail	Markup
Jimmy 2WD 2dr. SLS	$19,270	10%
Jimmy 4WD 2dr. SLS	$22,270	12%
Jimmy 4WD 4dr. SLT	$30,225	12%
Envoy 4WD (2000 model)	$34,370	10%

Competition 2001

Model	POOR					GOOD	pg.
GMC Jimmy		■					240
Honda Passport	■						252
Infiniti QX4						■	276
Ford Explorer				■			224

'00 and '99 Models

There were few changes in 1999 and 2000 for these sport utilities. Both the Jimmy and its more luxurious sibling, the Envoy, got GM's AutoTrac four-wheel drive system and some new color choices. Dual de-powered airbags and ABS are standard on both models.

Price Ranges 2000–1999

4WD	$33-35,000
2WD 2dr.SLS	$18-19,000
4WD 2dr. SLS	$19-22,000
4WD 4dr. SLT	$27-30,000

2000 GMC Jimmy

1999 GMC Envoy

GMC Jimmy — Mid-Size Sport Utility

	2001	2000	1999

RATINGS

	2001 (POOR→GOOD)	2000 (POOR→GOOD)	1999 (POOR→GOOD)
Comparative Rating	2	1	1
Frontal Crash Tests	4	4	4
Safety Features	6	8	6
Preventive Maintenance	5	4	5
Repair Costs	4	6	5
Warranty	2	2	2
Fuel Economy	2	2	2
Rollover (based on SSF; see pg. 30)	4	3	4
Complaints	4	4	1
Insurance Costs	10	5	5

SAFETY

	2001	2000	1999
Frontal Crash Tests	Poor	Poor	Poor
Side Crash Tests	No Govt Results	No Govt Results	No Govt Results
Airbags	Dual/Side	Dual/Side	Dual
Anti-Lock Brakes	4-Wheel	4-Wheel	4-Wheel
Day Running Lamps	Standard	Standard	Standard
Built-In Child Seats	None	None	None
Pretensioners	None	None	None

SPECIFICATIONS

	2001		2000		1999	
Fuel Economy (cty/hwy)	15/20	Vry. Poor	16/21	Vry. Poor	16/21	Vry. Poor
Driving Range (miles)	332.5	Vry. Short	351.5	Vry. Short	351.5	Vry. Short
Bumpers						
Parking Index	Easy		Easy		Easy	
Head/Leg Room (in.)	39.6/42.4	Roomy	39.6/42.4	Roomy	39.6/42.4	Roomy
Interior Space (cu. ft.)						
Cargo Space (cu. ft.)	66.9	Large	66.9	Large	66.9	Large
Tow Rating (lbs.)	5600	High	5600	High	5000	Average

Honda Accord   Intermediate

The Accord received its most dramatic makeover in its 22-year history in 1998, and there aren't any major changes for 2001. At that time, changes were made to structure, engine, suspension, interior, and exterior. The Accord now has more interior room and trunk space, a smoother transmission, and a more distinctively styled coupe. The Accord rates highly against its main competitors, the Taurus and Camry.

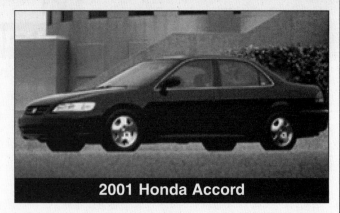
2001 Honda Accord

General Information

New for 2001: No major changes		**Year of Production:**	4
Twins:		**Seating:**	5
Where Made: U.S.		**Theft Rating:**	Very Low

Prices 2001

Model	Retail	Markup
4-cyl. DX Sedan auto	$16,200	12%
4-cyl. LX Coupe man.	$18,790	12%
V6 LX Coupe auto	$22,400	6%
V6 EX Sedan	$25,100	11%

Competition 2001

Model	POOR				GOOD	pg.
Honda Accord			■			**242**
Chev. Malibu		■				170
Ford Taurus					■	234
Toyota Camry				■		420

'00 and '99 Models

The standard engine on the base DX is a 2.3-liter engine which cranks out 135 hp. The LX and EX get the peppier version of the same engine with 150 hp. But many will want the optional VTEC V6 engine.

Price Ranges 2000–1999

4-cyl. DX Sedan	$15-16,000
4-cyl. LX Coupe	$18-19,000
6-cyl. LX Coupe	$21-22,000
6-cyl. EX Sedan	$24-25,000

2000 Honda Accord

1999 Honda Accord

Honda Accord — Intermediate

	2001	2000	1999

RATINGS

	2001 (POOR→GOOD)	2000 (POOR→GOOD)	1999 (POOR→GOOD)
Comparative Rating	5	6	6
Frontal Crash Tests*	7	8	8
Safety Features	5	6	5
Preventive Maintenance	3	2	3
Repair Costs	8	7	6
Warranty	1	1	1
Fuel Economy	7	5	5
Rollover (based on SSF, see pg. 25)	7	7	8
Complaints	6	6	8
Insurance Costs	5	5	5

SAFETY

	2001	2000	1999
Frontal Crash Tests	Good (2dr./4dr.)	Good	Good
Side Crash Tests[1]	Good (4dr.)[2]	Good	Good
Airbags	Dual (nextgen)	Dual (nextgen)	Dual (nextgen)
Anti-Lock Brakes	4-Wheel (optional)	4-Wheel (optional)	4-Wheel (optional)
Day Running Lamps	None	Standard	None
Built-In Child Seats	None	None	None
Pretensioners	None	None	None

SPECIFICATIONS

	2001		2000		1999	
Fuel Economy (cty/hwy)	26/32	Good	25/31	Average	25/31	Average
Driving Range (miles)	495.9	Vry. Long	478.8	Vry. Long	478.8	Vry. Long
Bumpers	Strong		Strong		Strong	
Parking Index	Average		Average		Easy	
Head/Leg Room (in.)	40/42.1	Roomy	40/42.1	Roomy	39.7/42.6	Roomy
Interior Space (cu. ft.)	102	Roomy	101.7	Roomy	92.7	Cramped
Cargo Space (cu. ft.)	14	Small	14.1	Small	13.6	Small
Tow Rating (lbs.)						

*To be tested in 2001; [1]Very good with side airbags; [2]2dr. good with no side airbags/very good with side airbags.

Honda Civic   Subcompact

All-new for 2001, this is the seventh generation of the Civic. There are a coupe and sedan in three basic models; notable is the high mileage HX version, and the GX which comes with a natural gas engine. To get the fancier options, you have to move up in the model series: DX to LX to EX. The Civic is larger than previous editions and starts to come close to the Accord, at least older Accords. The new 1.7L engine increases both power and fuel efficiency. The front side airbags have a cut-off switch.

2001 Honda Civic

General Information

New for 2001: All-new		**Year of Production:**	1
Twins:		**Seating:**	5
Where Made: U.S.		**Theft Rating:**	Average

Prices 2001

Model	Retail	Markup
DX Coupe man.	$12,960	9%
HX Cpe. w/Side Airbags man.	$13,800	9%
LX Sedan auto.	$15,800	9%
EX Sdn. w/Side Airbags auto.	$17,460	9%

Competition 2001

Model	POOR				GOOD		pg.
Honda Civic					■		244
Toyota Corolla						■	424
Saturn SL					■		400
VW Beetle					■		446

'00 and '99 Models

The 2000 Civic was unchanged from '99. The 1.6-liter engine gets good mileage and provides adequate power. Also available is a 1.6-liter 4 cylinder compressed natural gas engine that meets ULEV standards. The 1999 Civics got new bumpers, but not much else. The engines include a 1.6-liter that can be upgraded to more powerful engines with 115 or 127 hp on higher trim levels.

Price Ranges 2000–1999

CX Hatchback	$10-11,000
DX Coupe	$12-13,000
EX Sedan	$16-17,000

2000 Honda Civic

1999 Honda Civic

Honda Civic | Subcompact

Honda Civic   Subcompact

	2001	2000	1999

RATINGS

	POOR → GOOD (2001)	POOR → GOOD (2000)	POOR → GOOD (1999)
Comparative Rating	7	7	7
Frontal Crash Tests	10	8	8
Safety Features	5	6	5
Preventive Maintenance	3	2	3
Repair Costs	8	8	8
Warranty	1	1	1
Fuel Economy	9	8	8
Rollover (based on SSF; see pg. 30)	7	7	7
Complaints	5	9	9
Insurance Costs	1	1	1

SAFETY

	2001	2000	1999
Frontal Crash Tests	Very Good*	Good	Good
Side Crash Tests	Very Good*	Average	Average
Airbags	Dual and Optional Side	Dual (nextgen)	Dual (nextgen)
Anti-Lock Brakes	Optional	4-Wheel (optional)	4-Wheel (optional)
Day Running Lamps	None	Standard	None
Built-In Child Seats	None	None	None
Pretensioners	None	None	None

SPECIFICATIONS

	2001		2000		1999	
Fuel Economy (cty/hwy)	32/39	Vry. Good	32/37	Vry. Good	32/37	Vry. Good
Driving Range (miles)	462	Vry. Long	410.55	Average	410.55	Average
Bumpers	Strong		Strong		Strong	
Parking Index	Vry. Easy		Vry. Easy		Vry. Easy	
Head/Leg Room (in.)	39.8/42.2	Roomy	39.8/42.7	Roomy	39.8/42.7	Roomy
Interior Space (cu. ft.)	91	Cramped	89.8	Cramped	89.8	Cramped
Cargo Space (cu. ft.)	13	Vry. Small	11.9	Vry. Small	11.9	Vry. Small
Tow Rating (lbs.)						

*2dr. and 4dr.

C A R   B O O K   2 0 0 1   245

Another year with very few changes; this small sport utility is based on the Civic platform and rides and drives like the Civic. Dual airbags are standard; ABS is optional. The CR-V comes in either 2- or 4-wheel drive for the LX, and 4 wheel drive for the EX. The 2.0-liter engine gets an additional 20 hp, bringing the total to 145. The CR-V has become a popular contender in the small SUV category.

2001 Honda CR-V

General Information

New for 2001: No major changes	**Year of Production:** 4
Twins:	**Seating:** 5
Where Made: Japan	**Theft Rating:** Very Low

Prices 2001

Model	Retail	Markup
LX 2WD auto.	$18,800	9%
LX 4WD man.	$19,150	9%
EX 4WD man.	$20,750	8%
SE 4WD auto.	$22,800	8%

Competition 2001

Model	POOR				GOOD	pg.
Honda CR-V					■	246
Jeep Wrangler	■					288

'00 and '99 Models

The CR-V's interior is well designed, roomy, and has plenty of room for five. The cargo space is well designed and has a unique feature in the rear cargo floor that can be used as a picnic table.

Price Ranges 2000–1999

LX 2WD	$17-18,700
LX 4WD	$18,900-19,100
EX 4WD	$19,900-20,600

2000 Honda CR-V

1999 Honda CR-V

Honda CR-V — Small Sport Utility

	2001	2000	1999

RATINGS

	2001 (POOR → GOOD)	2000 (POOR → GOOD)	1999 (POOR → GOOD)
Comparative Rating	7	7	6
Frontal Crash Tests	8	8	9
Safety Features	5	6	5
Preventive Maintenance	3	2	2
Repair Costs	6	5	4
Warranty	1	1	1
Fuel Economy	5	4	4
Rollover (based on SSF; see pg. 30)	5	5	5
Complaints	10	10	10
Insurance Costs	10	10	10

SAFETY

	2001	2000	1999
Frontal Crash Tests	Good	Good	Very Good
Side Crash Tests	Very Good	Very Good	Very Good
Airbags	Dual (nextgen)	Dual (nextgen)	Dual (nextgen)
Anti-Lock Brakes	4-Wheel (optional)	4-Wheel (optional)	4-Wheel (optional)
Day Running Lamps	None	Standard	None
Built-In Child Seats	None	None	None
Pretensioners	None	None	None

SPECIFICATIONS

	2001		2000		1999	
Fuel Economy (cty/hwy)	22/25	Poor	22/25	Poor	22/25	Poor
Driving Range (miles)	359.55	Vry. Short	359.55	Vry. Short	359.55	Vry. Short
Bumpers	Weak		Weak			
Parking Index	Easy		Easy		Easy	
Head/Leg Room (in.)	40.5/41.5	Roomy	40.5/41.5	Roomy	40.5/41.5	Roomy
Interior Space (cu. ft.)	98	Average	98	Average	98	Average
Cargo Space (cu. ft.)	67.2	Large	67.2	Large	67.2	Large
Tow Rating (lbs.)	1000	Vry. Low	1000	Vry. Low	1000	Vry. Low

Honda Insight   Subcompact

The Insight, introduced in late 2000, has not been changed for 2001. The Insight gets 61 miles per gallon in the city and 68 on the highway. This amazing fuel economy in generated by Honda's Integrated Motor Assist system, combining a 1.0 liter 3-cylinder gasoline engine with an electric motor. The only real competition in this class of vehicle is the Toyota Prius. While there are various differences, the most obvious is the dramatic style of the Insight.

2001 Honda Insight

General Information

New for 2001: No major changes	**Year of Production:**	2
Twins:	**Seating:**	2
Where Made: Japan	**Theft Rating:**	

Prices 2001

Model	Retail	Markup
Hatchback w/o air	$18,880	12%
Hatchback w/ air	$20,080	12%

Competition 2001

Model	POOR				GOOD	pg.
Honda Insight						**248**
Toyota Prius						432

'00 and '99 Models

Introduced in 2000, this is essentially the same vehicle being sold in 2001.

Price Ranges 2000–1999

2000 Honda Insight

MODEL WAS NOT PRODUCED THIS YEAR

1999 Model

Honda Insight — Subcompact

	2001	2000	1999

RATINGS

	POOR — GOOD	POOR — GOOD	POOR — GOOD
Comparative Rating			
Frontal Crash Tests	8	8	
Safety Features	5	6	
Preventive Maintenance			
Repair Costs			
Warranty	1	1	
Fuel Economy	10	10	
Rollover (based on SSF; see pg. 30)	7	7	
Complaints	5		
Insurance Costs	5		

SAFETY

	2001	2000	1999
Frontal Crash Tests	Good	Good	
Side Crash Tests	No Govt Results	No Govt Results	
Airbags	Dual (nextgen)	Dual (nextgen)	
Anti-Lock Brakes	4-Wheel	4-Wheel	
Day Running Lamps	None	Standard	
Built-In Child Seats	None	None	
Pretensioners	None	None	

SPECIFICATIONS

	2001		2000		1999
Fuel Economy (cty/hwy)	61/68	Vry. Good	61/70	Vry. Good	
Driving Range (miles)	683.7	Vry. Long	694.3	Vry. Long	
Bumpers					
Parking Index					
Head/Leg Room (in.)	38.8/42.9	Average	38.8/42.9	Average	
Interior Space (cu. ft.)	47.4	Vry. Cramp.	47.4	Vry. Cramp.	
Cargo Space (cu. ft.)					
Tow Rating (lbs.)					

The Odyssey received a major overhaul in 1999 and remains essentially the same this year. Two sliding doors and a longer wheelbase are now available, and the interior grew in size. Traction control comes standard on the EX. The 3.5-liter 210 hp engine is a great boost in power, one of the most powerful for minivans. The ride is firm and above average for a minivan, and a touch-screen navigational system is optional. The EX also has power rear doors, automatic climate control, a security system, and upgraded stereo with a CD player.

2001 Honda Odyssey

General Information

New for 2001: No major changes	Year of Production:	3
Twins:	Seating:	7
Where Made: Canada	Theft Rating:	Very Low

Prices 2001

Model	Retail	Markup
LX	$23,900	12%
EX	$26,400	12%

Competition 2001

Model	POOR				GOOD		pg.
Honda Odyssey			■				250
Chev. Venture				■			184
Olds Silhouette					■		378
Toyota Sienna			■				438

'00 and '99 Models

Introduced in late 1999, this revamped Odyssey quickly became hard to find, with wait lists and full prices. The powerful engine, full array of custom features, and interior size and space like the other minivans only increased the popularity of this vehicle. The Odyssey has a low floor which makes it easier for kids to get in and out.

Price Ranges 2000–1999

LX	$23,000-23,400
EX	$25,800-26,000

2000 Honda Odyssey

1999 Honda Odyssey

Honda Odyssey — Minivan

	2001	2000	1999

RATINGS

	POOR — GOOD (2001)	POOR — GOOD (2000)	POOR — GOOD (1999)
Comparative Rating	4	3	3
Frontal Crash Tests	10	10	10
Safety Features	5	6	6
Preventive Maintenance	3	2	2
Repair Costs	6	3	4
Warranty	1	1	1
Fuel Economy	4	3	3
Rollover (based on SSF; see pg. 30)	7	7	6
Complaints	1	1	2
Insurance Costs	10	10	10

SAFETY

	2001	2000	1999
Frontal Crash Tests	Very Good	Very Good	Very Good
Side Crash Tests	Very Good	Very Good	Very Good
Airbags	Dual (nextgen)	Dual (nextgen)	Dual (nextgen)
Anti-Lock Brakes	4-Wheel	4-Wheel	4-Wheel
Day Running Lamps	None	Standard	None
Built-In Child Seats	None	None	None
Pretensioners	None	None	None

SPECIFICATIONS

	2001		2000		1999	
Fuel Economy (cty/hwy)	18/25	Poor	18/25	Poor	18/26	Poor
Driving Range (miles)	430	Long	430	Long	440	Long
Bumpers	Strong		Strong		Strong	
Parking Index	Hard		Hard		Hard	
Head/Leg Room (in.)	41.2/41	Roomy	41.2/41	Roomy	41.2/41	Roomy
Interior Space (cu. ft.)	170.7	Vry. Roomy	170.7	Vry. Roomy	170.7	Vry. Roomy
Cargo Space (cu. ft.)	146.11	Vry. Large	146.11	Vry. Large	146.11	Vry. Large
Tow Rating (lbs.)	3500	Low	3500	Low	3500	Low

Honda Passport

With no major changes for 2001, the Passport continues with standard dual airbags and 4-wheel ABS. The Passport comes with a 3.2-liter V6 engine, which should provide good power, but don't expect much in terms of gas mileage. You have your choice between two trim levels, a base LX or up-level EX, and you can also choose between two- and four-wheel drive. You will find that the cargo space is small and the payload is quite low.

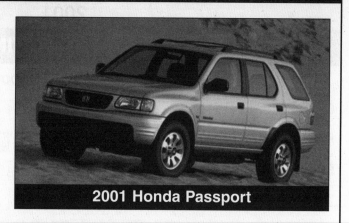

2001 Honda Passport

General Information

New for 2001:	No major changes	Year of Production:	4
Twins:	Isuzu Rodeo	Seating:	5
Where Made:	U.S.	Theft Rating:	Very High

Prices 2001

Model	Retail	Markup
LX 2WD man.	$23,000	12%
LX 2WD auto.	$24,200	12%
LX 4WD man.	$26,200	12%
EX 4WD auto. w/Luxury Pkg.	$30,100	12%

Competition 2001

Model	POOR						GOOD	pg.
Honda Passport	■							**252**
Ford Explorer					■			224
Jeep Gr. Cher.			■					286
Olds Bravada		■						374

'00 and '99 Models

Actually made by Isuzu, the Passport is the twin of the Rodeo. Ride and handling are what you would expect from a sport utility, and it does get noisy during acceleration. The Passport performed only averagely on frontal crash tests, but excellently on side crash tests.

Price Ranges 2000–1999

LX 2WD manual	$19-22,200
LX 2WD automatic	$19,600-22,800
LX 4WD manual	$21,200-25,400
LX 4WD automatic	$21,800-26,000

2000 Honda Passport

1999 Honda Passport

	2001	2000	1999

RATINGS

(POOR → GOOD)	2001	2000	1999
Comparative Rating	1	1	1
Frontal Crash Tests	6	5	5
Safety Features	5	6	5
Preventive Maintenance	5	4	5
Repair Costs	1	7	2
Warranty	1	1	1
Fuel Economy	2	2	2
Rollover (based on SSF; see pg. 30)	4	4	4
Complaints	1	1	1
Insurance Costs	5	5	5

SAFETY

	2001	2000	1999
Frontal Crash Tests	Average	Average	Average
Side Crash Tests	Very Good	Very Good	Very Good
Airbags	Dual (nextgen)	Dual (nextgen)	Dual (nextgen)
Anti-Lock Brakes	4-Wheel	4-Wheel	2-Wheel (4-whl opt.)
Day Running Lamps	None	Standard	None
Built-In Child Seats	None	None	None
Pretensioners	None	None	None

SPECIFICATIONS

	2001		2000		1999	
Fuel Economy (cty/hwy)	17/20	Vry. Poor	16/20	Vry. Poor	18/20	Poor
Driving Range (miles)	390.35	Short	379.8	Short	400.9	Average
Bumpers	Weak		Weak		Average	
Parking Index	Hard		Hard			
Head/Leg Room (in.)	38.9/42.1	Average	38.9/42.1	Average	38.9/42.1	Average
Interior Space (cu. ft.)	97.1	Average	97.1	Average	90.4	Cramped
Cargo Space (cu. ft.)	81.1	Large	81.1	Large	81.1	Large
Tow Rating (lbs.)	4500	Average	4500	Average	4500	Average

Essentially unchanged from its introduction five years ago, the Prelude is a mix of luxury and performance. The Prelude is surprisingly roomy and has a standard 2.2-liter 4-cylinder engine that offers a powerful, firm driving experience. Test driving the Prelude is a must for sports car enthusiasts. The back seat, as expected, is virtually non-existent—but that's not what you buy a sports car for!

2001 Honda Prelude

General Information

New for 2001: No major changes	**Year of Production:** 5
Twins:	**Seating:** 4
Where Made: Japan	**Theft Rating:** Very High

Prices 2001

Model	Retail	Markup
Base man.	$23,600	12%
Base auto.	$24,600	12%
SH Coupe man.	$26,100	3%

Competition 2001

Model	POOR				GOOD	pg.
Honda Prelude						254
Chev. Camaro			■			164
Ford Mustang				■		230
Pontiac Gr. Prix				■		386

'00 and '99 Models

The Prelude received a slightly stronger engine with the addition of 5 horses to bring it to 200 hp in 1999. The standard engine for both the base model and the SH is a 2.2-liter 4-cylinder engine, which is plenty to power this compact car.

Price Ranges 2000–1999

Manual Base	$23-24,000
Automatic Base	$25-26,000
Coupe	$21,800-26,000

2000 Honda Prelude

1999 Honda Prelude

Honda Prelude — Compact

	2001	2000	1999

RATINGS

	2001 (POOR → GOOD)	2000 (POOR → GOOD)	1999 (POOR → GOOD)
Comparative Rating			
Frontal Crash Tests			
Safety Features	5	6	6
Preventive Maintenance	3	2	3
Repair Costs	6	4	5
Warranty	1	1	1
Fuel Economy	5	4	4
Rollover (based on SSF; see pg. 30)	8	8	8
Complaints	6	6	7
Insurance Costs	1	5	5

SAFETY

	2001	2000	1999
Frontal Crash Tests	No Govt Results	No Govt Results	No Govt Results
Side Crash Tests	No Govt Results	No Govt Results	No Govt Results
Airbags	Dual (nextgen)	Dual (nextgen)	Dual (nextgen)
Anti-Lock Brakes	4-Wheel	4-Wheel	4-Wheel
Day Running Lamps	None	Standard	None
Built-In Child Seats	None	None	None
Pretensioners		None	None

SPECIFICATIONS

	2001		2000		1999	
Fuel Economy (cty/hwy)	22/27	Average	22/27	Average	22/27	Average
Driving Range (miles)	389.55	Short	389.55	Short	389.55	Short
Bumpers	Strong		Strong		Strong	
Parking Index	Easy		Easy		Easy	
Head/Leg Room (in.)	37.9/43	Average	37.9/43	Average	37.9/43	Average
Interior Space (cu. ft.)	78	Vry. Cramp.	78.4	Vry. Cramp.	78.4	Vry. Cramp.
Cargo Space (cu. ft.)	9	Vry. Small	8.7	Vry. Small	8.7	Vry. Small
Tow Rating (lbs.)						

Honda S2000 Subcompact

Last year's new S2000 roadster continues into 2001 unchanged. Its 4-cylinder engine has a 240-horsepower output. The engine won't start though unless you push the electronic start button. Although performance is the focus with this sports car, dual airbags and seat belt pretensioners are standard. Controls are positioned where the driver will intuitively seek them out and can focus on the road. The soft top raises or lowers in six seconds and A/C and leather are standard.

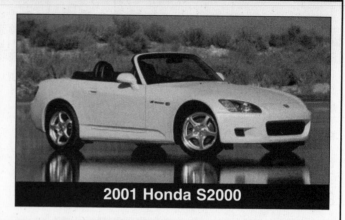

2001 Honda S2000

General Information

New for 2001: No major changes	Year of Production:	2
Twins:	Seating:	2
Where Made: Japan	Theft Rating:	

Prices 2001

Model	Retail	Markup
Roadster	$32,300	7%

Competition 2001

Model	POOR					GOOD	pg.
Honda S2000							**256**
Chev. Camaro				■			164
Ford Mustang					■		230
VW Beetle						■	446

'00 and '99 Models

Introduced in 2000, this distinctive-looking sports car is aimed squarely at the market longing for the old-style European sports cars. There is a standard theft prevention system, and the stereo/CD hides behind a retractable panel. The suspension is racing style, the engine powerful, and the steering is power assisted.

Price Ranges 2000–1999

2000 Honda S2000

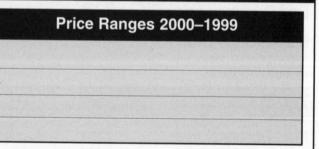

MODEL WAS NOT PRODUCED THIS YEAR

1999 Model

	2001	2000	1999

RATINGS

	POOR — GOOD	POOR — GOOD	POOR — GOOD
Comparative Rating	—	—	—
Frontal Crash Tests	—	—	—
Safety Features	6	7	—
Preventive Maintenance	—	—	—
Repair Costs	—	—	—
Warranty	1	1	—
Fuel Economy	5	4	—
Rollover (based on SSF; see pg. 30)	9	9	—
Complaints	5	—	—
Insurance Costs	5	1	—

SAFETY

	2001	2000	1999
Frontal Crash Tests	No Govt Results	No Govt Results	
Side Crash Tests	No Govt Results	No Govt Results	
Airbags	Dual (nextgen)	Dual (nextgen)	
Anti-Lock Brakes	4-Wheel	4-Wheel	
Day Running Lamps	None	Standard	
Built-In Child Seats	None	None	
Pretensioners	Standard	None	

SPECIFICATIONS

	2001		2000		1999
Fuel Economy (cty/hwy)	20/26	Poor	20/26	Poor	
Driving Range (miles)	303.6	Vry. Short	303.6	Vry. Short	
Bumpers	Strong		Strong		
Parking Index	Vry. Easy		Vry. Easy		
Head/Leg Room (in.)	34.6/44.3	Vry. Cramp.	34.6/44.3	Vry. Cramp.	
Interior Space (cu. ft.)	48.4	Vry. Cramp.	48.4	Vry. Cramp.	
Cargo Space (cu. ft.)	5	Vry. Small	5	Vry. Small	
Tow Rating (lbs.)					

Hyundai Accent   Subcompact

The low-priced Accent moves to 2001 with no changes. All Accents are powered by a 1.5-liter 4 cylinder engine with 92 horses. It still has three trim levels though—the three-door hatchback L and GS, and the 4-door GL. It has an amazing 10-year/100,000-mile powertrain warranty, and second generation de-powered airbags and belt pretensioners will help keep you safe. Hyundai's main competitive feature is their low price, and the Accent is one of the least expensive new cars you can buy.

2001 Hyundai Accent

General Information

New for 2001: No major changes	**Year of Production:**	2
Twins:	**Seating:**	5
Where Made: Korea	**Theft Rating:**	Average

Prices 2001

Model	Retail	Markup
L man.	$9,000	7%
GL man.	$9,900	8%
GS auto.	$10,000	9%
GL auto.	$10,500	7%

Competition 2001

Model	POOR					GOOD		pg.
Hyundai Accent								**258**
Mazda Protégé			■					334
Subaru Impreza						■		404
Saturn SL						■		400

'00 and '99 Models

The 2000 model was redesigned and improved over the 1999. Available in three trim levels: Accent L three-door, GS three-door hatchback, and GL four-door sedan. ABS is optional only on the GS and GL. The 1.5-liter 4-cylinder engine that comes on all Accents is adequate for this light car and is fuel efficient.

Price Ranges 2000–1999

L	$7,600-9,100
GS	$8,300-10,100
GL	$8,700-10,400

2000 Hyundai Accent

1999 Hyundai Accent

Hyundai Accent   Subcompact

	2001	2000	1999

RATINGS

	2001 (POOR–GOOD)	2000 (POOR–GOOD)	1999 (POOR–GOOD)
Comparative Rating			8
Frontal Crash Tests			6
Safety Features	5	5	5
Preventive Maintenance	10	10	10
Repair Costs	8	8	9
Warranty	9	10	10
Fuel Economy	6	7	7
Rollover (based on SSF; see pg. 30)	7	7	7
Complaints	5		7
Insurance Costs	1	1	1

SAFETY

	2001	2000	1999
Frontal Crash Tests	No Govt Results	No Govt Results	Average
Side Crash Tests	No Govt Results	No Govt Results	No Govt Results
Airbags	Dual (nextgen)	Dual (nextgen)	Dual
Anti-Lock Brakes	4-Wheel (optional)	4-Wheel (optional)	4-Wheel
Day Running Lamps	None	None	None
Built-In Child Seats	None	None	None
Pretensioners	None	None	None

SPECIFICATIONS

	2001		2000		1999	
Fuel Economy (cty/hwy)	18/36	Average	28/36	Good	28/37	Good
Driving Range (miles)	321.3	Vry. Short	380.8	Short	386.75	Short
Bumpers	Strong		Strong		Strong	
Parking Index	Vry. Easy		Vry. Easy		Vry. Easy	
Head/Leg Room (in.)	38.9/42.6	Average	38.9/42.6	Average	38.7/42.6	Average
Interior Space (cu. ft.)	89	Cramped	88	Cramped	88	Cramped
Cargo Space (cu. ft.)	12	Vry. Small	10.7	Vry. Small	10.7	Vry. Small
Tow Rating (lbs.)						

Hyundai Elantra — Compact

All-new for 2001, the Elantra is on a longer wheelbase than its predecessor which should make for a smoother ride. Side airbags are standard as are A/C, power locks/windows/mirrors, and a tilt steering column. The longer wheelbase also allows for more room inside. A new 2.0L engine should be peppier than last year's, and the new look is more aerodynamic. Front side air bags are standard as are seat belt pretensioners, which automatically take up slack when needed.

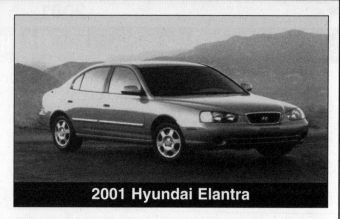

2001 Hyundai Elantra

General Information

New for 2001: All-new		**Year of Production:**	1
Twins:		**Seating:**	5
Where Made: Korea		**Theft Rating:**	Average

Prices 2001

Model	Retail	Markup
GLS man.	$12,500	7%
GLS auto.	$13,300	10%

Competition 2001

Model	POOR					GOOD	pg.
Hyundai Elantra							260
Chev. Cavalier				■			166
VW Golf						■	448
Toyota Corolla					■		424

'00 and '99 Models

The Elantra continues through 1999 and 2000 with no major changes. As either a sedan or wagon, the Elantra comes with plenty of options. The front seats are comfortable, but adults will feel cramped in the back. Average crash test results keep the 1999-2000 models from being top choices, but for value it's a decent selection.

Price Ranges 2000–1999

GLS manual	$9700-11,100
GLS automatic	$10,200-12,400

2000 Hyundai Elantra

1999 Hyundai Elantra

	2001	2000	1999

RATINGS

	2001 (POOR–GOOD)	2000 (POOR–GOOD)	1999 (POOR–GOOD)
Comparative Rating		7	6
Frontal Crash Tests		5	5
Safety Features	7	6	6
Preventive Maintenance	10	10	10
Repair Costs	8	8	9
Warranty	9	10	10
Fuel Economy	7	6	6
Rollover (based on SSF; see pg. 30)	7	7	7
Complaints	5	5	6
Insurance Costs	1	1	1

SAFETY

	2001	2000	1999
Frontal Crash Tests	To Be Tested	Average	Average
Side Crash Tests	No Govt Results	No Govt Results	No Govt Results
Airbags	Dual/Side	Dual	Dual
Anti-Lock Brakes	Optional	4-Wheel (optional)	4-Wheel (optional)
Day Running Lamps	None	None	None
Built-In Child Seats	None	None	None
Pretensioners	Standard	Standard	Standard

SPECIFICATIONS

	2001		2000		1999	
Fuel Economy (cty/hwy)	25/33	Good	24/33	Average	24/33	Average
Driving Range (miles)	420.5	Average	413.25	Average	413.25	Average
Bumpers	Strong		Strong		Strong	
Parking Index	Average		Vry. Easy		Vry. Easy	
Head/Leg Room (in.)	39.6/43.2	Roomy	38.6/43.2	Average	38.6/43.2	Average
Interior Space (cu. ft.)	95	Average	105	Roomy	93.6	Cramped
Cargo Space (cu. ft.)	13	Vry. Small	11.4	Vry. Small	11.4	Vry. Small
Tow Rating (lbs.)			1500	Vry. Low	1500	Vry. Low

Hyundai Santa Fe
Small Sport Utility

Like everyone else, Hyundai is entering the SUV field with the all-new Santa Fe. Built on a version of the Sonata platform, it has a choice of front wheel drive or full-time 4WD. There are two engine choices, a base 2.4L 4-cylinder and a more powerful 2.7L V6. Leather seats, ABS, and traction control are options. A/C, power windows, roof rack, and privacy glass are standard. 16-inch wheels are standard and designed to give the Santa Fe the strong SUV look.

2001 Hyundai Sante Fe

General Information

New for 2001: All-new		**Year of Production:**	1
Twins:		**Seating:**	5
Where Made: Korea		**Theft Rating:**	

Prices 2001

Model	Retail	Markup
4 cyl. 2WD man.	$16,500	7%
V6 2WD auto.	$18,300	7%
4 cyl. 2WD auto.	$17,300	9%
V6. 4WD auto.	$19,800	8%

Competition 2001

Model	POOR				GOOD	pg.
Hyun. Santa Fe						**262**
Jeep Wrangler		■				288
Honda CR-V				■		246

'00 and '99 Models

Price Ranges 2000–1999

MODEL WAS NOT PRODUCED THIS YEAR

2000 Model

MODEL WAS NOT PRODUCED THIS YEAR

1999 Model

Hyundai Santa Fe

Small Sport Utility

	2001	2000	1999

RATINGS

	POOR — GOOD	POOR — GOOD	POOR — GOOD
Comparative Rating			
Frontal Crash Tests			
Safety Features	4		
Preventive Maintenance	10		
Repair Costs	9		
Warranty	9		
Fuel Economy	5		
Rollover (based on SSF; see pg. 30)	5		
Complaints	5		
Insurance Costs	5		

SAFETY

Frontal Crash Tests	No Govt Results		
Side Crash Tests	No Govt Results		
Airbags	Dual		
Anti-Lock Brakes	Optional		
Day Running Lamps	None		
Built-In Child Seats	None		
Pretensioners	None		

SPECIFICATIONS

Fuel Economy (cty/hwy)	21/28 Average		
Driving Range (miles)	421.4 Average		
Bumpers			
Parking Index	Average		
Head/Leg Room (in.)	39.6/41.6 Average		
Interior Space (cu. ft.)	101 Average		
Cargo Space (cu. ft.)	31 Average		
Tow Rating (lbs.)			

Essentially unchanged for 2001, you still can choose between a 2.4-liter 4 cylinder engine or an aluminum 2.5-liter V6. Thicker glass and a redesigned cabin contribute to a quieter ride in the Sonata. The Sonata is also much safer than models from past years with standard side airbags and a system which detects the presence of a passenger in the front seat. Standard features include A/C, cruise control, power windows/locks/mirrors, and remote releases for the trunk, hood, and fuel door.

2001 Hyundai Sonata

General Information

New for 2001: No major changes	**Year of Production:** 7
Twins:	**Seating:** 5
Where Made: Korea	**Theft Rating:**

Prices 2001

Model	Retail	Markup
Base man.	$15,000	12%
Base auto.	$15,500	12%
GLS man.	$17,000	10%
GLS auto.	$17,500	10%

Competition 2001

Model	POOR					GOOD	pg.
Hyundai Sonata							**264**
Chev. Malibu			■				170
Honda Accord				■			242
Toyota Camry					■		420

'00 and '99 Models

The Sonata has a relatively sophisticated suspension system, which is designed to provide the feel of a luxury car and the handling of a sports sedan. The upgraded models have a split, folding rear seat, map lights, illuminated ignition key slot, and a rear center armrest.

Price Ranges 2000–1999

Base manual	$11-14,000
Base automatic	$11,500-15,000
GLS manual	$12,400-14,500
GLS automatic	$12,900-15,000

2000 Hyundai Sonata

1999 Hyundai Sonata

	2001	2000	1999

RATINGS

	POOR — GOOD (2001)	POOR — GOOD (2000)	POOR — GOOD (1999)
Comparative Rating		8	9
Frontal Crash Tests		5	5
Safety Features	8	6	6
Preventive Maintenance	10	10	10
Repair Costs	7	7	8
Warranty	9	10	10
Fuel Economy	6	4	5
Rollover (based on SSF; see pg. 30)	7	8	7
Complaints	5	5	6
Insurance Costs	1	1	1

SAFETY

	2001	2000	1999
Frontal Crash Tests	No Govt Results	Average	Average
Side Crash Tests	Very Good	No Govt Results	No Govt Results
Airbags	Dual/Side (nextgen)	Dual (nextgen)	Dual
Anti-Lock Brakes	4-Wheel (optional)	4-Wheel (optional)	4-Wheel (optional)
Day Running Lamps	None	None	None
Built-In Child Seats	None	None	None
Pretensioners	Standard	Standard	Standard

SPECIFICATIONS

	2001		2000		1999	
Fuel Economy (cty/hwy)	22/30	Average	21/29	Average	21/30	Average
Driving Range (miles)	447.2	Long	430	Long	438.6	Long
Bumpers	Strong		Strong		Strong	
Parking Index	Easy		Easy		Easy	
Head/Leg Room (in.)	39.3/43.3	Roomy	39.3/43.3	Roomy	38.5/43.3	Average
Interior Space (cu. ft.)	100	Average	100	Average	101.3	Average
Cargo Space (cu. ft.)	13	Vry. Small	13.2	Small	13.2	Small
Tow Rating (lbs.)						

Hyundai Tiburon

The Tiburon continues in 2001 with no changes. This is the sportiest car among the Hyundai offerings, with a 2.0-liter 4-cylinder engine that produces 140 horsepower. Handling and performance are good, in part due to a suspension system designed by Porsche engineers. The controls are well placed and easy to read. Pricewise, the Tiburon is an attractive choice among sporty compacts.

2001 Hyundai Tiburon

General Information

New for 2001: No major changes	**Year of Production:** 5
Twins:	**Seating:** 5
Where Made: Korea	**Theft Rating:** Average

Prices 2001

Model	Retail	Markup
Base man.	$14,500	10%
Base auto.	$15,300	12%

Competition 2001

Model	POOR				GOOD	pg.
Hyundai Tiburon						**266**
Audi A8					■	132
Ford Mustang			■			230
Pontiac Gr. Prix				■		386

'00 and '99 Models

With its Porsche-designed suspension, expect the ride to be good on smooth roads; get onto something bumpy and you won't have much fun. The Tiburon is aimed for car buyers looking for a sporty, inexpensive small car.

Price Ranges 2000–1999

Base manual	$11,300-13,500
Base automatic	$11,800-14,000

2000 Hyundai Tiburon

1999 Hyundai Tiburon

Hyundai Tiburon — Compact

	2001	2000	1999

RATINGS

	2001 (POOR–GOOD)	2000 (POOR–GOOD)	1999 (POOR–GOOD)
Comparative Rating	—	—	—
Frontal Crash Tests	—	—	—
Safety Features	4	4	4
Preventive Maintenance	10	10	10
Repair Costs	8	9	9
Warranty	9	10	10
Fuel Economy	6	5	5
Rollover (based on SSF; see pg. 30)	8	8	8
Complaints	3	3	5
Insurance Costs	1	1	1

SAFETY

	2001	2000	1999
Frontal Crash Tests	No Govt Results	No Govt Results	No Govt Results
Side Crash Tests	No Govt Results	No Govt Results	No Govt Results
Airbags	Dual	Dual	Dual
Anti-Lock Brakes	4-Wheel (optional)	4-Wheel (optional)	4-Wheel (optional)
Day Running Lamps	None	None	None
Built-In Child Seats	None	None	None
Pretensioners	None	None	None

SPECIFICATIONS

	2001		2000		1999	
Fuel Economy (cty/hwy)	23/31	Average	23/32	Average	22/31	Average
Driving Range (miles)	391.5	Short	398.75	Average	384.25	Short
Bumpers	Strong		Strong		Strong	
Parking Index	Vry. Easy		Vry. Easy		Vry. Easy	
Head/Leg Room (in.)	38/43.1	Average	38/43.1	Average	38/43.1	Average
Interior Space (cu. ft.)	80	Vry. Cramp.	80	Vry. Cramp.	80	Vry. Cramp.
Cargo Space (cu. ft.)	13	Vry. Small	12.8	Vry. Small	12.8	Vry. Small
Tow Rating (lbs.)						

Hyundai XG300 Large

All-new for 2001, the XG300 is Hyundai's flagship model and larger than the Sonata. This five-passenger sedan is designed to compete in the "almost" luxury sedan market. Standard are ABS, A/C, cruise control, keyless entry, and front and side airbags. Hyundai is trying to offer a more affordable Toyota Avalon. Only one engine is available, but it appears more than adequate at 3L and 192 horsepower. Other features included heated mirrors, power seats, and a trip computer.

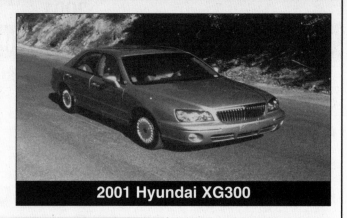

2001 Hyundai XG300

General Information

New for 2001: All-new		**Year of Production:**	1
Twins:		**Seating:**	5
Where Made: Korea		**Theft Rating:**	

Prices 2001

Model	Retail	Markup
Base	$23,499	11%
L Sedan	$25,000	11%

Competition 2001

Model	POOR			GOOD		pg.
Hyundai XG300					■	268
Lincoln Town Car				■		322
Cadillac DeVille			■			152
Acura RL				■		124

'00 and '99 Models

Price Ranges 2000–1999

MODEL WAS NOT PRODUCED THIS YEAR

2000 Model

MODEL WAS NOT PRODUCED THIS YEAR

1999 Model

	2001	2000	1999

RATINGS

	POOR — GOOD	POOR — GOOD	POOR — GOOD
Comparative Rating			
Frontal Crash Tests			
Safety Features	6		
Preventive Maintenance	10		
Repair Costs	9		
Warranty	9		
Fuel Economy	5		
Rollover (based on SSF; see pg. 30)	8		
Complaints	5		
Insurance Costs	5		

SAFETY

	2001	2000	1999
Frontal Crash Tests	No Govt Results		
Side Crash Tests	No Govt Results		
Airbags	Dual/Side		
Anti-Lock Brakes	Standard		
Day Running Lamps	None		
Built-In Child Seats	None		
Pretensioners	None		

SPECIFICATIONS

	2001	2000	1999
Fuel Economy (cty/hwy)	19/27 Poor		
Driving Range (miles)	425.5 Long		
Bumpers	Strong		
Parking Index	Average		
Head/Leg Room (in.)	39.7/43.4 Roomy		
Interior Space (cu. ft.)	103 Roomy		
Cargo Space (cu. ft.)	15 Small		
Tow Rating (lbs.)			

Infiniti G20 — Compact

Since its inception in 1999, there have not been any substantial changes to the Infiniti G20. An all-aluminum 140 hp 2.0-liter 4-cylinder engine powers both the base and a touring model known as the G20t. A multi-link suspension system and advanced steering give the G20 great handling. You choose between a 4-speed automatic and a 5-speed manual transmission. Inside, the G20 is roomy, thoughtfully designed, and quiet.

2001 Infiniti G20

General Information

New for 2001: No major changes	**Year of Production:** 3
Twins:	**Seating:** 5
Where Made: Japan	**Theft Rating:**

Prices 2001

Model	Retail	Markup
Luxury Sedan man.	$21,400	9%
Touring Sedan man.	$24,100	11%
Luxury Sedan auto.	$22,200	9%
Touring Sedan auto.	$24,900	11%

Competition 2001

Model	POOR	GOOD	pg.
Infiniti G20			**270**
Olds Alero			370
Mitsu. Galant			350
Pontiac Gr. Am			384

'00 and '99 Models

Dual and side airbags come standard for front occupants. ABS is also a standard feature. The G20t gives you a limited slip differential, fog lights, and automatic temperature control. This model has yet to be crash tested.

Price Ranges 2000–1999

Luxury	$18,800-21,400
Touring	$19,500-22,100

2000 Infiniti G20

1999 Infiniti G20

	2001	2000	1999

RATINGS

	POOR — GOOD	POOR — GOOD	POOR — GOOD
Comparative Rating			
Frontal Crash Tests			
Safety Features	8	8	8
Preventive Maintenance	6	5	6
Repair Costs	3	5	4
Warranty	9	9	10
Fuel Economy	6	5	5
Rollover (based on SSF; see pg. 30)	7	7	7
Complaints	10	10	10
Insurance Costs	5	5	5

SAFETY

	2001	2000	1999
Frontal Crash Tests	No Govt Results	No Govt Results	No Govt Results
Side Crash Tests	No Govt Results	No Govt Results	No Govt Results
Airbags	Dual/Side (nextgen)	Dual/Side (nextgen)	Dual/Side (nextgen)
Anti-Lock Brakes	4-Wheel	4-Wheel	4-Wheel
Day Running Lamps	None	None	None
Built-In Child Seats	None	None	None
Pretensioners	Standard	Standard	Standard

SPECIFICATIONS

	2001		2000		1999	
Fuel Economy (cty/hwy)	24/31	Average	23/30	Average	23/31	Average
Driving Range (miles)	437.25	Long	421.35	Average	429.3	Long
Bumpers	Strong		Strong			
Parking Index	Average		Average		Average	
Head/Leg Room (in.)	40/41.5	Average	40/41.5	Average	40/41.5	Average
Interior Space (cu. ft.)	91	Cramped	91	Cramped	91	Cramped
Cargo Space (cu. ft.)	14	Small	13.5	Small	13.5	Small
Tow Rating (lbs.)						

Infiniti I30 — Large

Redesigned in 2000, the I30 is essentially unchanged. It has a highly rated 3.0-liter V6 that produces 227 horsepower and last year's new styling, including increased dimensions and an all new interior. In addition to standard ABS, driver and front passenger airbags and side airbags, there is now head protection. It also has rear child seat tethers, which ensure your child seat is secured properly. The optional navigation system is 3-D and rises from the dash for easy visibility.

2001 Infiniti I30

General Information

New for 2001: No major changes	**Year of Production:** 2
Twins: Nissan Maxima	**Seating:** 5
Where Made: Japan	**Theft Rating:** Very High

Prices 2001

Model	Retail	Markup
Luxury Sedan	$29,500	11%
Touring Sedan	$31,500	13%

Competition 2001

Model	POOR				GOOD		pg.
Infiniti I30					■		**272**
Ford Cr. Victoria						■	216
Buick Regal				■			148
Audi A8						■	132

'00 and '99 Models

Revised in 2000, the newer model has improved on the highly rated 1999. Changes include better visibility, a new engine with a 100,000-mile tune-up schedule, and some different color choices. The seven speaker sound system comes with steering-mounted controls. Leather is standard, as is the fancy analog dash clock and a power rear window shade.

Price Ranges 2000–1999

Model	Price Range
Luxury Sedan	$22,600-29,500
Touring Sedan	$23,300-30,200

2000 Infiniti I30

1999 Infiniti I30

	2001	2000	1999

RATINGS

	POOR — GOOD	POOR — GOOD	POOR — GOOD
Comparative Rating	7	7	9
Frontal Crash Tests*	8	8	7
Safety Features	8	8	8
Preventive Maintenance	6	5	6
Repair Costs	2	1	2
Warranty	9	9	10
Fuel Economy	4	4	4
Rollover (based on SSF, see pg. 25)	7	7	7
Complaints	5		10
Insurance Costs	5	5	5

SAFETY

	2001	2000	1999
Frontal Crash Tests	Good	Good	Good
Side Crash Tests	Very Good	No Govt Results	No Govt Results
Airbags	Dual/Side (nextgen)	Dual/Side (nextgen)	Dual/Side (nextgen)
Anti-Lock Brakes	4-Wheel	4-Wheel	4-Wheel
Day Running Lamps	None	None	None
Built-In Child Seats	None	None	None
Pretensioners	Standard	Standard	Standard

SPECIFICATIONS

	2001		2000		1999	
Fuel Economy (cty/hwy)	18/26	Poor	20/28	Average	21/26	Poor
Driving Range (miles)	407	Average	444	Long	434.75	Long
Bumpers	Strong		Strong		Strong	
Parking Index	Average		Average		Easy	
Head/Leg Room (in.)	40.5/43.9	Vry. Roomy	40.5/43.9	Vry. Roomy	40.1/43.9	Vry. Roomy
Interior Space (cu. ft.)	102	Roomy	102	Roomy	99.6	Average
Cargo Space (cu. ft.)	15	Small	14.9	Small	14.1	Small
Tow Rating (lbs.)	1000	Vry. Low	1000	Vry. Low	1000	Vry. Low

*To be tested in 2001.

The Q45 continues on unchanged in anticipation of the all-new version to be announced later in 2001. Plushness and comfort are what you would expect from the top of the luxury line, and the ride is very smooth. Like other Infinitis the Q45 offers a pop-up navigational system, but you'll lose the signature analog dash clock. The power driver's seat has a two-person memory system, and temperature control is automatic. The Q45 is prewired for an optional 6 CD changer and cell phone, and the sound system's volume turns down when directions are spoken by the navigational system.

2001 Infiniti Q45

General Information

New for 2001: No major changes	**Year of Production:** 5
Twins:	**Seating:** 5
Where Made: Japan	**Theft Rating:** Very High

Prices 2001

Model	Retail	Markup
Base Luxury Sedan	$48,900	10%
T Luxury Performance Sdn.	$50,600	10%

Competition 2001

Model	POOR			GOOD	pg.
Infiniti Q45				■	274
Ford Cr. Victoria			■		216
Buick Century		■			142
Audi A8				■	132

'00 and '99 Models

The 1998 version (the base for the 1999 and 2000 models) has great safety features including dual airbags, 4-wheel ABS, pretensioners, and side airbags. The Q45 features a powerful 4.1-liter V8 which produces over 260 horsepower.

Price Ranges 2000–1999

Base Luxury Sedan	$36,200-48,900
T Luxury Performance Sedan	$36,800-50,600

2000 Infiniti Q45

1999 Infiniti Q45

	2001	2000	1999

RATINGS

	POOR → GOOD (2001)	POOR → GOOD (2000)	POOR → GOOD (1999)
Comparative Rating			
Frontal Crash Tests			
Safety Features	8	8	8
Preventive Maintenance	6	5	6
Repair Costs	1	1	1
Warranty	9	9	10
Fuel Economy	3	3	3
Rollover (based on SSF; see pg. 30)	7	7	7
Complaints	9	9	9
Insurance Costs	10	10	10

SAFETY

	2001	2000	1999
Frontal Crash Tests	No Govt Results	No Govt Results	No Govt Results
Side Crash Tests	No Govt Results	No Govt Results	No Govt Results
Airbags	Dual/Side (nextgen)	Dual/Side (nextgen)	Dual/Side (nextgen)
Anti-Lock Brakes	4-Wheel	4-Wheel	4-Wheel
Day Running Lamps	None	None	None
Built-In Child Seats	None	None	None
Pretensioners	Standard	Standard	Standard

SPECIFICATIONS

	2001		2000		1999	
Fuel Economy (cty/hwy)	18/23	Poor	18/23	Poor	17/24	Poor
Driving Range (miles)	438.7	Long	438.7	Long	438.7	Long
Bumpers	Strong		Strong		Strong	
Parking Index	Average		Average		Average	
Head/Leg Room (in.)	37.6/43.6	Average	37.6/43.6	Average	37.6/43.6	Average
Interior Space (cu. ft.)	97.4	Average	97.4	Average	97.4	Average
Cargo Space (cu. ft.)	12.6	Vry. Small	12.6	Vry. Small	12.6	Vry. Small
Tow Rating (lbs.)	1000	Vry. Low	1000	Vry. Low	1000	Vry. Low

Infiniti QX4   Mid-Size Sport Utility

With no changes for 2001, Infiniti continues to sell its parent company's Nissan Pathfinder as an upscale luxury vehicle, the QX4. The QX4, like the Pathfinder, comes standard with dual de-powered airbags and 4-wheel ABS. A 3.3-liter V6 is your only engine choice on the QX4, though it will do a decent job at moving this mid-size sport utility. The luxury makes the QX4 a very comfortable SUV, but at a significant price increase over the Pathfinder.

2001 Infiniti QX4

General Information

New for 2001: No major changes		**Year of Production:**	5
Twins: Nissan Pathfinder		**Seating:**	5
Where Made: Japan		**Theft Rating:**	Very High

Prices 2001

Model	Retail	Markup
2WD	$34,200	8%
4WD	$35,600	12%

Competition 2001

Model	POOR					GOOD	pg.
Infiniti QX4						■	276
Ford Explorer				■			224
Merc-Bz M-Class		■					340
Olds Bravada	■						374

'00 and '99 Models

Handling on the QX4 is quite good, better than most other sport utilities but still below the mark set by the better cars. Cargo space is only average, and you will find that the room inside is adequate for five. Ride should be good on smooth roads, and the interior noise level is acceptable.

Price Ranges 2000–1999

2WD	$27,500-35,500
4WD	$28,800-35,600

2000 Infiniti QX4

1999 Infiniti QX4

Infiniti QX4 — Mid-Size Sport Utility

	2001	2000	1999

RATINGS

	2001 (Poor–Good)	2000 (Poor–Good)	1999 (Poor–Good)
Comparative Rating	8	7	7
Frontal Crash Tests	9	9	9
Safety Features	8	8	6
Preventive Maintenance	6	5	6
Repair Costs	2	2	2
Warranty	9	9	10
Fuel Economy	2	2	2
Rollover (based on SSF; see pg. 30)	3	3	3
Complaints	9	10	10
Insurance Costs	10	5	5

SAFETY

	2001	2000	1999
Frontal Crash Tests	Very Good	Very Good	Very Good
Side Crash Tests	Very Good	Very Good	Very Good
Airbags	Dual/Side (nextgen)	Dual/Side (nextgen)	Dual (nextgen)
Anti-Lock Brakes	4-Wheel	4-Wheel	4-Wheel
Day Running Lamps	None	None	None
Built-In Child Seats	None	None	None
Pretensioners	Standard	Standard	Standard

SPECIFICATIONS

	2001		2000		1999	
Fuel Economy (cty/hwy)	15/19	Vry. Poor	15/18	Vry. Poor	15/19	Vry. Poor
Driving Range (miles)	358.7	Vry. Short	348.15	Vry. Short	358.7	Vry. Short
Bumpers	Strong		Strong		Strong	
Parking Index	Average		Average		Average	
Head/Leg Room (in.)	39.5/41.7	Average	39.5/41.7	Average	39.5/41.7	Average
Interior Space (cu. ft.)	92.9	Cramped	92.9	Cramped	92.9	Cramped
Cargo Space (cu. ft.)	38	Large	38	Large	38	Large
Tow Rating (lbs.)	5000	Average	5000	Average	5000	Average

Isuzu Rodeo Mid-Size Sport Utility

The Rodeo and its twin, the Honda Passport, carryover into 2001 with few changes. Dual airbags and height adjustable seat belts are standard. This year 4-wheel ABS is standard on all models. The base engine is a 2.2-liter 130 hp engine. The optional 3.2-liter V6 will give you 205 hp.

2001 Isuzu Rodeo

General Information

New for 2001: No major changes	**Year of Production:** 4
Twins: Honda Passport	**Seating:** 5
Where Made: U.S.	**Theft Rating:** Average

Prices 2001

Model	Retail	Markup
S 2WD	$17,990	12%
Sport S Hardtop V6 4WD	$20,360	16%
LS 4WD	$26,690	16%

Competition 2001

Model	POOR				GOOD	pg.
Isuzu Rodeo		■				**278**
Chev. Blazer		■				162
Ford Explorer				■		224
Jeep Cherokee		■				284

'00 and '99 Models

Following a major update in 1998, the Rodeo has changed little in 1999 and 2000. The engines were reworked and upgraded, and the suspension was improved. As for the exterior, Isuzu tried to maintain a truck-like quality for the Rodeo.

Price Ranges 2000–1999

S 2WD	$14,100-18,000
Sport S Hardtop V6	$15,600-20,900
LS 4WD	$19,600-$26,100

2000 Isuzu Rodeo

1999 Isuzu Rodeo

	2001	2000	1999
RATINGS (POOR → GOOD)			
Comparative Rating	3	3	2
Frontal Crash Tests	6	6	5
Safety Features	5	5	5
Preventive Maintenance	5	4	5
Repair Costs	7	10	5
Warranty	8	7	7
Fuel Economy	2	2	2
Rollover (based on SSF; see pg. 30)	4	4	5
Complaints	1	1	1
Insurance Costs	5	5	5

SAFETY

	2001	2000	1999
Frontal Crash Tests	Average	Average	Average
Side Crash Tests	Very Good	Very Good	Very Good
Airbags	Dual	Dual	Dual
Anti-Lock Brakes	4-Wheel	4-Wheel	4-Wheel
Day Running Lamps	None	None	None
Built-In Child Seats	None	None	None
Pretensioners	None	None	None

SPECIFICATIONS

	2001		2000		1999	
Fuel Economy (cty/hwy)	17/20	Vry. Poor	16/20	Vry. Poor	16/20	Vry. Poor
Driving Range (miles)	390.35	Short	379.8	Short	379.8	Short
Bumpers						
Parking Index	Average		Average		Average	
Head/Leg Room (in.)	38.9/42.1	Average	38.9/42.1	Average	38.9/42.1	Average
Interior Space (cu. ft.)						
Cargo Space (cu. ft.)	81.1	Large	81.1	Large	81.1	Large
Tow Rating (lbs.)	4500	Average	4500	Average	4500	Average

Isuzu Trooper

The Trooper enters 2001 with no changes since 1998's makeover. Standard features include dual airbags, 4-wheel ABS, and an anti-theft system. The standard 3.5-liter V6 comes in twin-cam form. The Trooper is available in an S model, with the option of a "Performance-" or "Luxury-Package". The interior remains roomy, and the cargo space is nicely designed.

2001 Isuzu Trooper

General Information

New for 2001: No major changes		**Year of Production:**	10
Twins:		**Seating:**	5
Where Made: Japan		**Theft Rating:**	Very High

Prices 2001

Model	Retail	Markup
S 5-spd. man. 4WD	$27,620	17%
LS 4-spd. auto. 2WD	$28,765	18%
S 4-spd. auto. 4WD	$29,170	17%
Limited 4-spd. auto. 4WD	$34,813	7%

Competition 2001

Model	POOR						GOOD	pg.
Isuzu Trooper								**280**
Ford Explorer				■				224
GMC Jimmy		■						240
Nissan Xterra				■				368

'00 and '99 Models

Consumers Union has found the Trooper, and its twin the Acura SLX, to be highly susceptible to turning over on sharp turns or corners, a phenomenon that is a major concern with sport utilities. No crash test scores are available.

Price Ranges 2000–1999

S 5-speed man. 4WD	$19,200-26,800
LS 4-speed auto. 2WD	$28,000-29,000
S 4-speed auto. 4WD	$19,800-26,900
Limited 4-sp. auto. 4WD	$34,000-35,000

2000 Isuzu Trooper

1999 Isuzu Trooper

	2001	2000	1999

RATINGS

	POOR → GOOD	POOR → GOOD	POOR → GOOD
Comparative Rating			
Frontal Crash Tests			
Safety Features	5	5	5
Preventive Maintenance	5	4	5
Repair Costs	3	2	2
Warranty	8	7	7
Fuel Economy	2	2	2
Rollover (based on SSF; see pg. 30)	1	1	1
Complaints	8	8	8
Insurance Costs	10	10	10

SAFETY

	2001	2000	1999
Frontal Crash Tests	No Govt Results	No Govt Results	No Govt Results
Side Crash Tests	No Govt Results	No Govt Results	No Govt Results
Airbags	Dual	Dual	Dual
Anti-Lock Brakes	4-Wheel	4-Wheel	4-Wheel
Day Running Lamps	None	None	None
Built-In Child Seats	None	None	None
Pretensioners	None	None	None

SPECIFICATIONS

	2001		2000		1999	
Fuel Economy (cty/hwy)	15/19	Vry. Poor	15/19	Vry. Poor	16/19	Vry. Poor
Driving Range (miles)	382.5	Short	382.5	Short	393.75	Short
Bumpers						
Parking Index	Hard		Hard		Hard	
Head/Leg Room (in.)	39.8/40.8	Cramped	39.8/40.8	Cramped	39.8/40.8	Cramped
Interior Space (cu. ft.)						
Cargo Space (cu. ft.)	90.2	Vry. Large	90.2	Vry. Large	90.2	Vry. Large
Tow Rating (lbs.)	5000	Average	5000	Average	5000	Average

The Isuzu VehiCROSS, unchanged since its introduction in 1999, is powered by a 3.5-liter V6 with 215 horsepower, but fuel economy isn't very good. For off-roading, the VehiCROSS' 4WD traction system helps grip the road and prevent slippage by instantly determining any slippage. Isuzu's warranty has improved over the years as well. While the VehiCROSS is a different looking SUV, from the inside, the dash and interior look like any passenger car.

2001 Isuzu VehiCROSS

General Information

New for 2001: No major changes		**Year of Production:**	3
Twins:		**Seating:**	5
Where Made: Japan		**Theft Rating:**	

Prices 2001

Model	Retail	Markup
2dr./4WD	$30,350	17%

Competition 2001

Model	POOR				GOOD	pg.
Isu. VehiCROSS						282
Ford Explorer			■			224
GMC Jimmy	■					240
Nissan Xterra			■			368

'00 and '99 Models

Isuzu introduced the VehiCROSS hoping to attract younger buyers with flashier design and styling and a special off-road suspension system. Watch out—repair costs will be on the high side. Four-wheel ABS should improve control in sudden stopping.

Price Ranges 2000–1999

2dr./4WD	$25,600-30,300

2000 Isuzu VehiCROSS

1999 Isuzu VehiCROSS

Isuzu VehiCROSS — Mid-Size Sport Utility

	2001	2000	1999

RATINGS

(Scale: POOR ... GOOD, 1–10)

Rating	2001	2000	1999
Comparative Rating			
Frontal Crash Tests			
Safety Features	5	5	5
Preventive Maintenance	5		
Repair Costs	1		
Warranty	8	7	7
Fuel Economy	2	2	2
Rollover (based on SSF; see pg. 30)	4	4	4
Complaints	5		
Insurance Costs	5	5	5

SAFETY

	2001	2000	1999
Frontal Crash Tests	No Govt Results	No Govt Results	No Govt Results
Side Crash Tests	No Govt Results	No Govt Results	No Govt Results
Airbags	Dual	Dual	Dual
Anti-Lock Brakes	4-Wheel	4-Wheel	4-Wheel
Day Running Lamps	None	None	None
Built-In Child Seats	None	None	None
Pretensioners	None	None	None

SPECIFICATIONS

	2001		2000		1999	
Fuel Economy (cty/hwy)	15/19	Vry. Poor	15/19	Vry. Poor	15/19	Vry. Poor
Driving Range (miles)	382.5	Short	382.5	Short	382.5	Short
Bumpers						
Parking Index	Vry. Easy		Vry. Easy		Vry. Easy	
Head/Leg Room (in.)	38.2/43.1	Average	38.2/43.1	Average	38.2/43.1	Average
Interior Space (cu. ft.)						
Cargo Space (cu. ft.)	50.4	Large	50.4	Large	50.4	Large
Tow Rating (lbs.)						

Jeep Cherokee

Mid-Size Sport Utility

The main difference in this year's Cherokee is the option of buying the 4L inline 6-cylinder engine that is offered with the Grand Cherokee. The Sand color available in 2000 will be replaced with Steel Blue. The dual airbags are standard but to get ABS, you must pay extra and buy the model with a 4.0-liter engine. The standard engine, a 2.5-liter 4-cylinder, should provide good power. A child seat tether anchor has also been added for 2001.

2001 Jeep Cherokee

General Information

New for 2001: No major changes	**Year of Production:** 18
Twins:	**Seating:** 5
Where Made: U.S.	**Theft Rating:** Very High

Prices 2001

Model	Retail	Markup
Sport 2WD 2dr.	$19,370	11%
Limited 2WD 4dr.	$21,870	10%
Sport 4WD 4dr.	$21,915	10%
Limited 4WD 4-dr.	$23,385	10%

Competition 2001

Model	POOR						GOOD		pg.
Jeep Cherokee		■							**284**
Ford Explorer				■					224
GMC Jimmy	■								240
Infiniti QX4						■			276

'00 and '99 Models

A 4-liter V6 with automatic overdrive is optional on the SE and standard on the Sport and Country models. The handling is among the best of utility vehicles. The front seat is roomy and comfortable, but the rear seat is cramped for adults.

Price Ranges 2000–1999

SE 2WD 2dr.	$12,400-17,400
Sport 2WD 2dr.	$13,800-18,900
Limited 2WD 4dr.	$17-23,100
Sport 4WD 4dr.	$17,200-21,400

2000 Jeep Cherokee

1999 Jeep Cherokee

Jeep Cherokee — Mid-Size Sport Utility

	2001	2000	1999

RATINGS

	2001 (POOR→GOOD)	2000 (POOR→GOOD)	1999 (POOR→GOOD)
Comparative Rating	3	3	2
Frontal Crash Tests	4	4	4
Safety Features	6	6	6
Preventive Maintenance	6	6	6
Repair Costs	9	10	10
Warranty	1	1	2
Fuel Economy	3	2	2
Rollover (based on SSF; see pg. 30)	3	2	2
Complaints	6	6	4
Insurance Costs	5	5	5

SAFETY

	2001	2000	1999
Frontal Crash Tests	Poor	Poor	Poor
Side Crash Tests	Very Good	Very Good	Very Good
Airbags	Dual/Side (nextgen)	Dual/Side (nextgen)	Dual/Side (nextgen)
Anti-Lock Brakes	4-Wheel (optional)	4-Wheel (optional)	4-Wheel (optional)
Day Running Lamps	None	None	None
Built-In Child Seats	None	None	None
Pretensioners	None	None	None

SPECIFICATIONS

	2001		2000		1999	
Fuel Economy (cty/hwy)	17/22	Poor	18/20	Poor	18/20	Poor
Driving Range (miles)	390	Short	380	Short	380	Short
Bumpers						
Parking Index	Easy		Easy		Easy	
Head/Leg Room (in.)	37.7/41.4	Vry. Cramp.	37.7/41.4	Vry. Cramp.	37.7/41.4	Vry. Cramp.
Interior Space (cu. ft.)						
Cargo Space (cu. ft.)	34	Average	34	Average	34	Average
Tow Rating (lbs.)	2000	Vry. Low	2000	Vry. Low	2000	Vry. Low

The popular Grand Cherokee remains unchanged from 2001. It comes with a 4-liter V6 or a more powerful 5.2-liter V8. You can choose two-wheel drive, or one of three four-wheel drive systems. Handling is good for a sport utility vehicle, and improves with the optional Up Country suspension. Front seats are comfortable, but the rear seat isn't as pleasant or spacious. Cargo room is adequate.

2001 Jeep Grand Cherokee

General Information

New for 2001: No major changes	**Year of Production:** 3
Twins:	**Seating:** 5
Where Made: U.S.	**Theft Rating:** High

Prices 2001

Model	Retail	Markup
Laredo 2WD	$27,300	11%
Laredo 4WD	$29,270	11%
Limited 2WD	$32,665	11%
Limited 4WD	$35,095	11%

Competition 2001

Model	POOR				GOOD	pg.
Jeep Gr. Cher.	■					**286**
Ford Explorer			■			224
Infiniti QX4				■		276
Merc-Bz M-Class	■					340

'00 and '99 Models

Redesigned in 1999, the Grand Cherokee had a slightly different look than past years' models. It was made over inside and out. Jeep offered a new automatic transmission, a new 4-wheel drive Quadra-Drive system, and an all-new suspension, steering, and braking system. Dual airbags are standard along with 4-wheel ABS.

Price Ranges 2000–1999

Laredo 2WD	$24,800-23,800
Laredo 4WD	$23,300-26,200
Limited 2WD	$25,000-28,400
Limited 4WD	$27,200-30,800

2000 Jeep Grand Cherokee

1999 Jeep Grand Cherokee

Jeep Grand Cherokee — Mid-Size Sport Utility

	2001	2000	1999

RATINGS

	2001 (POOR–GOOD)	2000 (POOR–GOOD)	1999 (POOR–GOOD)
Comparative Rating	2	1	2
Frontal Crash Tests	4	4	5
Safety Features	5	6	5
Preventive Maintenance	6	6	6
Repair Costs	9	10	10
Warranty	1	1	2
Fuel Economy	2	2	2
Rollover (based on SSF; see pg. 30)	3	3	3
Complaints	1	1	2
Insurance Costs	10	5	5

SAFETY

	2001	2000	1999
Frontal Crash Tests	Poor	Poor	Average
Side Crash Tests	Very Good	Very Good	Very Good
Airbags	Dual (nextgen)	Dual (nextgen)	Dual
Anti-Lock Brakes	4-Wheel	4-Wheel	4-Wheel
Day Running Lamps	None	None	None
Built-In Child Seats	None	None	None
Pretensioners	None	None	None

SPECIFICATIONS

	2001		2000		1999	
Fuel Economy (cty/hwy)	16/20	Vry. Poor	16/21	Vry. Poor	16/21	Vry. Poor
Driving Range (miles)	369	Vry. Short	379.25	Short	379.25	Short
Bumpers					Average	
Parking Index	Average		Average			
Head/Leg Room (in.)	39.7/41.4	Average	39.7/41.4	Average	39.7/41.4	Average
Interior Space (cu. ft.)						
Cargo Space (cu. ft.)	39	Large	39	Large	39	Large
Tow Rating (lbs.)	2000	Vry. Low	2000	Vry. Low	2000	Vry. Low

CAR BOOK 2001

287

There are no major changes to this vehicle, based on the original Jeep but introduced in 1987. This 4-wheel drive off-road vehicle has been a good seller for Chrysler. Dual de-powered airbags are standard, and 4-wheel ABS is an option. The standard 2.5-liter 4-cylinder engine will provide adequate power; if you are looking for something with more zing, choose the 4.0-liter 6-cylinder. This is a minimalist vehicle, which is what makes it popular. Nevertheless, with an adequate A/C and heating system, you don't have to worry about the elements.

2001 Jeep Wrangler

General Information

New for 2001: No major changes	**Year of Production:** 5
Twins:	**Seating:** 2-4
Where Made: U.S.	**Theft Rating:** Very High

Prices 2001

Model	Retail	Markup
SE	$14,890	4%
Sport	$19,155	11%
Sahara	$22,435	11%

Competition 2001

Model	POOR				GOOD	pg.
Jeep Wrangler	■					**288**
Honda CR-V				■		246

'00 and '99 Models

Ride and comfort have both been improved over previous years; however, don't expect the Wrangler to drive as smoothly as a car. Road noise is less noticeable in the hardtop than the softtop. The control panel has been redone, making it more convenient.

Price Ranges 2000–1999

SE	$14,300-15,500
Sport	$18,400-18,700
Sahara	$20,300-20,600

2000 Jeep Wrangler

1999 Jeep Wrangler

Jeep Wrangler — Small Sport Utility

	2001	2000	1999

RATINGS

	POOR → GOOD (2001)	POOR → GOOD (2000)	POOR → GOOD (1999)
Comparative Rating		2	4
Frontal Crash Tests		7	7
Safety Features	5	5	5
Preventive Maintenance	6	6	6
Repair Costs	9	9	10
Warranty	1	1	2
Fuel Economy	3	2	2
Rollover (based on SSF; see pg. 30)	2	2	2
Complaints	4	4	9
Insurance Costs	1	1	1

SAFETY

	2001	2000	1999
Frontal Crash Tests	No Govt Results	Good	Good
Side Crash Tests	No Govt Results	No Govt Results	No Govt Results
Airbags	Dual (nextgen)	Dual (nextgen)	Dual (nextgen)
Anti-Lock Brakes	4-Wheel (optional)	4-Wheel (optional)	4-Wheel (optional)
Day Running Lamps	None	None	None
Built-In Child Seats	None	None	None
Pretensioners	None	None	None

SPECIFICATIONS

	2001		2000		1999	
Fuel Economy (cty/hwy)	19/20	Poor	18/20	Poor	18/20	Poor
Driving Range (miles)	370.5	Short	361	Vry. Short	361	Vry. Short
Bumpers						
Parking Index	Vry. Easy		Vry. Easy		Vry. Easy	
Head/Leg Room (in.)	40.9/41.1	Roomy	40.9/41.1	Roomy	40.9/41.1	Roomy
Interior Space (cu. ft.)						
Cargo Space (cu. ft.)	37.7	Average	37.7	Average	37.7	Average
Tow Rating (lbs.)	2000	Vry. Low	2000	Vry. Low	2000	Vry. Low

The all-new Kia Rio is the least expensive sedan in the U.S. In spite of the low price you get a very good warranty. Standard features are limited and basically include a rear window defroster and tinted glass. If you want power steering, tilt steering wheel, A/C, or an automatic transmission, you have to upgrade. The one engine choice is a 1.5L 4-cylinder model. Other options include ABS, full wheel covers, and special body trim. Interior space is impressive for such a small vehicle. Basic.

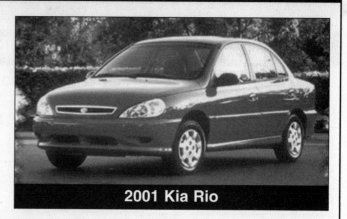
2001 Kia Rio

General Information

New for 2001: All-new	**Year of Production:**	1
Twins:	**Seating:**	4
Where Made: Korea	**Theft Rating:**	

Prices 2001

Model	Retail	Markup
Manual	$8,595	9%
Automatic	$9,470	9%

Competition 2001

Model	POOR						GOOD	pg.
Kia Rio								**290**
Ford Focus						■		228
Dodge Neon				■				214
VW Beetle						■		446

'00 and '99 Models

Price Ranges 2000–1999

MODEL WAS NOT PRODUCED THIS YEAR

2000 Acura CL

MODEL WAS NOT PRODUCED THIS YEAR

1999 Model

	2001	2000	1999

RATINGS

	POOR — GOOD	POOR — GOOD	POOR — GOOD
Comparative Rating			
Frontal Crash Tests			
Safety Features	4		
Preventive Maintenance	7		
Repair Costs	8		
Warranty	10		
Fuel Economy	6		
Rollover (based on SSF; see pg. 30)			
Complaints	5		
Insurance Costs	5		

SAFETY

	2001		
Frontal Crash Tests	To Be Tested		
Side Crash Tests	No Govt Results		
Airbags	Dual		
Anti-Lock Brakes	4-Wheel (optional)		
Day Running Lamps	None		
Built-In Child Seats	None		
Pretensioners	None		

SPECIFICATIONS

	2001		
Fuel Economy (cty/hwy)	22/30	Average	
Driving Range (miles)	309.4	Vry. Short	
Bumpers	Weak		
Parking Index			
Head/Leg Room (in.)	39.4/42.8	Roomy	
Interior Space (cu. ft.)	88	Cramped	
Cargo Space (cu. ft.)	13	Vry. Small	
Tow Rating (lbs.)			

The Sephia, unchanged for 2001, still comes in several trim levels—RS, LS, and GS but is available only as a sedan, unlike its competitors. The styling is similar to the old Mazda 323, which is no surprise as Mazda is a part-owner of Kia. The Sephia's low price tag and good crash test results have yet to make it a major player in the small sedan market.

2001 Kia Sephia

General Information

New for 2001: No major changes	**Year of Production:** 2
Twins:	**Seating:** 4
Where Made: Korea	**Theft Rating:** Low

Prices 2001

Model	Retail	Markup
Manual	$10,595	10%
Automatic	$11,570	11%
LS manual	$12,195	11%
LS automatic	$13,170	11%

Competition 2001

Model	POOR				GOOD	pg.
Kia Sephia					■	**292**
Mazda Protégé		■				334
Subaru Impreza				■		404
Saturn SL					■	400

'00 and '99 Models

The '99 and '00 models ride on the changes from 1998s major update to the Sephia. Slightly longer, and roomier inside, the Sephia also got a new 1.8-liter 4-cylinder engine, with 125 hp. Dual airbags are standard and ABS is optional.

Price Ranges 2000–1999

Base man.	$7,800-8,700
Base auto.	$8,200-9,200
LS man.	$8,200-9,400
LS auto.	$8,600-9,900

2000 Kia Sephia

1999 Kia Sephia

Kia Sephia — Subcompact

	2001	2000	1999

RATINGS

	2001 (POOR→GOOD)	2000 (POOR→GOOD)	1999 (POOR→GOOD)
Comparative Rating	8	3	2
Frontal Crash Tests*	7	7	7
Safety Features	4	4	4
Preventive Maintenance	7	6	6
Repair Costs	7	6	5
Warranty	10	6	5
Fuel Economy	6	5	5
Rollover (based on SSF, see pg. 25)	7	7	7
Complaints	5		1
Insurance Costs	1	1	1

SAFETY

	2001	2000	1999
Frontal Crash Tests	Good	Good	Good
Side Crash Tests	No Govt Results	No Govt Results	No Govt Results
Airbags	Dual	Dual	Dual
Anti-Lock Brakes	4-Wheel (optional)	4-Wheel (optional)	4-Wheel (optional)
Day Running Lamps	None	None	None
Built-In Child Seats	None	None	None
Pretensioners	None	None	None

SPECIFICATIONS

	2001		2000		1999	
Fuel Economy (cty/hwy)	24/29	Average	23/29	Average	24/31	Average
Driving Range (miles)	349.8	Vry. Short	343.2	Vry. Short	349.25	Vry. Short
Bumpers	Weak		Weak		Strong	
Parking Index	Vry. Easy		Vry. Easy		Vry. Easy	
Head/Leg Room (in.)	39.6/43.3	Roomy	39.6/43.3	Roomy	38.2/42.9	Average
Interior Space (cu. ft.)	93	Cramped	94.1	Cramped	93	Cramped
Cargo Space (cu. ft.)	10	Vry. Small	10.4	Vry. Small	11	Vry. Small
Tow Rating (lbs.)						

*To be tested in 2001.

Introduced in late 2000, the Spectra enters 2001 unchanged. This four-door, five-passenger car comes in two trim levels, the GS and GSX. The rear seats split, offering a variety of cargo configurations. The only engine is a 1.8L 4-cylinder 125 hp model. Standard are remote control mirrors, tachometer, and an AM/FM/cassette stereo. Better front brakes, dual vanity mirrors, and a gas-cap tether were added for 2001.

2001 Kia Spectra

General Information

New for 2001: No major changes	**Year of Production:**
Twins:	**Seating:**
Where Made: Korea	**Theft Rating:**

Prices 2001

Model	Retail	Markup
GS manual	$10,995	10%
GS automatic	$11,970	10%
GSX manual	$13,195	10%
GSX automatic	$14,170	10%

Competition 2001

Model	POOR					GOOD		pg.
Kia Spectra						▓		**294**
Ford Focus							▓	228
Mazda Protégé			▓					334
Ddge/Plym. Neon				▓				214

'00 and '99 Models

The manual transmission is standard, and a 4-speed automatic is an option. Introduced in 2000, this hatchback is designed to compete with the Ford Focus and Dodge Neon. Designed for three in the back, if they're all adults they won't be too comfortable. A/C, rear wiper/washer, and cruise control are options.

Price Ranges 2000–1999

GS man.	$10,200-10,300
GS auto.	$10,700-10,800
GSX man.	$12,400-12,500
GSX auto.	$12,900-13,000

PHOTO NOT AVAILABLE

2000 Model

MODEL NOT PRODUCED THIS YEAR

1999 Model

Kia Spectra — Subcompact

	2001	2000	1999

RATINGS

	2001 (POOR–GOOD)	2000 (POOR–GOOD)	1999 (POOR–GOOD)
Comparative Rating			
Frontal Crash Tests			
Safety Features	4	4	
Preventive Maintenance			
Repair Costs			
Warranty	10	10	
Fuel Economy	6	6	
Rollover (based on SSF; see pg. 30)			
Complaints	5	5	
Insurance Costs	5	5	

SAFETY

	2001	2000	1999
Frontal Crash Tests	No Govt Results	No Govt Results	
Side Crash Tests	No Govt Results	No Govt Results	
Airbags	Dual	Dual	
Anti-Lock Brakes	4-Wheel (optional)	4-Wheel (optional)	
Day Running Lamps	None	None	
Built-In Child Seats	None	None	
Pretensioners	None	None	

SPECIFICATIONS

	2001		2000		1999
Fuel Economy (cty/hwy)	24/29	Average	24/29	Average	
Driving Range (miles)	349.8	Vry. Short	349.8	Vry. Short	
Bumpers	Weak		Weak		
Parking Index					
Head/Leg Room (in.)	39.6/43.1	Roomy	39.6/43.1	Roomy	
Interior Space (cu. ft.)	93	Cramped	93	Cramped	
Cargo Space (cu. ft.)	10	Vry. Small	10	Vry. Small	
Tow Rating (lbs.)					

Kia Sportage   Mid-Size Sport Utility

Unchanged for 2001, the 2-liter 4-cylinder engine is the Sportage's only choice. Fuel economy is just average for this segment of vehicles. A more powerful engine would be nice; unfortunately, none is offered. The model lineup is fairly simple, with only a base model and an optional EX package that comes with some luxury amenities. Four-wheel drive is optional. This is a small sport utility vehicle, so don't expect room for more than 4 people or large amounts of luggage.

2001 Kia Sportage

General Information

New for 2001: No major changes		**Year of Production:**	7
Twins:		**Seating:**	5
Where Made: Korea		**Theft Rating:**	Very High

Prices 2001

Model	Retail	Markup
2WD Base man.	$15,295	10%
2WD Base auto.	$16,295	10%
4WD Base man.	$16,795	10%
4WD Base auto.	$17,795	11%

Competition 2001

Model	POOR				GOOD		pg.
Kia Sportage							**296**
Chev. Blazer		■					162
Ford Explorer			■				224
Isuzu Rodeo		■					278

'00 and '99 Models

New for the Kia Sportage in '99 was a two-door softtop model. The five-door version is likely the most available in the used market. Dual airbags are standard; 4-wheel ABS is optional.

Price Ranges 2000–1999

2WD man.	$12,300-14,300
2WD auto.	$12,800-14,800
4WD man.	$14,200-15,800
4WD auto.	$14,700-16,300

2000 Kia Sportage

1999 Kia Sportage

Kia Sportage — Mid-Size Sport Utility

	2001	2000	1999

RATINGS

	2001 (Poor→Good)	2000 (Poor→Good)	1999 (Poor→Good)
Comparative Rating	—	—	1
Frontal Crash Tests	—	—	4
Safety Features	4	4	4
Preventive Maintenance	7	6	6
Repair Costs	3	3	3
Warranty	10	6	5
Fuel Economy	4	3	3
Rollover (based on SSF; see pg. 30)	4	4	4
Complaints	1	1	1
Insurance Costs	1	5	5

SAFETY

	2001	2000	1999
Frontal Crash Tests	No Govt Results	No Govt Results	Poor
Side Crash Tests	No Govt Results	No Govt Results	No Govt Results
Airbags	Dual	Dual	Dual
Anti-Lock Brakes	4-Wheel (optional)	4-Wheel (optional)	4-Wheel (optional)
Day Running Lamps	None	None	None
Built-In Child Seats	None	None	None
Pretensioners	None	None	None

SPECIFICATIONS

	2001		2000		1999	
Fuel Economy (cty/hwy)	20/22	Poor	19/22	Poor	19/23	Poor
Driving Range (miles)	331.8	Vry. Short	323.9	Vry. Short	331.8	Vry. Short
Bumpers	Weak		Weak			
Parking Index	Vry. Easy		Vry. Easy		Vry. Easy	
Head/Leg Room (in.)	39.6/44.5	Vry. Roomy	39.6/44.5	Vry. Roomy	39.6/44.5	Vry. Roomy
Interior Space (cu. ft.)	125.7	Vry. Roomy	125.7	Vry. Roomy	126	Vry. Roomy
Cargo Space (cu. ft.)	55.4	Large	55.4	Large	55	Large
Tow Rating (lbs.)	2000	Vry. Low	2000	Vry. Low	2000	Vry. Low

Land Rover Discovery Series II — Mid-Size Sport Utility

The Discovery Series II rolls into 2001 unchanged and with the same powerful, 3.9-liter V8. But, with the vehicle alone weighing over two tons, it may strain under heavy loads. Though it officially seats seven, the two seats in the rear are uncomfortable and only for children. Four-wheel drive is standard, as is just about everything else you could possibly want. The Land Rover Discovery makes you feel like you're on a safari when all you're doing is the car pool and grocery shopping.

2001 Land Rover Discovery

General Information

New for 2001: No major changes		**Year of Production:**	3
Twins:		**Seating:**	5
Where Made: United Kingdom		**Theft Rating:**	High

Prices 2001

Model	Retail	Markup
SD	$33,400	12%
LE	$34,400	12%
SE	$36,400	12%

Competition 2001

Model	POOR				GOOD	pg.
LR Disc. Series II						**298**
Ford Explorer			■			224
Merc-Bz M-Class		■				340
Toyota 4Runner				■		416

'00 and '99 Models

The Series II was introduced in '99. Like its close sibling the Range Rover, the Discovery is geared toward the upscale sport utility buyer. Although it's slightly smaller than the Range Rover, you should have no problem doing any suburban hauling in comfort.

Price Ranges 2000–1999

Base	$31,300-34,200

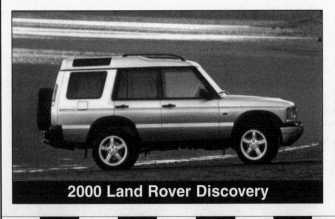

2000 Land Rover Discovery

1999 Land Rover Discovery

Land Rover Discovery Series II | Mid-Size Sport Utility

	2001	2000	1999

RATINGS

	POOR — GOOD	POOR — GOOD	POOR — GOOD
Comparative Rating			
Frontal Crash Tests			
Safety Features	7	7	6
Preventive Maintenance	1	1	1
Repair Costs	2	1	1
Warranty	6	7	7
Fuel Economy	1	1	1
Rollover (based on SSF; see pg. 30)	1	1	1
Complaints	5		2
Insurance Costs	5	5	5

SAFETY

	2001	2000	1999
Frontal Crash Tests	No Govt Results	No Govt Results	No Govt Results
Side Crash Tests	No Govt Results	No Govt Results	No Govt Results
Airbags	Dual (nextgen)	Dual (nextgen)	Dual (nextgen)
Anti-Lock Brakes	4-Wheel	4-Wheel	4-Wheel
Day Running Lamps	Optional	Optional	Optional
Built-In Child Seats	None	None	None
Pretensioners	Standard	Standard	None

SPECIFICATIONS

	2001		2000		1999	
Fuel Economy (cty/hwy)	13/17	Vry. Poor	14/17	Vry. Poor	14/17	Vry. Poor
Driving Range (miles)	351	Vry. Short	362.7	Vry. Short	362.7	Vry. Short
Bumpers						
Parking Index	Hard		Hard		Hard	
Head/Leg Room (in.)	37.4/38.5	Vry. Cramp.	37.4/38.5	Vry. Cramp.	37.4/38.5	Vry. Cramp.
Interior Space (cu. ft.)						
Cargo Space (cu. ft.)	69.8	Large	69.8	Large	69.8	Large
Tow Rating (lbs.)	5500	High	5500	High	5500	High

Land Rover Range Rover　　Large Sport Utility

Around since 1970, the Range Rover remains unchanged for 2001. Dual airbags, height adjustable seat belts for front and rear passengers, and 4-wheel ABS are standard. The naming changed slightly on these large sport utility vehicles in '99. You can now buy a 4.0SE or a 4.6HSE, with the numbers corresponding to their engine sizes. The 4.6HSE will allow you to tow almost four tons.

2001 Land Rover Range Rover

General Information

New for 2001: No major changes	**Year of Production:**	15
Twins:	**Seating:**	5
Where Made: United Kingdom	**Theft Rating:**	

Prices 2001

Model	Retail	Markup
SE	$62,000	13%
HSE	$68,000	13%

Competition 2001

Model	POOR			GOOD	pg.
LR Range Rover					**300**
Linc. Navigator				■	320
Ford Expedition			■		222

'00 and '99 Models

Four-wheel drive and an automatic transmission are standard. A Range Rover weighs roughly 4,500 pounds, so acceleration is fairly slow and fuel economy is dismal. Typical of this class of vehicles, handling is on the sluggish side, though the ride is comfortable.

Price Ranges 2000–1999

SE	$44,600-59,000
HSE	$51,300-67,300

2000 Land Rover Range Rover

1999 Land Rover Range Rover

Land Rover Range Rover — Large Sport Utility

	2001	2000	1999

RATINGS

	POOR — GOOD	POOR — GOOD	POOR — GOOD
Comparative Rating			
Frontal Crash Tests			
Safety Features	6	7	7
Preventive Maintenance	1	1	1
Repair Costs	1	1	1
Warranty	6	7	7
Fuel Economy	1	1	1
Rollover (based on SSF; see pg. 30)	3	3	3
Complaints	5	5	2
Insurance Costs	5	5	5

SAFETY

	2001	2000	1999
Frontal Crash Tests	No Govt Results	No Govt Results	No Govt Results
Side Crash Tests	No Govt Results	No Govt Results	No Govt Results
Airbags	Dual (nextgen)	Dual (nextgen)	Dual (nextgen)
Anti-Lock Brakes	4-Wheel	4-Wheel	4-Wheel
Day Running Lamps	Optional	Optional	Optional
Built-In Child Seats	None	None	None
Pretensioners	None	Standard	Standard

SPECIFICATIONS

	2001		2000		1999	
Fuel Economy (cty/hwy)	13/17	Vry. Poor	13/17	Vry. Poor	13/17	Vry. Poor
Driving Range (miles)	369	Vry. Short	369	Vry. Short	369	Vry. Short
Bumpers						
Parking Index	Hard		Hard		Hard	
Head/Leg Room (in.)	38.1/42.6	Cramped	38.1/42.6	Cramped	38.1/42.6	Cramped
Interior Space (cu. ft.)						
Cargo Space (cu. ft.)	58	Large	58	Large	58	Large
Tow Rating (lbs.)	6500	Vry. High	6500	Vry. High	6500	Vry. High

Lexus ES300 Large

The Lexus ES300 enters 2001 unchanged. Dual airbags and 4-wheel ABS are standard. Last year the ES300 added standard side airbags to its automatic crash protection features. The new standard engine for the ES300 is a 3.0-liter V6 which produces 210 horsepower, slightly more powerful than the previous engine. Fancy features include a remote control for windows, moon roof, and door locks in the key. Automatic temperature control and a sound system that adjusts to ambient noise are standard.

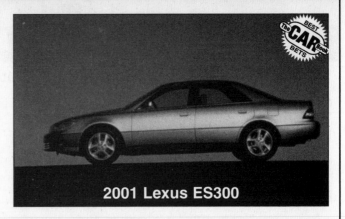

2001 Lexus ES300

General Information

New for 2001: No major changes	**Year of Production:** 5
Twins: Toyota Camry	**Seating:** 5
Where Made: Japan	**Theft Rating:** Very High

Prices 2001

Model	Retail	Markup
4-spd. auto FWD	$31,505	16%

Competition 2001

Model	POOR					GOOD	pg.
Lexus ES300						■	302
Chrys. Concorde				■			188
Audi A8						■	132
Ford Taurus						■	234

'00 and '99 Models

The ES300 is a solid, affordable luxury sedan, but if you can live without the nameplate, a fully loaded Camry will be just as good and costs less, too. In '99 a new drive train, electronic traction control, and skid control systems were added.

Price Ranges 2000–1999

4-sp. auto./FWD	$29,500-31,400

2000 Lexus ES300

1999 Lexus ES300

	2001	2000	1999

RATINGS

	POOR — GOOD	POOR — GOOD	POOR — GOOD
Comparative Rating	10	10	10
Frontal Crash Tests	9	9	9
Safety Features	8	9	9
Preventive Maintenance	6	5	6
Repair Costs	3	2	3
Warranty	8	8	8
Fuel Economy	4	4	4
Rollover (based on SSF; see pg. 30)	8	8	8
Complaints	10	10	10
Insurance Costs	10	10	10

SAFETY

	2001	2000	1999
Frontal Crash Tests	Very Good	Very Good	Very Good
Side Crash Tests	Very Good	Very Good	Very Good
Airbags	Dual/Side	Dual/Side (nextgen)	Dual/Side (nextgen)
Anti-Lock Brakes	4-Wheel	4-Wheel	4-Wheel
Day Running Lamps	Standard	Standard	Standard
Built-In Child Seats	None	None	None
Pretensioners	Standard	Standard	Standard

SPECIFICATIONS

	2001		2000		1999	
Fuel Economy (cty/hwy)	19/26	Poor	19/26	Poor	19/26	Poor
Driving Range (miles)	416.25	Average	416.25	Average	416.25	Average
Bumpers	Weak		Weak		Strong	
Parking Index	Average		Average		Average	
Head/Leg Room (in.)	38/43.5	Average	38/43.5	Average	38/43.5	Average
Interior Space (cu. ft.)	92	Cramped	92.1	Cramped	92.1	Cramped
Cargo Space (cu. ft.)	13	Vry. Small	13	Vry. Small	13	Vry. Small
Tow Rating (lbs.)			2000	Vry. Low	2000	Vry. Low

Lexus GS300/400　　　　　　　　　Large

Fully revised in 1999, the GS sedans zip into 2001 unchanged. Taking on the BMW 5 Series and Mercedes-Benz E-Class, the GS sedans have improved engines, a better suspension, and a more aggressive exterior design. The GS300 has a 3.0-liter 225 hp engine. Most sports car enthusiasts will want the bigger 4.0-liter V8 engine on the GS400. These are well-built, tight, thoughtfully appointed luxury cars that compete well against their European counterparts.

2001 Lexus GS300

General Information

New for 2001: No major changes		**Year of Production:**	4
Twins:		**Seating:**	5
Where Made: Japan		**Theft Rating:**	Very High

Prices 2001

Model	Retail	Markup
GS 300 Luxury Perf. Sedan	$38,555	15%
GS 430 Luxury Perf. Sedan	$47,355	16%

Competition 2001

Model	POOR			GOOD	pg.
Lexus GS300/400				■	304
Lincoln Town Car				■	322
Audi A8				■	132
Infiniti I30			■		272

'00 and '99 Models

An increased wheelbase allows for more interior room and a bigger trunk. On the GS sedans, 13 onboard computers are linked through a local area network that lets you customize electronic features like interior lights.

Price Ranges 2000–1999

GS300 5ECT-I RWD	$37,600-38,200
GS400 5ECT-I RWD	$43,300-46,000

2000 Lexus GS300

1999 Lexus GS300

	2001	2000	1999

RATINGS

	POOR — GOOD	POOR — GOOD	POOR — GOOD
Comparative Rating			
Frontal Crash Tests			
Safety Features	8	9	9
Preventive Maintenance	6	5	6
Repair Costs	2	2	3
Warranty	8	8	8
Fuel Economy	4	3	4
Rollover (based on SSF; see pg. 30)	7	7	7
Complaints	10	10	9
Insurance Costs	5	10	10

SAFETY

	2001	2000	1999
Frontal Crash Tests	No Govt Results	No Govt Results	No Govt Results
Side Crash Tests	No Govt Results	No Govt Results	No Govt Results
Airbags	Dual/Side (nextgen)	Dual/Side (nextgen)	Dual/Side (nextgen)
Anti-Lock Brakes	4-Wheel	4-Wheel	4-Wheel
Day Running Lamps	Standard	Standard	Standard
Built-In Child Seats	None	None	None
Pretensioners	Standard	Standard	Standard

SPECIFICATIONS

	2001		2000		1999	
Fuel Economy (cty/hwy)	18/24	Poor	19/25	Poor	20/25	Poor
Driving Range (miles)	415.8	Average	435.6	Long	445.5	Long
Bumpers			Weak		Strong	
Parking Index	Average		Average		Average	
Head/Leg Room (in.)	39/44.5	Vry. Roomy	39/44.5	Vry. Roomy	39/44.5	Vry. Roomy
Interior Space (cu. ft.)	100	Average	100	Average	100	Average
Cargo Space (cu. ft.)	15	Small	14.8	Small	14.8	Small
Tow Rating (lbs.)			2000	Vry. Low	2000	Vry. Low

This all-new vehicle is Lexus' challenge to European sport sedans however this year it will only be available as an automatic. One of the few rear wheel drive vehicles, this has many of the design features of the larger GS300. The console contains gauges designed to look like sport watches, and plenty of information. A six-disc CD changer is standard as are side airbags and an inside the trunk safety release handle. Heated mirrors and tilt steering wheel are also standard in this vehicle, designed to compete with the A4 and BMW 328i.

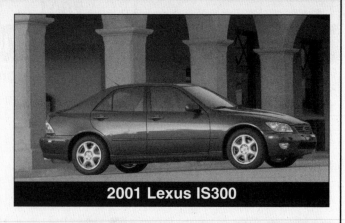

2001 Lexus IS300

General Information

New for 2001: All-new	**Year of Production:** 1
Twins:	**Seating:** 5
Where Made: Japan	**Theft Rating:**

Prices 2001

Model	Retail	Markup
Luxury Sport Sedan	$30,805	16%

Competition 2001

Model	POOR			GOOD	pg.
Lexus IS300					**306**
Lincoln Town Car				■	322
Chrys. Concorde			■		188
Audi A8				■	132

'00 and '99 Models

Price Ranges 2000–1999

MODEL WAS NOT PRODUCED THIS YEAR

2000 Model

MODEL WAS NOT PRODUCED THIS YEAR

1999 Model

	2001	2000	1999

RATINGS

	POOR — GOOD (2001)	POOR — GOOD (2000)	POOR — GOOD (1999)
Comparative Rating			
Frontal Crash Tests			
Safety Features	8		
Preventive Maintenance	6		
Repair Costs	4		
Warranty	8		
Fuel Economy	3		
Rollover (based on SSF; see pg. 30)	7		
Complaints	5		
Insurance Costs	5		

SAFETY

Frontal Crash Tests	To Be Tested		
Side Crash Tests	No Govt Results		
Airbags	Dual/Side		
Anti-Lock Brakes	4-Wheel		
Day Running Lamps	Standard		
Built-In Child Seats	None		
Pretensioners	Standard		

SPECIFICATIONS

Fuel Economy (cty/hwy)	18/23	Poor	
Driving Range (miles)	358.75	Vry. Short	
Bumpers	Strong		
Parking Index	Vry. Easy		
Head/Leg Room (in.)	39.1/42.7	Average	
Interior Space (cu. ft.)	89	Cramped	
Cargo Space (cu. ft.)	11	Vry. Small	
Tow Rating (lbs.)			

For 2001, Lexus' flagship sedan receives a redesign and a new designation. With a longer wheelbase, but the same length vehicle, the inside gets bigger and the ride yet smoother. The LS430 engine has what Lexus calls VVTi, Variable Valve Timing. This system provides better performance while improving fuel economy and reducing over-all emissions output. The cruise control system has a feature that senses vehicles in front of you and warns about obstacles at the car's corners when parking. Standard features include a garage door opening system, and power seats.

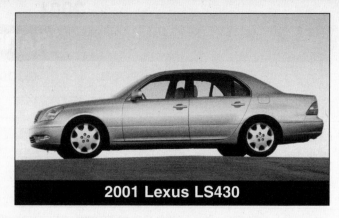

2001 Lexus LS430

General Information

New for 2001: All-new	**Year of Production:**	1
Twins:	**Seating:**	5
Where Made: Japan	**Theft Rating:**	Very High

Prices 2001

Model	Retail	Markup
Luxury Sedan	$54,005	16%

Competition 2001

Model	POOR					GOOD	pg.
Lexus LS430							**308**
Ford Cr. Victoria						▮	216
Lincoln Town Car						▮	322
Buick Regal					▮		148

'00 and '99 Models

Even though the 2001 is larger, the 1999-2000 LS400 has a smooth ride and an extremely roomy rear seat. But trunk space is rather small when compared to other large cars. An anti-theft system is standard and a computer navigation system is an option. For 2000, daytime running lights, interior trim changes, and new exterior colors were added.

Price Ranges 2000–1999

5-sp. auto./ RWD	$47,300-54,000

2000 Lexus LS400

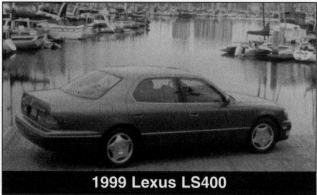

1999 Lexus LS400

Lexus LS430 — Large

	2001	2000	1999
RATINGS	POOR — GOOD	POOR — GOOD	POOR — GOOD
Comparative Rating			
Frontal Crash Tests			
Safety Features	8	9	9
Preventive Maintenance	6	5	6
Repair Costs	1	1	2
Warranty	8	8	8
Fuel Economy	4	3	3
Rollover (based on SSF; see pg. 30)	7	8	8
Complaints	10	10	9
Insurance Costs	10	10	10

SAFETY

	2001	2000	1999
Frontal Crash Tests	No Govt Results	No Govt Results	No Govt Results
Side Crash Tests	No Govt Results	No Govt Results	No Govt Results
Airbags		Dual/Side (nextgen)	Dual/Side (nextgen)
Anti-Lock Brakes		4-Wheel	4-Wheel
Day Running Lamps	Standard	Standard	Standard
Built-In Child Seats	None	None	None
Pretensioners	Standard	Standard	Standard

SPECIFICATIONS

	2001		2000		1999	
Fuel Economy (cty/hwy)	18/25	Poor	18/25	Poor	18/25	Poor
Driving Range (miles)	477.3	Vry. Long	470.85	Vry. Long	483.75	Vry. Long
Bumpers			Strong		Weak	
Parking Index	Hard		Average		Average	
Head/Leg Room (in.)	39.6/44	Vry. Roomy	38.9/43.7	Roomy	38.9/43.7	Roomy
Interior Space (cu. ft.)	107	Roomy	102	Roomy	102	Roomy
Cargo Space (cu. ft.)	16	Small	13.4	Small	13.9	Small
Tow Rating (lbs.)			2000	Vry. Low	2000	Vry. Low

This Toyota Land Cruiser twin moves into 2001 unchanged. The LX470 is designed to combine luxury and comfort with the ability to go off-road. You will find many of the luxurious amenities that you would expect in a Lexus, but the ride is not as smooth. Powering this heavy vehicle is a 4.7-liter V8 engine, which can produce 230 horsepower. The optional DVD navigation system allows DVD movies to be shown while the transmission is in park; otherwise you can listen to DVDs through the system.

2001 Lexus LX470

General Information

New for 2001: No major changes		**Year of Production:**	3
Twins: Toyota Land Cruiser		**Seating:**	8
Where Made: Japan		**Theft Rating:**	

Prices 2001

Model	Retail	Markup
Luxury SUV 4WD	$61,405	16%

Competition 2001

Model	POOR					GOOD	pg.
Lexus LX470						■	310
Lincoln Navigator					■		320
Ford Expedition			■				222

'00 and '99 Models

Like the Land Cruiser, the LX470 is fairly comfortable. The seats are roomy, and the cargo area is a good size. Handling, like in most sport utilities, is a bit sluggish. Power, heated seats, leather trim, and heated mirrors are standard as well as a tool and first aid kit.

Price Ranges 2000–1999

Luxury SUV 4WD	$52,000-59,000

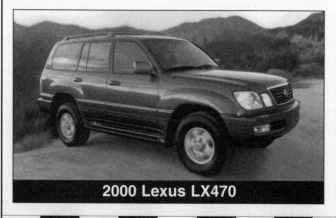

2000 Lexus LX470

1999 Lexus LX470

Lexus LX470 — Large Sport Utility

	2001	2000	1999

RATINGS

	2001 (POOR–GOOD)	2000 (POOR–GOOD)	1999 (POOR–GOOD)
Comparative Rating			
Frontal Crash Tests			
Safety Features	8	8	8
Preventive Maintenance	6	4	4
Repair Costs	2	3	3
Warranty	8	8	8
Fuel Economy	1	1	1
Rollover (based on SSF; see pg. 30)	4	4	4
Complaints	10	10	10
Insurance Costs	10	5	5

SAFETY

	2001	2000	1999
Frontal Crash Tests	No Govt Results	No Govt Results	No Govt Results
Side Crash Tests	No Govt Results	No Govt Results	No Govt Results
Airbags	Dual/Side	Dual (nextgen)	Dual (nextgen)
Anti-Lock Brakes	4-Wheel	4-Wheel	4-Wheel
Day Running Lamps	Standard	Standard	Standard
Built-In Child Seats	None	None	None
Pretensioners	Standard	Standard	Standard

SPECIFICATIONS

	2001		2000		1999	
Fuel Economy (cty/hwy)	13/16	Vry. Poor	13/16	Vry. Poor	13/16	Vry. Poor
Driving Range (miles)	368.3	Vry. Short	368.3	Vry. Short	368.3	Vry. Short
Bumpers	Weak		Weak			
Parking Index	Vry. Hard		Vry. Hard		Vry. Hard	
Head/Leg Room (in.)	40/42.3	Roomy	40/42.3	Roomy	40/42.3	Roomy
Interior Space (cu. ft.)						
Cargo Space (cu. ft.)	90.4	Vry. Large	90.4	Vry. Large	90.4	Vry. Large
Tow Rating (lbs.)	6500	Vry. High	6500	Vry. High	6500	Vry. High

New in 1999, the RX300 is unchanged for 2001. Clearly, this is a sport utility for the buyer looking more for luxury than rugged off-road conditions. It comes with an optional moonroof, heated outside mirrors, and cruise control. Seat belt height adjusters and pretensioners, dual and side airbags for front occupants, and 4-wheel ABS are all standard safety features. Under the hood, the RX300 sports a respectable 3.0L V6 that can give 220hp while meeting California Low Emission Vehicle standards.

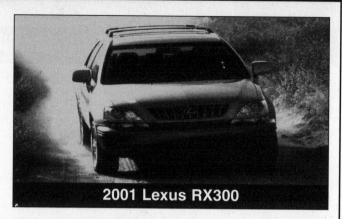

2001 Lexus RX300

General Information

New for 2001: No major changes	**Year of Production:**	3
Twins:	**Seating:**	5
Where Made: Japan	**Theft Rating:**	Very High

Prices 2001

Model	Retail	Markup
FWD	$33,905	15%
4WD	$35,655	15%

Competition 2001

Model	POOR					GOOD	pg.
Lexus RX300							**312**
Infiniti QX4						■	276
Jeep Gr. Cher.	■						286
Merc-Bz M-Class		■					340

'00 and '99 Models

The RX300 is available with full-time four-wheel drive, or front wheel drive. This is a class of vehicles which the carmakers call "car-based" SUV's. That means they are based on the design of a car, rather than a truck. This usually means unibody construction rather than a stiff frame system.

Price Ranges 2000–1999

FWD	$32,000-32,500
4WD	$33,900-34,100

2000 Lexus RX300

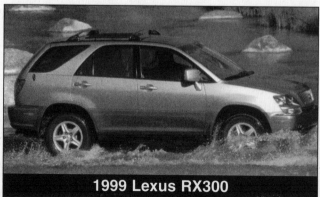

1999 Lexus RX300

	2001	2000	1999

RATINGS

	POOR — GOOD	POOR — GOOD	POOR — GOOD
Comparative Rating			
Frontal Crash Tests			
Safety Features	8	9	9
Preventive Maintenance	6	5	6
Repair Costs	2	3	3
Warranty	8	8	8
Fuel Economy	3	3	3
Rollover (based on SSF; see pg. 30)	5	5	5
Complaints	4	4	6
Insurance Costs	10	5	5

SAFETY

	2001	2000	1999
Frontal Crash Tests	To Be Tested	No Govt Results	No Govt Results
Side Crash Tests	No Govt Results	No Govt Results	No Govt Results
Airbags	Dual/Side	Dual/Side (nextgen)	Dual/Side (nextgen)
Anti-Lock Brakes	4-Wheel	4-Wheel	4-Wheel
Day Running Lamps	Standard	Standard	Standard
Built-In Child Seats	None	None	None
Pretensioners	Standard	Standard	Standard

SPECIFICATIONS

	2001		2000		1999	
Fuel Economy (cty/hwy)	18/22	Poor	18/22	Poor	14/22	Poor
Driving Range (miles)	396	Short	344	Vry. Short	353	Vry. Short
Bumpers	Weak		Weak			
Parking Index	Vry. Hard		Vry. Hard		Vry. Hard	
Head/Leg Room (in.)	39.5/40.7	Cramped	39.5/40.7	Cramped	39.5/40.7	Cramped
Interior Space (cu. ft.)	104	Roomy	140.6	Vry. Roomy	140.6	Vry. Roomy
Cargo Space (cu. ft.)	32	Average	39.8	Large	39.8	Large
Tow Rating (lbs.)			3500	Low		

Lexus SC300/400   Large

These two luxury coupes are due to be phased out this year but should be in showrooms for a while. They differ only in standard engines and luxury appointments; many items standard on the SC400 will cost extra on the SC300. The SC300 has a powerful 3-liter 6-cylinder engine and the SC400 has a 4-liter V8. A 6-CD changer is standard, and the SC has special door hinges, which make it easier to get out of the car in tight spots. Everything power is standard, except the tilt/telescoping steering wheel, which is an option on the 300. Be sure to get traction control.

2001 Lexus SC400

General Information

New for 2001: No major changes	**Year of Production:** 10
Twins:	**Seating:** 4
Where Made: Japan	**Theft Rating:**

Prices 2001

Model	Retail	Markup
SC300 Luxury Sport Cpe.	$43,805	15%
SC 400 Luxury Sport Cpe.	$56,305	16%

Competition 2001

Model	POOR				GOOD	pg.
Lexus SC300/400					■	**314**
Buick LeSabre				■		144
Acura RL					■	124
Lincoln Town Car				■		322

'00 and '99 Models

For both models the handling is excellent, and the ride is comfortably firm. All SC models have dual airbags and ABS. Inexplicably, side airbags aren't even an option for this class of car. Daytime running lamps were added in 1999.

Price Ranges 2000–1999

Base auto.	$38,800-43,400

2000 Lexus SC300

1999 Lexus SC400

Lexus SC300/400 — Large

	2001	2000	1999

RATINGS

	POOR → GOOD	POOR → GOOD	POOR → GOOD
Comparative Rating			
Frontal Crash Tests			
Safety Features	7	8	8
Preventive Maintenance	6	5	6
Repair Costs	10	3	3
Warranty	8	8	8
Fuel Economy	4	3	3
Rollover (based on SSF; see pg. 30)	8	8	8
Complaints	1	1	
Insurance Costs	5	5	5

SAFETY

	2001	2000	1999
Frontal Crash Tests	No Govt Results	No Govt Results	No Govt Results
Side Crash Tests	No Govt Results	No Govt Results	No Govt Results
Airbags	Dual (nextgen)	Dual (nextgen)	Dual (nextgen)
Anti-Lock Brakes	4-Wheel	4-Wheel	4-Wheel
Day Running Lamps	Standard	Standard	Standard
Built-In Child Seats	None	None	None
Pretensioners	Standard	Standard	Standard

SPECIFICATIONS

	2001		2000		1999	
Fuel Economy (cty/hwy)	19/23	Poor	19/23	Poor	19/24	Poor
Driving Range (miles)	432.6	Long	432.6	Long	442.9	Long
Bumpers	Strong		Strong		Strong	
Parking Index	Average		Average		Average	
Head/Leg Room (in.)	38.3/44.1	Roomy	38.3/44.1	Roomy	38.3/44.1	Roomy
Interior Space (cu. ft.)	75.4	Vry. Cramp.	75.4	Vry. Cramp.	75.4	Vry. Cramp.
Cargo Space (cu. ft.)	9.3	Vry. Small	9.3	Vry. Small	9.3	Vry. Small
Tow Rating (lbs.)	2000	Vry. Low	2000	Vry. Low	2000	Vry. Low

The Continental remains the same for 2001. The 4.6-liter V8 engine was beefed up last year for a total of 275 horsepower. There is plenty of interior space, and the Continental's mufflers were upgraded in '99 to be quieter. As for the ride, you can get an optional suspension system that lets you select from three different ride settings. Not exactly like the European cars that it was designed to compete against, this Lincoln is loaded with luxury touches.

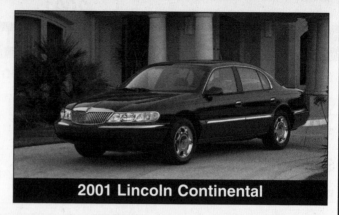
2001 Lincoln Continental

General Information

New for 2001: No major changes		**Year of Production:**	4
Twins:		**Seating:**	6
Where Made: U.S.		**Theft Rating:**	Average

Prices 2001

Model	Retail	Markup
Sedan	$39,380	8%

Competition 2001

Model	POOR					GOOD	pg.
Linc. Continental							**316**
Cadillac DeVille					■		152
Audi A8						■	132
Ford Cr. Victoria					■		216

'00 and '99 Models

The changes in '98, which brought a more aerodynamic exterior, rounding the front and rear ends, were continued through '99 and '00. Inside, you can get front and rear bench seats for up to six people, but most buyers opt for the two single bucket seats up front.

Price Ranges 2000–1999

Sedan	$25,800-38,900

2000 Lincoln Continental

1999 Lincoln Continental

Lincoln Continental — Large

	2001	2000	1999

RATINGS

	POOR — GOOD	POOR — GOOD	POOR — GOOD
Comparative Rating			
Frontal Crash Tests			
Safety Features	7	7	6
Preventive Maintenance	6	5	6
Repair Costs	3	3	3
Warranty	5	6	6
Fuel Economy	4	3	3
Rollover (based on SSF; see pg. 30)	8	8	8
Complaints	6	7	9
Insurance Costs	10	10	10

SAFETY

	2001	2000	1999
Frontal Crash Tests	No Govt Results	No Govt Results	No Govt Results
Side Crash Tests	No Govt Results	No Govt Results	No Govt Results
Airbags	Dual/Side (nextgen)	Dual/Side (nextgen)	Dual/Side
Anti-Lock Brakes	4-Wheel	4-Wheel	4-Wheel
Day Running Lamps	None	None	None
Built-In Child Seats	None	None	None
Pretensioners	None	None	None

SPECIFICATIONS

	2001		2000		1999	
Fuel Economy (cty/hwy)	17/25	Poor	17/25	Poor	17/25	Poor
Driving Range (miles)	420	Average	420	Average	420	Average
Bumpers	Strong		Strong		Strong	
Parking Index	Vry. Hard		Vry. Hard		Vry. Hard	
Head/Leg Room (in.)	39.2/41.9	Average	39.2/41.9	Average	39.2/41.9	Average
Interior Space (cu. ft.)	101	Average	102	Roomy	102	Roomy
Cargo Space (cu. ft.)	19	Average	18.4	Average	18.4	Average
Tow Rating (lbs.)	1000	Vry. Low	1000	Vry. Low	1000	Vry. Low

Lincoln LS Large

Introduced last year, this Jaguar S twin is unchanged for 2001. The LS is the lowest priced vehicle in the luxury Lincoln line. Standard is a 3.0-liter V6, with the option of manual or automatic transmission, but the optional 3.9-liter V8 comes with only automatic transmission. Standard are next-generation airbags and front seat-mounted side airbags in addition to 4-wheel ABS. Standard features include A/C, cruise control, ABS, remote keyless entry, and power everything.

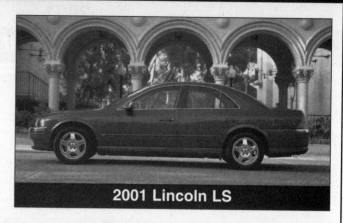

2001 Lincoln LS

General Information

New for 2001: No major changes	**Year of Production:** 2
Twins: Jaguar S-Type	**Seating:** 5
Where Made: U.S.	**Theft Rating:**

Prices 2001

Model	Retail	Markup
V6 auto.	$31,665	8%
V6 man.	$33,445	8%
V8 Sedan auto.	$35,695	8%

Competition 2001

Model	POOR					GOOD	pg.
Lincoln LS							**318**
Acura RL						■	124
Audi A8						■	132
Infiniti I30				■			272

'00 and '99 Models

With plenty of room for four, this rear wheel drive vehicle is designed to compete with European sedans. Ride and handling are not exactly the same, but the luxury touches are. While it doesn't look like its Jaguar twin, it drives like it.

Price Ranges 2000–1999

V6 auto.	$30-31,000
V6 man.	$31-32,000
V8 Sedan auto.	$34-35,000

2000 Lincoln LS

MODEL WAS NOT PRODUCED THIS YEAR

1999 Model

Lincoln LS

Large

	2001	2000	1999

RATINGS

	2001 (POOR–GOOD)	2000 (POOR–GOOD)	1999 (POOR–GOOD)
Comparative Rating			
Frontal Crash Tests			
Safety Features	6	6	
Preventive Maintenance	6		
Repair Costs	10		
Warranty	5	6	
Fuel Economy	4	4	
Rollover (based on SSF; see pg. 30)	8	8	
Complaints	5		
Insurance Costs	5	5	

SAFETY

	2001	2000	1999
Frontal Crash Tests	To Be Tested	No Govt Results	
Side Crash Tests	No Govt Results	No Govt Results	
Airbags	Dual/Side	Dual/Side	
Anti-Lock Brakes	4-Wheel	4-Wheel	
Day Running Lamps	None	None	
Built-In Child Seats	None	None	
Pretensioners	None	None	

SPECIFICATIONS

	2001		2000		1999
Fuel Economy (cty/hwy)	18/25	Poor	24/24	Average	
Driving Range (miles)	393.45	Short	439.2	Long	
Bumpers	Strong		Strong		
Parking Index	Hard		Hard		
Head/Leg Room (in.)	40.4/42.8	Vry. Roomy	40.4/42.8	Vry. Roomy	
Interior Space (cu. ft.)	104	Roomy	117.3	Vry. Roomy	
Cargo Space (cu. ft.)	13	Vry. Small	13.5	Small	
Tow Rating (lbs.)					

The Navigator is relatively unchanged for 2001. A modified Ford Expedition, the Lincoln Navigator gives the rugged off-road feel of an enormous sport utility, coupled with leather seats, walnut trim, power everything, and other amenities reserved for luxury sedans. Dual airbags and 4-wheel ABS are standard. The standard engine is a 5.4-liter V8 that now gives 260 hp, and look for another increase in horsepower later this year.

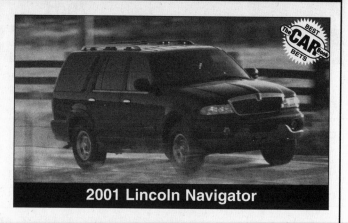

2001 Lincoln Navigator

General Information

New for 2001: No major changes		**Year of Production:**	4
Twins: Ford Expedition		**Seating:**	7
Where Made: U.S.		**Theft Rating:**	Very High

Prices 2001

Model	Retail	Markup
2WD	$43,645	13%
4WD	$47,395	13%

Competition 2001

Model	POOR				GOOD	pg.
Linc. Navigator					■	**320**
Infiniti QX4					■	276
Jeep Gr. Cher.	■					286
Toyota 4Runner			■			416

'00 and '99 Models

This is more than enough power for this sport utility. However, the fuel efficiency is very poor. The interior is spacious and luxurious, but storage does not match the Suburban.

Price Ranges 2000–1999

2WD	$28,800-33,700
4WD	$30,900-35,800

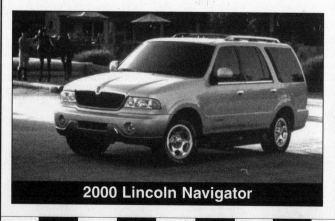

2000 Lincoln Navigator

1999 Lincoln Navigator

Lincoln Navigator | Large Sport Utility

	2001	2000	1999

RATINGS

	POOR → GOOD	POOR → GOOD	POOR → GOOD
Comparative Rating	8	5	4
Frontal Crash Tests*	8	8	9
Safety Features	6	6	5
Preventive Maintenance	8	8	7
Repair Costs	10	7	4
Warranty	5	6	6
Fuel Economy	7	1	1
Rollover (based on SSF, see pg. 25)	4	4	4
Complaints	2	2	3
Insurance Costs	10	10	10

SAFETY

	2001	2000	1999
Frontal Crash Tests	Good	Good	Very Good
Side Crash Tests	No Govt Results	No Govt Results	No Govt Results
Airbags	Dual/Side	Dual/Side	Dual
Anti-Lock Brakes	4-Wheel	4-Wheel	4-Wheel
Day Running Lamps	None	None	None
Built-In Child Seats	None	None	None
Pretensioners	None	None	None

SPECIFICATIONS

	2001		2000		1999	
Fuel Economy (cty/hwy)	12/17	Vry. Poor	14/18	Vry. Poor	14/18	Vry. Poor
Driving Range (miles)	420	Vry. Long	480	Vry. Long	480	Vry. Long
Bumpers						
Parking Index	Vry. Hard		Vry. Hard		Vry. Hard	
Head/Leg Room (in.)	39.7/40.9	Cramped	39.7/40.9	Cramped	39.8/41	Average
Interior Space (cu. ft.)						
Cargo Space (cu. ft.)	118.3	Vry. Large	118.3	Vry. Large	118.3	Vry. Large
Tow Rating (lbs.)	6600	Vry. High	6600	Vry. High	6600	Vry. High

*To be tested in 2001.

Lincoln Town Car

Large

For 2001, the Town Car carries over features from last year including standard side and de-powered dual airbags, a keyless entry system, rear window defroster, and traction assistance. 4-wheel ABS is standard. The new aerodynamic look may be hard for traditional Town Car lovers to take. The engine is a 4.6-liter V8 found on previous versions of the Town Car. It has been strengthened and now produces 225 hp and is more than adequate to power this over 4,000 lb, six-passenger sedan.

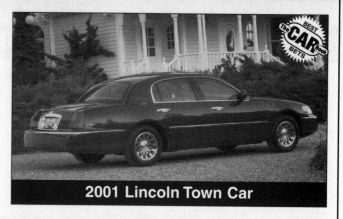
2001 Lincoln Town Car

General Information

New for 2001: No major changes	**Year of Production:** 4
Twins: Crown Vic., Grand Marquis	**Seating:** 6
Where Made: U.S.	**Theft Rating:** Very High

Prices 2001

Model	Retail	Markup
Executive	$39,145	8%
Signature	$41,315	8%
Cartier	$43,700	8%

Competition 2001

Model	POOR				GOOD		pg.
Linc. Town Car						■	**322**
Cadillac DeVille					■		152
Buick LeSabre						■	144
Chrys. Concorde			■				188

'00 and '99 Models

The interior space was decreased, but you won't notice it. The trunk space also decreased as well, but the Town Car still remains America's executive car of choice.

Price Ranges 2000–1999

Executive	$24,300-38,600
Signature	$25,900-40,600
Cartier	$42,800-43,100

2000 Lincoln Town Car

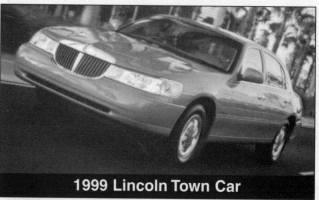
1999 Lincoln Town Car

	2001	2000	1999

RATINGS

	POOR — GOOD	POOR — GOOD	POOR — GOOD
Comparative Rating	9	9	9
Frontal Crash Tests	8	8	10
Safety Features	7	7	7
Preventive Maintenance	6	5	6
Repair Costs	10	7	1
Warranty	5	6	6
Fuel Economy	4	3	3
Rollover (based on SSF; see pg. 30)	8	8	8
Complaints	6	6	7
Insurance Costs	10	10	10

SAFETY

	2001	2000	1999
Frontal Crash Tests	Good	Good	No Govt Results
Side Crash Tests	Very Good	Very Good	Very Good
Airbags	Dual/Side (nextgen)	Dual/Side (nextgen)	Dual/Side (nextgen)
Anti-Lock Brakes	4-Wheel	4-Wheel	4-Wheel
Day Running Lamps	None	None	None
Built-In Child Seats	None	None	None
Pretensioners	None	None	None

SPECIFICATIONS

	2001		2000		1999	
Fuel Economy (cty/hwy)	18/25	Poor	17/24	Poor	17/24	Poor
Driving Range (miles)	408.5	Average	389.5	Short	389.5	Short
Bumpers	Strong		Strong		Strong	
Parking Index	Vry. Hard		Vry. Hard		Vry. Hard	
Head/Leg Room (in.)	39.2/42.6	Average	39.2/42.6	Average	39.2/42.6	Average
Interior Space (cu. ft.)	112	Roomy	112.3	Roomy	112.3	Roomy
Cargo Space (cu. ft.)	21	Average	20.6	Average	20.6	Average
Tow Rating (lbs.)	1000	Vry. Low	1000	Vry. Low	1000	Vry. Low

The 626 is Mazda's alternative to the Accord and doesn't change for 2001. Over the past few years, it has done fairly well against stiff competition. Dual airbags are now standard, but you'll still pay extra for ABS. Look for crash tests later this year. The base 2.0-liter 4-cylinder engine is adequate and reasonably economical. For more power, consider the 2.5-liter V6, available on the LX and ES. Room, comfort, and trunk space are good for four.

2001 Mazda 626

General Information

New for 2001: No major changes		**Year of Production:**	4
Twins:		**Seating:**	5
Where Made: U.S.		**Theft Rating:**	Average

Prices 2001

Model	Retail	Markup
LX	$18,740	10%
LX-V6	$19,940	10%
ES	$20,740	10%
ES-V6	$22,940	10%

Competition 2001

Model	POOR				GOOD	pg.
Mazda 626				■		**324**
Olds Alero				■		370
Mitsu. Galant		■				350
Toyota Corolla					■	424

'00 and '99 Models

With more room up front and a smaller price tag, the 626 competes fairly well against the more popular competition. Handling is fine, and the fit and finish rival that of Honda.

Price Ranges 2000–1999

Model	Price
LX	$13,500-18,300
LX V6	$15,100-19,500
ES	$14,300-20,500
ES V6	$16,600-22,500

2000 Mazda 626

1999 Mazda 626

Mazda 626 — Compact

	2001	2000	1999

RATINGS

	POOR → GOOD	POOR → GOOD	POOR → GOOD
Comparative Rating	5	6	7
Frontal Crash Tests	9	9	9
Safety Features	5	6	4
Preventive Maintenance	4	4	4
Repair Costs	9	9	8
Warranty	4	3	4
Fuel Economy	7	6	6
Rollover (based on SSF; see pg. 30)	7	7	7
Complaints	4	4	8
Insurance Costs	1	1	1

SAFETY

	2001	2000	1999
Frontal Crash Tests	Very Good	Very Good	Very Good
Side Crash Tests	Average	Average	Average
Airbags	Dual and Opt. Side	Dual and opt. Side	Dual
Anti-Lock Brakes	4-Wheel (optional)	4-Wheel (optional)	4-Wheel (optional)
Day Running Lamps	None	None	None
Built-In Child Seats	None	None	None
Pretensioners	None	None	None

SPECIFICATIONS

	2001		2000		1999	
Fuel Economy (cty/hwy)	26/32	Good	26/33	Good	26/33	Good
Driving Range (miles)	490.1	Vry. Long	498.55	Vry. Long	469.05	Vry. Long
Bumpers	Strong		Strong		Strong	
Parking Index	Average		Average		Easy	
Head/Leg Room (in.)	39.2/43.6	Roomy	39.2/43.6	Roomy	39.2/43.5	Roomy
Interior Space (cu. ft.)	97	Average	97.1	Average	97.2	Average
Cargo Space (cu. ft.)	14	Small	14.2	Small	13.8	Small
Tow Rating (lbs.)						

This version of the Ford Ranger does not change for 2001. Both front passengers benefit from the dual airbags, but 4-wheel ABS is still only an option. You get three engines to choose from: a 4.0-liter V8, a 3.0-liter V6, or a base 2.5-liter 4-cylinder. Mazda offers both regular and extended cabs. CD player, power door locks and windows, cruise control, and a theft deterrent system are a few of the available options.

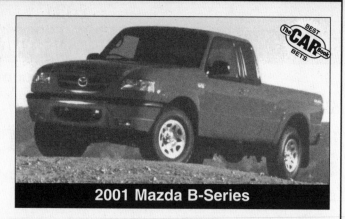

2001 Mazda B-Series

General Information

New for 2001: No major changes	Year of Production:	8
Twins: Ranger	Seating:	3
Where Made: Japan, U.S.	Theft Rating:	Very Low

Prices 2001

Model	Retail	Markup
B2500 SX 2WD	$12,230	7%
B3000 DS 2WD	$14,760	7%
B3000 SE 4WD	$18,250	11%
B4000 SE4WD	$22,220	11%

Competition 2001

Model	POOR					GOOD	pg.
Mazda B-Series			■				326
Ford Ranger				■			232
Chev. S-Series		■					174

'00 and '99 Models

Ride and handling have improved with the new suspension, and there's plenty of room inside. In 1998, the B-Series received a new grille, suspension, and steering system, all of which carried forward for 1999 and 2000.

Price Ranges 2000–1999

B2500 SX 2WD	$9,200-11,500
B3000 SX 2WD	$11,900-12,000
B3000 SE 4WD	$15,900-17,700
B4000 SE 4WD	$16,900-22,500

2000 Mazda B-Series

1999 Mazda B-Series

Mazda B-Series — Compact Pickup

	2001	2000	1999

RATINGS

	POOR — GOOD	POOR — GOOD	POOR — GOOD
Comparative Rating	5	5	4
Frontal Crash Tests*	9	9	9
Safety Features	4	4	4
Preventive Maintenance	8	8	7
Repair Costs	6	8	10
Warranty	4	3	4
Fuel Economy	2	3	3
Rollover (based on SSF, see pg. 25)	3		3
Complaints	8	8	4
Insurance Costs	1	1	1

SAFETY

	2001	2000	1999
Frontal Crash Tests	Very Good	Very Good	Very Good
Side Crash Tests	No Govt Results	No Govt Results	No Govt Results
Airbags	Dual	Dual	Dual
Anti-Lock Brakes	2-Wheel (4-whl opt.)	2-Wheel (4-whl opt.)	2-Wheel (4-whl opt.)
Day Running Lamps	None	None	None
Built-In Child Seats	None	None	None
Pretensioners	None	None	None

SPECIFICATIONS

	2001		2000		1999	
Fuel Economy (cty/hwy)	17/20	Vry. Poor	18/24	Poor	18/24	Poor
Driving Range (miles)	314.5	Vry. Short	357	Vry. Short	357	Vry. Short
Bumpers						
Parking Index	Hard		Hard		Hard	
Head/Leg Room (in.)	39.2/54.5	Vry. Roomy	39.2/54.5	Vry. Roomy	39.2/54.5	Vry. Roomy
Interior Space (cu. ft.)						
Cargo Space (cu. ft.)						
Tow Rating (lbs.)	2300	Low	2300	Low	2300	Low

*To be tested in 2001.

Mazda Miata   Subcompact

This Euro-styled sports car zips into 2001 unchanged. The 1.8-liter 4-cylinder engine develops 170 horsepower, which provides enough acceleration for most drivers. Brakes are good, even better with ABS. Controls and displays are sensibly designed. You won't get a soft, quiet ride, a spacious interior, or much of a trunk in a Miata, but you aren't buying it for any of those reasons either. You do get crisp, responsive handling, a peppy engine, and a car that will turn heads with the top down.

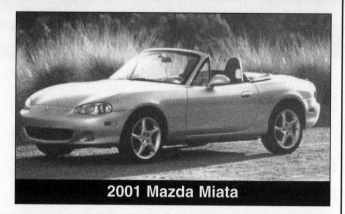
2001 Mazda Miata

General Information

New for 2001:	No major changes	Year of Production:	3
Twins:		**Seating:**	2
Where Made:	Japan, U.S.	**Theft Rating:**	

Prices 2001

Model	Retail	Markup
Base	$21,200	9%
LS Convertible	$23,930	9%

Competition 2001

Model	POOR				GOOD	pg.
Mazda Miata						**328**
Chev. Camaro			■			164
Ford Mustang				■		230
Pontiac Sunfire				■		390

'00 and '99 Models

Redesigned in 1999, the Miata remains a popular roadster. The new bodywork gives the Miata a more modern look, but it still retains the classic features that made it such a hit when it was originally introduced.

Price Ranges 2000–1999

Base	$17,500-21,200
LS Conv.	$21,300-24,000

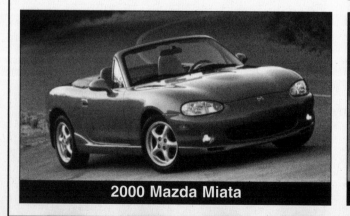
2000 Mazda Miata

1999 Mazda Miata

	2001	2000	1999

RATINGS

	POOR — GOOD (2001)	POOR — GOOD (2000)	POOR — GOOD (1999)
Comparative Rating			
Frontal Crash Tests			
Safety Features	4	4	4
Preventive Maintenance	4	4	4
Repair Costs	3	7	5
Warranty	4	3	4
Fuel Economy	6	5	5
Rollover (based on SSF; see pg. 30)	9	9	9
Complaints	2	2	2
Insurance Costs	5	5	5

SAFETY

	2001	2000	1999
Frontal Crash Tests	To Be Tested	No Govt Results	No Govt Results
Side Crash Tests	No Govt Results	No Govt Results	No Govt Results
Airbags	Dual	Dual	Dual
Anti-Lock Brakes	4-Wheel (optional)	4-Wheel (optional)	4-Wheel (optional)
Day Running Lamps	None	None	None
Built-In Child Seats	None	None	None
Pretensioners	None	None	None

SPECIFICATIONS

	2001		2000		1999	
Fuel Economy (cty/hwy)	23/28	Average	25/29	Average	25/29	Average
Driving Range (miles)	323.85	Vry. Short	342.9	Vry. Short	342.9	Vry. Short
Bumpers						
Parking Index	Vry. Easy		Vry. Easy		Vry. Easy	
Head/Leg Room (in.)	37.1/42.7	Cramped	37.1/42.7	Cramped	37.1/42.7	Cramped
Interior Space (cu. ft.)						
Cargo Space (cu. ft.)	5.1	Vry. Small	5.1	Vry. Small	5.1	Vry. Small
Tow Rating (lbs.)						

For 2001, the Millenia's substance remains unchanged, but a new grille, headlights, and front end give it a different look. The standard 2.5-liter V6 found on the base model is more than adequate; however, the Millenia S comes with the more powerful and responsive supercharged 2.3-liter V6. The base engine runs on regular fuel, while the S version requires premium fuel, which will increase your operating costs. This front wheel drive sedan is small, though it still should be quite comfortable for 4 passengers, 5 in a pinch.

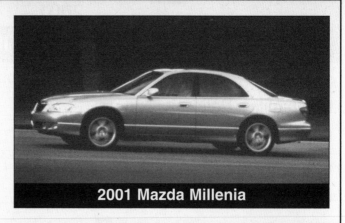

2001 Mazda Millenia

General Information

New for 2001: No major changes		**Year of Production:**	7
Twins:		**Seating:**	5
Where Made: U.S.		**Theft Rating:**	Very High

Prices 2001

Model	Retail	Markup
P Sedan	$28,000	9%
S Sedan	$31,000	9%

Competition 2001

Model	POOR				GOOD	pg.
Mazda Millenia				■		330
Chrys. Concorde			■			188
Lexus ES300					■	302
Ford Taurus					■	234

'00 and '99 Models

In 1999, the Millenia was restyled in hopes that it would be a winner in the competitive intermediate market. A well-designed car with good crash test scores, the Millenia deserves a close look in spite of its high maintenance costs.

Price Ranges 2000–1999

Base	$19,400-25,000
Premium	$20,600-27,000
Supercharged	$22,900-30,000

2000 Mazda Millenia

1999 Mazda Millenia

Mazda Millenia — Intermediate

	2001	2000	1999

RATINGS

	POOR — GOOD	POOR — GOOD	POOR — GOOD
Comparative Rating	7	5	5
Frontal Crash Tests	10	10	10
Safety Features	5	5	5
Preventive Maintenance	4	4	4
Repair Costs	1	1	1
Warranty	4	3	4
Fuel Economy	5	4	4
Rollover (based on SSF; see pg. 30)	8	8	8
Complaints	9	9	8
Insurance Costs	5	1	1

SAFETY

	2001	2000	1999
Frontal Crash Tests	No Govt Results	Very Good	Very Good
Side Crash Tests	No Govt Results	No Govt Results	No Govt Results
Airbags	Dual	Dual	Dual
Anti-Lock Brakes	4-Wheel	4-Wheel	4-Wheel
Day Running Lamps	None	None	None
Built-In Child Seats	None	None	None
Pretensioners	None	None	None

SPECIFICATIONS

	2001		2000		1999	
Fuel Economy (cty/hwy)	20/27	Poor	20/27	Poor	20/28	Average
Driving Range (miles)	423	Long	423	Long	432	Long
Bumpers	Weak		Weak		Weak	
Parking Index	Easy		Easy		Hard	
Head/Leg Room (in.)	39.3/43.3	Roomy	39.3/43.3	Roomy	39.3/43.3	Roomy
Interior Space (cu. ft.)	92	Cramped	93.8	Cramped	93.8	Cramped
Cargo Space (cu. ft.)	13	Vry. Small	13.3	Small	13.3	Small
Tow Rating (lbs.)						

The 2001 MPV, introduced as all-new last year, continues unchanged. Mazda is the first to offer dual sliding doors with power windows in the MPV's class. They are also challenging the idea that larger is better, which makes the MPV easier to drive and park while offering larger than passenger car interior space. An all-new 2.5-liter V6 engine offers more power. This is a small minivan for people who don't need the extra space—beware if you're expecting the interior size of a GM or DaimlerChrysler product.

2001 Mazda MPV

General Information

New for 2001: No major changes		**Year of Production:**	2
Twins:		**Seating:**	7-8
Where Made: U.S.		**Theft Rating:**	

Prices 2001

Model	Retail	Markup
DX	$20,700	9%
LX	$22,800	9%
ES	$26,300	9%

Competition 2001

Model	POOR				GOOD	pg.
Mazda MPV						332
Chev. Venture			■			184
Honda Odyssey		■				250
Toyota Sienna		■				438

'00 and '99 Models

The Mazda MPV, or multi-purpose passenger vehicle, does not have an official 1999 model; the '98 simply continued selling in '99. One feature of note: the '99 MPV comes with swing-out sedan-style side doors.

Price Ranges 2000–1999

DX	$19-20,000
LX	$22-23,000
ES	$25-26,000

2000 Mazda MPV

MODEL WAS NOT PRODUCED THIS YEAR

1999 Model

Mazda MPV — Minivan

	2001	2000	1999

RATINGS

	POOR — GOOD	POOR — GOOD	POOR — GOOD
Comparative Rating	3	3	
Frontal Crash Tests	7	7	
Safety Features	6	6	
Preventive Maintenance	4	3	
Repair Costs	4	4	
Warranty	4	3	
Fuel Economy	3	3	
Rollover (based on SSF; see pg. 30)	4	4	
Complaints	5		
Insurance Costs	5	5	

SAFETY

	2001	2000	1999
Frontal Crash Tests	Good	Good	
Side Crash Tests	Very Good	No Govt Results	
Airbags	Dual and Opt. Side (ng)	Dual and Opt. Side (ng)	
Anti-Lock Brakes	4-Wheel	4-Wheel	
Day Running Lamps	None	None	
Built-In Child Seats	None	None	
Pretensioners	None	None	

SPECIFICATIONS

	2001		2000		1999
Fuel Economy (cty/hwy)	18/23	Poor	18/23	Poor	
Driving Range (miles)	401.8	Average	401.8	Average	
Bumpers					
Parking Index	Hard		Hard		
Head/Leg Room (in.)	41/40.8	Average	41/40.8	Average	
Interior Space (cu. ft.)					
Cargo Space (cu. ft.)	127	Vry. Large	127	Vry. Large	
Tow Rating (lbs.)					

No changes in the Protégé for 2001. The ride surprisingly good for a car at this price level. Dual airbags are standard, and ABS can be found on higher models. The Protégé comes in three trim levels. DX and LX models come standard with a 1.5-liter 4-cylinder engine that is relatively weak, although quite fuel-efficient.

2001 Mazda Protégé

General Information

New for 2001: No major changes	Year of Production:	3
Twins:	Seating:	5
Where Made: U.S.	Theft Rating:	Very Low

Prices 2001

Model	Retail	Markup
DX	$12,215	5%
LX	$13,515	7%
ES	$15,315	9%

Competition 2001

Model	POOR				GOOD	pg.
Mazda Protégé			■			**334**
Ford Focus					■	228
VW Beetle					■	446
Saturn SL					■	400

'00 and '99 Models

In '99, Protégé was tweaked to offer more room inside than you might expect from a subcompact car. The fancier ES comes with a 1.8-liter engine—more powerful, but less fuel efficient. The Protégé faces tough competition in a crowded subcompact market with the Civic.

Price Ranges 2000–1999

DX	$11-12,000
LX	$11,800-13,400
ES	$13-15,000

2000 Mazda Protege

1999 Mazda Protege

Mazda Protegé — Subcompact

	2001	2000	1999

RATINGS

	2001 (POOR–GOOD)	2000 (POOR–GOOD)	1999 (POOR–GOOD)
Comparative Rating	4	4	5
Frontal Crash Tests*	7	7	7
Safety Features	5	6	4
Preventive Maintenance	4	4	4
Repair Costs	5	5	4
Warranty	4	3	4
Fuel Economy	8	7	7
Rollover (based on SSF, see pg. 25)	7	7	7
Complaints	5	5	7
Insurance Costs	1	1	1

SAFETY

	2001	2000	1999
Frontal Crash Tests	Good	Good	Good
Side Crash Tests	Good	No Govt Results	No Govt Results
Airbags	Dual and Opt. Side	Dual and Opt. Side	Dual
Anti-Lock Brakes	4-Wheel (optional)	4-Wheel (optional)	4-Wheel (optional)
Day Running Lamps	None	None	None
Built-In Child Seats	None	None	None
Pretensioners	None	None	None

SPECIFICATIONS

	2001		2000		1999	
Fuel Economy (cty/hwy)	29/34	Good	29/34	Good	29/34	Good
Driving Range (miles)	415.8	Average	415.8	Average	456.75	Vry. Long
Bumpers						
Parking Index	Vry. Easy		Vry. Easy		Vry. Easy	
Head/Leg Room (in.)	39.2/42.2	Average	39.2/42.2	Average	39.2/42.2	Average
Interior Space (cu. ft.)	93	Cramped	92.6	Cramped	95.5	Average
Cargo Space (cu. ft.)	13	Vry. Small	12.9	Vry. Small	13.1	Vry. Small
Tow Rating (lbs.)						

*To be tested in 2001.

Mercedes-Benz C-Class Intermediate

All new for 2001, the C-Class gets a longer wheelbase, more rear seat room, and head and side airbags. Mercedes has engineered away much of the exterior sound through creative aerodynamics for a much quieter interior. A memory system covers personal adjustments in seats, steering wheel, mirrors, and temperature. A sensor deactivates the dual stage airbags if no one is in the front seat, to reduce crash repair costs. If you want to shift, the C-Class offers a 6-speed manual transmission. The number after the "C" designates the size of the engine.

2001 Mercedes-Benz C-Class

General Information

New for 2001: All-new		**Year of Production:**	1
Twins:		**Seating:**	5
Where Made: U.S.		**Theft Rating:**	Average

Prices 2001

Model	Retail	Markup
C240	$29,950	8%
C320	$36,950	8%

Competition 2001

Model	POOR					GOOD	pg.
Merc-Bz C-Class							336
Chrys. Concorde					■		188
Honda Accord				■			242
Toyota Camry					■		420

'00 and '99 Models

Mercedes added a new engine with more horsepower to both the C230 and the C430 in 1999. Traction control is standard, which automatically aids driving on slippery surfaces. Mercedes' Electronic Stability Program, a high-tech feature that prevents spins or slides, is standard in the C430 and optional on the C280.

Price Ranges 2000–1999

C230	$29,100-31,700
C280	$32,900-35,900
C430	$46,400-53,000

2000 Mercedes-Benz C-Class

1999 Mercedes-Benz C-Class

Mercedes-Benz C-Class — Intermediate

	2001	2000	1999

RATINGS

(POOR → GOOD)	2001	2000	1999
Comparative Rating	—	6	4
Frontal Crash Tests	—	7	7
Safety Features	7	8	8
Preventive Maintenance	2	1	2
Repair Costs	2	3	2
Warranty	3	4	4
Fuel Economy	5	4	4
Rollover (based on SSF; see pg. 30)	7	7	7
Complaints	5	8	4
Insurance Costs	10	10	10

SAFETY

	2001	2000	1999
Frontal Crash Tests	No Govt Results	Good	Good
Side Crash Tests	No Govt Results	Good	Good
Airbags	Dual/Side	Dual/Side	Dual/Side
Anti-Lock Brakes	4-Wheel	4-Wheel	4-Wheel
Day Running Lamps	None	None	None
Built-In Child Seats	None	None	None
Pretensioners	Standard	Standard	Standard

SPECIFICATIONS

	2001		2000		1999	
Fuel Economy (cty/hwy)	20/26	Poor	21/29	Average	21/27	Average
Driving Range (miles)	377.2	Short	410	Average	393.6	Short
Bumpers	Weak		Weak		Weak	
Parking Index	Easy		Easy		Easy	
Head/Leg Room (in.)	38.8/41.4	Cramped	37.2/41.5	Vry. Cramp.	37.2/41.5	Vry. Cramp.
Interior Space (cu. ft.)	89	Cramped	88	Cramped	88	Cramped
Cargo Space (cu. ft.)	12	Vry. Small	12.9	Vry. Small	12.9	Vry. Small
Tow Rating (lbs.)						

Moving into 2001 unchanged, the E-Class has a full-curtain side airbag system. Working with side and front airbags, this intricate automatic crash protection system is a standard feature. The E-Class has distinctive styling with oval headlamps and a molded hood. Available engines include a 3-liter diesel (E300), a new 3.2-liter V6 (E320), and a new 4.3-liter V8 (E430). With Mercedes' new nomenclature, the E stands for the mid-level size, and the number stands for the engine size. The transmission is a five-speed automatic.

2001 Mercedes-Benz E-Class

General Information

New for 2001: No major changes		**Year of Production:**	6
Twins:		**Seating:**	5
Where Made: Germany		**Theft Rating:**	Very High

Prices 2001

Model	Retail	Markup
E320 2WD	$47,900	8%
E320 AWD Wagon	$48,650	8%
E430 2WD	$53,200	8%
E430 AWD	$56,100	8%

Competition 2001

Model	POOR					GOOD	pg.
Merc-Bz E-Class							**338**
Cadillac DeVille				■			152
Ford Cr. Victoria					■		216
Audi A8						■	132

'00 and '99 Models

Notable features include a unique brake system which shortens braking distances and a special child seat system that will detect a special child seat and deactivate the passenger-side airbag.

Price Ranges 2000–1999

E320 2WD	$42,200-47,100
E320 AWD Wagon	$44,900-49,000
E430 2WD	$47,200-52,500
E430 AWD	$55,200-55,300

2000 Mercedes-Benz E-Class

1999 Mercedes-Benz E-Class

	2001	2000	1999

RATINGS

	POOR → GOOD (2001)	POOR → GOOD (2000)	POOR → GOOD (1999)
Comparative Rating			
Frontal Crash Tests			
Safety Features	7	8	8
Preventive Maintenance	1	1	1
Repair Costs	1	1	2
Warranty	3	4	4
Fuel Economy	5	5	5
Rollover (based on SSF; see pg. 30)	7	7	7
Complaints	9	9	10
Insurance Costs	10	10	10

SAFETY

	2001	2000	1999
Frontal Crash Tests	No Govt Results	No Govt Results	No Govt Results
Side Crash Tests	No Govt Results	No Govt Results	No Govt Results
Airbags	Dual/Side	Dual/Side	Dual/Side
Anti-Lock Brakes	4-Wheel	4-Wheel	4-Wheel
Day Running Lamps	None	None	None
Built-In Child Seats	None	None	None
Pretensioners	Standard	Standard	Standard

SPECIFICATIONS

	2001		2000		1999	
Fuel Economy (cty/hwy)	20/28	Average	21/30	Average	21/30	Average
Driving Range (miles)	506.4	Vry. Long	538.05	Vry. Long	538.05	Vry. Long
Bumpers	Weak		Weak		Weak	
Parking Index	Hard		Hard		Hard	
Head/Leg Room (in.)	37.6/37.2	Vry. Cramp.	37.6/41.3	Vry. Cramp.	37.6/41.3	Vry. Cramp.
Interior Space (cu. ft.)	95	Average	95	Average	95	Average
Cargo Space (cu. ft.)	15	Small	15.3	Small	15.3	Small
Tow Rating (lbs.)						

The M-Class, unchanged for 2001, as expected, offers a luxury experience in an SUV and an optional four-foot-long sunroof. The safety features for both the ML430 and the ML320 include dual and side airbags for the front occupants, belt adjusters in front and back seats, and standard 4-wheel ABS. The interior is luxurious, though small when matched with its competition. The ML430 gets 268 hp from its 3.2L V8 engine. The cheaper, though still over $30K, 320 runs on a V6. For a little less money, you may want to look at a fully loaded Explorer.

2001 Mercedes-Benz M-Class

General Information

New for 2001: No major changes	**Year of Production:**	4
Twins:	**Seating:**	5
Where Made: Germany, U.S.	**Theft Rating:**	High

Prices 2001

Model	Retail	Markup
ML320	$35,300	8%
ML430	$43,750	8%
ML55 AMG	$64,900	8%

Competition 2001

Model	POOR					GOOD	pg.
Merc-Bz M-Class		■					**340**
Infiniti QX4						■	276
Ford Explorer				■			224
Olds Bravada	■						374

'00 and '99 Models

In 1998, Mercedes entered the high-profit luxury sport utility market with the much-anticipated M-Class. Built in the U.S. and Germany, the M-Class boasts the styling and craftsmanship typical of Mercedes.

Price Ranges 2000–1999

ML320	$33,900-35,300
ML430	$43,700-43,800
ML55 AMG	$64-65,000

2000 Mercedes-Benz M-Class

1999 Mercedes-Benz M-Class

	2001	2000	1999

RATINGS

	POOR → GOOD	POOR → GOOD	POOR → GOOD
Comparative Rating	3	3	3
Frontal Crash Tests	9	9	9
Safety Features	7	8	8
Preventive Maintenance	1	1	1
Repair Costs	3	1	2
Warranty	3	4	4
Fuel Economy	3	2	2
Rollover (based on SSF; see pg. 30)	3	3	3
Complaints	3	3	5
Insurance Costs	10	10	10

SAFETY

	2001	2000	1999
Frontal Crash Tests	Very Good	Very Good	Very Good
Side Crash Tests	No Govt Results	No Govt Results	No Govt Results
Airbags		Dual/Side	Dual/Side
Anti-Lock Brakes		4-Wheel	4-Wheel
Day Running Lamps	None	None	None
Built-In Child Seats	None	None	None
Pretensioners	Standard	Standard	None

SPECIFICATIONS

	2001		2000		1999	
Fuel Economy (cty/hwy)	17/21	Poor	16/20	Vry. Poor	17/21	Poor
Driving Range (miles)	361	Vry. Short	342	Vry. Short	361	Vry. Short
Bumpers			Weak			
Parking Index	Average		Average		Average	
Head/Leg Room (in.)	39.8/40.3	Cramped	39.8/40.3	Cramped	39.8/40.3	Cramped
Interior Space (cu. ft.)						
Cargo Space (cu. ft.)	81.2	Large	85.4	Vry. Large	85.4	Vry. Large
Tow Rating (lbs.)	5000	Average	5000	Average	5000	Average

Mercury relaunched the Mercury Cougar in 1999, based on the updated Mystique platform, and keeps it going into 2001 unchanged. Powering the car is a 2.0-liter 4-cylinder engine, or a 2.5-liter V6. The I4 comes with only a 5-speed automatic transmission, while the V6 offers a 4-speed automatic as well. For 2001, a new edition Cougar S model is available offering 200 hp. The Cougar offers de-powered airbags for the front occupants and the option of side airbags as well. ABS is optional for both models, and traction assistance is also an available extra for the V6.

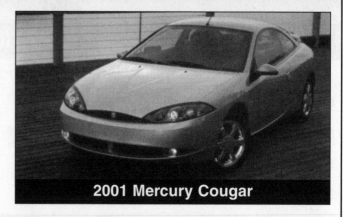

2001 Mercury Cougar

General Information

New for 2001: No major changes		**Year of Production:**	3
Twins:		**Seating:**	4
Where Made: U.S.		**Theft Rating:**	Low

Prices 2001

Model	Retail	Markup
I4	$16,700	8%
V6 Base	$17,200	8%
V6 S Coupe	$22,050	9%

Competition 2001

Model	POOR						GOOD	pg.
Mercury Cougar						■		342
Buick LeSabre						■		144
Audi A8							■	132
Infiniti I30					■			272

'00 and '99 Models

The Cougar plodded into 1999 unchanged until a 1999 1/2 redesign which became the current model. The older Cougar was a good crash test performer and offered a smooth ride and plenty of interior space.

Price Ranges 2000–1999

I4	$15,300-16,500
V6 Base	$16,700-16,900
V6 S Coupe	$18,000-19,000

2000 Mercury Cougar

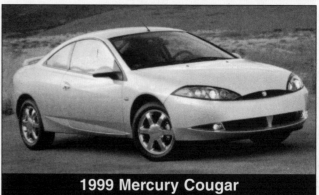

1999 Mercury Cougar

Mercury Cougar — Large

	2001	2000	1999

RATINGS

	POOR → GOOD (2001)	POOR → GOOD (2000)	POOR → GOOD (1999)
Comparative Rating			
Frontal Crash Tests			
Safety Features	5	5	5
Preventive Maintenance	6	6	6
Repair Costs	9	10	4
Warranty	4	2	2
Fuel Economy	7	6	6
Rollover (based on SSF; see pg. 30)	8	8	8
Complaints	1	1	1
Insurance Costs	1	5	5

SAFETY

	2001	2000	1999
Frontal Crash Tests	No Govt Results	No Govt Results	No Govt Results
Side Crash Tests	No Govt Results	No Govt Results	No Govt Results
Airbags	Dual (nextgen)	Dual (nextgen)	Dual (nextgen)
Anti-Lock Brakes	4-Wheel (optional)	4-Wheel (optional)	4-Wheel (optional)
Day Running Lamps	None	None	None
Built-In Child Seats	None	None	None
Pretensioners	None	None	None

SPECIFICATIONS

	2001		2000		1999	
Fuel Economy (cty/hwy)	23/34	Average	24/34	Good	24/34	Good
Driving Range (miles)	441.75	Long	449.5	Long	449.5	Long
Bumpers						
Parking Index	Average		Average		Average	
Head/Leg Room (in.)	37.8/42.5	Cramped	37.8/42.5	Cramped	37.8/42.5	Cramped
Interior Space (cu. ft.)	87	Cramped	84.2	Vry. Cramp.	84.2	Vry. Cramp.
Cargo Space (cu. ft.)	14	Small	14.5	Small	14.5	Small
Tow Rating (lbs.)	1000	Vry. Low	1000	Vry. Low	1000	Vry. Low

Mercury Villager | Minivan

Unchanged for 2001, the Villager was developed jointly with Nissan and built in Ohio, and is available in three trim levels: base, Sport, and Estate. Last year a restyled front grille and rear liftgate was added. The Villager's resemblance to the Dodge Caravan is no coincidence; Villager designers know who they need to beat. This year, Villager adds a standard driver- side sliding door and increases interior space. The 3.0-liter V6, with automatic overdrive, is acceptably responsive. Go for the towing package if you'll be hauling anything at all.

2001 Mercury Villager

General Information

New for 2001: No major changes	**Year of Production:**	3
Twins: Nissan Quest	**Seating:**	7
Where Made: U.S.	**Theft Rating:**	

Prices 2001

Model	Retail	Markup
Base	$22,510	10%
Sport	$25,737	10%
Estate	$27,210	6%

Competition 2001

Model	POOR					GOOD		pg.
Mercury Villager				■				**344**
Olds Silhouette					■			378
Honda Odyssey			■					250
Toyota Sienna			■					438

'00 and '99 Models

The Villager has received only minor revisions during the 1999-2000 model years. Unfortunately, no government crash test results are currently available, but it's scheduled to be tested in 2001.

Price Ranges 2000–1999

Base	$18,100-22,400
Sport	$20,200-25,400
Estate	$20,400-27,100

2000 Mercury Villager

1999 Mercury Villager

Mercury Villager — Minivan

	2001	2000	1999

RATINGS

	POOR — GOOD	POOR — GOOD	POOR — GOOD
Comparative Rating	5	5	4
Frontal Crash Tests	10	6	7
Safety Features	5	5	6
Preventive Maintenance	9	9	9
Repair Costs	8	8	4
Warranty	4	2	2
Fuel Economy	3	3	3
Rollover (based on SSF; see pg. 30)	5	5	5
Complaints	2	2	2
Insurance Costs	10	10	10

SAFETY

	2001	2000	1999
Frontal Crash Tests	Very Good	Good	Good
Side Crash Tests	Very Good	Very Good	No Govt Results
Airbags	Dual (nextgen)	Dual (nextgen)	Dual (nextgen)
Anti-Lock Brakes	4-Wheel (optional)	4-Wheel (optional)	4-Wheel (optional)
Day Running Lamps	None	None	None
Built-In Child Seats	None	None	Optional
Pretensioners	None	None	None

SPECIFICATIONS

	2001		2000		1999	
Fuel Economy (cty/hwy)	17/23	Poor	17/24	Poor	17/24	Poor
Driving Range (miles)	400	Average	410	Average	410	Average
Bumpers						
Parking Index	Vry. Hard		Vry. Hard		Hard	
Head/Leg Room (in.)	39.7/39.9	Vry. Cramp.	39.7/39.9	Vry. Cramp.	39.7/39.9	Vry. Cramp.
Interior Space (cu. ft.)						
Cargo Space (cu. ft.)	127.6	Vry. Large	127.6	Vry. Large	126	Vry. Large
Tow Rating (lbs.)	2000	Vry. Low	2000	Vry. Low	2000	Vry. Low

The Diamante continues forward with no changes. Powering the new Diamante is a refined 3.5-liter V6 engine, which is good enough for this mid-size sedan. As with past Diamantes, the ride should be smooth and comfortable. Great safety features include an optional fold-down child safety seat and a standard 3-point seat belt for the middle of the back seat. The new Cold Weather package offers traction control and heated front seats. Adherence to California's Low Emission Vehicle standards is optional.

2001 Mitsubishi Diamante

General Information

New for 2001: No major changes		**Year of Production:**	5
Twins:		**Seating:**	5
Where Made: U.S.		**Theft Rating:**	Very High

Prices 2001

Model	Retail	Markup
ES 4-spd. auto.	$25,387	10%
LS 4-spd. auto.	$27,407	6%

Competition 2001

Model	POOR				GOOD	pg.
Mitsu. Diamante						**346**
Cadillac DeVille			■			152
Ford Cr. Victoria				■		216
Audi A8					■	132

'00 and '99 Models

In 1999, the Diamante was reduced to only one trim level replacing the ES and the LS of previous years. The Diamante was improved greatly in 1997 with a redesign. But, unfortunately, it lacks government crash test results.

Price Ranges 2000–1999

ES 4-sp. auto.	$20,500-25,000
LS 4-sp. auto.	$27-28,000

2000 Mitsubishi Diamante

1999 Mitsubishi Diamante

	2001	2000	1999

RATINGS

	POOR — GOOD (2001)	POOR — GOOD (2000)	POOR — GOOD (1999)
Comparative Rating			
Frontal Crash Tests			
Safety Features	6	6	7
Preventive Maintenance	2	1	2
Repair Costs	4	2	2
Warranty	4	7	5
Fuel Economy	4	3	3
Rollover (based on SSF; see pg. 30)	8	8	8
Complaints	7	7	10
Insurance Costs	5	5	5

SAFETY

	2001	2000	1999
Frontal Crash Tests	No Govt Results	No Govt Results	No Govt Results
Side Crash Tests	No Govt Results	No Govt Results	No Govt Results
Airbags	Dual	Dual	Dual
Anti-Lock Brakes	4-Wheel	4-Wheel	4-Wheel
Day Running Lamps	None	None	None
Built-In Child Seats	None	None	Optional
Pretensioners	Standard	Standard	Standard

SPECIFICATIONS

	2001		2000		1999	
Fuel Economy (cty/hwy)	18/25	Poor	18/24	Poor	18/24	Poor
Driving Range (miles)	408.5	Average	399	Average	399	Average
Bumpers	Strong		Strong		Strong	
Parking Index	Average		Average		Average	
Head/Leg Room (in.)	39.4/43.6	Roomy	39.4/43.6	Roomy	39.4/43.6	Roomy
Interior Space (cu. ft.)	101	Average	100.9	Average	100.9	Average
Cargo Space (cu. ft.)	14	Small	14.2	Small	14.2	Small
Tow Rating (lbs.)						

The exterior was completely redesigned on the 2000 Eclipse and the engines have more power. After such a major overhaul, the 2001 Eclipse is little changed. The RS and GS models come with a 2.4-liter 4-cylinder engine standard, and the GT has a 3.0-liter V6. All three come with a manual transmission standard with the option of automatic but the GS and GT have an optional Sportronic auto/manual transmission. Dual airbags are standard, and this car has greater front and side impact protection, but side airbags and ABS are also options on the GT model.

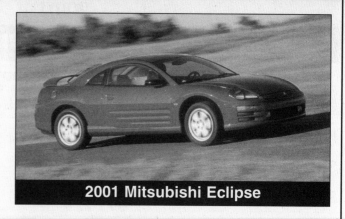

2001 Mitsubishi Eclipse

General Information

New for 2001: No major changes		**Year of Production:**	2
Twins:		**Seating:**	4
Where Made: U.S.		**Theft Rating:**	Very High

Prices 2001

Model	Retail	Markup
RS 5-spd. man.	$17,987	9%
RS 4-spd. auto.	$18,787	9%
Spyder GS 5-spd. man.	$23,407	9%
Spyder GS 4-spd. sportronic	$24,407	9%

Competition 2001

Model	POOR				GOOD		pg.
Mitsu. Eclipse							**348**
Dodge Intrepid					■		208
Ford Mustang					■		230
Chev. Camaro				■			164

'00 and '99 Models

There are few changes for the 1999 Eclipse: a sunroof and a security system with keyless entry are standard for the GS-T, and ABS and limited slip rear differential are standard on the GSX. The Eclipse does have a back seat, but it's not really meant for adults.

Price Ranges 2000–1999

RS 5-sp. man.	$13,100-17,100
RS 4-sp. auto.	$13,700-17,700
Spyder GS 5-sp. man.	$17,500-18,500
Spyder GS 4-sp. Sportronic	$18,100-20,200

2000 Mitsubishi Eclipse

1999 Mitsubishi Eclipse

Mitsubishi Eclipse — Compact

	2001	2000	1999

RATINGS

	2001 (POOR–GOOD)	2000 (POOR–GOOD)	1999 (POOR–GOOD)
Comparative Rating	—	—	—
Frontal Crash Tests	—	—	—
Safety Features	6	6	4
Preventive Maintenance	7	6	6
Repair Costs	8	8	8
Warranty	4	7	5
Fuel Economy	6	5	5
Rollover (based on SSF; see pg. 30)	8	8	10
Complaints	5	—	5
Insurance Costs	1	1	1

SAFETY

	2001	2000	1999
Frontal Crash Tests	No Govt Results	No Govt Results	No Govt Results
Side Crash Tests	No Govt Results	No Govt Results	No Govt Results
Airbags	Dual and Opt. Side	Dual and Opt. Side	Dual
Anti-Lock Brakes	4-Wheel	4-Wheel	4-wheel (optional)
Day Running Lamps	None	None	None
Built-In Child Seats	None	None	None
Pretensioners	None	None	None

SPECIFICATIONS

	2001		2000		1999	
Fuel Economy (cty/hwy)	22/30	Average	23/31	Average	22/33	Average
Driving Range (miles)	426.4	Long	442.8	Long	437.25	Long
Bumpers	Strong		Strong		Strong	
Parking Index	Easy		Easy		Average	
Head/Leg Room (in.)	37.9/42.3	Cramped	37.9/42.3	Cramped	37.9/43.3	Average
Interior Space (cu. ft.)	79	Vry. Cramp.	79.3	Vry. Cramp.	79.1	Vry. Cramp.
Cargo Space (cu. ft.)	17	Average	16.9	Average	16.6	Small
Tow Rating (lbs.)						

Carrying forward unchanged, the Galant comes in four trim levels. The DE comes with a 2.4-liter 4-cylinder engine, with either manual or automatic transmission. The LS and GTZ have a 3.0-liter V6 and an automatic transmission. The ES comes with either of these engines. Front airbags are standard on all models, for both driver and passenger. The LS and GTZ offer front side airbags. ABS is not available on the DE, costs extra with the ES 4-cylinder, and is standard on the ES V6, LS and GTZ. Rear headrests are available on the ES, LS, and GTZ.

2001 Mitsubishi Galant

General Information

New for 2001: No major changes	**Year of Production:** 3
Twins:	**Seating:** 5
Where Made: U.S.	**Theft Rating:** Very High

Prices 2001		
Model	**Retail**	**Markup**
DE	$17,557	9%
ES	$18,407	10%
LS-V6	$23,907	10%
GTZ-V6	$24,007	10%

Competition 2001	POOR				GOOD		pg.
Mitsu. Galant		■					**350**
Chev. Cavalier				■			166
Ford Focus						■	228
Toyota Corolla				■			424

'00 and '99 Models

The Galant received a complete remake in 1999 to help it compete against the Cavalier and Civic. The result was an attractive compact that costs a bit more than its competitors. However, the Galant performed excellently on frontal and side crash tests.

Price Ranges 2000–1999	
DE	$13,200-15,100
ES	$13,900-15,900
LS V6	$17,900-23,200
GTZ V6	$18,100-23,300

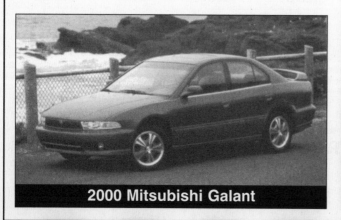

2000 Mitsubishi Galant

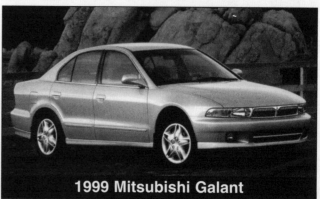

1999 Mitsubishi Galant

Mitsubishi Galant   Compact

	2001	2000	1999

RATINGS

	POOR → GOOD (2001)	POOR → GOOD (2000)	POOR → GOOD (1999)
Comparative Rating	3	6	6
Frontal Crash Tests	9	9	9
Safety Features	6	6	6
Preventive Maintenance	2	1	2
Repair Costs	7	8	9
Warranty	4	7	5
Fuel Economy	5	5	5
Rollover (based on SSF; see pg. 30)	7	7	7
Complaints	1	1	1
Insurance Costs	1	5	5

SAFETY

	2001	2000	1999
Frontal Crash Tests	Very Good	Very Good	Very Good
Side Crash Tests	Very Good	Very Good	Very Good
Airbags	Dual	Dual	Dual
Anti-Lock Brakes	4-Wheel	4-Wheel	4-Wheel
Day Running Lamps	None	None	None
Built-In Child Seats	None	None	None
Pretensioners	Standard	Standard	Standard

SPECIFICATIONS

	2001		2000		1999	
Fuel Economy (cty/hwy)	21/28	Average	23/31	Average	23/31	Average
Driving Range (miles)	399.35	Average	440.1	Long	440.1	Long
Bumpers	Strong		Strong			
Parking Index	Easy		Easy		Easy	
Head/Leg Room (in.)	39.9/43.5	Vry. Roomy	39.9/43.5	Vry. Roomy	39.9/43.5	Vry. Roomy
Interior Space (cu. ft.)	96	Average	97.3	Average	97.3	Average
Cargo Space (cu. ft.)	14	Small	12.5	Vry. Small	12.5	Vry. Small
Tow Rating (lbs.)						

Mitsubishi Mirage

Subcompact

The 2001 Mirage is unchanged from last year. All Mirages have dual airbags, but ABS is optional. The 1.5-liter 4-cylinder engine that comes with the base model Mirage DE is not very powerful, though you'll be pleased with its fuel economy. The 1.8-liter engine on the LS coupes and sedans is much more powerful, but gas mileage suffers dramatically.

2001 Mitsubishi Mirage

General Information

New for 2001: No major changes	**Year of Production:** 5
Twins:	**Seating:** 5
Where Made: U.S.	**Theft Rating:** Average

Prices 2001

Model	Retail	Markup
Coupe DE 5-spd. man.	$11,877	9%
Coupe DE 4-spd. auto.	$12,677	9%
Sedan ES 5-spd. man.	$13,627	9%
Sedan LS 4-spd. auto.	$15,267	9%

Competition 2001

Model	POOR				GOOD		pg.
Mitsu. Mirage							**352**
Mazda Protégé			■				334
Subaru Impreza						■	404
Saturn SL						■	400

'00 and '99 Models

In 1999 and 2000 the Mirage only received minor cosmetic changes such as tail lamps, new seat fabric, and exterior colors.

Price Ranges 2000–1999

Coupe DE 5-sp. man.	$8,700-10,000
Coupe DE 4-sp. auto.	$9,100-10,500
Sedan LS 5-sp. man.	$10,300-12,000
Sedan LS 4-sp. auto.	$10,700-12,500

2000 Mitsubishi Mirage

1999 Mitsubishi Mirage

Mitsubishi Mirage — Subcompact

	2001	2000	1999

RATINGS

(Scale: POOR → GOOD, 1–10)

	2001	2000	1999
Comparative Rating	—	—	—
Frontal Crash Tests	—	—	—
Safety Features	6	5	5
Preventive Maintenance	2	1	2
Repair Costs	7	6	6
Warranty	4	7	5
Fuel Economy	9	8	8
Rollover (based on SSF; see pg. 30)	8	8	8
Complaints	6	7	7
Insurance Costs	1	1	1

SAFETY

	2001	2000	1999
Frontal Crash Tests	No Govt Results	No Govt Results	No Govt Results
Side Crash Tests	No Govt Results	No Govt Results	No Govt Results
Airbags	Dual	Dual	Dual
Anti-Lock Brakes	4-Wheel	4-Wheel	4-Wheel
Day Running Lamps	None	None	None
Built-In Child Seats	None	None	None
Pretensioners	None	None	None

SPECIFICATIONS

	2001		2000		1999	
Fuel Economy (cty/hwy)	32/39	Vry. Good	33/40	Vry. Good	33/40	Vry. Good
Driving Range (miles)	462	Vry. Long	481.8	Vry. Long	481.8	Vry. Long
Bumpers	Strong		Strong		Strong	
Parking Index	Vry. Easy		Vry. Easy		Vry. Easy	
Head/Leg Room (in.)	38.6/43	Average	38.6/43	Average	38.6/43	Average
Interior Space (cu. ft.)	91	Cramped	85.6	Vry. Cramp.	85.6	Vry. Cramp.
Cargo Space (cu. ft.)	11	Vry. Small	11.5	Vry. Small	11.5	Vry. Small
Tow Rating (lbs.)						

Mitsubishi Montero

Mid-Size Sport Utility

The all-new Montero gets a longer wheelbase, wider track, and lower height which provide a bigger overall footprint but a smaller turning radius. The space inside is larger with more room for each of the 7 passengers and a bit larger cargo area. The third seat folds flat into the rear floor and when upright leaves a covered storage space. Standard features include side airbags, a CD player, multiple power outlets and removable tool box with flashlight. Options include leather, power seats, and a power sunroof. A 200 hp engine is standard.

2001 Mitsubishi Montero

General Information

New for 2001: All-new	**Year of Production:** 1
Twins:	**Seating:** 5
Where Made: Australia	**Theft Rating:** Very High

Prices 2001

Model	Retail	Markup
ES Sport 2WD	$22,747	10%
ES Sport 4WD	$24,947	10%
XLS SUV 4WD	$31,297	10%
Limited SUV 4WD	$35,297	10%

Competition 2001

Model	POOR					GOOD		pg.
Mitsu. Montero								**354**
Infiniti QX4						■		276
Merc-Bz M-Class			■					340
Olds Bravada		■						374

'00 and '99 Models

There are a variety of packages to pick from. The engine is a 3.5-liter V6. This engine should provide good power for this heavy vehicle. Gas mileage is abysmal, automatic overdrive is standard on the SR, optional on the LS, and you can choose between 2- and 4-wheel drive. The Montero and the Montero Sport are offered for 1999 with several option packages.

Price Ranges 2000–1999

ES Sport 2WD	$14,400-17,000
LS Sport 4WD	$20,400-22,000
XLS SUV 4WD	$21,100-23,000
Limited SUV 4WD	$24,000-31,400

2000 Mitsubishi Montero

1999 Mitsubishi Montero

Mitsubishi Montero — Mid-Size Sport Utility

	2001	2000	1999

RATINGS

	2001 (POOR→GOOD)	2000 (POOR→GOOD)	1999 (POOR→GOOD)
Comparative Rating			
Frontal Crash Tests		6	6
Safety Features	6	4	4
Preventive Maintenance	2	2	2
Repair Costs	10	2	1
Warranty	4	7	5
Fuel Economy	1	2	2
Rollover (based on SSF; see pg. 30)	3	2	1
Complaints	5	1	6
Insurance Costs	1	1	1

SAFETY

	2001	2000	1999
Frontal Crash Tests	To Be Tested	Average	Average
Side Crash Tests	No Govt Results	No Govt Results	No Govt Results
Airbags	Dual/Side	Dual	Dual
Anti-Lock Brakes	4-Wheel	4-Wheel (optional)	4-Wheel (optional)
Day Running Lamps	None	None	None
Built-In Child Seats	None	None	None
Pretensioners	None	None	None

SPECIFICATIONS

	2001		2000		1999	
Fuel Economy (cty/hwy)	14/17	Vry. Poor	17/20	Vry. Poor	16/19	Vry. Poor
Driving Range (miles)	368.9	Vry. Short	449.55	Long	425.25	Long
Bumpers						
Parking Index	Vry. Hard		Hard		Hard	
Head/Leg Room (in.)	41.4/42.7	Vry. Roomy	38.9/42.8	Average	40.9/40.3	Average
Interior Space (cu. ft.)	104.6	Roomy	137	Vry. Roomy	131	Vry. Roomy
Cargo Space (cu. ft.)	42.1	Large	79.3	Large	79.3	Large
Tow Rating (lbs.)	5000	Average	5000	Average	5000	Average

The 2001 Altima is unchanged from last year's model. Standard dual airbags have been de-powered, and ABS is still optional. A revised 2.4-liter 4-cylinder engine powers the new Altima. Four trim levels are available with a variety of new options packages. Be sure to look over the options list carefully. A remote keyless entry and security system is standard on the SE and GLE models.

2001 Nissan Altima

General Information

New for 2001: No major changes		**Year of Production:**	4
Twins:		**Seating:**	5
Where Made: U.S.		**Theft Rating:**	Average

Prices 2001

Model	Retail	Markup
XE Sedan man.	$15,140	4%
XE Sedan auto.	$15,940	4%
SE Sedan man.	$18,640	10%
SE Sedan auto.	$19,440	10%

Competition 2001

Model	POOR						GOOD	pg.
Nissan Altima							■	356
Ford Taurus								■	234
Honda Accord				■				242
Toyota Camry					■			420

'00 and '99 Models

For 2000, the Altima received new front and rear fascias and noise filtering was improved during driving. After the all-new model was released in 1998, there were only a few changes for the 1999 Altima. These included new windshield wipers, an improved stereo system, and new wheels on GLE models.

Price Ranges 2000–1999

Model	Price
XE Sedan man.	$13,000-14,500
XE Sedan auto.	$13,600-15,300
SE Sedan man.	$14,500-18,000
SE Sedan auto.	$15,000-18,600

2000 Nissan Altima

1999 Nissan Altima

	2001	2000	1999

RATINGS

	2001 (POOR–GOOD)	2000 (POOR–GOOD)	1999 (POOR–GOOD)
Comparative Rating	9	6	6
Frontal Crash Tests	10	6	6
Safety Features	6	6	6
Preventive Maintenance	7	6	6
Repair Costs	7	5	5
Warranty	7	4	4
Fuel Economy	6	5	5
Rollover (based on SSF; see pg. 30)	7	7	7
Complaints	9	9	9
Insurance Costs	1	1	1

SAFETY

	2001	2000	1999
Frontal Crash Tests	Very Good	Average	Average
Side Crash Tests	Average	Average	Average
Airbags	Dual (nextgen)	Dual (nextgen)	Dual (nextgen)
Anti-Lock Brakes	4-Wheel (optional)	4-Wheel (optional)	4-Wheel (optional)
Day Running Lamps	None	None	None
Built-In Child Seats	None	None	None
Pretensioners	Standard	Standard	Standard

SPECIFICATIONS

	2001		2000		1999	
Fuel Economy (cty/hwy)	23/31	Average	23/31	Average	24/31	Average
Driving Range (miles)	429.3	Long	429.3	Long	437.25	Long
Bumpers	Weak		Weak		Strong	
Parking Index	Average		Average		Average	
Head/Leg Room (in.)	39.4/42	Average	39.4/42	Average	39.4/42	Average
Interior Space (cu. ft.)	94	Cramped	94	Cramped	94	Cramped
Cargo Space (cu. ft.)	14	Small	13.8	Small	13.8	Small
Tow Rating (lbs.)	1000	Vry. Low	1000	Vry. Low	1000	Vry. Low

No major improvements for the Frontier in 2001. The base 2.4-liter is still the norm on other models. Dual de-powered airbags, 4-wheel ABS, and front height adjustable seat belts are standard. Fuel economy is low, but you'll find increased head and legroom inside. The Frontier still benefits from last year's increase in interior space. The truck's bed is one of the biggest around. A regular cab and King Cab are available.

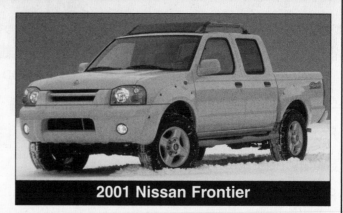

2001 Nissan Frontier

General Information

New for 2001: No major changes		**Year of Production:**	4
Twins:		**Seating:**	2
Where Made: U.S.		**Theft Rating:**	Very Low

Prices 2001

Model	Retail	Markup
XE 2WD man.	$11,699	6%
XE 2WD auto.l	$12,750	6%
SC V6 man. 4WD King Cab	$22,599	10%
SC V6 auto. 4WD King Cab	$23,649	10%

Competition 2001

Model	POOR				GOOD	pg.
Nissan Frontier						**358**
Chev. S-Series	■					174
Ford Ranger				■		232
Mazda B-Series				■		326

'00 and '99 Models

For 1999, Nissan's four-wheel drive Frontier pickups received a more powerful 3.3-liter V6 with 170 hp, inherited from the Pathfinder.

Price Ranges 2000–1999

XE 2WD man.	$11,000-11,600
XE 2WD auto.	$11,400-11,600
SC V6 man. 4WD King Cab	$17,300-21,200
SC V6 auto. 4WD King Cab	$17,800-21,700

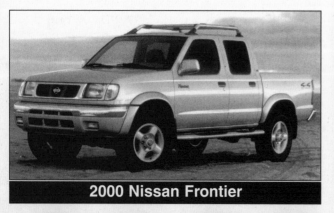

2000 Nissan Frontier

1999 Nissan Frontier

	2001	2000	1999

RATINGS

	POOR — GOOD	POOR — GOOD	POOR — GOOD
Comparative Rating		4	4
Frontal Crash Tests		6	6
Safety Features	5	6	6
Preventive Maintenance	4	3	4
Repair Costs	10	10	9
Warranty	7	4	4
Fuel Economy	5	4	3
Rollover (based on SSF; see pg. 30)	4	4	4
Complaints	7	7	8
Insurance Costs	5	5	5

SAFETY

	2001	2000	1999
Frontal Crash Tests	To Be Tested	Average	Average
Side Crash Tests	No Govt Results	No Govt Results	No Govt Results
Airbags	Dual (nextgen)	Dual (nextgen)	Dual (nextgen)
Anti-Lock Brakes	2-Wheel (4-whl opt.)	2-Wheel (4-whl opt.)	2-Wheel (4-whl opt.)
Day Running Lamps	None	None	None
Built-In Child Seats	None	None	None
Pretensioners	Standard	Standard	Standard

SPECIFICATIONS

	2001		2000		1999	
Fuel Economy (cty/hwy)	22/26	Average	22/26	Average	20/24	Poor
Driving Range (miles)	381.6	Short	381.6	Short	349.8	Vry. Short
Bumpers	Weak		Weak			
Parking Index	Easy		Easy		Easy	
Head/Leg Room (in.)	39.3/40.4	Cramped	39.3/40.4	Cramped	39.3/40.4	Cramped
Interior Space (cu. ft.)			50	Vry. Cramp.	50	Vry. Cramp.
Cargo Space (cu. ft.)	45.7	Large	45.7	Large	45.7	Large
Tow Rating (lbs.)	3500	Low	3500	Low	2000	Vry. Low

Nissan Maxima Intermediate

Other than a twentieth anniversary edition with a 227 hp engine, the Maxima moves into 2001 unchanged. The Maxima has grown inside and out to offer more space to its passengers and make for an even more comfortable ride. Tweaking the engine has increased horsepower on this 3-liter V6 from 190 to 222. The GXE and SE models still come standard with a 5-speed manual transmission, and the GLE has an automatic. ABS is standard now along with dual airbags, and there is now the option of side-impact airbags. The Maxima also has child seat tether anchors.

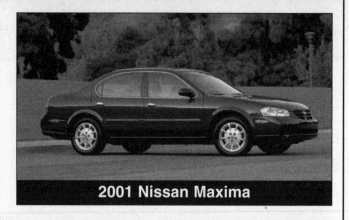
2001 Nissan Maxima

General Information

New for 2001: No major changes		**Year of Production:**	2
Twins: Inifiniti I30		**Seating:**	5
Where Made: Japan		**Theft Rating:**	Very High

Prices 2001

Model	Retail	Markup
GXE man.	$21,249	9%
GXE auto.	$22,949	11%
SE man.	$23,849	11%
GLE auto.	$26,449	11%

Competition 2001

Model	POOR				GOOD	pg.
Nissan Maxima			■			**360**
Dodge Intrepid				■		208
Honda Accord			■			242
Toyota Camry					■	420

'00 and '99 Models

Dual airbags are standard, and you'll have to pay extra for ABS and traction control. Side airbags are an option and optimal. The 3-liter V6 is powerful and quite fuel-efficient. You'll have the typical Nissan variety of trim levels and option packages, so shop carefully.

Price Ranges 2000–1999

GXE man.	$17,100-21,500
GXE auto.	$17,700-21,200
GLE auto.	$20,500-26,200
SE auto.	$19,900-23,500

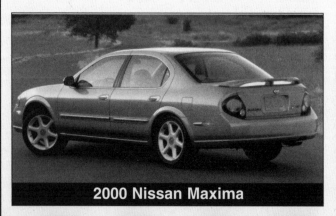
2000 Nissan Maxima

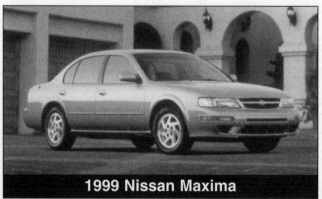
1999 Nissan Maxima

Nissan Maxima
Intermediate

	2001	2000	1999

RATINGS

	POOR → GOOD (2001)	POOR → GOOD (2000)	POOR → GOOD (1999)
Comparative Rating	5	5	5
Frontal Crash Tests*	8	8	7
Safety Features	8	6	6
Preventive Maintenance	5	5	5
Repair Costs	2	1	2
Warranty	7	4	4
Fuel Economy	5	4	4
Rollover (based on SSF, see pg. 25)	7	7	7
Complaints	5		9
Insurance Costs	1	1	1

SAFETY

	2001	2000	1999
Frontal Crash Tests	Good	Good	Good
Side Crash Tests	Very Good	No Govt Results	Good
Airbags	Dual (nextgen)[1]	Dual (nextgen)	Dual (nextgen)
Anti-Lock Brakes	4-Wheel	4-Wheel	4-Wheel (optional)
Day Running Lamps	None	None	None
Built-In Child Seats	None	None	None
Pretensioners	Standard	Standard	Standard

SPECIFICATIONS

	2001		2000		1999	
Fuel Economy (cty/hwy)	22/27	Average	22/28	Average	22/27	Average
Driving Range (miles)	453.25	Long	462.5	Vry. Long	453.25	Long
Bumpers	Weak		Weak		Strong	
Parking Index	Easy		Easy		Easy	
Head/Leg Room (in.)	40.1/43.9	Vry. Roomy	40.1/43.9	Vry. Roomy	40.1/43.9	Vry. Roomy
Interior Space (cu. ft.)	102	Roomy	102.5	Roomy	99.6	Average
Cargo Space (cu. ft.)	15	Small	15.1	Small	14.5	Small
Tow Rating (lbs.)	1000	Vry. Low	1000	Vry. Low	1000	Vry. Low

*To be tested in 2001; [1]Optional side/head airbags.

CAR BOOK 2001   361

This version of the Pathfinder debuted in 1996 and was an instant hit in the sport utility market. It enters 2001 with few changes. Dual airbags and 4-wheel ABS are standard. A 3.3-liter V6 is the only engine choice on the Pathfinder, which should give you good performance on and off the road. The base XE and mid-level SE models come with either manual or automatic transmission; the up-level LE comes only as an automatic.

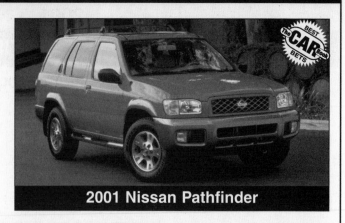

2001 Nissan Pathfinder

General Information

New for 2001: No major changes		**Year of Production:**	6
Twins: Infiniti QX4		**Seating:**	2
Where Made: Japan		**Theft Rating:**	Very High

Prices 2001

Model	Retail	Markup
XE auto. 2WD	$27,649	10%
SE auto. 2WD	$28,349	10%
XE auto. 4WD	$29,649	10%
SE auto. 4WD	$30,349	10%

Competition 2001

Model	POOR						GOOD		pg.
Nissan Pathfind.						■			**362**
Ford Explorer					■				224
Jeep Gr. Cher.		■							286
Merc-Bz M-Class		■							340

'00 and '99 Models

Handling, like the Jeep Cherokee's, is about as good as it gets for a utility vehicle. Comfort inside is good for four passengers, though the back seat will get tight with one more passenger. Typical of Nissan, there are plenty of options to choose from, so shop wisely.

Price Ranges 2000–1999

Model	Price
XE 2WD auto.	$20,300-26,400
SE 2WD auto.	$23,000-27,300
XE 4WD auto.	$22,400-28,400
SE 4WD auto.	$23,900-29,300

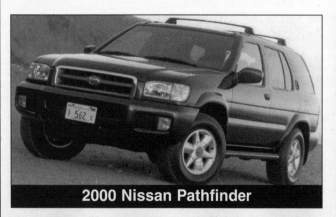

2000 Nissan Pathfinder

1999 Nissan Pathfinder

Nissan Pathfinder — Mid-Size Sport Utility

	2001	2000	1999
RATINGS	POOR — GOOD	POOR — GOOD	POOR — GOOD
Comparative Rating	6	4	4
Frontal Crash Tests	9	9	9
Safety Features	8	6	6
Preventive Maintenance	4	3	4
Repair Costs	3	3	2
Warranty	7	4	4
Fuel Economy	2	2	2
Rollover (based on SSF; see pg. 30)	3	3	4
Complaints	9	9	9
Insurance Costs	5	5	5

SAFETY

	2001	2000	1999
Frontal Crash Tests	Very Good	Very Good	Very Good
Side Crash Tests	Very Good	Very Good	Very Good
Airbags	Dual (nextgen)	Dual (nextgen)	Dual (nextgen)
Anti-Lock Brakes	4-Wheel	4-Wheel	4-Wheel
Day Running Lamps	None	None	None
Built-In Child Seats	None	None	None
Pretensioners	Standard	Standard	Standard

SPECIFICATIONS

	2001		2000		1999	
Fuel Economy (cty/hwy)	15/19	Vry. Poor	15/19	Vry. Poor	16/18	Vry. Poor
Driving Range (miles)	358.7	Vry. Short	358.7	Vry. Short	358.7	Vry. Short
Bumpers	Weak		Weak			
Parking Index	Average		Average		Average	
Head/Leg Room (in.)	39.5/41.7	Average	39.5/41.7	Average	39.5/41.7	Average
Interior Space (cu. ft.)	92.9	Cramped	92.9	Cramped	92.9	Cramped
Cargo Space (cu. ft.)	38	Large	38	Large	85	Vry. Large
Tow Rating (lbs.)	3500	Low	3500	Low	3500	Low

Nissan Quest   Minivan

The Quest was totally revamped in 1999 so it comes into 2001 unchanged. A new exterior, a roomier interior, and the popular driver-side sliding door were among the dramatic changes. The new engine is a 3.3-liter V6, with 170 hp; acceleration and power are good with poor fuel economy. You'll find the ride and handling are good by minivan standards. On the interior, seating is comfortable, and the Quest offers integrated child safety seats, which is a great option for parents.

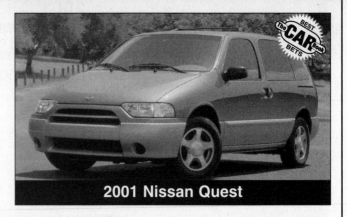
2001 Nissan Quest

General Information

New for 2001: No major changes	**Year of Production:** 9
Twins: Mercury Villager	**Seating:** 7
Where Made: U.S.	**Theft Rating:**

Prices 2001

Model	Retail	Markup
GXE	$22,260	10%
SE	$24,400	11%
GLE	$26,400	11%

Competition 2001

Model	POOR				GOOD	pg.
Nissan Quest					■	**364**
Chev. Venture			■			184
Honda Odyssey		■				250
Toyota Sienna		■				438

'00 and '99 Models

With Nissan's flexible seating system, you should be able to arrange the seating to suit most any purpose. The Quest competes well with the industry leaders like the Windstar, Venture, Silhouette, and, Montana.

Price Ranges 2000–1999

GXE	$19,500-22,200
SE	$20,600-24,400
GLE	$21,200-26,400

2000 Nissan Quest

1999 Nissan Quest

Nissan Quest

Minivan

	2001	2000	1999

RATINGS

	2001 (POOR–GOOD)	2000 (POOR–GOOD)	1999 (POOR–GOOD)
Comparative Rating	9	7	6
Frontal Crash Tests	10	7	7
Safety Features	10	6	7
Preventive Maintenance	1	9	9
Repair Costs	3	6	5
Warranty	9	4	4
Fuel Economy	4	3	3
Rollover (based on SSF, see pg. 25)	8	6	6
Complaints	5	6	3
Insurance Costs	10	10	10

SAFETY

	2001	2000	1999
Frontal Crash Tests	Average	Good	Good
Side Crash Tests	Very Good	No Govt Results	No Govt Results
Airbags	Dual (nextgen)	Dual (nextgen)	Dual (nextgen)
Anti-Lock Brakes	4-Wheel	4-Wheel	4-Wheel
Day Running Lamps	None	None	None
Built-In Child Seats	Optional	None	Optional
Pretensioners	Standard	Standard	Standard

SPECIFICATIONS

	2001		2000		1999	
Fuel Economy (cty/hwy)	17/23	Poor	17/24	Poor	17/24	Poor
Driving Range (miles)	400	Average	410	Average	410	Average
Bumpers	Weak		Weak			
Parking Index	Vry. Hard		Vry. Hard		Vry. Hard	
Head/Leg Room (in.)	39.7/39.9	Vry. Cramp.	39.7/39.9	Vry. Cramp.	39.7/39.9	Vry. Cramp.
Interior Space (cu. ft.)	135.6	Vry. Roomy	135.6	Vry. Roomy	135.6	Vry. Roomy
Cargo Space (cu. ft.)	125	Vry. Large	125	Vry. Large	125	Vry. Large
Tow Rating (lbs.)	3500	Low	3500	Low	3500	Low

All-new last year, the Sentra enters 2001 unchanged. This year there are four trim levels and two engine choices and two new colors. To get additional options, you'll have to move up the trim level ladder. Some models have a split rear seat, and the door has a place for a water bottle. Front seat side impact airbags are optional as is the automatic transmission. The CA (clean air) model has a very efficient engine and a special radiator that actually converts ozone into oxygen.

2001 Nissan Sentra

General Information

New for 2001: No major changes		**Year of Production:**	2
Twins:		**Seating:**	5
Where Made: Mexico		**Theft Rating:**	Average

Prices 2001

Model	Retail	Markup
XE man.	$11,650	6%
XE auto.	$12,400	6%
SE man.	$14,900	9%
SE auto.	$15,700	9%

Competition 2001

Model	POOR			GOOD	pg.
Nissan Sentra					366
Ford Focus				▮	228
Subaru Impreza				▮	404
Saturn SL				▮	400

'00 and '99 Models

A facelift for the '99 Sentra gave it new headlights and grille. You have five trim levels to choose from: base, XE, GXE, GLE, and the sporty SE. The 1.6-liter 4-cylinder engine, standard on all the trim levels except SE, is only adequate but gets good gas mileage. It was all-new for 2000 and offered a choice of 1.8-liter and 2.0-liter engines in three trim levels: XE, GXE, and SE.

Price Ranges 2000–1999

XE man.	$10,100-11,200
XE auto.	$10,600-11,600
SE man.	$14,400-15,600
SE auto.	$12,500-14,900

2000 Nissan Sentra

1999 Nissan Sentra

Nissan Sentra — Subcompact

	2001	2000	1999

RATINGS

	POOR — GOOD	POOR — GOOD	POOR — GOOD
Comparative Rating			5
Frontal Crash Tests			6
Safety Features	6	6	6
Preventive Maintenance	5	5	5
Repair Costs	6	6	6
Warranty	7	4	4
Fuel Economy	8	7	7
Rollover (based on SSF; see pg. 30)	7	7	7
Complaints	5		9
Insurance Costs	5	1	1

SAFETY

	2001	2000	1999
Frontal Crash Tests	To Be Tested	No Govt Results	Average
Side Crash Tests	No Govt Results	No Govt Results	Average
Airbags	Dual (nextgen)	Dual (nextgen)	Dual (nextgen)
Anti-Lock Brakes	4-Wheel (optional)	4-Wheel (optional)	4-Wheel (optional)
Day Running Lamps	None	None	None
Built-In Child Seats	None	None	None
Pretensioners	Standard	Standard	Standard

SPECIFICATIONS

	2001		2000		1999	
Fuel Economy (cty/hwy)	27/35	Good	29/39	Good	29/39	Good
Driving Range (miles)	409.2	Average	448.8	Long	448.8	Long
Bumpers	Weak		Weak		Strong	
Parking Index	Vry. Easy		Vry. Easy		Vry. Easy	
Head/Leg Room (in.)	39.1/42.3	Average	39.1/42.3	Average	39.1/42.3	Average
Interior Space (cu. ft.)	88	Cramped	87.2	Cramped	87.2	Cramped
Cargo Space (cu. ft.)	12	Vry. Small	10.7	Vry. Small	10.7	Vry. Small
Tow Rating (lbs.)	1000	Vry. Low	1000	Vry. Low	1000	Vry. Low

Introduced last year, the Xterra is unchanged for 2001. The Xterra is built on the Frontier's wheelbase and truck-style chassis. It is larger than the Cherokee and RAV4. It comes with ceiling hooks, floor tie-downs, and an interior bike rack. The rear seats are higher, which requires a raised roofline over the back of the vehicle. You can get a removable front accessory basket for wet or messy gear and an optional first aid kit. There are five engine/drive/trim configurations and standard 4-wheel ABS.

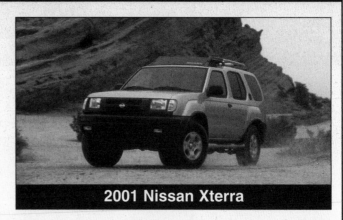

2001 Nissan Xterra

General Information

New for 2001: No major changes		**Year of Production:**	2
Twins:		**Seating:**	6
Where Made: U.S.		**Theft Rating:**	

Prices 2001

Model	Retail	Markup
XE man. 2WD	$17,999	2%
XE auto. 2WD	$19,050	2%
XE man. 4WD	$21,050	8%
XE auto. 4WD	$22,050	8%

Competition 2001

Model	POOR				GOOD	pg.
Nissan Xterra				■		**368**
Ford Explorer				■		224
Jeep Cherokee			■			284
Isuzu Rodeo		■				278

'00 and '99 Models

Strong enough for off-roading yet affordable, Nissan is aiming at adventure types with this utility vehicle. A 2.4-liter 4-cylinder comes standard and a 3.3-liter V6 offers more power. A choice of 5-speed manual or 4-speed automatic transmission is available. Rear-wheel or part-time 4-wheel drive are possible choices, and storage is ample.

Price Ranges 2000–1999

XE 2WD auto.	$18,400-18,500
XE 4WD auto.	$20,400-20,500

2000 Nissan Xterra

MODEL WAS NOT PRODUCED THIS YEAR

1999 Model

Nissan Xterra — Mid-Size Sport Utility

	2001	2000	1999

RATINGS

	2001 POOR → GOOD	2000 POOR → GOOD	1999 POOR → GOOD
Comparative Rating	5	4	
Frontal Crash Tests	9	9	
Safety Features	6	6	
Preventive Maintenance		5	
Repair Costs			
Warranty	7	4	
Fuel Economy	2	2	
Rollover (based on SSF; see pg. 30)	3	3	
Complaints	5		
Insurance Costs	5	5	

SAFETY

	2001	2000	1999
Frontal Crash Tests	Very Good	Very Good	
Side Crash Tests	Very Good	No Govt Results	
Airbags	Dual	Dual	
Anti-Lock Brakes	4-Wheel	4-Wheel	
Day Running Lamps	None	None	
Built-In Child Seats	None	None	
Pretensioners	Standard	Standard	

SPECIFICATIONS

	2001		2000		1999
Fuel Economy (cty/hwy)	15/19	Vry. Poor	16/18	Vry. Poor	
Driving Range (miles)	329.8	Vry. Short	329.8	Vry. Short	
Bumpers					
Parking Index	Easy		Easy		
Head/Leg Room (in.)	38.6/41.4	Cramped	38.6/41.4	Cramped	
Interior Space (cu. ft.)			50.2	Vry. Cramp.	
Cargo Space (cu. ft.)	44.5	Large	44.5	Large	
Tow Rating (lbs.)					

Unchanged for 2001, the Alero comes in three trim levels. The GX and the standard GL run on a 2.4-liter 4-cylinder engine, and the GLS uses a 3.4-liter V6. All have a 4-speed automatic transmission. Safety features standard on all models include de-powered airbags for front occupants, ABS, and traction control. Also available for all models are rear window defoggers, a theft deterrent system, and daytime running lamps. The more luxurious GLS offers leather interior, a CD player, remote keyless entry, and front fog lights as standard features.

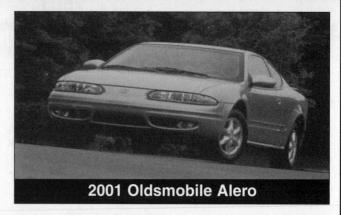

2001 Oldsmobile Alero

General Information

New for 2001: No major changes	**Year of Production:**	3
Twins: Pontiac Grand Am	**Seating:**	5
Where Made: U.S.	**Theft Rating:**	Very High

Prices 2001

Model	Retail	Markup
GX Sedan	$17,210	7%
GL1 Coupe	$18,620	9%
GL2 Sedan	$19,525	9%
GLS Coupe	$22,190	10%

Competition 2001

Model	POOR				GOOD		pg.
Olds Alero				■			**370**
VW Jetta					■		450
Pontiac Sunfire			■				390
Toyota Corolla					■		424

'00 and '99 Models

The all-new for 1999 Alero was Oldsmobile's answer to the Honda Accord. With great crash test scores, the Alero competes very well with the Taurus/Accord/Camry trio.

Price Ranges 2000–1999

GX Sedan	$12,300-14,000
GL Sedan	$13,200-15,100
GL Sedan V6	$13,600-15,600
GLS	$14,700-21,400

2000 Oldsmobile Alero

1999 Oldsmobile Alero

Oldsmobile Alero — Compact

	2001	2000	1999

RATINGS

	POOR — GOOD	POOR — GOOD	POOR — GOOD
Comparative Rating	5	5	7
Frontal Crash Tests	10	9	10
Safety Features	6	6	6
Preventive Maintenance	6	6	6
Repair Costs	5	4	6
Warranty	3	3	3
Fuel Economy	5	5	5
Rollover (based on SSF; see pg. 30)	8	8	8
Complaints	2	2	4
Insurance Costs	5	5	5

SAFETY

	2001	2000	1999
Frontal Crash Tests	Very Good	Very Good	Very Good
Side Crash Tests	Average	Average	Average
Airbags	Dual (nextgen)	Dual (nextgen)	Dual (nextgen)
Anti-Lock Brakes	4-Wheel	4-Wheel	4-Wheel
Day Running Lamps	Standard	Standard	Standard
Built-In Child Seats	None	None	None
Pretensioners	None	None	None

SPECIFICATIONS

	2001		2000		1999	
Fuel Economy (cty/hwy)	21/29	Average	21/29	Average	21/29	Average
Driving Range (miles)	375	Short	375	Short	375	Short
Bumpers	Weak		Weak			
Parking Index	Easy		Easy		Easy	
Head/Leg Room (in.)	38.2/42.1	Cramped	38.2/42.1	Cramped	38.2/42.1	Cramped
Interior Space (cu. ft.)	91	Cramped	92.6	Cramped	92.6	Cramped
Cargo Space (cu. ft.)	14	Small	14.6	Small	14.6	Small
Tow Rating (lbs.)						

All-new after a brief hiatus, the Aurora is Olds' flagship vehicle. With OnStar hardware standard, you can get your email, stock quotes, and help, all on a hands-free basis. Safety-wise, even the rear center passenger gets a shoulder belt, and side airbags are standard. There are two engine choices, V6 and V8, and a traction control system is available. Optional are automatic wipers, which sense when it is raining and how heavy the rain is for proper speed. Buying the V8 version gets you the most options, but leather seats and walnut trim are standard.

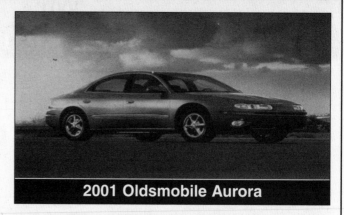

2001 Oldsmobile Aurora

General Information

New for 2001: All-new		**Year of Production:**	1
Twins: Cadillac Seville, Pontiac Bonneville, Buick LeSabre		**Seating:**	5
Where Made: U.S.		**Theft Rating:**	Very Low

Prices 2001

Model	Retail	Markup
3.5L Sedan	$30,470	9%
4.0L Sedan	$34,650	9%

Competition 2001

Model	POOR				GOOD	pg.
Olds Aurora				■		**372**
Ford Cr. Victoria					■	216
Audi A8					■	132
Lincoln Town Car					■	322

'00 and '99 Models

The 1999 model carried into 2000 with no changes. The '99 was a bigger but less refined version of the new model. Handling and performance of the older version, typical for larger sedans, are not as tight as the new model. The trunk was bigger than in the new model as were the gas bills.

Price Ranges 2000–1999

4 dr. Sedan	$23-24,000

PHOTO NOT AVAILABLE

2000 Model

PHOTO NOT AVAILABLE

1999 Model

Oldsmobile Aurora — Large

	2001	2000	1999

RATINGS

	2001 (POOR–GOOD)	2000 (POOR–GOOD)	1999 (POOR–GOOD)
Comparative Rating	7	7	7
Frontal Crash Tests*	10	5	5
Safety Features	6	7	7
Preventive Maintenance	6	5	5
Repair Costs	6	5	5
Warranty	3	7	7
Fuel Economy	5	2	2
Rollover (based on SSF, see pg. 25)	8	8	8
Complaints	5	7	7
Insurance Costs	10	10	10

SAFETY

	2001	2000	1999
Frontal Crash Tests	Very Good	Average	Average
Side Crash Tests	No Govt Results	No Govt Results	No Govt Results
Airbags	Dual	Dual	Dual
Anti-Lock Brakes	4-Wheel	4-Wheel	4-Wheel
Day Running Lamps	Standard	Standard	Standard
Built-In Child Seats	None	None	None
Pretensioners	None	None	None

SPECIFICATIONS

	2001		2000		1999	
Fuel Economy (cty/hwy)	19/28	Poor	17/26	Poor	17/26	Poor
Driving Range (miles)	434.75	Long	430	Long	430	Long
Bumpers						
Parking Index			Vry. Hard		Vry. Hard	
Head/Leg Room (in.)	38.6/42.5	Average	38.4/42.6	Average	38.4/42.6	Average
Interior Space (cu. ft.)	104	Roomy	102	Roomy	102	Roomy
Cargo Space (cu. ft.)	15	Small	16.1	Small	16.1	Small
Tow Rating (lbs.)			1000	Vry. Low	1000	Vry. Low

*To be tested in 2001.

Oldsmobile Bravada

Mid-Size Sport Utility

The Bravada carries over from 2001 unchanged. Oldsmobile's placeholder in the sport utility parade is the twin of the Chevrolet Blazer and the GMC Jimmy. The Bravada is designed to appeal to luxury sedan owners looking for the off-road feel. Dual airbags, 4-wheel ABS, and a power memory seat are standard. For cold weather climates you can get an optional engine block heater. Other options include OnStar and a sunroof.

2001 Oldsmobile Bravada

General Information

New for 2001: All-new	**Year of Production:**	1
Twins: Chevrolet Blazer, GMC Jimmy	**Seating:**	5
Where Made: U.S.	**Theft Rating:**	Average

Prices 2001

Model	Retail	Markup
SUV 4WD	$31,760	10%

Competition 2001

Model	POOR				GOOD		pg.
Olds Bravada	■						**374**
Ford Explorer				■			224
Infiniti QX4						■	276
Merc-Bz M-Class		■					340

'00 and '99 Models

Like the Blazer and Jimmy, the Bravada is powered by a 4.3-liter V6 engine that produces adequate power for this mid-sized sport utility. The Bravada only comes in a 4-door model, designed to seat five. The optional towing package goes a long way toward tailoring the ride and handling to the customer's preference.

Price Ranges 2000–1999

SUV 4WD	$21,700-23,100

2000 Oldsmobile Bravada

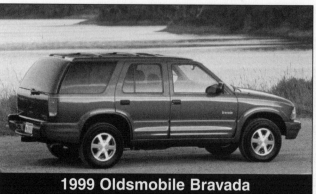

1999 Oldsmobile Bravada

Oldsmobile Bravada — Mid-Size Sport Utility

RATINGS

	2001 (POOR–GOOD)	2000 (POOR–GOOD)	1999 (POOR–GOOD)
Comparative Rating	2	3	2
Frontal Crash Tests	4	5	4
Safety Features	6	6	6
Preventive Maintenance	5	4	5
Repair Costs	4	6	5
Warranty	3	3	3
Fuel Economy	2	2	2
Rollover (based on SSF; see pg. 30)	4		4
Complaints		5	3
Insurance Costs	10	10	10

SAFETY

	2001	2000	1999
Frontal Crash Tests	Poor	Poor	Poor
Side Crash Tests	No Govt Results	Very Good	Very Good
Airbags	Dual	Dual (nextgen)	Dual (nextgen)
Anti-Lock Brakes	4-Wheel	4-Wheel	4-Wheel
Day Running Lamps	Standard	Standard	Standard
Built-In Child Seats	None	None	None
Pretensioners	None	None	None

SPECIFICATIONS

	2001		2000		1999	
Fuel Economy (cty/hwy)	15/20	Vry. Poor	16/20	Vry. Poor	16/20	Vry. Poor
Driving Range (miles)	325.5	Vry. Short	334.8	Vry. Short	334.8	Vry. Short
Bumpers			Weak			
Parking Index	Hard		Hard		Hard	
Head/Leg Room (in.)	39.6/42.4	Roomy	39.6/42.4	Roomy	39.6/42.4	Roomy
Interior Space (cu. ft.)						
Cargo Space (cu. ft.)	37.3	Average	37.3	Average	37.3	Average
Tow Rating (lbs.)	5000	Average	5000	Average	5000	Average

Oldsmobile Intrigue — Intermediate

Other than minor appearance changes, the Intrigue, designed to win over buyers who like the Toyota Camry, Honda Accord, and Nissan Maxima, is unchanged for 2001. A replacement for the geriatric Cutlass Supreme, the Intrigue shares a platform with the Buick Regal and Pontiac Grand Prix. You'll find a 3.8-liter V6 engine under the hood, which provides adequate power. Interior space is good, and trunk space is ample.

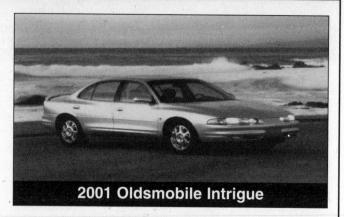

2001 Oldsmobile Intrigue

General Information

New for 2001: No major changes	**Year of Production:** 4
Twins: Century, Regal, Grand Prix	**Seating:** 5
Where Made: U.S.	**Theft Rating:** Very Low

Prices 2001

Model	Retail	Markup
GX	$22,390	9%
GL	$24,150	9%
GLS	$26,520	9%

Competition 2001

Model	POOR					GOOD	pg.
Olds Intrigue			■				**376**
Chrys. Concorde				■			188
Ford Taurus						■	234
Lexus ES300						■	302

'00 and '99 Models

Consider the Autobahn package which includes bigger tires, better steering, and a higher performance brake system. The Intrigue was an average performer on frontal crash tests, but very poor on side crash tests.

Price Ranges 2000–1999

GX	$14,100-16,800
GL	$14,900-18,100
GLS	$16,000-25,700

2000 Oldsmobile Intrigue

1999 Oldsmobile Intrigue

Oldsmobile Intrigue — Intermediate

	2001	2000	1999
RATINGS	POOR — GOOD	POOR — GOOD	POOR — GOOD
Comparative Rating	4	5	8
Frontal Crash Tests	6	6	5
Safety Features	6	6	6
Preventive Maintenance	6	5	6
Repair Costs	6	6	10
Warranty	3	3	3
Fuel Economy	5	4	4
Rollover (based on SSF; see pg. 30)	8	8	8
Complaints	2	2	5
Insurance Costs	10	10	10

SAFETY

	2001	2000	1999
Frontal Crash Tests	Average	Average	Average
Side Crash Tests	Very Poor	Very Poor	Very Poor
Airbags	Dual (nextgen)	Dual (nextgen)	Dual (nextgen)
Anti-Lock Brakes	4-Wheel	4-Wheel	4-Wheel
Day Running Lamps	Standard	Standard	Standard
Built-In Child Seats	None	None	None
Pretensioners	None	None	None

SPECIFICATIONS

	2001		2000		1999	
Fuel Economy (cty/hwy)	19/28	Poor	19/28	Poor	19/27	Poor
Driving Range (miles)	399.5	Average	399.5	Average	391	Short
Bumpers	Strong		Strong		Strong	
Parking Index					Average	
Head/Leg Room (in.)	39.3/42.4	Average	39.3/42.4	Average	39.3/42.4	Average
Interior Space (cu. ft.)	102	Roomy			101	Average
Cargo Space (cu. ft.)	17	Average			16.4	Small
Tow Rating (lbs.)					1000	Vry. Low

Oldsmobile Silhouette

Minivan

This is the upscale version of the GM minivan and didn't change in 2001. The Premier Edition which offers a TV screen, a video player, CD player, and four headphones leads the way in travel entertainment. The Silhouette has heated outside mirrors, an improved anti-theft system, and a more powerful engine. Side airbags and ABS are standard. There are four models available: the GL, GS, GLS, and the Premiere. The engine is a 3.4-liter V6 which should provide good acceleration. There are many different seating arrangements.

2001 Oldsmobile Silhouette

General Information

New for 2001: No major changes	**Year of Production:** 5
Twins: Chev. Venture, Pont. Montana	**Seating:** 7-8
Where Made: U.S.	**Theft Rating:** Very Low

Prices 2001

Model	Retail	Markup
GL	$26,290	10%
GLS	$30,190	10%
Premiere	$32,990	10%

Competition 2001

Model	POOR				GOOD		pg.
Olds Silhouette				■			**378**
Honda Odyssey			■				250
Ford Windstar						■	236
Toyota Sienna			■				438

'00 and '99 Models

Dual airbags are de-powered on the '98s and all future models. A handy option is the power assist right-side sliding door. The new Silhouette competes well with the upscale minivan market.

Price Ranges 2000–1999

GL	$20,000-21,200
GLS	$22,300-24,000
Premiere	$24,400-31,600

2000 Oldsmobile Silhouette

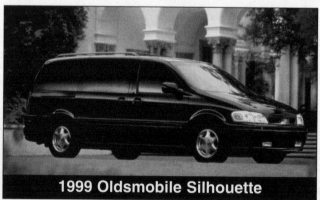

1999 Oldsmobile Silhouette

Oldsmobile Silhouette — Minivan

	2001	2000	1999

RATINGS

	POOR — GOOD (2001)	POOR — GOOD (2000)	POOR — GOOD (1999)
Comparative Rating	6	6	5
Frontal Crash Tests*	7	7	7
Safety Features	9	10	10
Preventive Maintenance	8	8	7
Repair Costs	5	5	5
Warranty	3	3	3
Fuel Economy	4	3	3
Rollover (based on SSF, see pg. 25)	5	5	5
Complaints	3	3	2
Insurance Costs	10	10	10

SAFETY

	2001	2000	1999
Frontal Crash Tests	Good	Good	Good
Side Crash Tests	Very Good	Very Good	Very Good
Airbags	Dual/Side (nextgen)	Dual/Side (nextgen)	Dual/Side (nextgen)
Anti-Lock Brakes	4-Wheel	4-Wheel	4-Wheel
Day Running Lamps	Standard	Standard	Standard
Built-In Child Seats	Optional	Optional	Optional
Pretensioners	Standard	Standard	Standard

SPECIFICATIONS

	2001		2000		1999	
Fuel Economy (cty/hwy)	19/26	Poor	18/25	Poor	18/25	Poor
Driving Range (miles)	450	Long	430	Long	430	Long
Bumpers	Weak		Weak		Weak	
Parking Index	Hard		Hard		Hard	
Head/Leg Room (in.)	39.9/39.9	Cramped	39.9/39.9	Cramped	39.9/39.9	Cramped
Interior Space (cu. ft.)						
Cargo Space (cu. ft.)						
Tow Rating (lbs.)	2000	Vry. Low	2000	Vry. Low	2000	Vry. Low

*To be tested in 2001.

Pontiac Aztek

This all-new vehicle is a high risk design; either you love it or you don't! There is a wide variety of seating configurations, including fold-down captain's seats in the second row. The fold-down tailgate has molded-in seating and cup holders for tailgating, not driving! The Aztek GT has a "heads up display" that shows speed, radio channel and other items at eye level. There are optional storage systems for the back that can be configured in up to 22 different ways and a tent system that attaches to the rear.

2001 Pontiac Aztek

General Information

New for 2001: All-new		**Year of Production:**	1
Twins:		**Seating:**	5
Where Made: Canada		**Theft Rating:**	

Prices 2001

Model	Retail	Markup
Base	$21,450	9%
GT Sport	$24,450	9%

Competition 2001

Model	POOR					GOOD	pg.
Pontiac Aztek							**380**
Jeep Cherokee			■				284
Chev. Blazer			■				162
Nissan Xterra				■			368

'00 and '99 Models

Price Ranges 2000–1999

MODEL WAS NOT PRODUCED THIS YEAR

2000 Model

MODEL WAS NOT PRODUCED THIS YEAR

1999 Model

	2001	2000	1999

RATINGS

	POOR — GOOD	POOR — GOOD	POOR — GOOD
Comparative Rating			
Frontal Crash Tests			
Safety Features	6		
Preventive Maintenance			
Repair Costs			
Warranty	2		
Fuel Economy	4		
Rollover (based on SSF; see pg. 30)	6		
Complaints	5		
Insurance Costs	5		

SAFETY

	2001		
Frontal Crash Tests	To Be Tested		
Side Crash Tests	No Govt Results		
Airbags	Dual		
Anti-Lock Brakes	Standard		
Day Running Lamps	Standard		
Built-In Child Seats	None		
Pretensioners	None		

SPECIFICATIONS

	2001		
Fuel Economy (cty/hwy)	19/26	Poor	
Driving Range (miles)	405	Average	
Bumpers	Strong		
Parking Index	Average		
Head/Leg Room (in.)	39.7/40.5	Cramped	
Interior Space (cu. ft.)	105.1	Roomy	
Cargo Space (cu. ft.)	45.4	Large	
Tow Rating (lbs.)	3500	Low	

The 2001 Bonneville, unchanged, carries forward some aggressive styling and safety features. ABS, daytime running lamps and dual airbags are still standard, and driver and front seat passenger side airbags are now standard. Standard on the SE and SLE models is a 3.8-liter V6, and the SSEi model has a supercharged version of this engine with 35 more horsepower. All have standard automatic transmission.

2001 Pontiac Bonneville

General Information

New for 2001: No major changes	Year of Production:	2
Twins: Buick LeSabre, Oldsmobile Aurora, Cadillac Seville	Seating:	5
Where Made: U.S.	Theft Rating:	Very Low

Prices 2001

Model	Retail	Markup
SE	$25,080	9%
SLE	$28,050	9%
SSEi	$32,420	9%

Competition 2001

Model	POOR					GOOD	pg.
Pont. Bonneville				■			**382**
Infiniti I30					■		272
Ford Cr. Victoria						■	216
Audi A8						■	132

'00 and '99 Models

For 1999-2000, the base model is the SE; the SSE is more refined. The SLE is a sporty package available on the SE. Traction control is available on the SSE, and a supercharged engine is offered on both the SE and SSE. The Bonneville is a viable alternative to the Japanese luxury sports sedans.

Price Ranges 2000–1999

SE	$16,100-23,700
SLE	$27,300-27,400
SSEi	$20,900-31,600

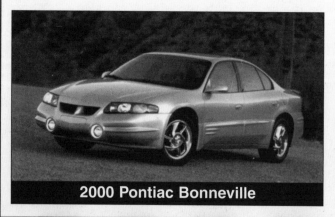

2000 Pontiac Bonneville

1999 Pontiac Bonneville

Pontiac Bonneville — Large

	2001	2000	1999
RATINGS (POOR → GOOD)			
Comparative Rating	6	9	7
Frontal Crash Tests*	10	10	7
Safety Features	7	8	6
Preventive Maintenance	6	6	6
Repair Costs	4	7	9
Warranty	2	2	2
Fuel Economy	5	4	4
Rollover (based on SSF, see pg. 25)	8	8	8
Complaints	5		4
Insurance Costs	10	10	10

SAFETY

	2001	2000	1999
Frontal Crash Tests	Very Good	Very Good	Good
Side Crash Tests	No Govt Results	No Govt Results	Poor
Airbags	Dual/Side	Dual/Side	Dual
Anti-Lock Brakes	4-Wheel	4-Wheel	4-Wheel
Day Running Lamps	Standard	Standard	Standard
Built-In Child Seats	None	None	None
Pretensioners	None	None	None

SPECIFICATIONS

	2001		2000		1999	
Fuel Economy (cty/hwy)	19/30	Average	19/30	Average	19/28	Poor
Driving Range (miles)	453.25	Long	453.25	Long	423	Long
Bumpers	Strong		Strong		Strong	
Parking Index	Vry. Hard		Vry. Hard		Vry. Hard	
Head/Leg Room (in.)	38.7/42.6	Average	38.7/42.6	Average	39.2/42.6	Average
Interior Space (cu. ft.)	104	Roomy	121.8	Vry. Roomy	126.8	Vry. Roomy
Cargo Space (cu. ft.)	18	Average	18	Average	18	Average
Tow Rating (lbs.)	1000	Vry. Low	1000	Vry. Low	1000	Vry. Low

*To be tested in 2001.

Pontiac Grand Am Compact

The Grand Am, which received an overhaul in 1999, gets no major changes for 2001. The wider wheelbase added in 1999 gave the Grand Am a more solid appearance. A stronger 170 horsepower 3.4-liter V6 engine is standard on the SE2 and GT models. The standard 2.4-liter twin cam engine for the SE and SE1 makes the Grand Am fun to drive, though fuel economy is poor.

2001 Pontiac Grand Am

General Information

New for 2001: No major changes		**Year of Production:**	3
Twins: Oldsmobile Alero, Chevrolet Malibu		**Seating:**	5
Where Made: U.S.		**Theft Rating:**	Average

Prices 2001

Model	Retail	Markup
SE Coupe	$16,140	9%
SE1 Sedan	$18,170	9%
GT Coupe	$20,240	9%
GT1 Sedan	$21,810	9%

Competition 2001

Model	POOR					GOOD	pg.
Pontiac Gr. Am		■					**384**
Pontiac Sunfire				■			390
Mitsu. Galant		■					348
Olds Alero			■				370

'00 and '99 Models

In '99, the Grand Am got a new cockpit design, redesigned bucket seats, four-wheel fully independent suspension, enhanced traction system, fog lamps, and standard ABS. Dual airbags and daytime running lamps are standard, and you can find height adjustable safety belts, which should improve comfort and safety.

Price Ranges 2000–1999

SE	$12,700-14,600
SE V6	$13,000-15,000
GT Sedan	$14,400-19,900
GT Coupe	$14,600-19,600

2000 Pontiac Grand Am

1999 Pontiac Grand Am

	2001	2000	1999

RATINGS

	POOR · · · GOOD	POOR · · · GOOD	POOR · · · GOOD
Comparative Rating	3	5	6
Frontal Crash Tests	9	9	9
Safety Features	6	6	6
Preventive Maintenance	6	6	6
Repair Costs	5	4	5
Warranty	2	2	2
Fuel Economy	5	5	5
Rollover (based on SSF; see pg. 30)	7	7	7
Complaints	2	2	3
Insurance Costs	1	5	5

SAFETY

Frontal Crash Tests	Very Good	Very Good	Very Good
Side Crash Tests	Average	Average	Average
Airbags	Dual (nextgen)	Dual (nextgen)	Dual (nextgen)
Anti-Lock Brakes	4-Wheel	4-Wheel	4-Wheel
Day Running Lamps	Standard	Standard	Standard
Built-In Child Seats	None	None	None
Pretensioners	None	None	None

SPECIFICATIONS

Fuel Economy (cty/hwy)	21/29 Average	22/30 Average	22/30 Average
Driving Range (miles)	357.5 Vry. Short	371.8 Short	395.2 Short
Bumpers	Strong	Strong	
Parking Index	Hard	Hard	Hard
Head/Leg Room (in.)	38.3/42.1 Cramped	38.3/42.1 Cramped	38.3/42.1 Cramped
Interior Space (cu. ft.)	90 Cramped	107.3 Roomy	107.3 Roomy
Cargo Space (cu. ft.)	13 Vry. Small	14.3 Small	14.3 Small
Tow Rating (lbs.)			

No major changes for the Grand Prix in 2001. A theft-deterrent system, CD player, and the optional OnStar communications system are some of the perks offered this year. The Grand Prix's dual airbags helped it perform well on the government's frontal crash tests. The Grand Prix is available in both coupe and sedan body styles with two trim levels: the base SE or the up-level GT.

2001 Pontiac Grand Prix

General Information

New for 2001: No major changes	**Year of Production:**	5
Twins: Chevrolet Impala/Monte Carlo	**Seating:**	5
Where Made: U.S.	**Theft Rating:**	Average

Prices 2001

Model	Retail	Markup
GT Coupe	$21,865	9%
GT Sedan	$22,015	9%
GTP Coupe	$25,355	9%
GTP Sedan	$25,535	9%

Competition 2001

Model	POOR					GOOD	pg.
Pontiac Gr. Prix					■		**386**
Dodge Intrepid				■			208
Ford Taurus						■	234
Nissan Altima						■	356

'00 and '99 Models

The standard 3.8-liter V6 engine got a 5 hp boost to make it 200 hp, which should be ample power for this car, though you can choose a supercharged version of the same engine and get 240 hp.

Price Ranges 2000–1999

GT Coupe	$16,300-17,900
GT Sedan	$16,300-17,900
GTP Coupe	$17,400-24,200
GTP Sedan	$17,400-24,200

2000 Pontiac Grand Prix

1999 Pontiac Grand Prix

Pontiac Grand Prix — Intermediate

	2001	2000	1999
RATINGS (POOR → GOOD)			
Comparative Rating	7	7	9
Frontal Crash Tests*	8	8	8
Safety Features	6	6	7
Preventive Maintenance	6	5	6
Repair Costs	9	5	7
Warranty	2	2	2
Fuel Economy	5	4	4
Rollover (based on SSF, see pg. 25)	8	8	8
Complaints	5	6	8
Insurance Costs	10	10	10

SAFETY

	2001	2000	1999
Frontal Crash Tests	Good	Good	Good
Side Crash Tests	No Govt Results	No Govt Results	No Govt Results
Airbags	Dual	Dual	Dual
Anti-Lock Brakes	4-Wheel	4-Wheel	4-Wheel
Day Running Lamps	Standard	Standard	Standard
Built-In Child Seats	None	None	Optional
Pretensioners	None	None	None

SPECIFICATIONS

	2001		2000		1999	
Fuel Economy (cty/hwy)	20/29	Average	20/29	Average	20/29	Average
Driving Range (miles)	441	Long	441	Long	441	Long
Bumpers	Strong		Strong		Strong	
Parking Index	Hard		Hard		Hard	
Head/Leg Room (in.)	38.3/42.4	Cramped	38.3/42.4	Cramped	38.3/42.4	Cramped
Interior Space (cu. ft.)	99	Average	115	Vry. Roomy	115	Vry. Roomy
Cargo Space (cu. ft.)	16	Small	16	Small	16	Small
Tow Rating (lbs.)	1000	Vry. Low	1000	Vry. Low	1000	Vry. Low

*To be tested in 2001.

Pontiac Montana | Minivan

The Montana is a twin of the Chevrolet Venture and Oldsmobile Silhouette and gets a bit of a restyling for 2001. Recently, the minivan received power sliding doors on extended wheelbase models, some new colors, and a sport performance package that includes all-weather traction control and specially tuned suspension. The second sliding door is available on models with either a regular or extended wheelbase. The standard engine is a 3.4-liter V6 which should provide ample power. Look for the new backup warning system.

2001 Pontiac Montana

General Information

New for 2001: No major changes	**Year of Production:** 3
Twins: Chevy Venture, Olds Silhouette	**Seating:** 7-8
Where Made: U.S.	**Theft Rating:**

Prices 2001

Model	Retail	Markup
Regular 7-Passenger	$25,875	10%
Extended 7-Passenger	$26,520	10%

Competition 2001

Model	POOR					GOOD	pg.
Pont. Montana				■			**388**
Honda Odyssey		■					250
Ford Windstar					■		236
Toyota Sienna		■					438

'00 and '99 Models

The Montana is marketed as your rugged, off-road family mover. There are five seating arrangements with a total capacity of eight. Good crash test results and numerous safety features make the Montana worth considering.

Price Ranges 2000–1999

Base	$18,800-20,200

2000 Pontiac Montana

1999 Pontiac Montana

	2001	2000	1999

RATINGS

	POOR — GOOD	POOR — GOOD	POOR — GOOD
Comparative Rating	6	7	6
Frontal Crash Tests	7	7	7
Safety Features	9	10	10
Preventive Maintenance	9	9	7
Repair Costs	5	9	6
Warranty	2	2	2
Fuel Economy	4	4	3
Rollover (based on SSF; see pg. 30)	5	5	5
Complaints	2	2	3
Insurance Costs	10	10	10

SAFETY

	2001	2000	1999
Frontal Crash Tests	Good	Good	Good
Side Crash Tests	Very Good	Very Good	Very Good
Airbags	Dual/Side (nextgen)	Dual/Side (nextgen)	Dual/Side (nextgen)
Anti-Lock Brakes	4-Wheel	4-Wheel	4-Wheel
Day Running Lamps	Standard	Standard	Standard
Built-In Child Seats	Optional	Optional	Optional
Pretensioners	Standard	Standard	Standard

SPECIFICATIONS

	2001		2000		1999	
Fuel Economy (cty/hwy)	19/26	Poor	19/26	Poor	18/25	Poor
Driving Range (miles)	562.5	Vry. Long	562.5	Vry. Long	537.5	Vry. Long
Bumpers	Strong		Strong		Strong	
Parking Index	Hard		Hard		Hard	
Head/Leg Room (in.)	39.9/39.9	Cramped	39.9/39.9	Cramped	39.9/39.9	Cramped
Interior Space (cu. ft.)						
Cargo Space (cu. ft.)	133	Vry. Large	133	Vry. Large	126.6	Vry. Large
Tow Rating (lbs.)	3500	Low	3500	Low	3500	Low

Pontiac Sunfire — Compact

The unchanged Sunfire is the higher-priced version of the Cavalier and borrows heavily from the Firebird's design, hoping to cater to young drivers looking for an affordable sporty car. The SE coupe, sedan, and convertible come standard with a 2.2-liter engine that is adequate. The GT coupe has a 2.4-liter dual-cam engine with 25% more power. Unfortunately, while the Sunfire performs well on frontal crash tests, it does poorly on the side crash tests. The convertible was dropped for 2001.

2001 Pontiac Sunfire

General Information

New for 2001: No major changes	**Year of Production:** 7
Twins: Chevrolet Cavalier	**Seating:** 5
Where Made: U.S.	**Theft Rating:** Very Low

Prices 2001

Model	Retail	Markup
SE Coupe	$14,175	8%
SE Sedan	$14,430	8%
GT Coupe	$16,295	8%

Competition 2001

Model	POOR					GOOD		pg.
Pontiac Sunfire					■			**390**
Mazda Protégé			■					334
Mitsu. Galant			■					350
Toyota Corolla					■			424

'00 and '99 Models

Ride is good on smooth roads, a little bumpy on anything else. Noise level is better than most competitors. Attractive styling and adequate performance make the Sunfire attractive among inexpensive sports cars, but note the poor side crash test results.

Price Ranges 2000–1999

SE Coupe	$10,400-12,300
SE Sedan	$10,500-12,400
GT Coupe	$12,400-14,700

2000 Pontiac Sunfire

1999 Pontiac Sunfire

Pontiac Sunfire — Compact

	2001	2000	1999

RATINGS

	POOR — GOOD (2001)	POOR — GOOD (2000)	POOR — GOOD (1999)
Comparative Rating	6	5	5
Frontal Crash Tests	7	7	7
Safety Features	6	6	6
Preventive Maintenance	6	6	6
Repair Costs	7	6	7
Warranty	2	2	2
Fuel Economy	6	5	6
Rollover (based on SSF; see pg. 30)	7	7	7
Complaints	8	8	8
Insurance Costs	1	1	1

SAFETY

	2001	2000	1999
Frontal Crash Tests	Good (2dr./4dr.)	Good (2dr./4dr.)	Poor (2dr./4dr.)
Side Crash Tests	Poor (4dr.) Vry. Pr. (2dr.)	Poor (4dr.) Vry. Pr. (2dr.)	Poor (4dr.) Vry. Pr. (2dr.)
Airbags	Dual	Dual	Dual
Anti-Lock Brakes	4-Wheel	4-Wheel	4-Wheel
Day Running Lamps	Standard	Standard	Standard
Built-In Child Seats	None	None	None
Pretensioners	None	None	None

SPECIFICATIONS

	2001		2000		1999	
Fuel Economy (cty/hwy)	23/32	Average	23/33	Average	24/34	Good
Driving Range (miles)	393.25	Short	400.4	Average	435	Long
Bumpers	Strong		Strong		Strong	
Parking Index	Easy		Easy		Easy	
Head/Leg Room (in.)	38.9/42.1	Average	38.9/42.1	Average	37.6/42.1	Cramped
Interior Space (cu. ft.)	90	Cramped	91.6	Cramped	87.2	Cramped
Cargo Space (cu. ft.)	13	Vry. Small	13.1	Vry. Small	12.4	Vry. Small
Tow Rating (lbs.)						

Saab 9-3 Intermediate

The unchanged Saab 9-3 model line includes a coupe, a 5-door, and a convertible. A 2.0-liter turbo engine powers all models, though a 200 hp version comes with the SE models. Other models have the 185 hp engine. A 5-speed transmission is standard and comes with a hydraulically operated clutch for easy use. Seats in the Saab are wider than in earlier models; large trunk room and a large cabin space make for a comfortable ride. Now a GM product, you can get the OnStar system as an option.

2001 Saab 9-3

General Information

New for 2001: No major changes	**Year of Production:** 3
Twins:	**Seating:** 5
Where Made: Sweden	**Theft Rating:**

Prices 2001

Model	Retail	Markup
Base Hatchback 3-dr.	$26,495	6%
SE Hot Hatchback 5-dr.	$32,595	7%
Viggen convertible 2-dr.	$44,995	10%

Competition 2001

Model	POOR			GOOD	pg.
Saab 9-3					**392**
Lexus ES300				■	302
Honda Accord		■			242
Toyota Camry			■		420

'00 and '99 Models

The 9-3 replaces the Saab 900 line. In 1999, Saab unleashed a whiplash protection system, which uses a padded head restraint to catch a passenger's head as it snaps backward in a frontal collision.

Price Ranges 2000–1999

Coupe 3-door	$20,400-25,900
SE Sedan	$23,200-31,900
Conv. 2-door Viggen	$44,900-45,000

2000 Saab 9-3

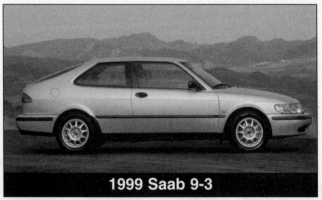
1999 Saab 9-3

	2001	2000	1999

RATINGS

	POOR — GOOD	POOR — GOOD	POOR — GOOD
Comparative Rating			
Frontal Crash Tests			
Safety Features	8	8	8
Preventive Maintenance	8	8	8
Repair Costs	5	5	2
Warranty	6	8	7
Fuel Economy	6	5	4
Rollover (based on SSF; see pg. 30)	7	7	7
Complaints	2	2	3
Insurance Costs	5	10	10

SAFETY

	2001	2000	1999
Frontal Crash Tests	No Govt Results	No Govt Results	No Govt Results
Side Crash Tests	No Govt Results	No Govt Results	No Govt Results
Airbags	Dual (nextgen)	Dual (nextgen)	Dual (nextgen)
Anti-Lock Brakes	4-Wheel	4-Wheel	4-Wheel
Day Running Lamps	Standard	Standard	Standard
Built-In Child Seats	Optional	None	Optional
Pretensioners	Standard	Standard	Standard

SPECIFICATIONS

	2001	2000	1999
Fuel Economy (cty/hwy)	22/30 Average	22/29 Average	20/27 Poor
Driving Range (miles)	442 Long	433.5 Long	423 Long
Bumpers	Strong	Strong	
Parking Index	Easy	Easy	Easy
Head/Leg Room (in.)	39.3/42.3 Average	39.3/42.3 Average	39.3/42.3 Average
Interior Space (cu. ft.)	90 Cramped	111.3 Roomy	111.3 Roomy
Cargo Space (cu. ft.)	22 Average	46 Large	49.8 Large
Tow Rating (lbs.)			

This year the 9-5, the replacement for the 9000, is unchanged. The 9-5 comes with a standard 2.3-liter 4-cylinder turbocharged engine with increased horsepower over last year, or an optional 3.0-liter 6-cylinder on the SE model. The 5 speed manual transmission comes with a hydraulic clutch to aid shifting. ABS is standard, as are driver and passenger front and side airbags. The Saab Active Head Restraint, also found on the 9-3, protects against whiplash in the event of a frontal collision.

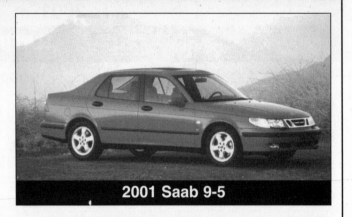
2001 Saab 9-5

General Information

New for 2001: No major changes		**Year of Production:**	3
Twins:		**Seating:**	5
Where Made: Finland		**Theft Rating:**	

Prices 2001

Model	Retail	Markup
2.3t Base Sedan	$33,995	8%
2.3t Wagon	$34,695	8%
SE V6t	$38,650	8%
Aero Wagon	$40,875	8%

Competition 2001

Model	POOR					GOOD	pg.
Saab 9-5							**394**
Chrys. Concorde			■				188
Lexus ES300						■	302
Nissan Altima					■		356

'00 and '99 Models

Interior features include automatic climate control with separate temperature controls for the driver and passenger, heated mirrors, front and rear fog lights, tinted heat-absorbing glass, and ample cabin space.

Price Ranges 2000–1999

2.3t Base	$25,700-32,600
2.3t Wagon	$27,300-32,600
SE V6t	$30,500-37,800
Aero Sedan	$27,600-39,800

2000 Saab 9-5

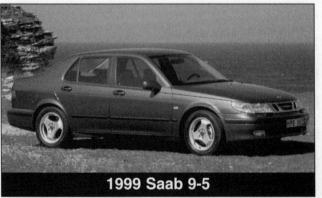
1999 Saab 9-5

Saab 9-5 — Intermediate

	2001	2000	1999

RATINGS

	POOR — GOOD	POOR — GOOD	POOR — GOOD
Comparative Rating			
Frontal Crash Tests			
Safety Features	8	8	8
Preventive Maintenance	7	7	7
Repair Costs	4	7	2
Warranty	6	8	7
Fuel Economy	6	4	5
Rollover (based on SSF; see pg. 30)	7	7	7
Complaints	9	9	9
Insurance Costs	10	5	5

SAFETY

	2001	2000	1999
Frontal Crash Tests	No Govt Results	No Govt Results	No Govt Results
Side Crash Tests	No Govt Results	No Govt Results	No Govt Results
Airbags	Dual (nextgen)	Dual (nextgen)	Dual (nextgen)
Anti-Lock Brakes	4-Wheel	4-Wheel	4-Wheel
Day Running Lamps	Standard	Standard	Standard
Built-In Child Seats	Optional	None	Optional
Pretensioners	Standard	Standard	Standard

SPECIFICATIONS

	2001		2000		1999	
Fuel Economy (cty/hwy)	21/30	Average	21/29	Average	21/30	Average
Driving Range (miles)	471.75	Vry. Long	462.5	Vry. Long	504.9	Vry. Long
Bumpers	Strong		Strong			
Parking Index	Average		Average		Easy	
Head/Leg Room (in.)	38.7/42.4	Average	38.7/42.4	Average	38.7/42.4	Average
Interior Space (cu. ft.)	99	Average	114.9	Vry. Roomy	114.9	Vry. Roomy
Cargo Space (cu. ft.)	16	Small	15.9	Small	15.9	Small
Tow Rating (lbs.)						

Saturn moves into 2001 with no changes to the L-Series. The sedan and wagon come standard with a 2.2-liter 4-cylinder engine and a 3.0-liter V6 is optional. The sedan comes standard with a 5-speed manual and the wagon has an automatic. To maintain its safety reputation, the L-Series has dual front reduced-force airbags and daytime running lamps with optional ABS. Saturn has also tried to offer a bit more luxury in its interior than in the past. With its attractive pricing, the L/LW should compete well.

2001 Saturn L

General Information

New for 2001: No major changes		**Year of Production:**	2
Twins:		**Seating:**	5
Where Made: U.S.		**Theft Rating:**	

Prices 2001

Model	Retail	Markup
L100 man.	$14,495	12%
L100 auto.	$15,355	12%
LW200 Wagon auto.	$18,835	12%
L300 auto.	$19,495	12%

Competition 2001

Model	POOR					GOOD		pg.
Saturn L100						■		**396**
Ford Taurus							■	234
Honda Accord			■					242
Toyota Camry				■				420

'00 and '99 Models

This is the largest of the Saturns and was added to expand the product line. One of the most popular aspects of buying a Saturn is that its dealers do not negotiate, which takes much of the hassle out of the buying process. This should cause used Saturns to hold their value more consistently.

Price Ranges 2000–1999

L100 man.	$14,500-14,600
L100 auto.	$15,000-15,100
LW200 Wagon auto.	$21,300-21,400
L300 auto.	$20,100-20,200

2000 Saturn LS

MODEL WAS NOT PRODUCED THIS YEAR

1999 Model

Saturn L/LW — Intermediate

	2001	2000	1999
RATINGS (POOR–GOOD)			
Comparative Rating	7	7	
Frontal Crash Tests	10	10	
Safety Features	4	6	
Preventive Maintenance	7		
Repair Costs	10		
Warranty	3	3	
Fuel Economy	7	5	
Rollover (based on SSF; see pg. 30)	7	7	
Complaints	5		
Insurance Costs	5	5	

SAFETY

	2001	2000	1999
Frontal Crash Tests	Very Good	Very Good	
Side Crash Tests	Average	Average	
Airbags		Dual (nextgen)	
Anti-Lock Brakes		4-Wheel (optional)	
Day Running Lamps	None	Standard	
Built-In Child Seats	None	None	
Pretensioners	None	None	

SPECIFICATIONS

	2001	2000	1999
Fuel Economy (cty/hwy)	25/33 Good	24/32 Average	
Driving Range (miles)	455.3 Long	366.8 Vry. Short	
Bumpers			
Parking Index		Average	
Head/Leg Room (in.)	39.3/42.3 Average	39.3/55.7 Vry. Roomy	
Interior Space (cu. ft.)	97 Average	96.9 Average	
Cargo Space (cu. ft.)	18 Average	17.5 Average	
Tow Rating (lbs.)			

Two years ago, Saturn introduced a 3-door coupe among its SCs. For all of its models, Saturn uses an improved 1.9-liter 4-cylinder engine, with a new crankshaft, pistons, rods, and a cover over the timing chain. The sleek-looking SC includes standard daytime running lamps, standard dual de-powered airbags, and optional ABS and side airbags. On the interior, the SC looks much like the SL/SW. The standard engine delivers 100 horsepower, which is not tops in this competitive market. Ride is fairly smooth, though less so on rough roads.

2001 Saturn SC

General Information

New for 2001: No major changes		**Year of Production:**	5
Twins:		**Seating:**	4
Where Made: U.S.		**Theft Rating:**	Very Low

Prices 2001

Model	Retail	Markup
SC1 man.	$12,535	15%
SC1 auto.	$13,395	15%
SC2 man.	$15,645	15%
SC2 auto.	$16,505	15%

Competition 2001

Model	POOR						GOOD	pg.
Saturn SC							■	**398**
Ford Focus						■		228
Mazda Protégé			■					334
VW Beetle							■	446

'00 and '99 Models

The SC received no major changes in 1999 or 2000. Models have two engine choices: a 1.9L inline 4-cylinder model and a 16-valve version that ups the horsepower from 100 to 124.

Price Ranges 2000–1999

SC1 man.	$11,800-12,100
SC1 auto.	$12,200-12,500
SC2 man.	$12,800-14,700
SC2 auto.	$13,200-15,100

2000 Saturn SC

1999 Saturn SC

Saturn SC — Subcompact

	2001	2000	1999

RATINGS

	POOR — GOOD	POOR — GOOD	POOR — GOOD
Comparative Rating			
Frontal Crash Tests			
Safety Features	5	6	6
Preventive Maintenance	3	2	3
Repair Costs	10	10	10
Warranty	3	3	3
Fuel Economy	9	7	8
Rollover (based on SSF; see pg. 30)	7	7	7
Complaints	8	8	9
Insurance Costs	1	1	1

SAFETY

	2001	2000	1999
Frontal Crash Tests	No Govt Results	No Govt Results	No Govt Results
Side Crash Tests	No Govt Results	No Govt Results	No Govt Results
Airbags		Dual (nextgen)	Dual (nextgen)
Anti-Lock Brakes		4-Wheel (optional)	4-Wheel (optional)
Day Running Lamps	Standard	Standard	Standard
Built-In Child Seats	None	None	None
Pretensioners	None	None	None

SPECIFICATIONS

	2001		2000		1999	
Fuel Economy (cty/hwy)	28/40	Good	28/40	Good	29/40	Vry. Good
Driving Range (miles)	399.3	Average	411.4	Average	417.45	Average
Bumpers			Strong		Strong	
Parking Index	Average		Average		Average	
Head/Leg Room (in.)	38.6/42.6	Average	38.6/42.6	Average	38.5/42.6	Average
Interior Space (cu. ft.)	84	Vry. Cramp.	84.1	Vry. Cramp.	84.1	Vry. Cramp.
Cargo Space (cu. ft.)	11	Vry. Small	11.4	Vry. Small	11.4	Vry. Small
Tow Rating (lbs.)						

No changes this year. Just as with the SC, Saturns sedan and wagon got adjustments under the hood to quiet the engine in 1999. The dual overhead cam engine available on the SL and SW is more powerful than the base 4-cylinder model and only reduces fuel efficiency slightly. The raised roofline adds headroom, which makes the sedan and wagon more comfortable, although the back seat is still tight for adults. Smaller and less expensive than the L-Series, side bags and ABS are optional on the S-Series.

2001 Saturn SL

General Information

New for 2001: No major changes	**Year of Production:**	6
Twins:	**Seating:**	4
Where Made: U.S.	**Theft Rating:**	Very Low

Prices 2001

Model	Retail	Markup
SL1 man.	$11,485	15%
SL1 auto.	$12,345	15%
SW2 man.	$14,290	15%
SW2 auto.	$15,150	15%

Competition 2001

Model	POOR				GOOD	pg.
Saturn SL					■	**400**
Ford Focus					■	228
Dodge Neon			■			214
VW Beetle					■	446

'00 and '99 Models

With top-notch frontal crash test results and great safety features, this economically priced car fares nicely against tough competition like the Ford Escort, Honda Civic, and Dodge/Plymouth Neon.

Price Ranges 2000–1999

SL1 man.	$11,000-11,100
SL1 auto.	$11,400-11,500
SW2 man.	$12,500-13,800
SW2 auto.	$12,900-14,300

2000 Saturn SL

1999 Saturn SW

	2001	2000	1999
RATINGS (POOR → GOOD)			
Comparative Rating	9	9	10
Frontal Crash Tests	10	10	10
Safety Features	5	6	6
Preventive Maintenance	7	3	3
Repair Costs	10	10	10
Warranty	3	3	3
Fuel Economy	9	8	8
Rollover (based on SSF; see pg. 30)	6	7	7
Complaints	8	8	9
Insurance Costs	5	10	10
SAFETY			
Frontal Crash Tests	Very Good	Very Good	Very Good
Side Crash Tests	Average	Average	Average
Airbags	Dual (nextgen)	Dual (nextgen)	Dual (nextgen)
Anti-Lock Brakes	4-Wheel (optional)	4-Wheel (optional)	4-Wheel (optional)
Day Running Lamps	Standard	Standard	Standard
Built-In Child Seats	None	None	None
Pretensioners	None	None	None
SPECIFICATIONS			
Fuel Economy (cty/hwy)	29/40 Vry. Good	29/40 Vry. Good	29/40 Vry. Good
Driving Range (miles)	399.3 Average	417.45 Average	417.45 Average
Bumpers	Strong	Strong	Strong
Parking Index	Average	Average	Easy
Head/Leg Room (in.)	39.3/42.5 Average	39.3/42.5 Average	39.3/42.5 Average
Interior Space (cu. ft.)	91 Cramped	91 Cramped	91 Cramped
Cargo Space (cu. ft.)	12 Vry. Small	12.1 Vry. Small	12.1 Vry. Small
Tow Rating (lbs.)			

Subaru Forester   Mid-Size Sport Utility

Unchanged for 2001, the Impreza-based Forester is designed to capitalize on the success of Subaru's Outback line of cars. The Forester is a mix of station wagon and sport utility. Dual airbags and front height adjustable seat belts are standard; 4-wheel ABS is optional. As is true for all Subarus, all-wheel drive comes standard. A 2.5-liter engine powers the Forester. Compared to other sport utilities, the Forester has a lower stance, which increases stability and makes getting in and out easier.

2001 Subaru Forester

General Information

New for 2001: No major changes	**Year of Production:** 4
Twins:	**Seating:** 5
Where Made: Japan	**Theft Rating:** Very Low

Prices 2001

Model	Retail	Markup
L man.	$20,295	10%
L auto.	$21,095	10%
S man.	$22,895	10%
S auto.	$23,695	10%

Competition 2001

Model	POOR					GOOD	pg.
Subaru Forester				■			402
Chev. Blazer			■				162
Ford Explorer				■			224
Honda Passport	■						252

'00 and '99 Models

Not meant for off-roading, the Forester will still appeal to the minivan crowd who don't need all that space, with its ample head- and legroom and all-wheel drive handling. With good crash test results, the Forester is a good choice for families.

Price Ranges 2000–1999

L man.	$18,100-19,500
L auto.	$18,800-20,100
S man.	$20,000-22,000
S auto.	$20,600-22,600

2000 Subaru Forester

1999 Subaru Forester

Subaru Forester — Mid-Size Sport Utility

	2001	2000	1999

RATINGS

	2001 (POOR→GOOD)	2000 (POOR→GOOD)	1999 (POOR→GOOD)
Comparative Rating	5	4	3
Frontal Crash Tests*	8	8	8
Safety Features	6	6	6
Preventive Maintenance	9	9	10
Repair Costs	5	5	4
Warranty	5	5	3
Fuel Economy	5	4	4
Rollover (based on SSF, see pg. 25)		5	4
Complaints	3	3	3
Insurance Costs	5	1	1

SAFETY

	2001	2000	1999
Frontal Crash Tests	Good	Good	Good
Side Crash Tests	No Govt Results	No Govt Results	No Govt Results
Airbags	Dual (nextgen)	Dual (nextgen)	Dual (nextgen)
Anti-Lock Brakes	4-Wheel	4-Wheel	4-Wheel
Day Running Lamps	None	None	None
Built-In Child Seats	None	None	None
Pretensioners	Standard	Standard	Standard

SPECIFICATIONS

	2001		2000		1999	
Fuel Economy (cty/hwy)	21/28	Average	21/27	Average	21/27	Average
Driving Range (miles)	389.55	Short	381.6	Short	381.6	Short
Bumpers	Strong		Strong			
Parking Index	Vry. Easy		Vry. Easy		Vry. Easy	
Head/Leg Room (in.)	40.6/43	Vry. Roomy	40.6/43	Vry. Roomy	40.6/43	Vry. Roomy
Interior Space (cu. ft.)	95.1	Average	95.1	Average	95.1	Average
Cargo Space (cu. ft.)	33.2	Average	33.2	Average	33.2	Average
Tow Rating (lbs.)	2000	Vry. Low	2000	Vry. Low	2000	Vry. Low

*To be tested in 2001.

The Impreza continues into 2001 with two basic models: the L, as a sedan, coupe, or wagon, and the RS, as a sedan or coupe. Last year's changes included more exterior colors and interior fabrics, a more powerful engine, and two improved transmissions. This year a single-disc CD is standard. All-wheel drive now comes standard on all models, which should please cold weather drivers. The base model has a 2.2-liter 4-cylinder engine. A 2.5-liter, 142 hp engine is available on the coupe RS.

2001 Subaru Impreza

General Information

New for 2001: No major changes	**Year of Production:** 9
Twins:	**Seating:** 5
Where Made: Japan	**Theft Rating:** Very Low

Prices 2001

Model	Retail	Markup
L man. Coupe	$15,995	9%
L Sport Wagon	$16,395	9%
L auto. Coupe	$16,795	9%
2.5 RS auto.	$20,300	9%

Competition 2001

Model	POOR				GOOD	pg.
Subaru Impreza					■	**404**
Ford Focus					■	228
Ddge/Plym. Neon			■			214
Saturn SL					■	400

'00 and '99 Models

On all models you have the option of a 4-speed automatic transmission or a manual 5-speed. The Impreza rates very well in terms of subcompacts and did well on frontal crash tests.

Price Ranges 2000–1999

Base man.	$13,100-15,500
Sport Wagon	$14,900-16,300
Base auto.	$13,700-15,900

2000 Subaru Impreza

1999 Subaru Impreza

Subaru Impreza — Subcompact

	2001	2000	1999

RATINGS

	POOR — GOOD	POOR — GOOD	POOR — GOOD
Comparative Rating	9	8	6
Frontal Crash Tests	8	8	8
Safety Features	6	6	6
Preventive Maintenance	9	9	9
Repair Costs	5	5	5
Warranty	5	5	3
Fuel Economy	6	5	5
Rollover (based on SSF; see pg. 30)	7	7	7
Complaints	10	10	8
Insurance Costs	1	1	1

SAFETY

	2001	2000	1999
Frontal Crash Tests	Good	Good	Good
Side Crash Tests	No Govt Results	No Govt Results	No Govt Results
Airbags	Dual (nextgen)	Dual (nextgen)	Dual (nextgen)
Anti-Lock Brakes	4-Wheel	4-Wheel	4-Wheel
Day Running Lamps	None	None	None
Built-In Child Seats	None	None	None
Pretensioners	Standard	Standard	Standard

SPECIFICATIONS

	2001		2000		1999	
Fuel Economy (cty/hwy)	23/29	Average	23/29	Average	22/29	Average
Driving Range (miles)	413.4	Average	413.4	Average	336.6	Vry. Short
Bumpers	Strong		Strong		Strong	
Parking Index	Vry. Easy		Vry. Easy		Vry. Easy	
Head/Leg Room (in.)	39.2/43.1	Roomy	39.2/43.1	Roomy	39.2/43.1	Roomy
Interior Space (cu. ft.)	84	Vry. Cramp.	84.4	Vry. Cramp.	84.4	Vry. Cramp.
Cargo Space (cu. ft.)	11	Vry. Small	11.1	Vry. Small	11.1	Vry. Small
Tow Rating (lbs.)	1500	Vry. Low	1500	Vry. Low	1500	Vry. Low

No significant changes for 2001. Last year's new engine and increased size were the key changes in this all-wheel drive vehicle. The Legacy's trim levels still include the Brighton Wagon, Sedan L, GT, and GT Limited. A 2.5-liter boxer engine comes standard on all models. This engine provides as much power as a V6. ABS, dual front airbags, and daytime running lamps come standard. You have the choice of manual or automatic. And this year power moonroof, leather seats, and climate control come standard on many models.

2001 Subaru Legacy

General Information

New for 2001: No major changes	**Year of Production:** 2
Twins:	**Seating:** 5
Where Made: U.S.	**Theft Rating:** Very Low

Prices 2001

Model	Retail	Markup
L Sedan man.	$19,295	10%
L Wagon man.	$19,995	10%
L Sedan auto.	$20,095	10%
GTWagon auto.	$24,595	10%

Competition 2001

Model	POOR					GOOD	pg.
Subaru Legacy						■	**406**
Chev. Cavalier				■			166
Mitsu. Galant		■					350
Toyota Corolla					■		424

'00 and '99 Models

The fresh styling the Legacy received in 1995 made this car a good seller. The GT model should please sportier buyers. Ride and comfort are both good, and the '99 Legacy performed well on government frontal crash tests; the later models even better.

Price Ranges 2000–1999

L Sedan man.	$15,100-19,600
L Wagon man.	$16,300-16,700
L Sedan auto.	$15,700-19,200
L Wagon auto.	$17,000-19,900

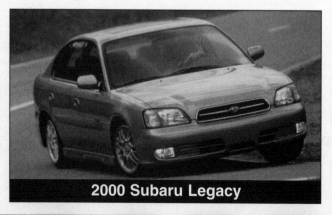

2000 Subaru Legacy

1999 Subaru Legacy

Subaru Legacy   Compact

	2001	2000	1999

RATINGS

	POOR → GOOD	POOR → GOOD	POOR → GOOD
Comparative Rating	9	8	6
Frontal Crash Tests	9	9	8
Safety Features	7	8	6
Preventive Maintenance	9	9	9
Repair Costs	9	9	6
Warranty	5	5	3
Fuel Economy	5	4	5
Rollover (based on SSF; see pg. 30)		7	7
Complaints	5		5
Insurance Costs	5	5	5

SAFETY

	2001	2000	1999
Frontal Crash Tests	Very Good	Very Good	Good
Side Crash Tests	Very Good	Very Good	No Govt Results
Airbags	Dual (nextgen)	Dual (nextgen)	Dual (nextgen)
Anti-Lock Brakes	4-Wheel	4-Wheel	4-Wheel
Day Running Lamps	Standard	Standard	None
Built-In Child Seats	None	None	None
Pretensioners	Standard	Standard	Standard

SPECIFICATIONS

	2001		2000		1999	
Fuel Economy (cty/hwy)	21/28	Average	21/28	Average	22/29	Average
Driving Range (miles)	414.05	Average	414.05	Average	405.45	Average
Bumpers	Strong		Strong		Strong	
Parking Index	Easy		Easy		Easy	
Head/Leg Room (in.)	38.9/43.3	Roomy	38.9/43.3	Roomy	38.9/43.3	Roomy
Interior Space (cu. ft.)	91	Cramped	91.4	Cramped	92.1	Cramped
Cargo Space (cu. ft.)	12	Vry. Small	12.4	Vry. Small	13	Vry. Small
Tow Rating (lbs.)	2000	Vry. Low	2000	Vry. Low	2000	Vry. Low

Subaru Outback

This popular Subaru line continues into 2001 with few changes. The redesigned 2.5-liter engine is standard, and manual transmission comes standard as well. New for this year, in the L.L. Bean model, are two high-performance 3-liter engines. ABS, dual airbags, and pretensioners supplement the all-wheel drive capability of these cars. The Outback Limited model comes equipped with the first front seat side airbags on a Subaru.

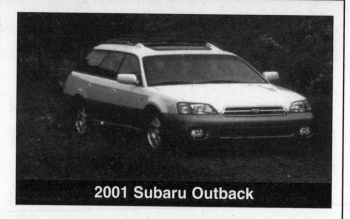

2001 Subaru Outback

General Information

New for 2001: No major changes	Year of Production:	2
Twins:	Seating:	5
Where Made: U.S.	Theft Rating:	Very Low

Prices 2001

Model	Retail	Markup
Base Wagon man.	$22,895	10%
Base Wagon auto.	$23,695	10%
Limited Sedan	$25,995	10%
HS-3.0L VDC auto.	$31,895	10%

Competition 2001

Model	POOR				GOOD	pg.
Subaru Outback						**408**
Ford Taurus					■	234
Honda Accord		■				242
Toyota Camry				■		420

'00 and '99 Models

In 1999, the Outback received a new grille, halogen headlights, and new bucket seats, and comes pre-wired for keyless entry. For many years very popular in New England, Subaru vehicles have spread throughout the U.S. and are readily available in most markets.

Price Ranges 2000–1999

Base Wagon man.	$19,600-25,300
Base Wagon auto.	$20,200-22,700
Limited Sedan	$19,100-25,900

2000 Subaru Outback

1999 Subaru Outback

Subaru Outback — Intermediate

	2001	2000	1999

RATINGS

Scale: POOR ← → GOOD

Rating	2001	2000	1999
Comparative Rating	—	—	—
Frontal Crash Tests	—	—	—
Safety Features	7	8	6
Preventive Maintenance	9	9	9
Repair Costs	10	7	6
Warranty	5	5	3
Fuel Economy	5	4	5
Rollover (based on SSF; see pg. 30)	—	6	5
Complaints	5	—	6
Insurance Costs	5	5	5

SAFETY

	2001	2000	1999
Frontal Crash Tests	No Govt Results	No Govt Results	No Govt Results
Side Crash Tests	No Govt Results	No Govt Results	No Govt Results
Airbags	Dual	Dual (nextgen)	Dual (nextgen)
Anti-Lock Brakes	4-Wheel	4-Wheel	4-Wheel
Day Running Lamps	Standard	Standard	None
Built-In Child Seats	Optional	None	None
Pretensioners	Standard	Standard	Standard

SPECIFICATIONS

	2001	2000	1999
Fuel Economy (cty/hwy)	22/27 Average	22/27 Average	22/29 Average
Driving Range (miles)	414.05 Average	414.05 Average	405.45 Average
Bumpers	Strong	Strong	Strong
Parking Index	Average	Average	Average
Head/Leg Room (in.)	38.1/43.3 Average	38.1/43.3 Average	40.2/43.3 Vry. Roomy
Interior Space (cu. ft.)	91.4 Cramped	91.4 Cramped	91.4 Cramped
Cargo Space (cu. ft.)	12.4 Vry. Small	12.4 Vry. Small	12.4 Vry. Small
Tow Rating (lbs.)	2000 Vry. Low	2000 Vry. Low	2000 Vry. Low

Debuting in 1997, the Esteem was revamped in 1999 and moves into 2001 unchanged. Three trim levels are available: GL, GLX, and the GLX+, and the Esteem comes as either a sedan or wagon. The 1.6-liter 4-cylinder engine is standard on all models, and you can choose between the 4-speed automatic and 5-speed manual transmission. The small engine may lack race car power, but it gives good gas mileage, and the manual transmission passes TLEV standards. Be sure to check out the larger, 1.8-liter engine.

2001 Suzuki Esteem

General Information

New for 2001: No major changes		**Year of Production:**	6
Twins:		**Seating:**	5
Where Made: Japan		**Theft Rating:**	

Prices 2001

Model	Retail	Markup
GL man. Sedan	$13,199	4%
GL man. Wagon	$13,699	4%
GL auto. Sedan	$14,199	4%
GL auto. Wagon	$14,699	4%

Competition 2001

Model	POOR						GOOD	pg.
Suzuki Esteem								**410**
Ford Focus						■		228
Mazda Protégé			■					334
Saturn SL							■	400

'00 and '99 Models

The Esteem has been Suzuki's subcompact sedan selection in a very competitive market. While the low price is attractive, you can get more for your money elsewhere. Changes in '99 included new sheet metal work, grille, fenders, and headlights.

Price Ranges 2000–1999

GL Sedan man.	$9,100-12,400
GL Wagon man.	$9,500-13,400
GL Sedan auto.	$9,600-12,800
GL Wagon auto.	$9,600-13,800

2000 Suzuki Esteem

1999 Suzuki Esteem

	2001	2000	1999

RATINGS

	POOR — GOOD	POOR — GOOD	POOR — GOOD
Comparative Rating			
Frontal Crash Tests			
Safety Features	5	6	6
Preventive Maintenance	4	4	4
Repair Costs	3	2	2
Warranty	1	1	1
Fuel Economy	9	7	7
Rollover (based on SSF; see pg. 30)	7	7	7
Complaints	7	7	6
Insurance Costs	1	1	1

SAFETY

	2001	2000	1999
Frontal Crash Tests	No Govt Results	No Govt Results	No Govt Results
Side Crash Tests	No Govt Results	No Govt Results	No Govt Results
Airbags	Dual	Dual	Dual
Anti-Lock Brakes	4-Wheel (optional)	4-Wheel (optional)	4-Wheel (optional)
Day Running Lamps	Standard	Standard	Standard
Built-In Child Seats	None	None	None
Pretensioners	None	None	None

SPECIFICATIONS

	2001		2000		1999	
Fuel Economy (cty/hwy)	30/37	Good	30/37	Good	30/37	Good
Driving Range (miles)	419.1	Average	425.45	Long	425.45	Long
Bumpers						Weak
Parking Index	Vry. Easy		Vry. Easy		Vry. Easy	
Head/Leg Room (in.)	39.1/42.3	Average	39.1/42.3	Average	39.1/42.3	Average
Interior Space (cu. ft.)	86	Cramped	110.3	Roomy	110.3	Roomy
Cargo Space (cu. ft.)	12	Vry. Small	24	Average	24	Average
Tow Rating (lbs.)						

Suzuki's unchanged Vitara line lies in between the rankings of Small and Mid-Size Sport Utility Vehicle. The smaller Vitara is available as a two or four-door model with a 2.0L 4-cylinder engine that offers 127 hp. But the Grand Vitara comes standard with a 155 hp 2.5L V6. The heavy engine merited a tough suspension and a rigid body—giving a more solid feeling. Passenger room inside is average, though cargo room is low. Not surprisingly fuel economy is poor, as is the warranty.

2001 Suzuki Grand Vitara

General Information

New for 2001: No major changes	**Year of Production:** 3
Twins: Chevy Tracker	**Seating:** 5
Where Made: Japan	**Theft Rating:**

Prices 2001

Model	Retail	Markup
JLS 2WD man.	$18,399	9%
JLS 2WD auto.	$19,399	9%
JLX 4WD man.	$19,599	9%
JLX 4WD auto.	$20,599	9%

Competition 2001

Model	POOR					GOOD	pg.
Suzuki Gr. Vitara							**412**
Chev. Blazer		■					162
Ford Explorer				■			224
Isuzu Rodeo		■					278

'00 and '99 Models

These are essentially two different vehicles, with different wheelbases. Unfortunately, the government has no current plans to crash test this vehicle. Popular with young drivers, care has to be taken to avoid rollover.

Price Ranges 2000–1999

JLS 2WD man.	$14,100-14,500
JLS 2WD auto.	$15,100-15,500
JLX 4WD man.	$15,800-20,000
JLX 4WD auto.	$16,200-17,900

2000 Suzuki Grand Vitara

1999 Suzuki Grand Vitara

Suzuki Grand Vitara — Mid-Size Sport Utility

	2001	2000	1999

RATINGS

	2001 POOR → GOOD	2000 POOR → GOOD	1999 POOR → GOOD
Comparative Rating			
Frontal Crash Tests			
Safety Features	5	6	6
Preventive Maintenance	1	4	4
Repair Costs	1	1	1
Warranty	1	1	1
Fuel Economy	3	3	3
Rollover (based on SSF; see pg. 30)	4	4	4
Complaints	3	3	5
Insurance Costs	5	5	5

SAFETY

	2001	2000	1999
Frontal Crash Tests	To Be Tested	No Govt Results	No Govt Results
Side Crash Tests	No Govt Results	No Govt Results	No Govt Results
Airbags	Dual	Dual	Dual
Anti-Lock Brakes	4-Wheel (optional)	4-Wheel (optional)	4-Wheel (optional)
Day Running Lamps	Standard	Standard	Standard
Built-In Child Seats	None	None	None
Pretensioners	None	None	None

SPECIFICATIONS

	2001		2000		1999	
Fuel Economy (cty/hwy)	19/22	Poor	19/21	Poor	19/21	Poor
Driving Range (miles)	356.7	Vry. Short	348	Vry. Short	348	Vry. Short
Bumpers						
Parking Index	Vry. Easy		Vry. Easy		Vry. Easy	
Head/Leg Room (in.)	39.9/41.4	Average	39.9/41.4	Average	39.9/41.4	Average
Interior Space (cu. ft.)	103.7	Roomy	103.7	Roomy	103.7	Roomy
Cargo Space (cu. ft.)	44.6	Large	44.6	Large	44.6	Large
Tow Rating (lbs.)						

CAR BOOK 2001 413

Suzuki Swift   Subcompact

While its twin, the Chevy Metro has been relegated to fleet-only sales, the Swift stays on the Suzuki shelf unchanged for 2001. The Swift's small 1.3-liter 4-cylinder engine provides great fuel economy and stellar emissions ratings with the manual transmission. Because fuel efficiency suffers dramatically with the optional automatic transmission, stick to the standard 5-speed. Room for two is tight; the rear seat is really only for children. The Swift is inexpensive but rates poorly overall due to high repair costs and a weak warranty.

2001 Suzuki Swift

General Information

New for 2001: No major changes	**Year of Production:** 7
Twins: Chevrolet Metro	**Seating:** 4
Where Made: Canada	**Theft Rating:**

Prices 2001

Model	Retail	Markup
GA man.	$9,299	6%
GA auto.	$9,949	6%
GL man.	$10,299	6%
GL auto.	$10,949	6%

Competition 2001

Model	POOR				GOOD	pg.
Suzuki Swift						**414**
Ford Focus					■	228
VW Beetle					■	446
Saturn SL					■	400

'00 and '99 Models

The original starting price of under $10,000 was very attractive; however this car is tiny, light, and does not handle very well. This is as basic as transportation gets. The Swift fares poorly against other subcompacts like the Saturns and the Civic.

Price Ranges 2000–1999

GL man.	$7,300-9,100
GL auto.	$7,800-9,600

2000 Suzuki Swift

1999 Suzuki Swift

Suzuki Swift — Subcompact

	2001	2000	1999

RATINGS

	2001 (POOR→GOOD)	2000 (POOR→GOOD)	1999 (POOR→GOOD)
Comparative Rating	—	—	—
Frontal Crash Tests	—	—	—
Safety Features	5	6	6
Preventive Maintenance	4	4	4
Repair Costs	2	2	3
Warranty	1	1	1
Fuel Economy	10	9	9
Rollover (based on SSF; see pg. 30)	6	6	6
Complaints	7	7	—
Insurance Costs	1	1	1

SAFETY

	2001	2000	1999
Frontal Crash Tests	No Govt Results	No Govt Results	No Govt Results
Side Crash Tests	No Govt Results	No Govt Results	No Govt Results
Airbags	Dual	Dual	Dual
Anti-Lock Brakes	4-Wheel (optional)	4-Wheel (optional)	4-Wheel (optional)
Day Running Lamps	Standard	Standard	Standard
Built-In Child Seats	None	None	None
Pretensioners	None	None	None

SPECIFICATIONS

	2001		2000		1999	
Fuel Economy (cty/hwy)	36/42	Vry. Good	36/42	Vry. Good	39/43	Vry. Good
Driving Range (miles)	401.7	Average	401.7	Average	422.3	Long
Bumpers						
Parking Index	Vry. Easy		Vry. Easy		Vry. Easy	
Head/Leg Room (in.)	39.1/42.5	Average	39.1/42.5	Average	39.1/42.5	Average
Interior Space (cu. ft.)	77	Vry. Cramp.	85.8	Cramped	85.8	Cramped
Cargo Space (cu. ft.)	8	Vry. Small	8.4	Vry. Small	8.4	Vry. Small
Tow Rating (lbs.)						

Toyota 4Runner

Mid-Size Sport Utility

Recently, the 4Runner received a new grille, redesigned front bumper, a new interior console, and a few other minor upgrades. Dual airbags are standard on all models. ABS is optional with the four-cylinder engine, standard with the V6. You have your choice between two engines, a 4-liter or 6-liter with the 6-liter providing more power. Beware, this is a very heavy vehicle and acceleration will be anything but fast, even with the larger engine.

2001 Toyota 4Runner

General Information

New for 2001: No major changes	**Year of Production:** 12
Twins:	**Seating:** 5
Where Made: Japan	**Theft Rating:** Very High

Prices 2001

Model	Retail	Markup
2WD SR5	$26,355	14%
4WD SR5	$28,895	14%
2WD Limited	$34,955	14%
4WD SR5	$37,605	14%

Competition 2001

Model	POOR				GOOD		pg.
Toyota 4Runner				■			**416**
Infiniti QX4					■		276
Ford Explorer			■				224
Olds Bravada	■						374

'00 and '99 Models

The 4Runner got few changes throughout the 1999-2000 model years. One of the heaviest of sport utilities, the 4Runner focuses on its distinctive looks and versatility. Despite strong crash test scores, the 4Runner is hurt by expensive repair costs, not many safety features, and a high insurance rate.

Price Ranges 2000–1999

2WD SR5	$24,400-26,000
4WD SR5	$26,600-28,000
2WD Limited	$28,700-33,900
4WD Limited	$30,900-36,500

2000 Toyota 4Runner

1999 Toyota 4Runner

Toyota 4Runner — Mid-Size Sport Utility

	2001	2000	1999
RATINGS (POOR → GOOD)			
Comparative Rating	6	3	3
Frontal Crash Tests*	9	9	9
Safety Features	6	6	6
Preventive Maintenance	4	3	4
Repair Costs	6	3	3
Warranty	2	2	3
Fuel Economy	2	3	2
Rollover (based on SSF, see pg. 25)	4	4	4
Complaints	10	10	8
Insurance Costs	5	1	1
SAFETY			
Frontal Crash Tests	Very Good	Very Good	Very Good
Side Crash Tests	Very Good	Very Good	Very Good
Airbags	Dual	Dual	Dual
Anti-Lock Brakes	4-Wheel (optional)	4-Wheel (optional)	4-Wheel (optional)
Day Running Lamps	Standard	Standard	Standard
Built-In Child Seats	None	None	None
Pretensioners	Standard	Standard	Standard
SPECIFICATIONS			
Fuel Economy (cty/hwy)	16/19 Vry. Poor	17/23 Poor	17/21 Poor
Driving Range (miles)	323.75 Vry. Short	370 Short	351.5 Vry. Short
Bumpers			
Parking Index	Hard	Hard	Average
Head/Leg Room (in.)	39.3/42.6 Average	39.3/42.6 Average	39.2/43.1 Roomy
Interior Space (cu. ft.)	44.6 Vry. Cramp.	44.6 Vry. Cramp.	44.6 Vry. Cramp.
Cargo Space (cu. ft.)	79.8 Large	79.8 Large	79.7 Large
Tow Rating (lbs.)	3500 Low	3500 Low	3500 Low

*To be tested in 2001.

Toyota Avalon

The 2001 Avalon adds more space and power to its already adequate levels of both. An improved 3.0-liter V6 produces 210 horsepower and still gets decent fuel economy, and automatic transmission is standard with both the base XL and XLS models. ABS, dual front and side airbags, and pretensioners will keep you safe. The new styling contributes to an even quieter ride.

2001 Toyota Avalon

General Information

New for 2001: No major changes	**Year of Production:** 2
Twins:	**Seating:** 5
Where Made: U.S.	**Theft Rating:** Average

Prices 2001

Model	Retail	Markup
XL Sedan w/bucket seats	$25,845	14%
XL Sedan w/bench seats	$26,665	14%
XLS Sedan w/bucket seats	$30,405	16%
XLS Sedan w/bench seats	$30,305	16%

Competition 2001

Model	POOR						GOOD	pg.
Toyota Avalon								**418**
Chrys. Concorde					■			188
Lexus ES300							■	302
VW Passat						■		452

'00 and '99 Models

This Toyota flagship is built in Georgetown, Kentucky—who would have imagined that twenty years ago? With more interior room and a higher price tag than the Camry, the Avalon is more upscale in design, competing with models like the Mercury Sable and Nissan Maxima.

Price Ranges 2000–1999

XL Sedan	$21,300-25,200
XLS Sedan	$23,300-29,700

2000 Toyota Avalon

1999 Toyota Avalon

Toyota Avalon — Intermediate

	2001	2000	1999

RATINGS

	POOR … GOOD	POOR … GOOD	POOR … GOOD
Comparative Rating			7
Frontal Crash Tests			9
Safety Features	8	8	8
Preventive Maintenance	2	2	3
Repair Costs	3	3	3
Warranty	2	2	3
Fuel Economy	5	4	4
Rollover (based on SSF; see pg. 30)	7	7	7
Complaints	5		6
Insurance Costs	10	10	10

SAFETY

	2001	2000	1999
Frontal Crash Tests	To Be Tested	No Govt Results	Very Good
Side Crash Tests	Very Good	Very Good	Very Good
Airbags	Dual/Side	Dual/Side	Dual/Side
Anti-Lock Brakes	4-Wheel	4-Wheel	4-Wheel
Day Running Lamps	Standard	None	None
Built-In Child Seats	None	None	None
Pretensioners	Standard	Standard	Standard

SPECIFICATIONS

	2001		2000		1999	
Fuel Economy (cty/hwy)	21/29	Average	21/29	Average	21/29	Average
Driving Range (miles)	462.5	Vry. Long	462.5	Vry. Long	462.5	Vry. Long
Bumpers	Strong		Strong		Strong	
Parking Index	Hard		Hard		Hard	
Head/Leg Room (in.)	38.7/41.7	Cramped	38.7/41.7	Cramped	39.1/44.1	Vry. Roomy
Interior Space (cu. ft.)	106	Roomy	121.5	Vry. Roomy	120.9	Vry. Roomy
Cargo Space (cu. ft.)	16	Small	15.9	Small	15.4	Small
Tow Rating (lbs.)	2000	Vry. Low	2000	Vry. Low	2000	Vry. Low

Camry continues its reign as best-seller going into this model year. You have your choice between three trim levels: CE, LE, and XLE; and there are many option packages. Side airbags are a great new safety feature from last year. The CE comes standard with a 2.2-liter 4-cylinder engine with 133 hp. Most will prefer the more powerful 3.0-liter V6 engine with a slight loss in fuel economy. The Camry rates very highly and is a Best Bet.

2001 Toyota Camry

General Information

New for 2001: No major changes		**Year of Production:**	5
Twins: Lexus ES300		**Seating:**	5
Where Made: U.S.		**Theft Rating:**	Average

Prices 2001

Model	Retail	Markup
CE man.	$17,675	13%
LE Auto	$20,415	14%
LE man. V6	$22,385	14%
XLE Auto V6	$26,225	14%

Competition 2001

Model	POOR					GOOD		pg.
Toyota Camry					■			420
Ford Taurus							■	234
Honda Accord			■					242
Nissan Altima						■		356

'00 and '99 Models

Every year, the Camry faces tough competition with the Accord and the popular Taurus. If you get a version with leather seating and high-performance engine, you essentially have a Lexus at a percentage of the cost.

Price Ranges 2000–1999

CE man.	$14,300-17,800
LE auto.	$15,500-18,200
LE V6 man.	$17,100-20,000
XLE V6 auto.	$19,400-26,000

2000 Toyota Camry

1999 Toyota Camry

Toyota Camry — Intermediate

	2001	2000	1999

RATINGS

	POOR — GOOD	POOR — GOOD	POOR — GOOD
Comparative Rating	7	7	8
Frontal Crash Tests	10	10	10
Safety Features	7	8	8
Preventive Maintenance	2	2	3
Repair Costs	5	4	4
Warranty	2	2	3
Fuel Economy	7	5	5
Rollover (based on SSF; see pg. 30)	8	8	8
Complaints	6	6	8
Insurance Costs	5	5	5

SAFETY

	2001	2000	1999
Frontal Crash Tests	Very Good	Very Good	Very Good
Side Crash Tests	Good	Good	Good
Airbags	Dual and Opt. Side	Dual and Opt. Side	Dual/Side
Anti-Lock Brakes	4-Wheel (optional)	4-Wheel (optional)	4-Wheel (optional)
Day Running Lamps	Optional	Optional	None
Built-In Child Seats	None	Optional	Optional
Pretensioners	Standard	Standard	Standard

SPECIFICATIONS

	2001		2000		1999	
Fuel Economy (cty/hwy)	24/33	Average	23/32	Average	23/32	Average
Driving Range (miles)	527.25	Vry. Long	508.75	Vry. Long	508.75	Vry. Long
Bumpers	Strong		Strong		Strong	
Parking Index	Easy		Easy		Easy	
Head/Leg Room (in.)	38.6/43.5	Roomy	38.6/43.5	Roomy	38.6/43.5	Roomy
Interior Space (cu. ft.)	97	Average	96.8	Average	96.9	Average
Cargo Space (cu. ft.)	14	Small	14.1	Small	14.1	Small
Tow Rating (lbs.)	2000	Vry. Low	2000	Vry. Low	2000	Vry. Low

With a shorter length, a longer wheelbase, and some serious new styling, the Celica was reinvented for 2000 and carries over into 2001 unchanged. The GT is powered by a 1.8-liter 4-cylinder that provides 140 horsepower. For more power, the GTS DOHC version gets 180 horsepower. A 5-speed manual is standard on the GT and a 6-speed manual is standard on the GTS, but a 4-speed automatic is available. Dual airbags are standard, and side airbags are available.

2001 Toyota Celica

General Information

New for 2001: No major changes	**Year of Production:** 2
Twins:	**Seating:** 4
Where Made: Japan	**Theft Rating:** Average

Prices 2001

Model	Retail	Markup
GT man.	$16,985	12%
GT Auto	$17,785	12%
GTS man.	$21,455	13%
GTS Auto	$22,155	13%

Competition 2001

Model	POOR					GOOD	pg.
Toyota Celica							**422**
Chev. Camaro				■			164
Ford Mustang					■		230
Pontiac Gr. Prix						■	386

'00 and '99 Models

For 1999, Toyota dropped the Celica GT coupe, leaving the GT liftback and convertible. The Celica is a mid-priced sports car, especially popular with women.

Price Ranges 2000–1999

GT man.	$16,100-18,900
GT Auto	$16,700-19,500
GTS man.	$20,800-20,900
GTS Auto	$21,100-21,200

2000 Toyota Celica

1999 Toyota Celica

Toyota Celica — Compact

	2001	2000	1999

RATINGS

	2001 (Poor–Good)	2000 (Poor–Good)	1999 (Poor–Good)
Comparative Rating			
Frontal Crash Tests			
Safety Features	8	6	6
Preventive Maintenance	2	2	3
Repair Costs	5	4	4
Warranty	2	2	3
Fuel Economy	7	6	4
Rollover (based on SSF; see pg. 30)	8	8	8
Complaints	5		10
Insurance Costs	1	1	1

SAFETY

	2001	2000	1999
Frontal Crash Tests	To Be Tested	No Govt Results	No Govt Results
Side Crash Tests	No Govt Results	No Govt Results	No Govt Results
Airbags	Dual and Opt. Side	Dual and Opt. Side	Dual
Anti-Lock Brakes	4-Wheel (optional)	4-Wheel (optional)	4-Wheel (optional)
Day Running Lamps	Standard	None	None
Built-In Child Seats	Optional	None	None
Pretensioners	Standard	Standard	Standard

SPECIFICATIONS

	2001		2000		1999	
Fuel Economy (cty/hwy)	28/33	Good	28/34	Good	22/28	Average
Driving Range (miles)	442.25	Long	523.9	Vry. Long	397.5	Average
Bumpers	Strong		Strong		Strong	
Parking Index	Easy		Easy		Vry. Easy	
Head/Leg Room (in.)	38.4/43.6	Roomy	38.4/33	Vry. Cramp.	38.3/44.2	Roomy
Interior Space (cu. ft.)	78	Vry. Cramp.	88	Cramped	93.4	Cramped
Cargo Space (cu. ft.)	17	Average	16.9	Average	16.2	Small
Tow Rating (lbs.)			2000	Vry. Low	2000	Vry. Low

The Corolla underwent a redesign in 1998 and hasn't changed much since then. Safety was a priority with the latest redesign, and the Corolla can come loaded with safety features. Dual airbags and daytime running lamps are standard; ABS and side airbags are optional. A new engine is a 1.8-liter 4-cylinder with 120 hp, which is more powerful than the previous 1.6-liter. Check out the Corolla's twin, the Prizm, and you can save some money.

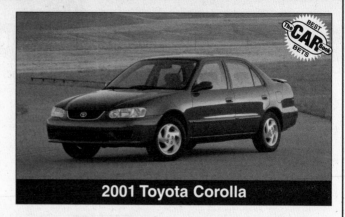
2001 Toyota Corolla

General Information

New for 2001: No major changes		**Year of Production:**	4
Twins: Chevrolet Prizm		**Seating:**	5
Where Made: U.S.		**Theft Rating:**	Average

Prices 2001

Model	Retail	Markup
CE Sedan man.	$12,568	10%
LE man.	$13,383	13%
S Sedan Auto	$13,608	13%
LE Auto	$14,198	13%

Competition 2001

Model	POOR					GOOD	pg.
Toyota Corolla					■		**424**
Ford Focus						■	228
Mitsu. Galant		■					350
Saturn SL						■	400

'00 and '99 Models

Good crash test results, both front and side, contribute to the car's overall safety. The Corolla continues to rate highly against its competitors.

Price Ranges 2000–1999

CE Sedan man.	$11,400-13,000
LE man.	$12,200-14,000
LE auto.	$12,700-14,500

2000 Toyota Corolla

1999 Toyota Corolla

Toyota Corolla — Compact

	2001	2000	1999

RATINGS

	2001 (POOR–GOOD)	2000 (POOR–GOOD)	1999 (POOR–GOOD)
Comparative Rating	7	7	8
Frontal Crash Tests	8	8	8
Safety Features	7	7	8
Preventive Maintenance	3	3	4
Repair Costs	4	4	4
Warranty	2	2	3
Fuel Economy	9	8	8
Rollover (based on SSF; see pg. 30)		7	7
Complaints	9	9	10
Insurance Costs	1	1	1

SAFETY

	2001	2000	1999
Frontal Crash Tests	Good	Good	Good
Side Crash Tests	Good	Good	Good
Airbags	Dual and Opt. Side	Dual and Opt. Side	Dual and Opt. Side
Anti-Lock Brakes	4-Wheel (optional)	4-Wheel (optional)	4-Wheel (optional)
Day Running Lamps	Standard	None	Standard
Built-In Child Seats	None	Optional	Optional
Pretensioners	Standard	Standard	Standard

SPECIFICATIONS

	2001		2000		1999	
Fuel Economy (cty/hwy)	31/38	Vry. Good	31/38	Vry. Good	31/38	Vry. Good
Driving Range (miles)	455.4	Vry. Long	455.4	Vry. Long	455.4	Vry. Long
Bumpers			Strong		Strong	
Parking Index	Vry. Easy		Vry. Easy		Vry. Easy	
Head/Leg Room (in.)	39.3/42.5	Average	39.3/42.5	Average	39.3/42.5	Average
Interior Space (cu. ft.)	88	Cramped	88	Cramped	88	Cramped
Cargo Space (cu. ft.)	12	Vry. Small	12.1	Vry. Small	12.1	Vry. Small
Tow Rating (lbs.)	1500	Vry. Low	1500	Vry. Low	1500	Vry. Low

The ECHO, Toyota's replacement for the Tercel,is unchanged for 2001 and offers almost the same passenger volume as the Corolla yet is priced significantly lower. And the exterior dimensions are those of a subcompact. It is meant to appeal to a young market. Its 1.5-liter 4-cylinder engine is one of the highest mileage vehicles ever offered. Manual transmission is standard, and ABS and daytime running lamps are optional. It is equipped with dual airbags, pretensioners, and child restraint top tether anchors.

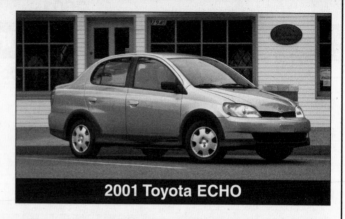

2001 Toyota ECHO

General Information

New for 2001: No major changes	**Year of Production:**	2
Twins:	**Seating:**	4
Where Made: Japan	**Theft Rating:**	

Prices 2001

Model	Retail	Markup
2 door man.	$9,995	8%
4 door man.	$10,525	8%
2 door auto.	$10,795	8%
4 door auto.	$11,325	8%

Competition 2001

Model	POOR					GOOD	pg.
Toyota ECHO						■	**426**
VW Beetle					■		446
Ford Focus							228
Saturn SL					■		400

'00 and '99 Models

Introduced in 2000, the ECHO is tiny, fuel efficient, and designed to compete with the Ford Focus and stripped-down Honda Civic. This is definitely a commuter car for those seeking basic, economical transportation.

Price Ranges 2000–1999

4-door man.	$9-800-9,900
2-door auto.	$9,900-10,000
4-door auto.	$10,200-10,300
2-door man.	$8,500-8,600

2000 Toyota Echo

MODEL WAS NOT PRODUCED THIS YEAR

1999 Model

	2001	2000	1999

RATINGS

	2001 (POOR → GOOD)	2000 (POOR → GOOD)	1999 (POOR → GOOD)
Comparative Rating			
Frontal Crash Tests			
Safety Features	6	6	
Preventive Maintenance			
Repair Costs			
Warranty	2	2	
Fuel Economy	10	9	
Rollover (based on SSF; see pg. 30)	6	6	
Complaints	5		
Insurance Costs	5	5	

SAFETY

	2001	2000	
Frontal Crash Tests	To Be Tested	No Govt Results	
Side Crash Tests	No Govt Results	No Govt Results	
Airbags	Dual	Dual	
Anti-Lock Brakes	4-Wheel (optional)	4-Wheel (optional)	
Day Running Lamps	Optional	Standard	
Built-In Child Seats	None	None	
Pretensioners	Standard	Standard	

SPECIFICATIONS

	2001		2000		
Fuel Economy (cty/hwy)	34/41	Vry. Good	34/41	Vry. Good	
Driving Range (miles)	446.25	Long	446.25	Long	
Bumpers			Strong		
Parking Index	Vry. Easy		Vry. Easy		
Head/Leg Room (in.)	39.9/41.1	Average	39.9/41.1	Average	
Interior Space (cu. ft.)	87	Cramped	87.4	Cramped	
Cargo Space (cu. ft.)	14	Small	13.6	Small	
Tow Rating (lbs.)					

Toyota Highlander

Small Sport Utility

This all-new SUV is built like a car with its unibody construction. The standard engine is a 4-cylinder average power system; the one they are pushing is a 220-horsepower V6. This is the fifth type of SUV you can get from Toyota.

2001 Toyota Highlander

General Information

New for 2001: All-new	**Year of Production:**	1
Twins:	**Seating:**	
Where Made: Japan	**Theft Rating:**	

Prices 2001

Model*	Retail	Markup
No prices available at press time.		

Competition 2001

Model	POOR				GOOD	pg.
Toy. Highlander						**428**
Honda CR-V				■		246
Jeep Wrangler	■					288

'00 and '99 Models

Price Ranges 2000–1999

MODEL WAS NOT PRODUCED THIS YEAR

2000 Model

MODEL WAS NOT PRODUCED THIS YEAR

1999 Model

Toyota Highlander

Small Sport Utility

	2001	2000	1999

RATINGS

	POOR → GOOD	POOR → GOOD	POOR → GOOD
Comparative Rating			
Frontal Crash Tests			
Safety Features	6		
Preventive Maintenance			
Repair Costs			
Warranty	2		
Fuel Economy			
Rollover (based on SSF; see pg. 30)	5		
Complaints	5		
Insurance Costs	5		

SAFETY

	2001	2000	1999
Frontal Crash Tests	No Govt Results		
Side Crash Tests	No Govt Results		
Airbags	Dual		
Anti-Lock Brakes			
Day Running Lamps	Optional		
Built-In Child Seats	None		
Pretensioners	Standard		

SPECIFICATIONS

	2001	2000	1999
Fuel Economy (cty/hwy)			
Driving Range (miles)			
Bumpers			
Parking Index			
Head/Leg Room (in.)			
Interior Space (cu. ft.)			
Cargo Space (cu. ft.)	16 Small		
Tow Rating (lbs.)			

The Land Cruiser has been around in various forms since the 1960s; the latest version does battle with the Jeep Grand Cherokee and the Range Rovers. Little has changed for 2001. The Land Cruiser is best known for its quality as well as its off-road prowess. Dual airbags and ABS are both standard equipment. The engine is a hefty, gas-guzzling 4.5-liter 6-cylinder with automatic transmission and all-wheel drive. Because the Land Cruiser tips the scales at 4,700 pounds, don't expect stunning acceleration.

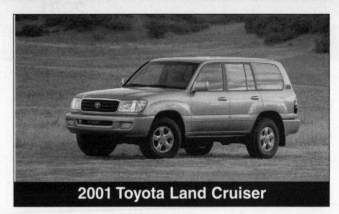

2001 Toyota Land Cruiser

General Information

New for 2001: No major changes		**Year of Production:**	11
Twins: Lexus LX470		**Seating:**	7
Where Made: Japan		**Theft Rating:**	

Prices 2001

Model	Retail	Markup
Base	$52,895	16%

Competition 2001

Model	POOR				GOOD	pg.
Toy. Land Cruis.						430
Ford Expedition			■			222
Linc. Navigator				■		320

'00 and '99 Models

There were no significant changes for the 1999-2000 model years. The lack of crash test results prevents us from rating the Land Cruiser.

Price Ranges 2000–1999

Base	$47-50,800

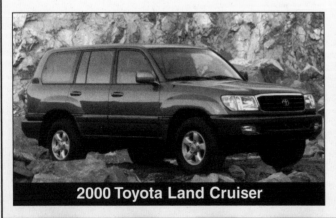

2000 Toyota Land Cruiser

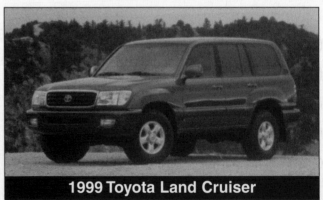

1999 Toyota Land Cruiser

Toyota Land Cruiser — Large Sport Utility

	2001	2000	1999

RATINGS

	2001 POOR→GOOD	2000 POOR→GOOD	1999 POOR→GOOD
Comparative Rating			
Frontal Crash Tests			
Safety Features	7	7	6
Preventive Maintenance	4	3	4
Repair Costs	10	3	2
Warranty	2	2	3
Fuel Economy	1	1	1
Rollover (based on SSF; see pg. 30)	4	4	3
Complaints	8	9	8
Insurance Costs	10	5	5

SAFETY

	2001	2000	1999
Frontal Crash Tests	No Govt Results	No Govt Results	No Govt Results
Side Crash Tests	No Govt Results	No Govt Results	No Govt Results
Airbags	Dual	Dual	Dual
Anti-Lock Brakes	4-Wheel	4-Wheel	4-Wheel
Day Running Lamps	Standard	Standard	None
Built-In Child Seats	None	None	None
Pretensioners	Standard	Standard	Standard

SPECIFICATIONS

	2001		2000		1999	
Fuel Economy (cty/hwy)	13/16	Vry. Poor	13/16	Vry. Poor	13/15	Vry. Poor
Driving Range (miles)	368.3	Vry. Short	368.3	Vry. Short	351.4	Vry. Short
Bumpers						
Parking Index	Vry. Hard		Vry. Hard		Vry. Hard	
Head/Leg Room (in.)	39.2/42.3	Average	39.2/42.3	Average	40.3/42.2	Roomy
Interior Space (cu. ft.)						
Cargo Space (cu. ft.)	90.8	Vry. Large	90.8	Vry. Large	91	Vry. Large
Tow Rating (lbs.)	6500	Vry. High	6500	Vry. High	5000	Average

The Prius, along with the Honda Insight, represents the next generation of fuel-efficient vehicles. Prius can run on either electricity or gasoline alone, or a combination of both. It is equipped with a 1.5-liter gasoline engine and an electric motor with permanent magnet design. It gets a combined fuel economy of 66 mpg. ABS and dual airbags are standard. The Prius was designed to meet or exceed all crash test standards, but, without crash test results, we cannot rate it

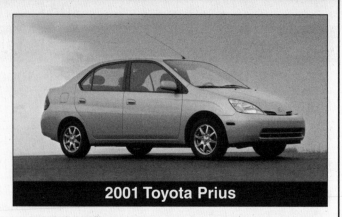

2001 Toyota Prius

General Information

New for 2001: All-new		**Year of Production:**	1
Twins:		**Seating:**	5
Where Made: Japan		**Theft Rating:**	

Prices 2001

Model	Retail	Markup
Base	$19,995	8%

Competition 2001

Model	POOR				GOOD	pg.
Toyota Prius						**432**
Honda Insight						248

'00 and '99 Models

Price Ranges 2000–1999

MODEL WAS NOT PRODUCED THIS YEAR

2000 Model

MODEL WAS NOT PRODUCED THIS YEAR

1999 Model

Toyota Prius

Subcompact

	2001	2000	1999

RATINGS

	POOR — GOOD	POOR — GOOD	POOR — GOOD
Comparative Rating			
Frontal Crash Tests			
Safety Features	6		
Preventive Maintenance			
Repair Costs	10		
Warranty	2		
Fuel Economy	10		
Rollover (based on SSF; see pg. 30)			
Complaints	5		
Insurance Costs	5		

SAFETY

	2001	2000	1999
Frontal Crash Tests	To Be Tested		
Side Crash Tests	No Govt Results		
Airbags	Dual		
Anti-Lock Brakes	4-Wheel		
Day Running Lamps	Optional		
Built-In Child Seats	None		
Pretensioners	Standard		

SPECIFICATIONS

	2001		2000	1999
Fuel Economy (cty/hwy)	52/45	Vry. Good		
Driving Range (miles)	640.2	Vry. Long		
Bumpers				
Parking Index				
Head/Leg Room (in.)	38.8/41.2	Cramped		
Interior Space (cu. ft.)	89	Cramped		
Cargo Space (cu. ft.)	12	Vry. Small		
Tow Rating (lbs.)				

This all-new 2001 model is the second generation of the RAV4. The new engine is still a 2L 4 cylinder model, but has more horsepower. A 5-speed manual transmission is standard; the automatic and ABS are options. Inside, you'll find a bit more cargo space, adjustable front cup holders, and a foot rest for the passenger. All the power options are available on the base model and standard on the L version. The rear bench seat is designed to be easily folded down or removed.

2001 Toyota RAV4

General Information

New for 2001: All-new	Year of Production:	1
Twins:	Seating:	5
Where Made: Japan	Theft Rating:	Average

Prices 2001

Model	Retail	Markup
2WD man.	$16,215	10%
2WD auto.	$17,265	10%
4WD man.	$17,615	12%
4WD auto.	$18,665	12%

Competition 2001

Model	POOR				GOOD	pg.
Toyota RAV4						434
Honda CR-V					■	246
Jeep Wrangler	■					288

'00 and '99 Models

For the 2000 model year, the 2-door RAV4 was dropped from the lineup. The RAV4 (Recreational Active Vehicle with 4WD) is designed to be a light, off-road vehicle that seats five. Toyota has equipped this new vehicle well with standard dual airbags and optional 4-wheel ABS. It has a wide stance, which gives it decent room inside for four.

Price Ranges 2000–1999

2WD man.	$15,800-16,200
2WD auto.	$15,300-16,700
4WD man.	$15,800-17,700
4WD auto.	$16,200-18,100

2000 Toyota RAV4

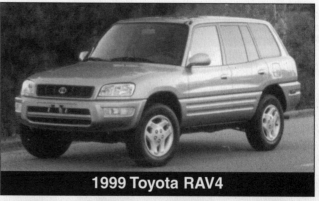

1999 Toyota RAV4

	2001	2000	1999

RATINGS

	POOR — GOOD	POOR — GOOD	POOR — GOOD
Comparative Rating	—	4	4
Frontal Crash Tests	—	9	9
Safety Features	6	6	6
Preventive Maintenance	4	3	4
Repair Costs	5	2	3
Warranty	2	2	3
Fuel Economy	7	5	5
Rollover (based on SSF; see pg. 30)	5	4	4
Complaints	5	9	8
Insurance Costs	1	5	5

SAFETY

	2001	2000	1999
Frontal Crash Tests	To Be Tested	Very Good	Very Good
Side Crash Tests	Very Good	Very Good	Very Good
Airbags	Dual	Dual	Dual
Anti-Lock Brakes	4-Wheel (optional)	4-Wheel (optional)	4-Wheel (optional)
Day Running Lamps	Optional	Optional	None
Built-In Child Seats	None	None	None
Pretensioners	Standard	Standard	Standard

SPECIFICATIONS

	2001		2000		1999	
Fuel Economy (cty/hwy)	25/31	Average	24/29	Average	24/28	Average
Driving Range (miles)	414.4	Average	405.45	Average	397.8	Average
Bumpers						
Parking Index	Vry. Easy		Vry. Easy		Vry. Easy	
Head/Leg Room (in.)	41.3/42.4	Vry. Roomy	40.3/39.5	Cramped	40.3/39.5	Cramped
Interior Space (cu. ft.)						
Cargo Space (cu. ft.)	23.9	Average	57.9	Large	57.9	Large
Tow Rating (lbs.)	1500	Vry. Low	1500	Vry. Low	1500	Vry. Low

All new for 2001, the Sequoia is Toyota's first full-size SUV, aimed at the Ford Expedition and Chevy Suburban. It beats the Expedition in cargo space but not the Suburban. The engine is a 4.7L 240 hp V8. In addition to traction control, the Sequoia has something called Vehicle Skid Control which, when sensing a sideways skid, reduces power and applies the brakes. ABS is standard, but side and head airbags are an option. The third seat splits in half and can be easily removed, one-half at a time. The rear window is electric and retracts into the hatch.

2001 Toyota Sequoia

General Information

New for 2001: All-new		**Year of Production:**	1
Twins:		**Seating:**	5-8
Where Made: U.S.		**Theft Rating:**	

Prices 2001

Model	Retail	Markup
Base	$31,295	12%
4WD Limited	$42,755	13%

Competition 2001

Model	POOR					GOOD	pg.
Toyota Sequoia							**436**
Ford Expedition				■			222
Linc. Navigator					■		320

'00 and '99 Models

Price Ranges 2000–1999

MODEL WAS NOT PRODUCED THIS YEAR

2000 Model

MODEL WAS NOT PRODUCED THIS YEAR

1999 Model

Toyota Sequoia | Large Sport Utility

	2001	2000	1999

RATINGS

	POOR — GOOD	POOR — GOOD	POOR — GOOD
Comparative Rating			
Frontal Crash Tests			
Safety Features	6		
Preventive Maintenance			
Repair Costs			
Warranty	2		
Fuel Economy	1		
Rollover (based on SSF; see pg. 30)	4		
Complaints	5		
Insurance Costs	5		

SAFETY

Frontal Crash Tests	No Govt Results		
Side Crash Tests	No Govt Results		
Airbags	Dual		
Anti-Lock Brakes	4-Wheel		
Day Running Lamps	Optional		
Built-In Child Seats	None		
Pretensioners	Standard		

SPECIFICATIONS

Fuel Economy (cty/hwy)	14/17	Vry. Poor		
Driving Range (miles)	409.2	Average		
Bumpers				
Parking Index	Vry. Hard			
Head/Leg Room (in.)	41.1/41.6	Roomy		
Interior Space (cu. ft.)				
Cargo Space (cu. ft.)	128.1	Vry. Large		
Tow Rating (lbs.)				

The addition of a second sliding door was a welcome option. The Sienna is Toyota's match for the Chrysler minivans, the philosophy being that if you can't beat 'em, copy 'em. The safety features are numerous. Dual airbags, height adjustable seat belts, pretensioners, and 4-wheel ABS are standard. An optional built-in child seat is a must for parents. The Camry's 3.0-liter V6 adequately powers the Sienna but, not surprisingly, gives poor mileage.

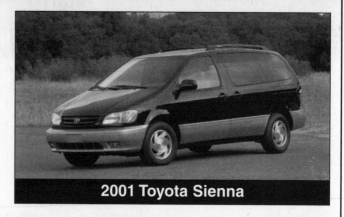
2001 Toyota Sienna

General Information

New for 2001: No major changes	Year of Production:	4
Twins:	Seating:	7
Where Made: U.S.	Theft Rating:	Very Low

Prices 2001

Model	Retail	Markup
CE	$23,905	13%
LE	$25,755	14%
XLE	$28,436	14%

Competition 2001

Model	POOR					GOOD	pg.
Toyota Sienna			■				438
Chev. Venture			■				184
Honda Odyssey		■					250
Ford Windstar					■		236

'00 and '99 Models

Standard on this minivan is Toyota's tire pressure monitor. Using the sensors already in place for ABS, the vehicle calculates tire pressure based on rotational speed. A dashboard light alerts you when pressure is low—both a great fuel saver and safety feature. The Sienna is worth a look.

Price Ranges 2000–1999

CE	$21,600-22,000
LE	$24,000-24,900
XLE	$25,800-26,900

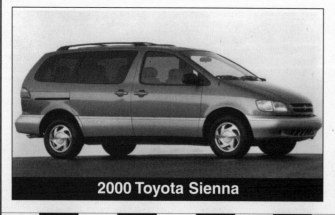
2000 Toyota Sienna

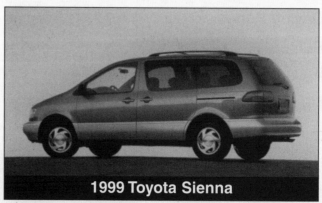
1999 Toyota Sienna

Toyota Sienna

Minivan

	2001	2000	1999

RATINGS

	POOR — GOOD	POOR — GOOD	POOR — GOOD
Comparative Rating	4	4	5
Frontal Crash Tests	10	10	10
Safety Features	7	7	7
Preventive Maintenance	2	2	2
Repair Costs	2	2	3
Warranty	2	2	3
Fuel Economy	4	3	3
Rollover (based on SSF; see pg. 30)	5	5	5
Complaints	3	3	4
Insurance Costs	10	10	10

SAFETY

	2001	2000	1999
Frontal Crash Tests	Very Good	Very Good	Very Good
Side Crash Tests	Very Good	Very Good	Very Good
Airbags	Dual	Dual	Dual
Anti-Lock Brakes	4-Wheel	4-Wheel	4-Wheel
Day Running Lamps	Standard	None	None
Built-In Child Seats	None	Optional	Optional
Pretensioners	Standard	Standard	Standard

SPECIFICATIONS

	2001		2000		1999	
Fuel Economy (cty/hwy)	19/24	Poor	18/24	Poor	18/24	Poor
Driving Range (miles)	451.5	Long	441	Long	441	Long
Bumpers					Strong	
Parking Index	Vry. Hard		Vry. Hard		Vry. Hard	
Head/Leg Room (in.)	40.6/41.9	Roomy	40.6/41.9	Roomy	40.6/41.9	Roomy
Interior Space (cu. ft.)						
Cargo Space (cu. ft.)	131	Vry. Large	131	Vry. Large	131	Vry. Large
Tow Rating (lbs.)						

A spin-off of the Camry, and introduced last year, this sports car was a joint U.S.-Japanese engineering concept, built in Canada. The Solara comes with either a 2.2-liter 4-cylinder engine or a 3.0-liter V6. 5-speed manual transmission or 4-speed automatic is an option for both. Though built on the same platform as the Camry, changes made to the struts, springs, and suspension mounts give the Solara a tighter, more responsive, and quieter ride, with more control on corners.

2001 Toyota Solara

General Information

New for 2001: No major changes	**Year of Production:** 3
Twins:	**Seating:** 4
Where Made: Canada	**Theft Rating:** Average

Prices 2001

Model	Retail	Markup
SE man. 4-cyl	$18,965	13%
SE Auto 4-cyl	$19,765	13%
SE man. V6	$21,675	13%
SLE Auto V6	$25,165	12%

Competition 2001

Model	POOR				GOOD	pg.
Toyota Solara					■	440
Ford Taurus						■ 234
Honda Accord			■			242
Dodge Intrepid		■				208

'00 and '99 Models

Safety features include standard dual airbags for front occupants, seat belt pretensioners, ABS on V6 models, and daytime running lamps. Front side airbags are optional on all models; traction control is optional for the SLE.

Price Ranges 2000–1999

SE man.	$17,200-18,500
SE auto.	$17,800-18,900
SE V6 man.	$19,400-21,600
SLE V6 auto.	$21,500-25,800

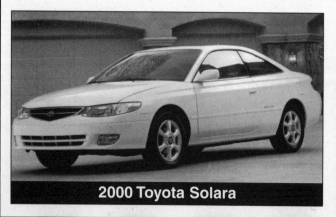
2000 Toyota Solara

1999 Toyota Solara

Toyota Solara — Intermediate

	2001	2000	1999

RATINGS

	POOR → GOOD (2001)	POOR → GOOD (2000)	POOR → GOOD (1999)
Comparative Rating			
Frontal Crash Tests			
Safety Features	7	8	8
Preventive Maintenance	2	2	3
Repair Costs	5	4	3
Warranty	2	2	3
Fuel Economy	7	5	5
Rollover (based on SSF; see pg. 30)	8	8	8
Complaints	5		5
Insurance Costs	5	1	1

SAFETY

	2001	2000	1999
Frontal Crash Tests	No Govt Results	No Govt Results	No Govt Results
Side Crash Tests	Good	No Govt Results	No Govt Results
Airbags	Dual and Opt. Side	Dual and Opt. Side	Dual and Opt. Side
Anti-Lock Brakes	4-Wheel (optional)	4-Wheel (optional)	4-Wheel
Day Running Lamps	Optional	None	Standard
Built-In Child Seats	None	None	None
Pretensioners	Standard	Standard	Standard

SPECIFICATIONS

	2001		2000		1999	
Fuel Economy (cty/hwy)	24/33	Average	23/32	Average	23/32	Average
Driving Range (miles)	527.25	Vry. Long	508.75	Vry. Long	508.75	Vry. Long
Bumpers	Strong		Strong			
Parking Index	Hard		Hard		Hard	
Head/Leg Room (in.)	38.3/43.3	Average	38.3/43.3	Average	38.3/43.3	Average
Interior Space (cu. ft.)	92	Cramped	92.1	Cramped	92.1	Cramped
Cargo Space (cu. ft.)	14	Small	13.8	Small	14.1	Small
Tow Rating (lbs.)	2000	Vry. Low	2000	Vry. Low	2000	Vry. Low

Toyota Tacoma

Compact Pickup

All-new this year, the Tacoma has added a 4-door double cab and S-Runner sport truck to the lineup. You can choose between 2WD and 4WD, and regular and extended-cab models. Take your pick of engines. There is the standard 2.4-liter 4-cylinder which will provide adequate power, or you can choose a more powerful 2.7-liter, or an even bigger 3.4-liter V6. High insurance costs and a high number of complaints hurt the Tacoma's rating.

2001 Toyota Tacoma

General Information

New for 2001: All-new	**Year of Production:** 1
Twins:	**Seating:** 3
Where Made: U.S.	**Theft Rating:** Very High

Prices 2001

Model	Retail	Markup
2WD Base Reg. Cab man.	$11,845	9%
2WD V6 Xtracab auto.	$18,185	10%
4WD Reg Cab man.	$16,255	10%
4WD Doublecab V6 auto.	$21,865	12%

Competition 2001

Model	POOR				GOOD		pg.
Toyota Tacoma							**442**
Chev. S-Series		■					174
Mazda B-Series				■			326
Ford Ranger					■		232

'00 and '99 Models

Seating inside is comfortable, and the ride is like most compact pickups, smooth on smooth roads. A new off-road package is available that allows you to shift into 4-wheel drive on the go.

Price Ranges 2000–1999

2WD Base Reg. Cab man.	$11,300-11,400
2WD V6 Xtracab auto.	$15,300-15,400
4WD Reg Cab man.	$15,100-15,900

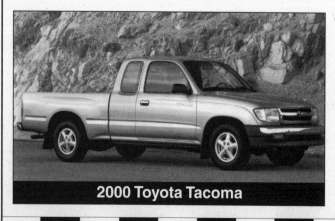

2000 Toyota Tacoma

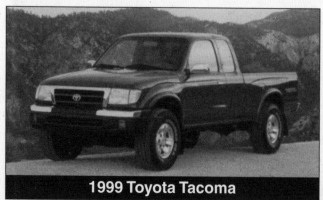

1999 Toyota Tacoma

Toyota Tacoma — Compact Pickup

	2001	2000	1999
RATINGS (POOR → GOOD)			
Comparative Rating		1	3
Frontal Crash Tests		8	8
Safety Features	6	6	6
Preventive Maintenance	4	3	4
Repair Costs	5	4	6
Warranty	2	2	3
Fuel Economy	3	4	4
Rollover (based on SSF; see pg. 30)	3	3	3
Complaints	5	4	8
Insurance Costs	1	1	1

SAFETY

	2001	2000	1999
Frontal Crash Tests	To Be Tested	Good	Good
Side Crash Tests	No Govt Results	No Govt Results	No Govt Results
Airbags	Dual	Dual	Dual
Anti-Lock Brakes	4-Wheel (optional)	4-Wheel (optional)	4-Wheel (optional)
Day Running Lamps	Optional	Optional	Optional
Built-In Child Seats	None	None	None
Pretensioners	Standard	Standard	Standard

SPECIFICATIONS

	2001		2000		1999	
Fuel Economy (cty/hwy)	19/21	Poor	22/26	Average	22/27	Average
Driving Range (miles)	370	Short	432	Long	441	Long
Bumpers						
Parking Index	Easy		Easy		Easy	
Head/Leg Room (in.)	38.5/53.9	Vry. Roomy	38.2/41.7	Cramped	38.2/41.7	Cramped
Interior Space (cu. ft.)						
Cargo Space (cu. ft.)						
Tow Rating (lbs.)	3500	Low	3500	Low	3500	Low

Toyota Tundra
Standard Pickup

New last year, the Tundra is designed to compete directly with the basic Ford, GM, and Chrysler full-size pickups. A 3.4-liter V6 will power the pickup, providing 190 horsepower, but if you want more, a 4.7-liter V8 can give you 245 hp. Automatic transmission is standard for both models, but a 5-speed manual is available. A strong truck, the Tundra also has driver comfort and convenience at heart. Many configurations are possible, including 2- and 4-wheel drive, different bed sizes and 2 or 4 doors. ABS and daytime running lamps are optional, but dual airbags are standard.

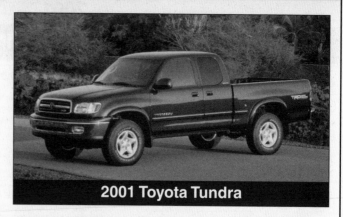

2001 Toyota Tundra

General Information

New for 2001: No major changes	**Year of Production:**	2
Twins:	**Seating:**	2
Where Made: U.S.	**Theft Rating:**	

Prices 2001

Model	Retail	Markup
2WD Base man.	$15,605	12%
2WD Access Cab man. V6	$20,895	12%
4WD Regular	$23,405	12%
4WD Access Cab LTD V8	$29,065	12%

Competition 2001

Model	POOR				GOOD	pg.
Toyota Tundra						**444**
Chev. Silverado		■				176
Dodge Ram		■				210
Ford F-Series				■		226

'00 and '99 Models

2000 Toyota Tundra

Price Ranges 2000–1999

2WD Base man.	$14,900-15,000
2WD Access Cab V6 man.	$20,100-20,200
4WD Regular	$22,700-22,800
4WD Access Cab LTD V8	$27,800-27,900

MODEL WAS NOT PRODUCED THIS YEAR

1999 Model

Toyota Tundra — Standard Pickup

	2001	2000	1999

RATINGS

	2001 (POOR → GOOD)	2000 (POOR → GOOD)	1999 (POOR → GOOD)
Comparative Rating			
Frontal Crash Tests			
Safety Features	6	6	
Preventive Maintenance			
Repair Costs			
Warranty	2	2	
Fuel Economy	2	2	
Rollover (based on SSF; see pg. 30)	5	5	
Complaints	5		
Insurance Costs	5	5	

SAFETY

	2001	2000	1999
Frontal Crash Tests	To Be Tested	No Govt Results	
Side Crash Tests	No Govt Results	No Govt Results	
Airbags	Dual	Dual	
Anti-Lock Brakes	4-Wheel (optional)	4-Wheel (optional)	
Day Running Lamps	Optional	Optional	
Built-In Child Seats	None	None	
Pretensioners	Standard	Standard	

SPECIFICATIONS

	2001		2000		1999
Fuel Economy (cty/hwy)	16/20	Vry. Poor	16/18	Vry. Poor	
Driving Range (miles)	475.2	Vry. Long	448.8	Long	
Bumpers					
Parking Index	Vry. Hard		Vry. Hard		
Head/Leg Room (in.)	40.3/41.5	Average	40.3/41.5	Average	
Interior Space (cu. ft.)	60.4	Vry. Cramp.	60.4	Vry. Cramp.	
Cargo Space (cu. ft.)					
Tow Rating (lbs.)	5250	High	5250	High	

The new Beetle is much more than the old bug. With standard front and side airbags for front occupants, it performed well in independent crash tests, though the government has yet to crash test the car. Volkswagen loaded the new Beetle with the current standard of safety features—virtually the opposite of its historic predecessor. The new Beetle comes with a 2.0-liter 115 hp 4-cylinder, inline gas engine or a 1.9-liter 90 hp 4-cylinder TDI inline diesel. The 2.0-liter meets LEV standards.

2001 Volkswagen Beetle

General Information

New for 2001: No major changes		**Year of Production:**	3
Twins:		**Seating:**	4
Where Made: Mexico		**Theft Rating:**	Very Low

Prices 2001

Model	Retail	Markup
GL man.	$15,900	5%
GL auto.	$16,775	5%
GLS man.	$16,850	7%
GLS auto.	$17,725	7%

Competition 2001

Model	POOR					GOOD	pg.
VW Beetle						■	**446**
Ford Focus						■	228
Mazda Protégé			■				334
Saturn SL						■	400

'00 and '99 Models

No major changes from 1999-2000 but none were really needed. The VW Beetle performed well on crash tests and should appeal to many car buyers.

Price Ranges 2000–1999

GL man.	$15,500-16,100
GL auto.	$15,900-16,600
GLS man.	$16,500-16,600
GLS auto.	$16,400-16,800

2000 Volkswagen Beetle

1999 Volkswagen Beetle

Volkswagen Beetle — Subcompact

	2001	2000	1999

RATINGS

	POOR — GOOD (2001)	POOR — GOOD (2000)	POOR — GOOD (1999)
Comparative Rating	9	8	8
Frontal Crash Tests	9	9	9
Safety Features	8	9	9
Preventive Maintenance	10	10	10
Repair Costs	6	3	3
Warranty	10	10	9
Fuel Economy	6	5	5
Rollover (based on SSF; see pg. 30)	6	6	6
Complaints	3	3	4
Insurance Costs	5	5	5

SAFETY

	2001	2000	1999
Frontal Crash Tests	Very Good	Very Good	Very Good
Side Crash Tests	No Govt Results	No Govt Results	No Govt Results
Airbags	Dual/Side (nextgen)	Dual/Side (nextgen)	Dual/Side (nextgen)
Anti-Lock Brakes	4-Wheel	4-Wheel	4-Wheel
Day Running Lamps	Standard	Standard	Standard
Built-In Child Seats	None	None	None
Pretensioners	Standard	Standard	Standard

SPECIFICATIONS

	2001		2000		1999	
Fuel Economy (cty/hwy)	24/31	Average	24/31	Average	42/49	Vry. Good
Driving Range (miles)	398.75	Average	398.75	Average	659.75	Vry. Long
Bumpers	Strong		Strong			
Parking Index	Vry. Easy		Vry. Easy		Vry. Easy	
Head/Leg Room (in.)	41.3/39.4	Cramped	41.3/39.4	Cramped	41.3/39.4	Cramped
Interior Space (cu. ft.)	85	Vry. Cramp.	85	Vry. Cramp.	85	Vry. Cramp.
Cargo Space (cu. ft.)	12	Vry. Small	12	Vry. Small	12	Vry. Small
Tow Rating (lbs.)						

Unchanged since its redesign in the 1999 model year, the Golf offers a five-door hatchback, and 2.0-liter 115 hp 4-cylinder engine on all models. Dual airbags and daytime running lamps are standard; ABS is optional. Traction control is a great feature available on some models. All models come with 5-speed manual or automatic overdrive. In addition to the industry-best 10-year/100,000-mile power train warranty, VW now includes all service, repairs and parts for the entire duration of the basic warranty of 2 years/24,000 miles.

2001 Volkswagen Golf

General Information

New for 2001: No major changes	**Year of Production:**	3
Twins: Volkswagen Jetta	**Seating:**	5
Where Made: Brazil	**Theft Rating:**	Low

Prices 2001

Model	Retail	Markup
GL man.	$14,900	7%
GL auto.	$15,775	7%
GLS man.	$16,350	7%
GLS auto.	$17,225	7%

Competition 2001

Model	POOR				GOOD	pg.
VW Golf					■	**448**
Chev. Cavalier				■		166
Mitsu. Galant		■				350
Toyota Corolla				■		424

'00 and '99 Models

In 1999 and 2000 the Golf came in a variety of packages: Golf, the sporty Golf Sport, or the GTI VR6. A Golf TDI, or turbo direct engine, was added, but they all have the same basic specs.

Price Ranges 2000–1999

GL man.	$14,700-14,900
GL auto.	$15,200-15,400
GLS man.	$15,500-16,300
GLS auto.	$16,000-16,800

2000 Volkswagen Golf

1999 Volkswagen Golf

Volkswagen Golf — Compact

	2001	2000	1999

RATINGS

	POOR — GOOD	POOR — GOOD	POOR — GOOD
Comparative Rating	8	9	9
Frontal Crash Tests	10	10	10
Safety Features	8	9	9
Preventive Maintenance	10	10	10
Repair Costs	4	5	6
Warranty	10	10	9
Fuel Economy	7	5	5
Rollover (based on SSF; see pg. 30)	7	7	7
Complaints	2	2	3
Insurance Costs	1	1	1

SAFETY

	2001	2000	1999
Frontal Crash Tests	Very Good	Very Good	Very Good
Side Crash Tests	No Govt Results	No Govt Results	No Govt Results
Airbags	Dual/Side (nextgen)	Dual/Side (nextgen)	Dual/Side (nextgen)
Anti-Lock Brakes	4-Wheel (optional)	4-Wheel (optional)	4-Wheel (optional)
Day Running Lamps	Standard	Standard	Standard
Built-In Child Seats	None	None	None
Pretensioners	Standard	Standard	Standard

SPECIFICATIONS

	2001		2000		1999	
Fuel Economy (cty/hwy)	25/31	Average	24/31	Average	24/31	Average
Driving Range (miles)	406	Average	398.75	Average	398.75	Average
Bumpers	Strong		Strong			
Parking Index	Vry. Easy		Vry. Easy		Vry. Easy	
Head/Leg Room (in.)	38.6/41.5	Cramped	38.6/41.5	Cramped	38.6/41.5	Cramped
Interior Space (cu. ft.)	88	Cramped	88	Cramped	88	Cramped
Cargo Space (cu. ft.)	18	Average	18	Average	18	Average
Tow Rating (lbs.)						

It was a busy year for Volkswagen 2 years ago as they introduced an all-new Golf and Jetta. Unchanged this year, the Jetta offers a 2-liter 4-cylinder engine in the GL and as a choice for the GLS. The second engine for the GLS is a 2.8-liter V6, which is the standard on the GLX model. All models come with 5-speed manual or automatic overdrive, and a 10-year/100,000-mile power train warranty. VW now includes all service, repairs and parts for the entire duration of the basic warranty of 2 years/24,000 miles.

2001 Volkswagen Jetta

General Information

New for 2001: No major changes		**Year of Production:**	3
Twins: Volkswagen Golf		**Seating:**	5
Where Made: Mexico		**Theft Rating:**	Low

Prices 2001

Model	Retail	Markup
GL man.	$16,700	10%
GL auto.	$17,575	9%
GLS man.	$17,650	10%
GLS auto.	$18,525	9%

Competition 2001

Model	POOR						GOOD	pg.
VW Jetta						■		450
Chev. Cavalier					■			166
Subaru Legacy							■	406
Toyota Corolla				■				424

'00 and '99 Models

The 1999 Jetta was introduced in three different trim levels, with a 2.0-liter or 2.8-liter V6 engine. Safety features include optional side airbags. With an industry-leading warranty, the Jetta is worth taking out for a test drive.

Price Ranges 2000–1999

GL man.	$13,500-16,200
GL auto.	$16,300-16,700
GLS man.	$16,300-17,200
GLS auto.	$16,800-17,700

2000 Volkswagen Jetta

1999 Volkswagen Jetta

	2001	2000	1999

RATINGS

	POOR — GOOD	POOR — GOOD	POOR — GOOD
Comparative Rating	7	9	
Frontal Crash Tests	10	10	10
Safety Features	3	8	8
Preventive Maintenance	10	10	10
Repair Costs	4	5	6
Warranty	10	10	9
Fuel Economy	7	5	5
Rollover (based on SSF; see pg. 30)	7	7	7
Complaints	3	3	4
Insurance Costs	1	1	1

SAFETY

	2001	2000	1999
Frontal Crash Tests	Very Good	Very Good	Very Good
Side Crash Tests	Very Good	Very Good	Very Good
Airbags	Dual and Opt. Side (ng)	Dual and Opt. Side (ng)	Dual and Opt. Side (ng)
Anti-Lock Brakes	4-Wheel (optional)	4-Wheel (optional)	4-Wheel (optional)
Day Running Lamps	Standard	Standard	Standard
Built-In Child Seats	None	None	None
Pretensioners	Standard	Standard	Standard

SPECIFICATIONS

	2001		2000		1999	
Fuel Economy (cty/hwy)	25/31	Average	24/31	Average	24/31	Average
Driving Range (miles)	406	Average	398.75	Average	398.75	Average
Bumpers	Strong		Strong			
Parking Index	Easy		Easy		Easy	
Head/Leg Room (in.)	38.6/41.5	Cramped	38.6/36.9	Vry. Cramp.	38.6/36.9	Vry. Cramp.
Interior Space (cu. ft.)	87	Cramped	87	Cramped	87	Cramped
Cargo Space (cu. ft.)	13	Vry. Small	13	Vry. Small	13	Vry. Small
Tow Rating (lbs.)						

The unchanged Passat, VW claims, gives car buyers German automobile excellence with a low price tag. Safety features abound. The GLS sedan and wagon have either a 1.8-liter engine with 4 cylinders, or a 2.8-liter V6. Both engines have a 5-speed manual transmission. The GLX model has a 2.8-liter V6 engine. Along with VW's industry-best 10-year/100,000-mile power train warranty, VW now includes all service, repairs and parts for the entire duration of the basic warranty of 2 years/24,000 miles.

2001 Volkswagen Passat

General Information

New for 2001: No major changes		**Year of Production:**	4
Twins:		**Seating:**	5
Where Made: Germany		**Theft Rating:**	Very Low

Prices 2001

Model	Retail	Markup
GLS man. Sedan	$21,450	10%
GLS man. Wagon	$22,250	10%
GLS auto. Sedan	$22,525	9%
GLS auto. Wagon	$23,325	9%

Competition 2001

Model	POOR					GOOD	pg.
VW Passat						■	**452**
Ford Taurus						■	234
Honda Accord			■				242
Toyota Camry				■			420

'00 and '99 Models

In 1999, all models met California's Transitional Low Emission Vehicles standards. No crash test results are available.

Price Ranges 2000–1999

GLS Sedan man.	$16,800-17,700
GLS Sedan auto.	$17,300-18,200

2000 Volkswagen Passat

1999 Volkswagen Passat

Volkswagen Passat — Intermediate

	2001	2000	1999

RATINGS

	2001 (POOR→GOOD)	2000 (POOR→GOOD)	1999 (POOR→GOOD)
Comparative Rating	8	9	
Frontal Crash Tests	10	10	10
Safety Features	9	9	9
Preventive Maintenance	10	10	10
Repair Costs	2	2	4
Warranty	10	10	9
Fuel Economy	6	5	5
Rollover (based on SSF; see pg. 30)	7	7	7
Complaints	1	1	1
Insurance Costs	5	5	5

SAFETY

	2001	2000	1999
Frontal Crash Tests	Very Good	Very Good	Very Good
Side Crash Tests	Good	Good	Good
Airbags	Dual/Side (nextgen)	Dual/Side (nextgen)	Dual/Side (nextgen)
Anti-Lock Brakes	4-Wheel	4-Wheel	4-Wheel
Day Running Lamps	Standard	Standard	Standard
Built-In Child Seats	None	None	None
Pretensioners	Standard	Standard	Standard

SPECIFICATIONS

	2001		2000		1999	
Fuel Economy (cty/hwy)	22/31	Average	23/32	Average	23/32	Average
Driving Range (miles)	434.6	Long	451	Long	508.75	Vry. Long
Bumpers	Strong		Strong		Strong	
Parking Index	Average		Average		Average	
Head/Leg Room (in.)	39.7/41.5	Average	39.7/41.5	Average	39.7/41.5	Average
Interior Space (cu. ft.)	95	Average	95	Average	95	Average
Cargo Space (cu. ft.)	15	Small	15	Small	15	Small
Tow Rating (lbs.)						

Volvo C70/V70   Intermediate

Despite the new name and smoother exterior, the wagon (V70) isn't radically different from the old 850. However, the C70 coupe's aggressive and sporty styling is a departure for Volvo, and a convertible is available. Safety is still Volvo's strength. Dual airbags, side airbags, daytime running lamps, pretensioners, and ABS are all standard.

2001 Volvo V70

General Information

New for 2001: No major changes	**Year of Production:**	4
Twins:	**Seating:**	5
Where Made: Sweden, Belgium	**Theft Rating:**	Average

Prices 2001

Model	Retail	Markup
C70 HT Coupe man.	$34,500	6%
C70 HT Convertible man.	$45,500	6%
V70 2.4 man.	$29,400	6%
V70 XC AWD auto.	$34,900	6%

Competition 2001

Model	POOR				GOOD	pg.
Volvo C70/V70						**454**
Chrys. Concorde			■			188
Lexus ES300					■	302
Buick Regal				■		148

'00 and '99 Models

The standard engine is a 2.4-liter, inline five that produces 168 hp. Turbo versions are optional and provide more power, and all-wheel drive is available on the V70 wagons. Interior room is spacious and comfortable, but five is a squeeze. The trunk space remains quite generous.

Price Ranges 2000–1999

HT M man.	$33,800-38,400
LT A CV auto.	$31,600-34,000
HT M Auto	$34,600-39,000

2000 Volvo C70

1999 Volvo V70

	2001	2000	1999

RATINGS

	POOR — GOOD	POOR — GOOD	POOR — GOOD
Comparative Rating			
Frontal Crash Tests			
Safety Features	9	10	10
Preventive Maintenance	1	1	1
Repair Costs	3	4	5
Warranty	9	9	9
Fuel Economy	5	4	4
Rollover (based on SSF; see pg. 30)	7	7	7
Complaints	5	5	7
Insurance Costs	10	5	5

SAFETY

	2001	2000	1999
Frontal Crash Tests	No Govt Results	No Govt Results	No Govt Results
Side Crash Tests	No Govt Results	No Govt Results	No Govt Results
Airbags	Dual/Side (nextgen)	Dual/Side (nextgen)	Dual/Side (nextgen)
Anti-Lock Brakes	4-Wheel	4-Wheel	4-Wheel
Day Running Lamps	Standard	Standard	Standard
Built-In Child Seats	Optional	Optional	Optional
Pretensioners	Standard	Standard	Standard

SPECIFICATIONS

	2001		2000		1999	
Fuel Economy (cty/hwy)	20/27	Poor	19/27	Poor	20/28	Average
Driving Range (miles)	420.65	Average	411.7	Average	444	Long
Bumpers			Strong		Weak	
Parking Index	Hard		Hard		Hard	
Head/Leg Room (in.)	39/41.3	Cramped	39/41.3	Cramped	39/41.3	Cramped
Interior Space (cu. ft.)	91	Cramped	79.6	Vry. Cramp.	79.6	Vry. Cramp.
Cargo Space (cu. ft.)	13	Vry. Small	13.1	Vry. Small	13.1	Vry. Small
Tow Rating (lbs.)	3300	Low	3300	Low	3300	Low

Unchanged, the S40/V40 targets a younger consumer with this sedan and wagon, which include the performance and safety features that have set standards in the industry at a more affordable price. A standard 1.9-liter, 4-cylinder 160 hp engine powers these front wheel drive vehicles, and a 4-speed automatic transmission is standard. Safety features are impressive, as should be expected: dual level deployment front airbags, side airbags, a Whiplash Protection System, seat belt pretensioners, and ABS.

2001 Volvo S40

General Information

New for 2001: No major changes		**Year of Production:**	2
Twins:		**Seating:**	5
Where Made: Netherlands		**Theft Rating:**	

Prices 2001

Model	Retail	Markup
S40 Sedan 4-dr.	$23,500	6%
V40 Wagon 4-dr.	$24,500	6%

Competition 2001

Model	POOR				GOOD		pg.
Volvo S40/V40							**456**
Ford Taurus						■	234
Honda Accord			■				242
Toyota Camry				■			420

'00 and '99 Models

Volvo introduced this aerodynamically designed S and V 40 series in 2000 to appeal to buyers unwilling to spend the extra dollars on the upscale 60 and 70 series. The lower price does not mean a compromise in safety features. With the option package, you won't have to sacrifice that much in terms of luxury either.

Price Ranges 2000–1999

2.4 M auto.	$22,800-22,900

2000 Volvo S40

MODEL WAS NOT PRODUCED THIS YEAR

1999 Model

Volvo S40/V40 — Intermediate

	2001	2000	1999

RATINGS

(POOR → GOOD)	2001	2000	1999
Comparative Rating			
Frontal Crash Tests			
Safety Features	9	10	
Preventive Maintenance		1	
Repair Costs			
Warranty	9	9	
Fuel Economy	6	4	
Rollover (based on SSF; see pg. 30)	7	7	
Complaints	5		
Insurance Costs	5	5	

SAFETY

	2001	2000	1999
Frontal Crash Tests	No Govt Results	No Govt Results	
Side Crash Tests	No Govt Results	No Govt Results	
Airbags	Dual/Side (nextgen)	Dual/Side (nextgen)	
Anti-Lock Brakes	4-Wheel	4-Wheel	
Day Running Lamps	Standard	Standard	
Built-In Child Seats	Optional	Optional	
Pretensioners	Standard	Standard	

SPECIFICATIONS

	2001		2000		1999
Fuel Economy (cty/hwy)	22/32	Average	21/28	Average	
Driving Range (miles)	426.6	Long	387.1	Short	
Bumpers	Weak		Weak		
Parking Index	Vry. Easy		Easy		
Head/Leg Room (in.)	38.7/41.4	Cramped	38.7/41.4	Cramped	
Interior Space (cu. ft.)	88	Cramped			
Cargo Space (cu. ft.)	13	Vry. Small	13.2	Small	
Tow Rating (lbs.)	2000	Vry. Low	2000	Vry. Low	

Volvo S60   Intermediate

Based on the same platform which serves the S80 and V70, this all-new vehicle seats five and tries to look like a coupe even though it actually seats five. Rear passengers have their own climate controls and the more aerodynamic shape contributes to less road noise. In addition to frontal, head, and side airbags, Volvo is including its Whiplash Protection System which causes the seat to move down and slightly backward in the event of a collision. Traction control is available, as are three engine choices. The S60 will replace its older and bit larger sibling, the S70.

2001 Volvo S60

General Information

New for 2001: All-new		**Year of Production:**	1
Twins:		**Seating:**	5
Where Made: Sweden		**Theft Rating:**	

Prices 2001

Model	Retail	Markup
2.4 Base Sedan man.	$26,500	6%
2.4T Sedan auto.	$29,800	6%
T5 Sedan man.	$31,800	6%

Competition 2001

Model	POOR				GOOD	pg.
Volvo S60					■	**458**
VW Passat				■		452
Lexus ES300					■	302
Dodge Intrepid		■				208

'00 and '99 Models

Price Ranges 2000–1999

MODEL WAS NOT PRODUCED THIS YEAR

2000 Model

MODEL WAS NOT PRODUCED THIS YEAR

1999 Model

	2001	2000	1999

RATINGS

	POOR GOOD	POOR GOOD	POOR GOOD
Comparative Rating			
Frontal Crash Tests			
Safety Features	7		
Preventive Maintenance	1		
Repair Costs	6		
Warranty	9		
Fuel Economy	5		
Rollover (based on SSF; see pg. 30)	8		
Complaints	5		
Insurance Costs	5		

SAFETY

	2001	2000	1999
Frontal Crash Tests	To Be Tested		
Side Crash Tests	No Govt Results		
Airbags	Dual		
Anti-Lock Brakes	Standard		
Day Running Lamps	Standard		
Built-In Child Seats	Optional		
Pretensioners	Standard		

SPECIFICATIONS

	2001	2000	1999
Fuel Economy (cty/hwy)	20/27 Poor		
Driving Range (miles)	495.85 Vry. Long		
Bumpers	Weak		
Parking Index			
Head/Leg Room (in.)	38.9/33.3 Vry. Cramp.		
Interior Space (cu. ft.)	94 Cramped		
Cargo Space (cu. ft.)	14 Small		
Tow Rating (lbs.)			

Volvo S80 Intermediate

The S80, unchanged this year, replaces Volvo's S90, and it's a giant departure from the boxy designs of old. The S80 offers a 2.9-liter 6 cylinder engine with 201 hp, or a 2.8-liter 6-cylinder twin turbo with 268 hp (known as the T6). The list of safety features is no surprise for a Volvo: de-powered airbags for driver and front passenger, side impact inflatable curtains, side impact airbags in all seats, safety belt pretensioners, daytime running lamps, and standard ABS.

2001 Volvo S80

General Information

New for 2001: No major changes	**Year of Production:**	3
Twins:	**Seating:**	5
Where Made: Sweden	**Theft Rating:**	

Prices 2001

Model	Retail	Markup
2.9 auto.	$36,900	6%
T-6 A auto.	$40,900	6%
T-6 Executive Sedan	$46,300	6%

Competition 2001

Model	POOR						GOOD	pg.
Volvo S80							■	460
Chrys. Concorde					■			188
Lexus ES300							■	302
Nissan Altima						■		356

'00 and '99 Models

A strong competitor with plenty of great safety features, but no crash tests results are available.

Price Ranges 2000–1999

2.9 auto.	$30,100-36,000
T6 A auto.	$34,700-40,500

2000 Volvo S80

1999 Volvo S80

Volvo S80

Intermediate

	2001	2000	1999

RATINGS

	POOR — GOOD	POOR — GOOD	POOR — GOOD
Comparative Rating	9	8	9
Frontal Crash Tests	10	10	10
Safety Features	10	10	10
Preventive Maintenance	1	1	1
Repair Costs	3	3	5
Warranty	9	9	9
Fuel Economy	4	3	4
Rollover (based on SSF; see pg. 30)	8	10	10
Complaints	5	5	7
Insurance Costs	10	8	8

SAFETY

	2001	2000	1999
Frontal Crash Tests	Very Good	Very Good	Very Good
Side Crash Tests	Very Good	Very Good	Very Good
Airbags	Dual/Side (nextgen)	Dual/Side (nextgen)	Dual/Side (nextgen)
Anti-Lock Brakes	4-Wheel	4-Wheel	4-Wheel
Day Running Lamps	Standard	Standard	Standard
Built-In Child Seats	Optional	Optional	Optional
Pretensioners	Standard	Standard	Standard

SPECIFICATIONS

	2001		2000		1999	
Fuel Economy (cty/hwy)	19/26	Poor	18/26	Poor	18/27	Poor
Driving Range (miles)	474.75	Vry. Long	464.2	Vry. Long	474.75	Vry. Long
Bumpers	Weak		Weak		Weak	
Parking Index	Average		Average		Average	
Head/Leg Room (in.)	37.5/42.2	Cramped	37.5/42.2	Cramped	38.9/42.2	Average
Interior Space (cu. ft.)	99	Average	114.1	Roomy	114.1	Roomy
Cargo Space (cu. ft.)	15	Small	31.2	Average	14.2	Small
Tow Rating (lbs.)	3300	Low	3300	Low	3300	Low

INDEX